No Cause For Indictment

No Cause For Indictment

An Autopsy of Newark

By Ron Porambo

HOLT, RINEHART AND WINSTON   New York·Chicago·San Francisco

309.1749
P832n

Grateful acknowledgment is made for permission to quote from:

New American Story. Copyright © 1965 by Donald M. Allen. Reprinted by permission of Grove Press, Inc.

"In New Jersey He's Mr. White Vigilante" by Myron Cope. Reprinted from *True* magazine. Copyright © 1969, Fawcett Publications, Inc.

"The Killing of Billy Furr" by Dale Wittner, *Life* magazine, July 28, 1967. Copyright © 1967 Time, Inc.

"Black People" by LeRoi Jones. Copyright © 1967 by LeRoi Jones. Reprinted from *Evergreen Review*, December 1967. Used with permission of the author and the Sterling Lord Agency.

To Carol, my loving wife, who for three years lived with an aggravating monk, and to the most wonderful mother and father a son could have.

And to the journalists who have devoted themselves to giving a voice to those who would otherwise be silent. They write for the victims, the powerless, rather than for those in power, the Nixons, Agnews, and Mitchells of the world. Every so often these journalists raise newspapers and periodicals above garbage can liners.

Acknowledgment

A book such as this can only be born through the efforts of those who care. A manuscript of 700 pages which needed considerable editing had to be read and appreciated. Sig Moglen undertook the challenge. This book evolved from his prodigious editorial talent and craftsmanship, and the skillful rewriting of Warren Sloat. Their sympathy was for the misery of the people whose story fills these pages; their dedication was to its revelation.

RON PORAMBO

Contents

PART I

The Smoke Clears

1

RUMBLE INTO THE MORNING

Visit to a Frustrated Rage

She was ghetto Newark and her brown arms glistened and drops of sweat covered her bare stomach. They formed trickles that dripped into her navel and on down into what little there was of the bottom half of her dancing costume, down into black Newark, a place where tattered kids play on dirty brick streets; where, at the first light of dawn, working people rise for another day's labor and junkies look for anything worth stealing to feed the needle; where locked warm thighs in the restless morning start the cycle all over again, bringing screaming infants into a cramped jungle that now must be called post-riot Newark.

Loud jukebox music enveloped the scene in noise and smoke, and the way the sweating girl danced and her pleased expression made black men up and down the bar forget about their drinks. Black knit stockings covered her moving hips and thighs. Full and wide they were, surely among those that would be doing their thing on some squeaky bed later in the night when that brown skin would become hot and moist, flesh on flesh, the sweat first slipping, then holding with a suction like soggy glue. Keep moving, brown-skinned girl, you are Newark and you are beautiful and the place you call home has a primitive beauty and allure of its own.

Friday night in downtown Newark begins with this low rumble, while a block away Springfield Avenue begins its slow, deliberate climb into the heart of the 1967 riot area. Half the riot's homicide victims were shot in this area and there are no monuments.

Springfield Avenue, which begins peaceably in the suburb of Springfield and runs through the white retreats of Short Hills, Millburn, and Maplewood, ends seven miles later in a frustrated rage. What was an avenue of transportation ends as a prison winding down into Newark's hardcore ghetto, "the Strip," with a string of bars, liquor stores, and barbecue shops with greasy windows. It perverts, it intimidates, and it finally suffocates

3

those who come in contact with it in a sea of movement, marijuana, heroin, and liquor. Pimps and prostitutes, thieves and junkies mix together with the people who work to live. They are all trapped in a culture of poverty—a combustion chamber sustained by the power structure.

Here Friday night's rumble grows louder. Bright colored lights attract junkies who make their buys at the corner of South 19th Street. Lithe, dark-skinned foxes in fine clothes who won't sell their bodies but give them away. The dealing swingers who carry loaded guns and heroin, their shiny cars burning rubber and squealing on the slippery cobblestone. And the fun-seeking people who work through the week for a chance to play on the weekend, exploding in rough laughter at the crowded bars, moving and grooving with the young, loose-hipped girls who do things on a dance floor that are kept behind locked doors in the white world.

Side streets lined with parked cars, garbage-strewn gutters, and three-story wooden firetraps that seem to lean in a stiff breeze have Springfield Avenue for a life-giving artery. Heavy-set mothers plod along with packages of wilted vegetables and meats of the lowest quality and the highest price. They shop one day at a time here where freezers are a status symbol. The rats, mice, roaches, and cats are often the first to eat and always the last.

These extra mouths come free. Everything else has a price in the ghetto, whether you want it or not. Many tenants pay thirty dollars a month extra for junk furniture that landlords refuse to remove. They live with gaping holes, cracks, and peeling paint. The peeling holes provide refuge to rats that scar children; the paint provides lead poisoning which kills them. The plumbing creaks, groans, and leaks. Fuses blow continually because of inadequate wiring. Naked light bulbs dangle from walls and ceilings on extension cords rather than electrical outlets, and every month people are burned and die in fires caused by overloaded circuits. Here women cook on coal and wood-burning iron stoves, relics of a past age, and families eat with a can of "No Roach" within reach. Where insects and rodents no longer flee the light, the battle against vermin goes on twenty-four hours a day. With garbage facilities inadequate or nonexistent, piles of debris accumulate in basements, hallways, and backyards. Slum landlords give their tenants the choice of chipping in to clean the building themselves, or moving out. Health inspectors peer, make notes, and then disappear, never to be heard from again. A few of the newer landlords offer them bribes, but the established ones know that it isn't necessary.

Newark has a battery of ordinances and codes designed to protect ghetto dwellers against substandard housing, each one less effective than the last. The latest effort came in January of 1967 when the City Council adopted an ordinance providing for rent controls as a weapon to force slum landlords to bring their shabby buildings up to decent living standards.

In the first fifty cases referred to the responsible official, the city health officer, no rent controls were imposed. Owners were given thirty days to make the necessary repairs and, in every instance, did. Since controls could only be imposed when the repairs weren't made, many of these landlords then raised their rents 75 to 100 percent, forcing tenants who had filed complaints out of the building.

The city's Housing Court can impose fines of one hundred dollars per day per violation against slum landlords who fail to correct code deficiencies. In practice, though, owners get one postponement after another and, three to five months later, appear in court to pay ninety dollars for as many as ten separate violations. It is cheaper for them to pay the fines than to make repairs. Electrical wires are taped up, pipes are soldered instead of replaced, plywood replaces plaster. Broken tenants are as easily replaced.

The average slum landlord began buying up property during the Depression at bargain prices. He paid nothing down, received low-interest financing, and has done nothing to the building since. Now landlords are sitting on a gold mine. Their tenements have returned ten times the investment and have plenty of profit potential left—as long as they're still standing. The average six-family tenement provides its owner with $6,062 net profit per year. As it deteriorates, the rents increase. The law of supply and demand works for the landlord. If the tenants don't like the rent gouging, there are always new families from the South ready to take their place.

Newark, in the throes of a critical housing shortage for years, has the *highest percentage* of substandard housing of any city in the country. Within the past fifty years, 100,000 rural black families have migrated to Newark. Since 1940 the black population has quadrupled. Poor and uneducated, scarred by discrimination in the racist South, they find more of the same here. They search for work as opportunities for unskilled labor dwindle. They seek health services and police protection as the city's resources erode. For living accommodations they are offered tenements forty to seventy years old which have never been maintained, much less modernized. More than 41,430 living units of the city total of 134,872 —a percentage of 32.5—were substandard in 1960, and since then the situation has worsened considerably. In slum Newark, 3,159 living units have no hot water, 7,097 have no flush toilets, and 28,795 have no built-in heating. Few meet minimum health and safety standards.

Deterioration from age and neglect—permitted by the Health and Public Welfare Department's tolerance and lack of code enforcement— has passed the point of no return. These tenements cannot be repaired or rehabilitated now. It is far too late.

If never visited, these dwellings cannot be imagined. Once seen, they can't be forgotten. Only 8 percent of whites questioned in a survey following the riot thought bad housing was the prime cause of the disturbance. But more than 50 percent of blacks listed poor housing and living conditions as the major cause of the violence. Unsurprisingly, the major areas of rioting were those with the worst living conditions.

One recent trend of Newark's absentee landlords is to convert homes into furnished apartments and larger apartments into smaller ones to meet the housing demand and make still more money. More than 1,000 such rooming houses are now operating illegally in Newark. These practices result in overcrowding, hasten deterioration, and spread blight. Wealthy landlords in the suburbs never bother to visit their tenements, but employ rent collectors and professional management organizations to intercept the complaints of tenants.

Some buildings have reached such advanced decay that their owners have finally departed. Some sell to black owners who often treat their tenants worse than their Jewish predecessors. Others, unable to find a buyer, abandon the tenements, leaving them for the city to tear down. More than 5,000 deserted housing units line Newark's ghettos. Yet, according to Louis Danzig, a former executive director of the Housing Authority, "housing conditions in Newark are now better than they have been in our time."

When one considers that the deterioration rate increases faster than the new housing rate, the city's future looks as unhappy as its past. If all the proposed twenty-seven urban renewal projects were completed on schedule —an impossible feat—and if all available federal aid were utilized, at most only half the housing need could be met by 1979. The Newark Community Renewal Program, proposed in 1968, calls for 18,317 buildings to be razed and another 2,683—many not substandard—to be demolished for highway construction. This would eliminate less than half of the 43,000 buildings already unfit for human habitation. Only 5,070 low-income public housing units are planned for 1979 and a thousand of these are intended for the elderly, with children excluded.

As it is, Newark has 13,000 public housing units, more per capita than any other U.S. city. They represent little more than brick high-rise prisons.

Despite Newark's highest percentage of substandard housing, the city's downtown construction is one of the most ambitious rebuilding programs in the nation. The Gateway project, a $50-million development near Penn Station, includes a ten-story motel, a thirty-story office tower, a shopping plaza, and a three-level underground parking facility. A second phase includes construction of the eighteen-story regional headquarters for an electric firm. The entire project would be connected by glass-enclosed bridges to link the buildings. Privately sponsored office construction downtown amounted to another $80-million outlay, with eleven new buildings in a decade helping to produce the second largest life insurance complex in the nation. Entire new campuses for Rutgers and the Newark College of Engineering also sprang up downtown, and it was expected that Seton Hall Law School and Essex County College would also build downtown facilities.

With many of these structures completed or underway the situation in Newark is a vivid contradiction: the structural beauty of new facades and the ugliness of decay and the waste of human lives. With the continuing cutback in manufacturing and other manual employment contributing to an unemployment rate twice that of the national average and with the new construction virtually adding nil to the plight of the ghetto, these structures even fostered a feeling of resentment and anger. This is particularly true of the $8 million being spent for construction of a new Essex County Jail. Surrounding this exquisite building were the dilapidated firetrap tenements and a culture of poverty which guaranteed that the new facility would be filled to capacity soon after a grand opening scheduled for 1971.

The ghetto's medical care is as good as its housing. The administration of City Hospital, sometimes called Martland Medical Center, has been beset by many troubles, including political ones. In 1962, Congressman Hugh J. Addonizio made it a major target in the mayoralty election, charging that a recent accreditation by the Joint Commission for the Accreditation of Hospitals had been politically timed by his opponent, then incumbent Mayor Leo Carlin. Addonizio, the election winner, charged that Carlin "had managed to whip through a desperate official blessing for this sorry institution."

Three years later it was the same institution, but a different mayor. City Magistrate Nicholas Castellano again made the hospital a political issue, calling for a grand jury investigation of its administration.

Reporting to no board of trustees, City Hospital's director and administrator were responsible only to the mayor and City Council. They made the rules and regulations governing management function, handling of patients, and duties of employees. Three hospital directors appointed by Mayor Addonizio resigned in rapid succession. Frequent changes in top personnel lowered administrative efficiency. Some of the results were listed by Albert Black, chairman of the Human Rights Commission, in a September 1967 report: shortages of staff; inadequate equipment; shortages of eating utensils and food; lack of staff doctors and hospital security; roaches in rooms; bats flying in hospital; lack of bedside curtains and exposure of patients.

Proportionally, Newark has the highest crime rate and the highest rates of venereal disease, maternal mortality, and tuberculosis in the nation. It is a city of more than 400,000 people with nearly 65 percent non-whites, a majority that increases yearly as more black babies arrive and white residents flee the city. It is the only major American city other than Washington, D.C., with a black majority.

Proportionally, Newark has the second highest birth rate and the *highest rate* of infant mortality. A particular source of community anger was a diarrhea epidemic in early 1965 that resulted in the deaths of twenty-eight infants, eighteen at City Hospital. The situation was aggravated when the hospital administration admitted it was unaware that the infants had died within its facilities—four dying in one day—until the epidemic was nearly over.

The public school system is in an advanced state of decay. There are seventy-five school buildings, with fifty-four of them more than a half century old. Although many have been altered extensively, they remain decrepit, functionally unsatisfactory and costly to maintain. As recently as November of 1967, the city notified the Board of Education that proposed school construction totaling $51 million would be postponed indefinitely. The school system was already $250 million behind in capital funds urgently needed to bring the present structures up to date. Inadequate buildings and lack of funds for improvements exist side by side with an ever-increasing school population. In September of 1966 there was room for 49,340 pupils in Newark's elementary schools—but there was an enrollment of 55,272, including 70 percent blacks and 7 percent Spanish speaking. The situation has since worsened, with facilities estimated as short by 10,000 places. One result has been part-time classes offering part-time education.

One third of these new pupils came from Georgia, Virginia, North and South Carolina, Florida, Puerto Rico, and Spanish Harlem, all urgently needing the best education for even a fair chance at life.

For them reading skills are all important, since lack of that ability cripples most other educational pursuits. Yet thousands of the city's pupils graduate from grade to grade as semiliterates. Only six out of a hundred pupils are above the normal reading level. Failing to acquire basic reading skills, they fall further and further behind. Alienation sets in and they are lost forever to education. Some drop out and become social dynamite. The cumulative high school dropout rate from 1962 to 1966 was 32 percent. The students who remain are just as dangerous—hostile, alienated, and often disturbed. Harassed teachers find increasing numbers of disruptive students and are forced to resort to discipline at the expense of instruction.

Harold J. Ashby, president of the Board of Education and a black man, made this summation: "I think somewhere along the line someone has to say 'Stop, this is it.' We are not doing a good job, professional educator or layman. Until such time as these reading levels and arithmetic levels come up, there isn't anyone who can say in the city of Newark, professional or otherwise, 'We are doing a good job,' because these children just can't read and do arithmetic. . . . I think we are going to have to call a sharp halt to all of the camouflage that has gone on for the past ten, fifteen and twenty years."

Newark illustrates the Moynihan report. Non-white births in 1967 were 37 percent illegitimate. Thousands of kids run wild, learning life on the streets before they start school. From the early lesson that force prevails come the knives and razors that teenagers carry in their pockets by habit. Use of the gun comes soon after. For those caught up in the fast life, carrying "a piece" or "heat" is a means of self-preservation.

I Didn't Go to Look at the Body

Graham's Restaurant sits dejectedly on the corner of South 10th Street and Springfield, just on the edge of what was the riot area six months before. There are eight stools in front of a clean formica counter and the top halves of the walls are painted gray. The two front windows broken by bullets of the State Police have been replaced.

William Graham, a fifty-three-year-old black man, has owned restaurants in Newark for more than eighteen years. Before the riot he was held up only once. Since then his restaurant has been visited by gunmen six times, the last two in quick succession. A thirty-year-old gunman, Billy Magwood, walked into the restaurant on a cold December night with a .38 caliber revolver and walked out minutes later with one hundred dollars. Less than twenty-four hours later he was back, ordering a chicken sandwich from the girl behind the counter and then walking for the kitchen door some thirty feet away where he knew the safe was. Graham, lying on a sofa, was in the kitchen with his wife.

"My wife saw him coming through the glass window in the door," Graham recalled. "She recognized him as the one who had robbed her the night before when I wasn't around. He was pulling out on the door and she was pulling in, trying to keep him out. It must have been close to two-thirty in the morning. I was lying down off to the side of the kitchen and I don't think he even saw me. He must have put his gun into his jacket when he was pulling on the door. When he came in I was standing about four feet away with my own thirty-eight. My first shot hit him around the chest and he ran for the outside door. He turned around there and tried to shoot and my second shot hit him in the face. It spun him around outside on the sidewalk and he still went about ten feet further before he dropped and just laid there. I didn't go to look at the body, I'm an expert shot. I just told my wife to call for the police.

"I feel sorry for that person, decidedly so," Graham went on. "At the same time I am sorry he caused blood to be on my hands. One thing, the police won't give me back my gun. Of course, I had a permit but they still won't give it back. First they told me they needed it for ballistics, then I went downtown and a detective told me I'd never get it back. I need that gun, I've been held up six times since the riot. Things have changed, there's something just been backfiring in people.

"I need that gun," he repeated. "It was right under my pillow right there on the sofa."

From South 10th Street the avenue creeps on its cobblestones downhill past forty boarded-up stores left as grim reminders of the summer explosion six months before, past bars and stores that have been the scenes of hundreds of armed robberies, past furniture stores with never-ending bargain sales, straight on down into a cramped jungle where anything can be bought on credit. A stop-off point is Jackson's Lounge at Howard Street, the Howard Street of Nathan Heard's novel. Heard wrote about his street while serving an eight-year sentence for armed robbery at Trenton State Prison. This bar may be the largest gathering place for lesbians and homosexuals in any city of Newark's size. The street is worse now than Heard remembered it.

Nigger, Wait Your Turn

Light from the front windows of the lounge touched the cold sidewalk with bits of color and bursts of wind frosted the avenue's soul. Every time its doors opened, music and laughter spilled out. The brown-skinned people inside were born into a world of skin-bleaching creams, hair-processing irons, and Dixie Peach.

"What do I like the best? I like to smoke reefers," Pap said.

"When you gonna give me my drink?" the man next to him yelled at the bartender.

"Nigger, wait your turn," the black bartender shouted back.

"That's right, you black motherfucker, wait your turn," Pap said, laughing. "Tonight is the best fun I've had since I got out of prison. Just come from Joliet in Illinois, served seven of a fifteen for armed robbery. Damned poor luck, damned poor. If you ain't a probation officer looking for me, we'll get along fine. I've got a wife somewhere up in these projects and a couple of kids I haven't seen for years.

"Is she pretty? She's a motherfucking dog," Pap shouted, laughing harder. "I wasn't in Newark during the trouble last summer, but it was a good thing. These people out there don't realize there's people trying to live in here 'til somethin' like that happens. A man had to be a man, we get tired of being walked on."

Liquor was being poured into the glasses as quickly as the three bartenders could do it, some of it slopping onto the bar. Everybody was buying drinks near closing time, and at 2 A.M. a crowd of about forty spilled outside onto the cold sidewalk. A bulldagger—a girl who acts like a man—and a fag began yelling at one another in front of the bar. They began fighting faggot-style, running up and down the sidewalk and around the parked cars, slapping at the air in a battle with lots of movement but no blood.

Pap and I crossed the avenue to buy Italian hotdogs from a vendor while the crowd of lesbians and homosexuals in blond wigs shouted encouragement to the fighters.

"Scratch her eyes out, Tiny!"

"Bust 'er baby, bust 'er good!"

"You rotten son of a bitch!" the bulldagger shouted at her opponent.

The bulldagger took the offensive. She sat down in the middle of Springfield Avenue and took off a shoe. Shoe in hand, she ran after the fag, kicking at him with her bare foot. Pap and I munched on the hot dogs and laughed at the battle, which had something to do with alienation of affections.

They Must Have Been Junkies

A few doors farther down the avenue on the same side of the street is the E & A Liquor Store, its shelves always well stacked. Liquor is a big commodity on The Strip with one culture selling it to make money, the other drinking it to live.

Eric Stewart, the forty-one-year-old white owner, feels differently about guns than Graham does. "I just try to mind my own business," Stewart said pleasantly. "Keeping a gun only breeds trouble. I've been lucky since I bought the store—only been hit once. That was just about a month after I moved in. Two guys had guns and they wanted money. I gave it to them. They must have been junkies. They took me into the back room and I figured the best that would happen was they'd conk me on the head to keep me down while they got away. But they didn't even touch me, just took the money and left. Police never did catch them, not that I ever heard of, anyway. I'm not scared, no, I just don't like to think about being here."

The neon sign in front said A & E LIQUOR STORE when Stewart bought the business after the former owner's wife had been shot to death during a holdup. The two gunmen also killed a customer. In January 1968, post-riot Newark saw two of its ghetto residents—Jesse Wilson, thirty-two, and Wilbur Sinclair, thirty-four—retried, reconvicted, and resentenced for the double killing. Wilson and Sinclair now reside in a special area at Trenton State Prison where the prisoners to be electrocuted are kept.

Is There Anything You Did Not Understand?

Our trip on the avenue ends, appropriately enough, at the stone majesty of the Essex County Courthouse a short distance away. It is a symbol of justice for Newark's white population and the rod of punishment for most everyone else.

On the fourth floor, a court officer guided the handcuffed Clyde Williams along the shadowy marble hallway to a large wine-colored door. JUDGE JOSEPH SUGRUE was painted in eloquent script on the door's plaque. The guard opened the door as Williams, twenty-three, father of six, drug addict, and an element of Newark's future, kept an appointment with justice. A heavy-set black woman sat with a little girl a few rows from the front of the courtroom. Her face lit up and she waved as she saw Williams walking down the aisle. Williams smiled in return and waved his handcuffs.

"You look good, son," she said.

"I'm all right, Mom," he answered.

Mrs. Williams at first was smiling and happy but later began crying. "Don't cry," he told her, patting his mother on the back and shoulders. Soon she was smiling again. Years of hard times have given some ghetto mothers nervous systems with built-in shock absorbers.

"Can I sit here with him?" the mother asked.

"No," the guard answered gently. "I'm not even supposed to allow you to talk to him."

Men like Clyde Williams are all over Newark and most of them end up here. Newark has the seventh highest total—and the highest *per capita*—of junkies in the nation. "I have a nice family," the prisoner said. "I don't blame anybody but myself for where I'm at."

Williams' lawyer, assigned from Legal Aid, conferred with the assistant prosecutor who had also been assigned to the case. The defendant was to plead guilty, a routine procedure. Williams signed the charge form after answering the questions and all was ready.

Maybe Clyde Williams had been living with his wife and kids on Belmont Avenue, maybe not. There had been a girl friend. She slapped him and he slugged her. It happens every day and few men end up here because of such an offense. The assault charge brought him to jail but the matter at hand was a charge of armed robbery.

Judge Sugrue entered his courtroom and the formality began. When his name was called Williams walked to the center and stood, head down, in front of the bench. He wore summer pants and a blue and yellow sports shirt. An old knife scar was visible on his cheek. His processed hair was frizzy after weeks in jail, and combed straight back. The story of his life was on the inside of both forearms just above the wrists, the insignia of the hardcore junkie—shiny black bumps commonly known as "tracks."

"Did you sign the form?" the judge asked.

"Yes," Williams answered.

"Did you read all the questions?"

"Yes, sir," Williams said.

"Can you read and write?"

"Yes."

"How far did you go in school?"

"The ninth grade." .

"Is everything on the form correct?" the judge asked.

"Everything but the money," the prisoner responded. "We didn't take the money. Nobody got any money. We went in there to get money, I admit that. But we didn't take any money and there wasn't any knife."

"Did one of the other men take the money?" the judge asked.

"No," Williams answered. "He was picked up for something else later. None of us got any money. That's the truth."

A cog was out of place and the legal process ground to a halt. A maximum fifteen-year sentence for Williams hung in the air. In the shadow of the courthouse other junkies were sticking needles in their arms and the ghetto from which he had come was falling apart. But inside justice had to wait. The judge looked at the prosecutor and the prosecutor looked at the defense counsel. Then the prosecutor looked back at the judge. Something was wrong. The assistant prosecutor conferred with the police officers who had worked on the case. It was the most fuss that had been made over Clyde Williams since he was born.

"It was a little grocery store on Bragaw Avenue in the Weequahic section," Williams told me, sitting at the prisoner's table again while they scurried to find the missing cog.

"Did you have a knife?"

"No," Williams said. "That's the truth. The other two guys grabbed him. We didn't need any knife or anything. They grabbed him, I didn't."

"What about the money? The grocer said you got away with nine hundred dollars."

"We looked for the money but we couldn't find any," Williams answered. "There wasn't any knife."

Judge Sugrue returned to the bench a few minutes later and began again from the beginning, the same questions, the same answers. To the last detail it had to be correct, precise—and official. When Williams was born they filled out a form. When he quit school for the Army there had been more forms. Now he had a judge calling him "Mr. Williams," a lawyer of his own, a prosecutor asking questions—and everyone listening to his answers. For once in his twenty-three years Clyde Williams was important.

He had stopped everything by mentioning a cog out of place and, for one of the few times in his life, he was right. He had told the truth. They reduced the charge on the form from armed robbery to "entered premises with intent to rob." The prosecutor had sought out the truth, the defense attorney had been provided to help, and a judge had patiently waited. Fair play had been exercised. Justice would once again triumph.

The white-haired judge looked benignly down upon the young man before him with the knife scar on his cheek.

"Now, did you do what was in the accusation?" the judge asked.

"Yes, sir," Williams responded.

"Were all your answers truthful?"

"Yes, sir," Williams said.

"Did anyone make any promise to you about your sentence?"

"No, sir."

"Now, is there anything I have said to you that you did not understand, Mr. Williams?"

"No, sir," the prisoner replied.

Judge Sugrue then told the prisoner he would be sentenced on March 26, with other men who would also have their forms correctly filled in.

"I can't claim police brutality or anything like that," Williams told me. "I'm getting what I deserve. This is the last time for me, I'm quitting the habit."

If he could do it, he would belong to an exclusive circle. Nonetheless he had made everyone happy. He turned to smile at his mother. She smiled back. Then he called to her that the worst he could get now was seven years.

I Got a Good Whore for You

Up on the hill the rumble of Friday night is pure black, but where Springfield Avenue grinds to a halt downtown, white men join it. They like the brown-skinned go-go girls and know that the black prostitutes frequent the South Broad and Washington Streets downtown. White men drift in and out of the black bars all night long, sitting for half an hour sipping a drink and watching the girls dance. They think it will be easy, but they seldom find it. For the girls in this part of Newark, white men aren't worth messing with unless they've got money.

"Thanks for stopping," he said getting into the car. "I've been trying to flag down a taxi for ten minutes. Just making it in from work. Tired, man, tired. I worked the day shift through and some cat didn't show for his shift, so I worked his too. Some bread for you," he said, taking out two dollar bills.

"No money, thanks just the same," he was told. "I'm passing through anyway. Just tell me where you want to go."

Richard, the passenger, was in his midtwenties and was dressed casually but neatly. He had a just-showered fresh look and an air of confidence. "Want a reefer?" he asked, offering one. "Give you a nice mild high."

"Don't mind if I do."

"Well, keep movin'," the light-skinned black said. "That's the worst thing you can do, stopping the car. I'm goin' up to South Fifteenth Street."

The car filled with that unmistakable aroma as we moved down Belmont and left on Avon Avenue, past the drugstore where Leroy Boyd had been shot during the riot. Then down Avon a block, past Mack Liquors where Billy Furr had been shotgunned the next afternoon. The car crossed the railroad tracks and up the slope, turning right on Bergen Street. The odor of marijuana became stronger. "Nice mild high, eh, puff easy," Richard said. "You're puffin' too fast." We continued out Bergen and across the big one, Springfield Avenue, past the tenement where another riot victim had died, and turned left on 16th Avenue, straight up the hill into a jungle of after-hours bars, marijuana, heroin and where women are available for a price.

"You want more, I got 'em," Richard said. "Got all the reefers you want, my man. Five bucks a bag, nickel bags is all I have."

"How about heroin, white stuff?"

"You can have that too, but not right away. I just met you, you know, and I don't know who the hell you are. Give me some time to check you out and it will be all right. . . . You want a woman, too?"

"Sure, I'd like to talk to one."

"Listen, my man, I got a good whore for you."

"Can she talk?"

"No, man, you don't understand. She's just a whore, a stone whore. Turn right onto Fifteenth, and I'll show you."

We were on South 15th Street, a long row of houses that all looked alike. A girl named Peaches was in one of them. "She's a damn good whore. I bring all the white guys up here from work all the time." He rapped on a door in the hallway and asked, "Hey, you awake?"

"Yes," a girl answered sleepily on the other side.

"You alone?" he asked.

"Yes," she replied.

Inside was a neat apartment and a pretty, light-skinned black girl of about eighteen who had just come north. Richard turned on a light in the kitchen and, walking back into the bedroom, lit another joint. The girl, in a short nightie, sat on the edge of the warm bed she had just left. "What did I tell you?" Richard asked. "Nice stuff, eh?" He went into the kitchen and started making a sandwich. The guy made himself at home. Hell, he was paying the rent.

Holdup men like Billy Magwood, the lonely and listless such as Pap, men who work in the white world by day but live by ghetto standards of success at home like Richard, and junkies like Clyde Williams personify much of black Newark as it was six months after its riot. Two societies overlap one another within the city. As white youths grow within a normal family structure, black children are squeezed into manhood by the constricting walls of an escape-proof ghetto. The ghetto streets throb and the fearful white areas nearby feel it. Black men sell women and white men buy them. Black children shoot heroin and white politicians give the city away to the mobsters who supply the narcotics.

Work Up a Sweat, Baby

The brown-skinned go-go dancer sat in the cage next to the bar's front window, with sweat running down her stomach, her legs, everywhere. Down the bar, past liquor bottles and bags of bacon rinds, a male go-go dancer in tights in a cage warmed up with deep knee bends.

"The guy's a dancer," the black bartender said. "He was out of work so he asked the boss if he could dance. We're short a girl so the boss said okay, what the hell."

The male dancer stood on his hands, wiggling his feet in the air. Men at the bar snickered, then laughed. Sugar, the big-hipped dancer in the black stockings, gave him a bad look. "It's about time he started doing *something*," she said. "I'm plumb wore out." She wiped the sweat from her arms and stomach, watching the male dancer, now back on his feet, ripple his breast muscles. The men laughed harder. Then he began to move his hips in semicircles while standing on his toes.

Big Scotti, brown as a bear, with a mean-looking scar down the side of his neck, walked in. He wore a heavy three-quarter coat with the collar turned up and his hat sat on top of his head like a bird on a boulder. He ordered a drink. He walked halfway down the bar to make certain he saw a male go-go dancer in tights standing on his head. Then he walked back to where Sugar was sitting.

"Umph, look at that woman," Big Scotti said, a gravelly voice coming from under a thick moustache. "Don't want to spend my money looking at a nigger standing on his head." He was looking at the sweating girl like he could eat her.

"Listen, man," Big Scotti said to the bartender, "what about the girl?" The bartender grinned.

"Five more minutes and I'll be back up," Sugar said.

"Shit, five more minutes and I'll be gone," the big man answered. "I want to look at a real woman and you are a real woman."

"Uh-huh," Sugar responded.

"Don't want you to catch cold, baby," Big Scotti said.

"Uh-huh," she answered again.

"Here's a dry towel," said the big man. "Now wipe some of that sweat off you and let's go."

"Why don't you have another drink and look at the other dancer?" the bartender asked.

"No matter how many drinks I take he won't look no better than what he looks right now," Big Scotti laughed. "Hell with a nigger standing on his head. Com'n, baby, get on up and really show me somethin'.

"Gim'me a roll of quarters," he shouted to the bartender, "I'm gonna keep that music machine going all night long. Baby, do your thing and next time I come down here I'm gonna bring you a new bathrobe."

"Uh-huh," Sugar said again.

She got to her feet and the sound of the Four Tops made her move, first down in her legs and on up to her hips and then she was moving all over. Then she started using her arms and even the male go-go dancer was watching. Big Scotti stood next to the cage with a drink in one hand, growling through his teeth, "Umphhh, look at that woman. . . . Work up a sweat, baby, you sure are lookin' good." She sure was. The smell of her perspiration and the smoke and the liquor mixed together into a euphoria in the cramped bar. Downtown and along the strip the swaying, throbbing rumble into the morning continued, but up on the hill were those who still lived with the riot. . . . Lord have mercy on my soul, how many chickens have I stole.

2

THE WEEPING AND GNASHING OF TEETH

We're Killing Innocent People

Livingston Street is a one-way road to nowhere lined with abandoned cars and litter that gusts of wind whipped into the clutches of a nearby wire fence. The street is as forgotten as those who live on it. One of them, a thirty-five-year-old man named Emerson Moss, lived with his wife and three sons in a grayish, dilapidated house near the Rose Street crossover. There had been another boy, ten-year-old Eddie, but he had been killed during the riot when a National Guard checkpoint opened fire on the family car.

Alive, Eddie Moss was just one of the thousands of kids in the Central and South Wards, but when he died he gained a special—if mute—importance. No one has faced up to what killed him.

"I thought it was just a street repair site," the boy's father related. "A gun went off and I mashed down on the gas. I thought they were trying to kill everyone in the car. . . . I'm sorry, I just can't talk about it again, going over and over it. I just can't stand it anymore. They called me down to the grand jury three times."

The notices of Eddie Moss's death had been faulty and inadvertent, if not outright lies:

"A ten-year-old boy, Edward Moss of 240 Livingston Street, was fatally shot by a sniper while riding in a car with his parents," the local press reported.

"Passenger in car at Hawthorne near Belmont," the boy's autopsy report read. "Homicide by shooting. Bullet wound back of right ear, passed through."

"The troops were instructed to act with the utmost restraint," John V. Spinale, assistant to Governor Richard J. Hughes, said in explanation, "and to shoot only when necessary, primarily in self-defense."

"I know how he died," Emerson Moss told me. "I just want to forget

18

about it. What difference does it make to go over it all again? It won't bring Eddie back."

The tall, thin man walked back to his crumbling house that wasn't numbered 240 and went inside.

In the cold scarred streets of Newark the winter after the riot stories that had never been published were gradually coming to light.

Broken glass on the dirty Bergen Street sidewalk crunched under my shoes in front of the ramshackle three-floor tenement where the Browns had lived. Months before the street had rung with shouts of violent chaos:

> Newark police, hold your fire! State Police, hold your fire! . . . You're shooting at each other! National Guardsmen, you're shooting at buildings and sparks fly so we think there are snipers! Be sure of your targets! . . . Tell those guardsmen to stop shooting at the roof. Those men they're firing at are policemen!

A stench hung in the air inside the hallway and the walk up the creaky stairs to the third floor ended in darkness. The apartment where Ozell and Rebecca Brown once lived with their four children was still vacant and silent as death. Mrs. Brown had stayed home from her job as a nurse's aide during the riot and her husband was late getting home from his construction job on the fateful night. His brother was with Mrs. Brown and the kids when the National Guard gunfire crashed through the front windows. As she ran to pull one of her children to safety, bullets ripped open her abdomen.

"Mrs. Rebecca Brown, about 30, of 298 Bergen St., died in City Hospital of gunshot wounds in the abdomen," the Newark *Evening News* of July 16 reported. "She had been sitting in her apartment yesterday when three bullets from a sniper's gun came through the windows and hit her."

During the winter, Ozell Brown returned to Newark from his mother-in-law's home near Alachua, Florida, where he took his children after his wife's death. His weight had dropped from 165 to 135 pounds and he nervously smoked one cigarette after another.

"They were shooting at everything that moved and I had a hard time getting home from work, ducking into doorways along Bergen Street," he related. "They wouldn't let me see her upstairs. They wouldn't let me go up. I knew she was dead when they carried her down. If you ever seen a dead body, you know when they're dead. Right after they took her away I went to the hospital and they even shot at my car. I had three tires but I didn't dare stop, I kept right on all the way to the hospital on three tires. I saw a guy get pulled from a car at Bergen and Sixteenth Avenue and the cops beating on him. The guardsmen were riding around in jeeps saying, 'Kennedy's not with you now,' and 'Let's kill all these black bastards.' They rode by the people saying these things.

"When I went back to the apartment there were bullet holes all through it and I found three big bullets lying around on the floor," Brown went on. "My brother-in-law was in Viet Nam and my brother was in Korea and they both told me they weren't allowed to shoot into huts where people may be living. We're American citizens, how could they shoot where they didn't know what was there?

"After it happened, I pretty near drunk myself to death," he continued. "Nothing meant anything anymore. When I went home to Florida I got married again. I was pretty near out of my head with worry and everybody told me to get married again because it would be easier on me. I stayed with my new wife a few weeks but it was no good. I was such a confused person, you can get so messed up so bad in the head. I still don't understand it, I never will. If this had happened to a white person there would be someone to come round to see how you're doin', somebody to say somethin'. I just can't figure it out. I just can't figure out how they can do a thing like that and not one person has even said anything."

It is a short walk to Hunterdon Street where, the summer before, the intersection had also been full of soldiers carrying guns. Mrs. Eloise Spellman had lived with her eleven children in the Hayes Homes, a mid-1950's slum clearance project in which 1,000 human beings are crowded into twelve floors. She had lived on the tenth floor, a height reached in small, slow-motion elevators, sometimes puddled with urine. In the smelly, unlighted stairwell, where the lightbulbs had either been stolen or broken, the walls were covered with grime and crayon drawings. The forty-one-year-old widow, shot to death inside her apartment, had also been reported in the press as a victim of elusive snipers.

"She looked out the window when we heard the shots," her young son said. "She screamed and then she fell to the floor. There was a lot of blood around her."

"She fell back and said, 'Oh, God,'" a thirteen-year-old daughter remembered. "She went out of her head and started talking baby talk."

Then the state troopers rushed into the building, firing into the corridors. "They told us to get our black asses out of there," a seventeen-year-old daughter said.

Of all the riot deaths none received more publicity than Mrs. Spellman's, because of her eleven children. The three over eighteen went to live with other relatives and the Essex County Welfare Department placed four others in a private home. Four others became state wards in a foster home. A committee raised $3,178 for the children, which was placed in a trust fund.

The compensation for losing a mother—$289 each—was more than other families of riot victims received.

Brenda Spellman, the oldest child at twenty-two, is an operator with the telephone company. She is a pleasant girl but a little tired of discussing the incident. *"Those poor Spellman kids, those poor Spellman kids,* that's all I've been hearing," she told me. "I just want everybody to forget about it and just let us live."

Still on Hunterdon Street just the other side of Springfield Avenue stands the six-family tenement where Mrs. Hattie Gainer died violently at age fifty-three. The building had been built with care but now it looked down on the littered pavement of Hunterdon through bullet-splattered windows, its boarded-up doors barring the life that teemed around it. "The reason they all moved out," said an old man in suspenders, "was because the heat broke down and then the water pipe busted and no one would fix it. Cold weather came and they all moved out."

He also remembered Hattie Gainer who was shot minutes after Mrs. Spellman. "She used to be sitting in the second-floor window looking out all the time," he said.

Breaking in through the basement door was easy. Light slanted through broken windows on the first floor. Piles of clothing, curtains, and an old chair with protruding stuffing were abandoned in the front rooms. On the third floor, someone who had tried to make off with a bathtub had quit at the hallway. Mrs. Gainer's twenty-four-year-old daughter, Mrs. Marie Evans, had lived just above her mother on the third floor. Tacked to a closet door in her front room was a New York *Sunday News* color photo of "Old Glory," clipped from the paper two weeks before the room had been further decorated with bullet holes. There were twenty-six of them sprayed on the adjacent wall, in a pattern and angle that could only have come from an automatic weapon at street level.

Mrs. Evans, living now in another part of the ghetto, delivered an epitaph for the ghost house.

"I was outside on the sidewalk, I looked up and saw my mother looking out her second-floor window. They were shooting at the projects then and I went upstairs with my girl friend to my apartment on the third floor. 'It looks like they're getting ready to shoot up here,' my girl friend said, and I ran downstairs to tell my mother and my kids to stay away from the windows. There was shooting by the time I got downstairs and my mother was laying in a puddle of blood and my kids were screaming. I kept yelling to her but she couldn't hear me. Then two state troopers with yellow stripes on their pants came in. 'We made a mistake,' one of them said. 'We shot the wrong person, we're killing innocent people.'

"They made the kids go into the bathroom and they made me go in there with them," she continued. "They told me they'd send for an ambulance. Every time I'd try to get to my mother the one trooper told me to stay in the bathroom. My mother was moaning there in a puddle of blood. They weren't trying to help her, there wasn't no first aid or nothin' for her, nothin'. They let her lay there in the blood until the ambulance came three hours later and then she was dead."

A picture frame with photos of her three children stood on Mrs. Evans' coffee table. A bullet had mangled one side. "I had it on the mantelpiece," she explained.

Michael Pugh was twelve years old when he died in the military occupation of Newark. National Guardsmen shot him in front of his tenement on 15th Avenue on Sunday night, while he took out the garbage. A boy with him had called the guardsmen names and they opened fire.

The press said his killers were unknown.

"Essentially there were two riots in Newark," said Eric Mann, ex-teacher[1] and ghetto organizer working with the Newark Community Union Project (NCUP). "One was started by black people and one by the State Police. The first riot was over in two days. It took very few lives but a hell of a lot of property. The second riot was pure retribution on the part of the National Guard and State Police. For instance, the first three days not a black store was touched. It can be documented that systematically, starting on Friday night and primarily on Saturday and Sunday nights, the State Police went to each black store and smashed in its windows. Some guardsmen told me that if they were not relieved they would have gone on strike, that they came to put down a riot and that the riot was over in two days. The State Police were accosting people, pulling them out of cars and hitting them over the head. A sniper would shoot from a roof and they'd shoot one or two shots at the sniper and he'd run away. Then they would empty three hundred rounds into the entire apartment building, shooting from the first floor to the fifth or sixth floors. The policy of the National Guard was to use the snipers—and there were very few by Friday—as an excuse to put down what they understood to be a very popular rebellion and as a result they felt that anybody in the neighborhood was fair game."

This view, a far different one from that found in the press, is confirmed by twenty-two-year-old Mack Tucker. We retraced the route that he and his

---

[1] The Board of Education fired Mann from his job as eighth grade teacher at Peshine Avenue School early in 1967. Charges included misconduct, insubordination, and conduct unbecoming a teacher. He was specifically charged with asking his Clinton Hill area students to write an essay on "My Christmas with the Rats and Roaches," with discussing birth control in class, and with injecting his personal views on the Viet Nam war into his teaching.

friend, Sam Malone, had taken after leaving the home of Malone's girl friend at Bergen and West Runyon.

"There were police barricades all down this street," he said, motioning with his hand. "We couldn't make a left turn on Jelliff and there were barricades on the left all the way down West Runyon. We went all the way down the hill and finally turned at Elizabeth Avenue and drove over to Bigelow. We turned left there to go back up the hill but National Guardsmen there stopped us and made us back up. All the cars were being turned back. Sam backed up and went back down Elizabeth Avenue the way we had just come. There were a lot of cars ahead of us, driving slow."

As their car crept forward, a police car pulled up on the left side. All Tucker remembers is hearing explosions.

"You can tell I wasn't looking at the police car," he said. "They weren't telling us to stop or nothing. See where the slugs hit." He ran his fingers over scars on the back of his neck and head. "I was looking straight ahead. Some of the windows were shattered and I felt glass all over me. My eyes were closed and I couldn't see. I couldn't talk, I couldn't do anything. I was paralyzed. Someone came over to the passenger side of the car and said 'Get out of there' but I couldn't move. He put something that felt like a gun barrel against my head and told me again to get out. The blood started dripping out my mouth and he said, 'This guy's dead.' Someone said it was an accident, the shotgun had gone off.

"I sat in the car for at least a couple of hours, and I could hear a big crowd standing there," Tucker continued. "The pain was terrible. Finally a truck or something pulled up and the police thought I was dead. They wouldn't touch me. They told Sam to take me out of the car and dump me in the truck. They told the driver to drop me off at the hospital but not to hurry."

Listed in critical condition for a time, Tucker was eventually released from City Hospital with four shotgun slugs still in his neck. No charges were made against him.

"We're just beginning to find out some of the things that happened in the city during the riot," Sam Freeman, Tucker's attorney, said. "I've filed a million-dollar law suit against [Police Director Dominick A.] Spina and the police department. They can't go around just shooting people like that."

We Have to Make Them Admit They Were Wrong

Most of them had filed into the meeting room by seven o'clock, and now it was eight-twenty on a soul-chilling, blustery winter night. About sixty black people, most of them women, shifted around in the folding chairs. Their dead had been buried months before. Their stitches had been removed. Their bruises and broken heads had healed and their shattered windows had been repaired.

Seven months before, a half-block away, two Newark policemen had dragged cab driver John Smith toward the Fourth Precinct and precipitated a riot. Now the worn ghetto people arrived to list grievances that the white world cared nothing about. White people, reading newspaper accounts fearfully in the suburbs, already had their own understanding of Newark's riot: a lot of niggers running around burning, looting, and killing a police detective and a fire captain. Twenty-one others had also been shot to death but they were black—either looters or killed by mysterious snipers.

"We have to make them admit they were wrong doing what they did," said Albert Black, chairman of the Newark Human Rights Commission. "That's all these people want. There is no communication between the people here and the police. If there is ever going to be communication, the police will have to be believed. The state troopers, police, and guardsmen must admit some of the things they did here were wrong or these people will never believe anybody again. We're going to make tapes and flood the governor with so much documentation they'll have to admit they were wrong.

"I don't know if we can do it or not but I've got to try," Black added. "I need this like I need a hole in my head. The Human Rights Commission was a bullshit thing for a long time. They made me chairman and didn't think I'd do anything, but if I'm going to do it, I might as well do it right. I walk through these dirty streets and see these poor devils who never had a chance at anything. . . . Somebody has to do something."

Six members of the commission sat at a long table. The officials, four of them administrative Negroes, listened gravely to the familiar stories as speakers came forward one by one.

It began with Al Black, a pleasant man with sad, sleepy eyes, rising to read in a mild voice:

"At approximately five-thirty P.M. on the fourteenth of July, most of the residents of Beacon Street were sitting on their porches watching their kids playing in the front. Without provocation, members of the State Police approached the corner and sprayed the street from left to right. They shot James Snead, thirty-six, in the stomach as he made repairs on his car out front. Karl Green, seventeen, was shot in the head as he stood on his sister's porch. Seventy-six residents of Beacon Street have signed this eyewitness petition."

Some of the signers in the audience nodded in agreement as a man stepped forward to speak. The hands of James Sanders, Sr., were clasped tightly behind his back. "We have ten kids," he told the group. "We did have eleven until the fourteenth of July. That's the day one got killed. . . .

I don't know how to say this. . . . We checked the police and hospitals and we couldn't find him for six days. He was in the morgue all shot up. It must have been a shotgun." There were murmurs from the audience as Sanders returned to his seat. Other hands were raised to be heard and Robert King and his pretty wife stepped to the front.

"I have a drycleaning store on Avon Avenue and South Eighteenth Street," he began. "At about three-thirty Sunday morning the sound of breaking glass woke us up. From our bedroom in the rear we could see state troopers come into the store."

"When we heard the glass break we got up to look," Mrs. King went on. "They took the clothes with the butts of their guns, knocked them off the rack, and just went knocking things around. . . . By accident they hit the cash register and they opened it. One came over and took the money and then they were looking around. One of them said, 'There's nothing else left here, let's go.' They got in the middle of Avon Avenue and fired back into the store. They shot up a candy store and a lounge, too."

Mrs. King had brought along shell casings found at the scene and photographs of the storefront where her husband had nailed a notice: GLASS WAS BROKEN BY STATE TROOPERS, CARS NO. 530, 535, 491.

One woman stepped forward to tell of a little girl who had lost an eye and an ear. Two women from Hunterdon Street related how State Police had broken into their homes. "Our doors were kicked in and we were forced into the street like animals," one of them said. "It was wet and women and children were forced to lie down on the wet sidewalk."

"I had this little sheriff sticker on my car window and my teaching credentials," said John Thomas, a forty-four-year-old high school teacher. "I had most of what us middle-class black men thought was gonna keep us safe." He told of being dragged from his car and being struck with a rifle butt. "I found out like the black businessmen in Newark," he went on. "I found out the big game. I found out that no matter how many white and colored children I taught, I was still nothing but a black nigger to white people. They made a mistake doing what they did. Now they know we're together."

"I went into John Smith's cell and he was laying there beaten up, groaning and crying," a woman told the audience. "The two arresting officers were there. They said Smith had attacked and kicked them. I asked them to roll up their pants legs to show me where Smith had kicked them but they wouldn't."

It went on into the night, they talked on and on and it all seemed unreal. The floor of the seamy auditorium was littered and overhead were red, green and gold decorations left from a Christmas dance. Black people, beaten and powerless, were speaking of blood and death and the decorations glittered in the light. It was the first time since the riot that these

things were finally being said at a public meeting but those present heard
nothing new. They had been there. All around them were brown faces who
had also been there. And in front of them were a group of administration
appointees—virtual puppets—who had brought along a tape recorder to record the messages of the beaten for posterity.

As far back as August, Black had submitted fourteen instances of unlawful police activity during the riot to state officials. Hundreds more statements and affidavits followed from the Rights Commission, from an ad hoc
committee headed by Dr. Renold E. Burch and more than 275 from Legal
Services Project workers.

"The statements we have indicate widespread police misconduct," said
Oliver Lofton, administrator of the Legal Services Project and a former
U.S. Attorney. "If these allegations are sustained they will warrant criminal
action."

"Every single one of them is valid," Black said. "They have to admit
they were wrong. It's so clear-cut."

"Police are guilty of wanton destruction and actual murder during the
disturbance," Dr. Burch's committee reported.

"The most shocking thing," said Dickinson Debevoise, Legal Services
Project president, "is that there is a tremendous out-pouring of rage and
determination to enforce the laws when it comes to the rioters, but no action whatsoever when the police are involved."

"There is a whole conspiracy of silence," said Henry di Suvero, executive director of the American Civil Liberties Union of New Jersey, "grim
hostility from public officials in response to charges against the police."

"The police were the instrument of a conspiracy to engage in a pattern
of systematic violence, terror, abuse, intimidation, and humiliation to keep
Negroes second-class citizens," a group of Newark lawyers and law pro-
fessors said. "The police seized on the initial orders as an opportunity and
pretext to perpetrate the most horrendous and widespread killing, violence,
torture and intimidation, not in response to any crime or civilian disorder,
but as a violent demonstration of the powerlessness of the plaintiffs and
their class."

Slowly, but with great fanfare, the mills of justice began to grind as the
smoke from Newark's riot started to clear. U.S. Attorney David M. Satz,
stationed in the city, began an investigation into whether anyone's civil
rights had been abused. The office of State Attorney General Arthur J.
Sills, it was announced, would see that all charges against the National
Guard and State Police were investigated. Essex County Prosecutor Brendan T. Byrne's office had already begun investigating the riot's homicides as
it would any other homicide in its jurisdiction. In addition, Governor
Hughes appointed a special commission to investigate the Newark riot and

its causes in detail. The FBI was also conducting special investigations into the arrests of John Smith and black playwright LeRoi Jones and the killing of James Rutledge, Jr.

Newark's unconvinced blacks waited. The whites read of the intentions of those in power and promptly forgot—which was the main intention of those in power. After all this fanfare the issue might have slid quietly away —had it not been for the blue-ribbon commission of the governor.

No Possible Justification

If Governor Hughes expected a whitewash from his commission, he was greatly disappointed. The unexpectedly bold report released on February 10, 1968, blamed the riot on long-neglected social ills, frustration, and white racism. "Excessive and unjustified force" had been used in putting down the eruption, it stated, and black-owned stores had been shot up, mostly by state troopers, in "a pattern of police action for which there is no possible justification."

After hearing more than 700 witnesses during its five months of study, and quoting 106 of them in the report, the commission recommended a grand jury probe of "corruption" in the Newark administration and called for an investigation of the Newark Police Department, a group regarded in the ghetto as "the single continuously lawless element operating in the community." The report commented on the official vengeance in the city's military occupation and found that accounts of snipers had been exaggerated.

> There is no doubt that some shooting that was reported as sniping was firing by police. The large numbers of armed men on the street and inadequate communication among the various units was a critical factor. In addition to Police Director Dominick Spina, one witness testified that on Friday from 10 P.M. on, and continuing sporadically until Saturday morning, he saw State Police located at Springfield Avenue and Bergen Street firing toward Hunterdon Street in the direction of his building. At about 3 A.M. Saturday he observed a National Guard unit behind the building exchanging fire with the first group. Coincidentally, State Police records show that State Police on Bergen and Springfield returned *sniper* fire twice on Saturday.

The report called for sweeping reforms to reconstruct the ghetto, at least emotionally. It recommended placing the city's horrendous school system and malfunctioning municipal courts under state control. It recommended a civilian review board—an explosive issue in Newark—and warned against a police K-9 corps that would only aggravate police-community relations in the ghetto. The report also recommended that Lieutenant Eddie Williams, the only ranking black officer in the department, be promoted to head one of the precincts.

The Hughes Report also stressed its discovery of a prevalent attitude toward Newark's public morality. One realtor had testified that new business wouldn't move into Newark because of the tense racial situation, taxes, and corruption. Another source said that Newark businessmen believed that "everything at City Hall was for sale." A former state official, a former city official, and an incumbent city official agreed: "There's a price on everything at City Hall."

As in any reputable whorehouse, everything had its price and was for sale.

Unfortunately, the most serious aspect of the riot was placed beyond the jurisdiction of the Hughes commissioners. As instructed by the governor, they were under orders not to undertake a case-by-case investigation of the homicides—this being the responsibility of law enforcement agencies. The report stated:

> Prosecutor Byrne testified that his office was inquiring into each of the deaths. Each case was assigned to an assistant prosecutor for an individual investigation, using homicide detectives who are part of the prosecutor's staff. As of January 10, 1968, these investigations are still pending. A letter from the U.S. Attorney indicates that his office has certain deaths under investigation and that these, too, were still pending when this report was written.
>
> The Commission views with concern the fact that such action has not yet been completed. These homicides are matters of grave concern and should be quickly and exhaustively investigated and resolved by the appropriate juries.

However, the commission did take note of a "special report" it had received three months after the riot from the Newark Police Department which stated that the Newark police were responsible for only ten deaths— seven justifiable and three accidental. A policeman and a fire captain had been shot by snipers, the police report added, and the eleven other homicides had resulted from undetermined sources. The Hughes Commissioners found this information hard to accept: "The location of death, the number of wounds, the manner in which the wounds were inflicted all raise grave doubts about the circumstances under which many of these people died."

I Don't Know What I Can Tell the People

And with the publication of the Hughes Report the search for justice petered out. The announcements of investigations all proved to be exercises in calculated futility. Attorney General Sills had assigned State Police detectives to investigate complaints about their own group. All reports went to

Colonel David B. Kelly, their superintendent. "I have checked all the complaints against our men at the request of Governor Hughes," Kelly reported. "There was no need to take disciplinary action. We found nothing to substantiate the charges. . . . Just remember one thing, the police didn't start the riots."

"My inspector general could find no proof that guardsmen were involved in any wrongdoing," stated Major General James F. Cantwell, commander of the New Jersey National Guard. Cantwell said that his inspector generals had checked incidents as the riot progressed and reported to him. He found no cause for action. "There was no major internal investigation after the riot, rather an evaluation and study of our procedures during the disturbance," he said.

"A good faith investigation was made," Attorney General Sills related. "Every attempt was made to try to track down the facts as presented. There is no evidence that State Police planned or ordered any attacks on stores with SOUL BROTHER signs. . . . The fact that you can't find somebody to punish doesn't mean it didn't occur."

"I want to assure the people that the State Police are not in the business of doing anything but protecting citizens," Governor Hughes offered.

Despite the words of hundreds of eyewitnesses, formal depositions, complaints, bloodstains, spent bullets, and hospital records, not *one charge* against the Newark police, National Guard, or State Police was conclusive enough—black people were told—to warrant even an admission of guilt, much less punishment. Many police had carried their own personal weapons, making ballistic reports uncheckable. Units or officers who might have been involved in specific incidents couldn't be identified, it was claimed. Out of hundreds of incidents in one of the most brutal domestic occupations in the nation's history, *not one* could be substantiated. "I don't know what I can tell the people if legal redress is unavailable," Oliver Lofton said.

With the Hughes Report, an independent body with no self-serving interests had delivered the only truth that the state would receive. The onslaught to discredit or neutralize it began immediately. Detective Anthony Giuliano, president of the Newark Patrolmen's Benevolent Association, called the charges of corruption and police abuses "unsubstantiated and un-American." Other PBA heads through the state, including the blustering state president, John Heffernan, followed suit. The Newark PBA was conducting a private "investigation" of its own and was given use of City Hall for its "hearings." The group wanted to prove that the riot was the result of a giant conspiracy. Newark's City Council expressed formal indignation that none of its members had been called upon to testify, after the Hughes Commission apparently dismissed the corrupt ruling body as irrelevant.

All over New Jersey, politicians turned the Hughes Report into a political prop, good for one or two press releases letting their white constituents know that they were staunchly behind "law and order"—though most of them admitted they hadn't read it. Elizabeth Mayor Thomas G. Dunn, for example, damned the report as "an open invitation to lawlessness." Whether he had even seen it is questionable. Whether Dunn's friendly associations with Mafia chieftains such as Simone "Sam the Plumber" De-Cavalcante are likewise an open invitation to lawlessness is a cogent question—though unlikely to be entertained by the Elizabeth *Daily Journal*.[2]

While others leaped to condemn the report before reading it, Governor Hughes secluded himself for three days to prepare "an analytical statement," perhaps hoping that his law and order constituents would forget that it was his commission.

"I'm studying it thoroughly," Sills announced. "I've got to talk to the governor on the views presented here." A day later, he told reporters, "I'm

[2] In January of 1968, I came to the Elizabeth *Daily Journal* to write a column for Joe Jennings, the newspaper's editor. The first result was a fifteen-part series on the post-riot situation in Newark, the embryo of this book and an effort that made me the subject of a formal investigation by the Newark Police Department. Once the Newark series was complete, I turned my attention to Elizabeth and Mayor Dunn, a man whose ego and inability to lead had done nothing to change miserable living conditions endured by the city's poor. A column on Dunn's seemingly bottomless campaign treasury made me an ex-columnist at the age of twenty-nine. I was put to work writing movie schedules. The shake-up went much deeper: Jennings, the only editor at the *Journal* who could comprehend and attempt meaningful journalism, was called to New York by owner Ralph Ingersoll, after which he continued as editor in name only, while the publisher, Harry Frank, assumed tight control of the paper's contents.

A postscript to this sorry affair came on June 10, 1969, when the FBI released thirteen volumes of transcripts on Mafia activity obtained from bugging devices. These transcripts disclosed the camaraderie of Dunn and DeCavalcante. The mayor of Elizabeth responded by saying he *didn't know* at the time who DeCavalcante was, but he admitted taking money from him. An answer to the question of where some of Dunn's extensive campaign funds came from had been provided. As could be expected, the *Journal* soft-pedaled Dunn's involvement as much as possible—as it had *Life* magazine's exposé on the Mafia affiliations of Congressman Cornelius Gallagher—and purposely ignored mention of other prominent area politicians in the FBI material. Frank personally killed a story being written on the shady dealings of Dominick Mirabelli, the Union County attorney, and County Judge Ralph DeVita. Despite the *Journal*'s blackout, the public eventually learned of the judge's activities when he was caught offering a bribe to the Somerset County prosecutor on behalf of gambling interests. DeVita was subsequently suspended and barred from practicing law on December 12, 1969.

A year later, Harry Frank retired to the applause of his many powerful friends to start his own public relations firm—the business he had been in for most of his more than fifty years with the Elizabeth *Daily Journal*. His successors, John Musgat and Gerald Coy, reduced editorial output, carrying on the low level of journalism that had become a tradition at the Elizabeth *Daily Journal*.

With the power of their office, Musgat and Coy, like Frank before them, sacrifice editorial substance to advertising linage. They sacrifice the public's right to know to a philosophy of "no news is good news" and to a jellyfish editorial policy regarding troubled race relations in Union County. The *Journal* shares responsibility for the ignorance of whites on this sensitive issue, a truth pointed out by the Kerner Report. The festering racism of Rahway, Linden, and Roselle reflect the *Journal's* irresponsibility.

not in a position to line up six hundred men and ask each one of them if they did it."

Nor was he ready to do much of anything. Nor was any official, federal, state, or local, ready to take a stand on behalf of the black people of Newark. Ironically, the Hughes Commission's effort to effect an intelligent reconstruction of Newark produced largely negative results. Newark was not allowed the convenience of a phony report and it couldn't live with a just one.

Fuck the Hughes Report

Livingston Street hadn't changed much in the six months since my last visit to see Emerson Moss. The street was still lost, weeds and litter were abundant, and the neighborhood men still met in the small used-tire shop across the street. However, the house where Moss lived had holes punched through its windows and stood deserted and desolate in a heavy rain. The Moss family, a man in the tire shop said, had moved some time before to Sterling Street. This is the street where LeRoi Jones resided, black Newark's writer and militant-in-residence. It seemed an irony that Emerson Moss, a man who hadn't quickly learned to hate after the death of his eleven-year-old son, had moved across the street from Jones's residence where hate and distrust of whites were passwords.

Hate, however, was a luxury for Moss who was too busy just trying to exist. He was found in the kitchen of his second-floor apartment, deep in thought over a bottle of cheap whiskey. My second visit was to get Moss's reaction to the Hughes Report and to find out if he was legally represented in his son's death, and, if not, to give him the name of a lawyer who was offering his services. By this time, the report, which Moss had never heard of and didn't express the slightest interest in, was history, filed away and as forgotten as Moss himself. With whiskey drowning out any reluctance, the tall, soft-spoken man candidly revealed how it looked from his side.

"The only people who count in Newark are the white man and colored women," he blurted. "Fuck the Hughes Report and fuck any money. I don't want any money behind the death of my son. Only thing I want is my son back. Can you give me that?"

Emerson Moss, who was still unemployed, refused this latest offer of help the same way he had refused to accept three dollars I had offered him on the first visit. Moss belonged to the ignorant and the uncivilized. He refused to accept payment for a dead son.

3

WELCOME HOME, LEROI

The "Black Militant"

A tour of black Newark wouldn't be complete without a stop at the residence of Everett LeRoi Jones, sometimes termed "the prince of the revolution" by his black brothers and "the famous nigger" by the Newark police. The black playwright lives among his people on one of those one-way streets that doesn't seem to go anywhere, the eleventh house down Sterling Street, around the corner from—of all places—the Essex County Courthouse. His house, three stories of weather-beaten gray, is set off from its equally shabby neighbors by a large banner begging the ghetto to ORGANIZE in blazing red letters.

Jones, who had managed to hate his way to a thirty-fourth birthday, was the darling of New York City's white literati in the early 1960's. He was the scowling black panther flush with success from what appeared—as far as most whites were concerned—a bent psyche. He hated whites, "cocasians" as he referred to them, for what they had done to his people.

The playwright's first impact on the white world came from the violence of his treatment of racial conflict. In one short play, *J-E-L-L-O,* Eddie "Rochester" Anderson, one of LeRoi's favorite "nee-grows," throws off his servile jester's role to kill his patronizing employer, Jack Benny.

The more usual situation of Jones's work, however, is the innocent black being ground up by animalistic whites—as in *Slaveship.* In that vein, his renowned play *Dutchman* was called the best American play of 1963–64.

Jones gave out doses of artistic hate and he was rewarded with the John Hay Whitney and Obie awards. He told everybody white to go screw themselves and they made him a Guggenheim Fellow. Jones was truly original in that he tired of the amusing game before his benefactors did. Shedding a white wife, he took up residence in Harlem in 1966 and completely shunned the white world. In Harlem, Jones put together the Black Arts Repertory Theatre School. Anti-white plays? LeRoi had just been warming up. In the blackness of Harlem he found nourishment. He latched onto $40,000 in anti-poverty funds and used it to finance his unsettling literary efforts. When politicians discovered that Jones was using the taxpayers' money to portray them as "degenerate homosexuals," they were somewhat peeved. There was a scandal. There was the predictable end to the project. Some people in Harlem wanted to congratulate Jones for his unique style of battling poverty. There were others who wanted money from him. Then there were those who would have settled for a few pints of his blood. "Now that the old world has crashed around me, and it's raining in early summer, I live in Harlem . . . and suffer for my decadence which kept me away so long," Jones had written after his arrival. Now it was winter and still raining. And now LeRoi thought perhaps the suffering would yield triumph in this minor metropolis 10 miles southwest of New York City on the banks of the polluted Passaic River.

Short and thin with slightly stooped shoulders, LeRoi Jones is, despite his press clippings, essentially a mild-mannered man with the gentle sensitivity of an artist. He often seems to suppress this side of his nature. His expressive eyes give it away while his frantic, often violent rhetoric furthers his public image. Beneath his bushy hair may be a devious mind, but beneath his colorful dashike beats a big heart. A group of actors he has gathered and sustained presents plays for the black community. He conducts classes in black history and culture for ghetto children, presenting them with an image of themselves that contradicts the life around them. Though police and the white public envision assembly line firebomb production at the Jones home, he is politically non-revolutionary. His message, to be found in any high school civics textbook, is that meaningful change in Newark will come only from the ballot box. Jones calls his home and headquarters The Spirit House. God knows what the Newark police call it.

Jones manifests the major change of his life in the symbolic handshake with which he greets his black brothers. Since shortly before the riot he has been a member of a sect close to the Sunni or Orthodox Muslim faith, one of the largest religious groups in the world, followers of the prophet Muhammad and the teachings of the Koran. (Orthodox Muslims are not to be confused with the Black Muslims, an anti-white sect peculiar to this country with mosques in many large cities, including Newark. The religion of Islam and the domestic sect are similar in some aspects, but basically Black Muslims are a racial phenomenon while the Sunni are religiously oriented.) The playwright is surrounded by his Muslim brothers, and their number grows steadily. Islam represents an alternative to the Christian "slave-religion" and to the ghetto process that leads so many of its residents to the Essex County Penitentiary or Trenton State Prison.

So "religious fanatic" may be added to "black militant" and the rest of the titles given Jones by the white press.

Having returned to where he was born and raised, Jones prospers—or seems to. The finer instincts of the Newark police have even given the playwright a new popularity, if only in the ghetto, where he puts out a steady flow of verse that could never be accused of excessive love for his white brothers or prudishness as far as the English language is concerned. As a matter of fact, Jones would have continued on in virtual anonymity as far as a majority of both whites and blacks are concerned except for a chance meeting with Newark's officers of the law in the early morning hours of the riot's second day.

Where Are the Guns?

The playwright and two companions, Barry Wynn, twenty-four, an actor residing at The Spirit House, and Charles McCray, the thirty-three-year-old head accountant for United Community Corporation (UCC), Newark's anti-poverty agency, had been riding through the riot-torn ghetto in Jones's VW camper when they encountered the police at South 7th Street and South Orange Avenue.

"We were told to come out of the camper bus," Jones said. "When I opened the door and stepped down, one detective, whom I recognized as having once attended Barringer High School while I was there, preached to me, screaming that we were 'the black bastards' who'd been shooting at him. I said that we hadn't been shooting at anyone. I told the officer that I thought I remembered him from high school—whereupon he hit me in the face and threw me against the side of the camper. The detective then began to jab me as hard as he could with his pistol in my stomach, asking, 'Where are the guns?' I told him that there were no guns. Suddenly it seemed that five or six officers surrounded me and began to beat me. I was hit perhaps five times on top of my head by nightsticks, and when I fell, some of the officers went about me methodically trying to break my hands, elbows and shoulders. One officer tried to kick me in the groin and there were many punches thrown. As they beat me they kept calling me 'animal' and asking me, 'Where are the guns?' "

"I was standing about thirty feet away," a black police officer related, "when they snatched him out of that little truck, knocked him to the ground and began to beat him so viciously that I don't know how that little man is still living today. I started to go over and butt in, but I just knew they were going to kill him from the way they were beating him and I figured they'd just kill me, too. Man, I was crying. That was all I could do without committing suicide."

The officer said he didn't testify at the trial because "it would have been just another nigger telling lies on the whole Newark police force."

Sitting behind the desk at the fourth precinct when Jones and his two companions were brought in was none other than Police Director Spina, who, noting the playwright's bloody appearance, thought the occasion rather humorous. Jones was taken to City Hospital, where a nasty cut on his forehead was stitched, and then to police headquarters, where he was fingerprinted. Police then announced Jones had been in possession of two revolvers. He and the other two men were charged with possession of the weapons and the prosecutor's office asked for $25,000 bail for Jones, an outlandish figure which the presiding magistrate allowed. The playwright was then transported to Essex County Penitentiary and put into solitary confinement where he remained for several days until bail was posted.

Jones, Wynn, and McCray filed a damage suit against Spina and seven officers who had participated in the attack. Police responded with a $200-million countersuit charging conspiracy to slander. The black men refused to give depositions in their case. When a federal court ordered them to do so, they took the Fifth Amendment. This led some to disbelieve the charges, but for them it was the only safe move. If they failed to convince a jury of their case, they could have ended up owing the police a lot of money. Both the suit and countersuit were eventually dropped but the state continued to press the criminal charge against Jones, a matter not to be finally resolved until two years later.

Black Political Agitator

Jones, almost solely because of the publicity surrounding his bloody arrest, was forced into a leading role in post-riot Newark. White middle-class families, largely of Italian extraction and unable to retreat before the spreading black migration from cramped ghettos, had been frightened senseless by the riot and regarded Jones and his ilk as all that was wrong with Newark. Unconcerned about the deaths of black women and children and machine guns ripping into cardboard tenements, they found it outrageous to read of an uppity nigger allegedly riding around the city with two revolvers. Their fears were fed by the fantasies of Dominick Spina, Newark's police director. Appearing before a legislative commission in Trenton on March 29, 1968, Spina called "guerrilla warfare" the current problem. "They're going to go to the downtown business section and into the white suburbs and start shooting and burning," he prophesied.

Given the new title of "black political agitator," Jones was thrust by whites into the political limelight. The playwright, who represented at most an aesthetic spokesman for young blacks, was now seen in white imaginations as the black Genghis Khan. White groups formed and armed themselves through fear and ignorance, guaranteeing that some blacks would react to confirm the whites' fears. Thus a poet with a practiced scowl and a mean pen—a man having difficulty even getting himself together—was regarded by the whites as the satanic chieftain of a united black horde ready to overrun Newark. The white population had whipped itself into a frenzy without having the least knowledge of the conditions that had nurtured a riot, the long-term and immediate causes, nor the ghosts created during the disturbance—ghosts that have been buried and must now be exhumed.

PART II

Sifting Through the Ashes

4

THE GHOST OF LESTER LONG

Oh My God, He Has Been Shot

Somewhere in the ashes of Newark's riot were the remains of 22-year-old Lester Long, Jr., who had died two years before at the corner of Oriental and Broadway, a good place to begin charting the course of an impending riot. Approximately fifteen yards up the block was the Happy Inn Tavern, whose departing patrons in the early morning hours of June 12, 1965, witnessed Long's last moments. On the other side of the street, eight huge pillars of Essex County High School recall an age when human sacrifices were even more popular.

At 1:15 A.M. Long and his friend Larry Northern, seventeen, were riding in Long's black 1955 Chevrolet on Broadway. Between Chester and Elwood Avenues—five blocks from Oriental Place—they passed an unmarked police car cruising in the opposite direction. In it were Patrolmen Henry Martinez, twenty-nine, and William Provost, thirty, members of the Crime Prevention Unit. Noticing Long's loud muffler, Martinez made a U-turn and followed the car. He later called it a chase, but Northern and other witnesses said the police car pulled up a minute after Long had turned into Oriental and parked near the corner. Martinez approached the car and Long handed over his license and registration when asked. Suspicious of the credentials, which were "marked up" in the age and height categories, Martinez told Long to get into the rear of the police car. Long again complied. Northern got out of the passenger side of Long's car and joined some friends on the corner. Martinez then backed his patrol car out on Broadway and drove thirty yards up the block and made another U-turn. This left the police car at the corner of Second Avenue and Broadway at an outdoor telephone booth, about eighty-five yards diagonally across from Long's car, which remained parked on Oriental Place.

Long's friend, Northern, waited fifteen minutes at the car for his release. During this period one patrolman was in the phone booth while one remained in the car with Long. A friend of Northern's came by and they took

a short ride, returning at 1:45 A.M. Long was still sitting in the back of
the unmarked car, but it had been moved a short distance up the block,
past the high school, and was parked directly across from Long's car on
Broadway. By this time the police had been informed of a contempt of
court action—four unanswered traffic violations—against Long, and they
were going to take him in. They were waiting for a tow truck to come for
Long's car.

As they waited the Happy Inn closed for the night, its customers spilling
out a few minutes before 2 A.M. Northern was standing with two others
on the corner and when a girl friend pulled up near the front of the tavern,
he went to speak with her. On the way he passed Horace Foote, a custodian
for the Board of Education, who had just left the tavern and was walking
toward the corner Northern had just left. At this moment and in the view
of this group, Long, after having been in the rear of the police car for forty-
five minutes, bolted from the rear seat. He ran toward the people on the
sidewalk less than forty feet away.

He reached the corner just as a .38 caliber bullet fired by Officer Martinez thudded into the back of his head. Long pitched forward and was
dead before he hit the sidewalk, twisting over onto his back a few feet past
the corner. The bullet, fired from some thirty feet behind the fleeing man,
passed through his head and came out between his eyes. The shocked
crowd, some of whom had been little more than an arm's length from Long,
watched his blood leak onto the sidewalk. The shaken Martinez reached
the corner and called back across Broadway for his partner to call an
ambulance.

The police supplied this version of the shooting to newspapers:

> A motorist, halted for an alleged traffic violation, was fatally shot early
> today by a Crime Prevention Unit patrolman. Police said the man had
> slashed the officer's partner with a knife and ran from the patrol car in
> which he was being questioned.
>
> Captain Anthony Kossup said the man was identified by a sister as Lester
> Long Jr., 22, of 44 Mount Pleasant Avenue. Long was pronounced dead on
> arrival at City Hospital of a bullet wound in the head. Patrolman Henry
> Martinez, who fired the shot, said he was not trying to hit Long but slipped
> as he drew his gun and the revolver went off.
>
> Kossup said Martinez and Patrolman William Provost were riding on
> Broadway about 1:15 A.M. when they heard a car with a noisy muffler. They
> halted the vehicle after a six-block chase to Oriental Street, where they told
> the driver, later identified as Long, and a companion, they faced several
> summonses.
>
> The driver gave them a license and registration in two different names,
> police said. Martinez and Provost said they told the driver to get into their
> police car and asked him for his social security number. They then radioed
> Police Headquarters for a record check on the man.

The second man, who was not identified, asked if he could leave. The pair told him he could and he walked away. The patrolman, meanwhile, issued the driver summonses for careless driving, having a loud muffler and having only one working headlight. The summonses were issued to the name on the license given them by the motorist.

A short time later, the patrolmen were notified that the social security number was in the name of Lester Junior Long, 22, and that Long was wanted on four traffic warrants. They said they asked Long for other identification and that when he took out his wallet, several social security and draft cards, a bill of sale and other papers spilled out, all with different names.

The patrolmen said Long had become increasingly angry and began cursing them when they told him he was under arrest for the traffic warrants.

"We told him we would have to have him fingerprinted to learn who he was," Martinez said. "He had his right hand in a pocket and when we told him we would have to routinely search him, he refused.

"When I reached over the front seat, he suddenly pulled out the knife from the pocket with the blade open and slashed at my throat. I raised my arm and my elbow hit his wrist and warded off the blow."

Police said that Provost was cut at this time.

The patrolmen said Long then ran from the car despite their shouts that he halt. *Martinez said he flung open his door, whipped out his revolver and then lost his balance as he jumped from the car.*

"The gun suddenly went off," Martinez said. *"The man was about thirty feet from me. I wasn't trying to shoot him but he was hit."* [1]

Detective Sergeant Frank Ardito said Long was arrested twice this year in Newark. He said Long was sentenced to 30 days in jail for atrocious assault and battery and was sentenced to time spent in jail on an assault and battery complaint.

Detectives Thomas Flanagan and John Conlan said later a driver for Dewey's Garage was sent to tow away the car after police left the scene. The detectives said a crowd of persons warned the tow truck driver against towing the car. He called his superior who, in turn, notified police. The car was gone when police arrived.

Police found the car almost four hours later, parked near Long's home.

No sooner had the black community read the first version of the shooting when another was reported, this one saying that Martinez had aimed and fired with every intention of hitting Long. Those who had seen the shooting knew the first story wasn't correct and, because it was such an obvious cover-up, wondered how much of the second version was true. The police blunder increased the anger of the black community. A police report conceivably would be falsified to change an intentional shooting to an accidental one, but to do the opposite was unheard of. Newark cared little for Long's life, but they tended carefully his obituary.

[1] Author's italics.

"If the police felt that Long had been legitimately shot," said Bob Curvin, then Newark CORE chairman, "they would never have created a phony report. . . . There were a number of people who *saw* what had happened, they *saw* the shooting. Martinez didn't stumble and that part about the other policeman getting cut was nonsense. He was supposed to have had a scratch, nothing more than a superficial scratch that could have come from anything. I spent countless hours out there trying to prevent a riot. These people had all that kind of nonsense they could stand."

The police were unaware that at noon on Sunday, Larry Northern, Horace Foote, and three other eyewitnesses to the shooting had assembled at the Mount Zion Baptist Church on Broadway, not far from the corner where Long had fallen thirty-four hours before. Curvin and three other Newark-Essex CORE leaders were also present, along with Newark attorney Irvin Solondz, and an official court reporter. The witnesses gave what amounted to sworn depositions.

A forty-page transcript was assembled, including these pertinent portions:

> This fellow came running past me and fell about a half-foot—not a half-foot, but about three feet in front by the car there. . . . He ran right past me, almost touched me. . . . Well, let us put it this way. If I had took another step me and him would have bumped into one another.
>
> QUESTION: Did you hear any voice shout anything at this figure or did this fellow say anything to you?
>
> ANSWER: No, I didn't hear anything. . . . After he fell somebody said, "Oh my God, he has been shot." Somebody hollered, "Foote, you almost got that."
>
> Q: When he ran past you, did you see the fellow who was shot? Did he have any weapon, knife or gun in his hands?
>
> A: No, he did not. Then I turned around and I saw Lester jump out of the car, slam the door, and run across the street . . .
>
> Q: Let me ask you this, was he [Martinez] standing with both feet flatfooted? Was he running when he took out his gun?
>
> A: He made two steps. He jumped out of the car, opened the door, made two steps and then he shot . . .
>
> Q: How far away from Lester were you?
>
> A: Foote was standing a little in front of me with two more guys, my cousin and I was standing a little over from the store. I would say that was about a good six or seven feet.
>
> Q: Were the police officers wearing short or long sleeve shirts?
>
> A: Short sleeve shirts.

Q: Was either of them bleeding?

A: I didn't see any blood. No, neither one, because I was standing very close. I went to see him [Long, now on the sidewalk], you know.

Q: You never heard the police officers say anything to Lester as he was running?

A: No, I didn't hear anything. I was standing right by the bar door.

Q: Who was with you?

A: My three sisters.

Q: Were there other people on this corner? Quite a number of you?

A: Yes, because they had closed and everybody was coming out. . . . My sister was standing on the corner and the other one was behind me. My sister turned to tell her to come on. A man [Foote] came up and told us that some cops were sitting across the street and they said they were taking everybody downtown and for us to get off the corner. . . . Right after he said that the boy came across the street running, the cop jumped out of the car and shot him.

Q: Did you hear any sounds that you could make out like words like "stop" or "halt"?

A: No.

Q: When you saw the boy, after the shot, was he still standing?

A: He stumbled. He was right by the curb, so I guess he was trying to run a little bit more, but he just fell.

Q: When you saw the boy running, did he have anything in his hands?

A: I did not see anything.

Q: How many people were there on the corner at the time the shot was fired? More than ten would you say?

A: Yes. I was standing right in front [of the Happy Inn]. I was talking to Mr. Horace Foote, and he was telling my sister and I that there was an unmarked police car across the street. . . . Just as I turned around, just as he got through saying it was an unmarked police car I turned around and I heard a shot—I mean I saw the boy running and I heard a shot. . . .

Q: Did he have anything in his hands that you could see?

A: I didn't see anything. . . .

Q: Did you hear the police officers yelling anything?

A: No. . . . He [Long] was coming and he fell just about at my oldest sister's feet. In fact, she had been standing there.

Q: Did you hear any yelling or shouting from that car toward the boy [Long]?

A: All I heard was the shot. . . . I thought it was my boy friend's cousin. I ran over. He was just lying there. I said, "Why don't they do something?" He was bleeding. Blood was coming out of his head. Then the police emergency took so long to get there. He had been lying there about twenty minutes.

Martinez had now admitted that his early version of Long's shooting was faulty. It was clear that the story had deliberately been reversed. Possibly, the police believed there had been too many witnesses to get away with the original version or perhaps the city's liability for accidental death litigation was the chief factor. At this point, with CORE pressing him, Mayor Addonizio "technically" suspended Martinez on June 18, pending an investigation.

This was the cue for the morality play's new characters to emerge. Anthony Imperiale, later to become an important figure in the city, made his first appearance in Newark, waving his fist in support of the police. While CORE held rallies for a civilian review board, the police and PBA demonstrated for five days at City Hall, with even Martinez's wife and children in the picket line. His supporters contrasted Martinez's job—maintaining the thin blue line against the jungle—to Long's record of arrests. They were saying in effect that *any action* was permissible if it maintained so-called law and order.

"This case is a morale buster for any man wearing a uniform who is trying to do his job," huffed John Heffernan. Newark PBA leader Giuliano said that his organization backed Martinez "one hundred percent."

What should have been an issue defined by facts had become an ideological conflict with "police morale" as the main issue. Before it ended the Human Rights Commission was firmly established as a spineless puppet of the city administration and a grand jury decision strengthened the conviction of non-whites that they were without legal redress.

The Human Rights Commission, the window-dressing of the city administration for the black population, held a quickie hearing. Without even calling Hy Kuperstein, who had written the first newspaper account of the shooting, it managed to vindicate Martinez in a single session. The commission concluded that race had not been a factor in the incident and called it a day. Martinez was returned to duty behind a desk. As it turned out, his announced suspension had indeed been technical since he had continued to collect his salary and no entry was made on his record.

The grand jury gave the matter more attention, or at least took a respectably longer time. In five days it heard some thirty witnesses, including

Larry Northern and ten other eyewitnesses of the shooting, Kuperstein, and—for two and a half hours—Martinez and Provost. The jury then retired to deliberate with these remarks from Judge Alexander P. Waugh, then Essex County assignment judge:

> Did the decedent commit a high misdemeanor in the car? If he did not, there is no legal justification for the shooting. If no crime was committed in the car, if Martinez aimed to kill, he was guilty of murder; if he aimed to maim, he was guilty of manslaughter. The motor vehicle violations, the contempt of court, the escape—which is a misdemeanor—are not offenses justifying shooting the decedent under any circumstances.

Facing certain uproar from the police and the city administration if it indicted Martinez, the grand jury returned "no bill" on July 1. Seven of the twenty-three jurors, according to a reliable leak, had voted for a manslaughter indictment. Even these seven jurors demonstrated Newark's sickness. They were saying that the bullet that went through Long's head was meant to maim him. Bob Curvin, who earned Martinez's endearing affection for years to come, described the situation crudely but aptly: "Martinez was sweating his ass off."

CORE, using this case as an argument for civilian review boards, helped direct national attention to the Newark situation. CORE National Director James Farmer said over NBC radio:

> This is of course conceivable that there may be a justifiable killing by a policeman but the facts in this case do not indicate that such was the case. Let me point out that the mayor himself, the mayor of Newark, has indicated that there were contradictory statements coming from the police department and he wants to find out why the police department contradicted themselves. . . . Now the mayor has said that the contradictory reports were the key to the current protests and threatened demonstrations by the Congress of Racial Equality and he is right. We still call for an independent review board in major cities, in New York City, in Newark, and this will be the focus of our activities of the situation. . . . I think the slashing of a person is not grounds for the policeman serving as jury and executioner. I think a policeman who is trained in marksmanship should be able to shoot to stop, to shoot for the leg, that will drop them and hold them, and not shoot to kill.

Farmer came to Newark on July 21 to lead a peaceful demonstration calling for a review board. As a result, he was soon one of ten defendants involved in a libel suit brought by Martinez after leaflets had been distributed locally calling him a murderer.

On various occasions, when subjected to severe criticism, the Newark police have resorted to this tactic. Such would later be the case with the $200-million suit against LeRoi Jones, a $16,500,000 suit against cab driver John Smith, and such was certainly the case with this $3.7-million suit. Its purpose was to intimidate and harass, which is why ten defendants were named. This tactic could be relied upon to curtail future demonstrations related to Long's death.

Lester Long Runs On

A year later, on July 19, 1966, Martinez appeared at the law office of Dickinson Debevoise, Newark attorney representing Farmer, for a deposition in the libel suit. It proceeded smoothly until Debevoise asked Martinez questions about how he had been supplied with recordings made the previous summer at rallies, whereupon Martinez had a sudden attack of amnesia. It appeared to Debevoise and Arnold Mytelka, attorney representing the nine other defendants, that the patrolman and his lawyer, Edward D'Alessandro, seemed to have the facilities of the entire Newark Police Department at their disposal in preparing their case.

The deposition of Martinez provided a third rendition of his account of the shooting, one with a good deal more animation—and imagination. In this version the dead youth had run thirty to forty feet beyond where everyone had seen him drop. And now, with the knife in his hand, Long "was hollering and screaming . . . acting like a wild man running down the street." Also more active was Martinez himself, now supposedly running after Long and calling on him to halt before he fired. Long was eighty to ninety feet away before he fired—according to Martinez—and the crowd along Broadway had now dwindled to "three or four" people nowhere within range of his shot.

Dialogue attributed to Long and the subsequent action in the police car was also interesting:

> "You ain't searching me, you white motherfucker. . . . You motherfuckers ain't going to take me and lock me up. No white motherfucker is going to lock me up."
>
> "Look out, Hank, he's got a knife!"
>
> As we were both trying to grab him, I grabbed for his pants belt and he slashed with the knife and I pulled my hands away because at this point he was taking his left hand and was starting to go out the car. I tried to grab him to keep him in the car and at the same time try to stop him from swinging the knife hand and we failed. He got out of the car and at that point I was stuck behind the steering wheel because I was turned sideways and I was attempting to get out of the car door.

As Martinez's perception and recollection had dramatically improved in some instances, however, the passage of time had eroded his memory in others. Even the reported "knife wound" suffered by Provost now escaped mention and the knife itself was nowhere to be seen because Martinez testified he had picked it up and handed it to Provost, telling him to place it in the back of their police car. He also told Provost to be careful not to smudge any fingerprints, telltale markings which then must have disappeared as there were none, at least none belonging to Lester Long.

The sworn testimony of his own deposition—with the slayer admitting he had removed evidence from the scene—should have been reason enough for immediate suspension in any reputable police department.

In the final analysis, the further Martinez said Long had run, so was the actual truth that much closer. Thirteen months after the black youth had gone down on the corner of Broadway and Oriental Place the deceased was still running—but only in the mind of Henry Martinez.

In November of 1966, four months after taking a deposition from Martinez, Debevoise and Mytelka visited Kuperstein, a reporter with seventeen years' experience, in the press room of the police department. After the meeting, Debevoise returned to his office and prepared a memorandum. This conversation made it clear that both Captain Kossup and Martinez had been present when the information was given out, with Kossup dominating the event. Martinez, Kuperstein said, had been present throughout, had heard the first version and had made the remarks attributed to him.

After forty years with the police department and four months after the Long shooting, Captain Anthony Kossup retired at age sixty-five. I visited him with the vague introduction that I was writing a book about Newark. At my first mention of Martinez, Kossup responded: "I did him the biggest favor of his life." The further Kossup was pressed about the circumstances of the "favor," the more difficult he found it to remember. "I testified before the grand jury during the hearing; I think that's a favor," he finally explained. Kossup's explanation lacked candor. As a police officer in charge at the scene of a shooting, he had little choice whether he would appear before a grand jury. The favor—whatever it was—remains with Kossup and the Newark police.

Meanwhile, the libel suit which had been a tactical maneuver was becoming more trouble for the police than it was worth. While testifying in a deposition for the plaintiffs' case, Reverend Seymour Everett of Newark's Blessed Sacrament Church reportedly testified that he had overheard conversations to the effect that the police themselves were going to provoke a major incident, if possible, on their own picket line at City Hall. D'Alessandro, in an embarrassing position, moved to suppress the deposition of his own witness. He did so by what was probably an illegal court order by

Superior Court Judge Lawrence A. Whipple, who issued it over the strenuous objections of both Mytelka and Debevoise. Had the suit proceeded, the attorneys would certainly have moved to make the entire deposition public and doubtless would have succeeded. This situation helped produce a settlement.

On June 13, 1967, almost two years to the day after the death of Lester Long, Jr., a verbal agreement between D'Alessandro and Debevoise set a settlement figure of a mere $3,500, a far cry from the $3,750,000 originally asked. Any claim that Martinez had "won" a libel suit was farfetched. The settlement figure was more than twice the cost of normal legal fees.

A final episode in the aftermath of Lester Long's death only typified the frustration that pervaded the entire affair. Unbeknown to the man who had shot him, one of the deceased's sisters contacted Solondz and the attorney began to prepare a damage suit against Martinez and the Newark Police Department. Long had died without a will, however, and to initiate such a suit it was necessary to first have the sister named administrator of his estate. Under the technicalities of law, each of Long's seven brothers and sisters had to agree to such a decision. Under the practicalities of ghetto life, three of them couldn't be found. In two years the statute of limitations ran out on Lester Long and justice.

Come and Get Me

Bernard Rich was the second black to die in the summer of 1965 at the hands of the police. The twenty-six-year-old man might have been dead when they took him from the second precinct that Sunday afternoon, but several police officers said he looked alive. Rich, wrapped tightly in a body bag, was certainly dead when they carried him into City Hospital less than fifteen minutes later. Though he had no history of mental disorder, Rich had suddenly gone berserk in cell five, police said, banging his head against the wall and setting fire to his shirt. He became an unwilling example of what can happen when Newark police run through fire drill and first aid at the same time.

A study of the corpse showed a four- to five-inch in diameter hematoma on the back of his skull, a blackened right eye, a one-inch cut on his left eyelid, and multiple abrasions on his forehead. Some of the injuries may have been self-inflicted. None caused his death. The "cause of death" blank on his death certificate was *unfilled* for more than five months. Then the Essex County medical examiner's office finally ruled that Rich had died when parts of his head had ceased to function properly, an amazing deduction. Explaining the delay, the office said it had been waiting for a toxological report, but a record showed that they had this information months before. The in-fighting between the medical examiner's office and Solondz, who represented Mrs. Elaine Rich, the widow, became fierce. Eventually Solondz disqualified himself as attorney since it appeared he would testify at the civil trial. Needless to say, the grand jury had routinely shuffled through Rich's death without taking any criminal action.

Two expert pathologists for the plaintiff finally determined that Rich had not died from a heart attack—the easiest translation of his death certificate —but from asphyxiation, a determination the medical examiner's office agreed with after all. Lack of oxygen in Rich's lungs could have resulted, they stated, from any two of five factors: smoke from the small fire, Rich's exhaustion after struggling with four police officers who were trying to save him from himself, pressure on Rich's diaphragm when one or two of them sat on him in the process, a body bag which was a bit too snug and, last but far from least, use of a fire extinguisher that may have deposited a bit too much carbon dioxide into Rich's face and further disturbed his health.

As fate would have it, Rich was in jail because of a seemingly forgotten, two-and-a-half-year-old warrant brought by his wife. He had been separated from her and their two children for some time and when Mrs. Rich applied for welfare she was obligated to first sign a warrant charging her husband with non-support. He was finally arrested during a routine Friday night check and the nature of the charge delayed bail. Rich's mother and sister brought him a change of underwear and cigarettes on Saturday afternoon.

"We'll get this straightened out Monday morning," the mother told her son when leaving.

"Rich was on the cell block floor banging his head and screaming incoherently," the jailer testified during pre-trial depositions. He related that he then ran to the precinct desk and said Rich should be hospitalized. The jailer returned to talk to Rich. "Then he reared back," the jailer said, "and had a container of coffee there partially filled with cigarette butts, he just threw it all over me; and that was in the cell, threw it over my shirt and trousers; and then he started to go into his act again, banging his head, the back of his head, against the cell block." The jailer returned to the desk, this time reporting, "We'll have to take him out of the cell now before he hurts himself."

Rich stood in the doorway of his open cell holding his burning shirt in front of him.

"Come on out!" he was told.

"Come and get me," he replied.

After a shot or two of water from a fire hose and a few blasts of carbon dioxide, the police obliged. Eventually four officers managed to fit into the cramped cell to rescue the prisoner. They had quickly put out the fire. Then they put out Bernard Rich.

Why Did You Shoot?

Near the intersection of Rose and Bergen Streets on the night of September 14—three months after the Long shooting and two weeks after Rich's death—Detectives Harold Schwankert and Joseph Tartaglia noticed a car occupied by four men driving erratically north on Bergen. Tartaglia, driving the unmarked police car, pulled alongside after four blocks. Schwankert identified himself as a police officer and told the driver, thirty-four-year-old James Sutton, to pull over just before the 18th Avenue intersection. The car shot off instead, making a sharp right turn on 18th Avenue with the detectives in close pursuit.

Schwankert fired two warning shots and two at the car as it sped down the hill. As it squealed around the Jelliff Avenue corner, a fifth shot hit Charles "Shirts" Kendrick in the back of the head, killing him instantly. "When they went around the corner the car was screeching on two wheels," Schwankert told me. "We thought they were going to turn over. I was shooting at the car and didn't aim to hit any of them."

Schwankert's bullet had finished a twenty-seven-year-old holdup man wanted for armed robberies in Jersey City, Morris County, and by the FBI, and who had a record going back to 1955. The three others in the car—Sutton, Marvin Boykins, twenty-two, and Albert Portee, nineteen—were part of the same holdup gang.

Kendrick's death, however, was badly timed, what with the deaths of Long and Rich. "My boss asked me, 'Why did you shoot?'" Schwankert said. "How would you like to do your job and have your boss ask you a question like that? When that car took off driving like that I knew they were dangerous. I've been a police officer for a long time. We were never even cited for the arrests, we were taken off the case. We were chastised."

Schwankert, a fifty-five-year-old veteran officer and a decent man, said he had seen Kendrick "playing with a gun" in his lap when their police car had pulled alongside. He also related that the gun was found in Sutton's belt after the chase, where Sutton said Kendrick had shoved it at the appearance of the police. Tartaglia told me he had never seen the gun but that Schwankert had told him of seeing "something that looked like a gun." Tartaglia also said he thought the gun, a .38 caliber English Webley revolver, had later been found underneath the seat. These statements should be evaluated with consideration to the episode's physical setting. Bergen Street is a poorly lit, two-lane street usually lined on both sides with parked cars. It is doubtful if Schwankert could have seen any gun. And, as there was no return fire from the fleeing auto, there is even doubt that a gun was there at all. It is possible that Kendrick, as so many before him, lost his life merely because he ran.

However, Schwankert's good record and Kendrick's past ruled out any sympathy for the deceased, least of all from the black community who had been paying the price for such as Kendrick and his accomplices for years.

Boykins was subsequently charged with seven armed robberies. In June of 1966 he was found guilty on one charge and the others were dismissed. He was sentenced to seven to ten years. Narcotics were found inside the car at the time of the arrest and Boykins was returned from Trenton State Prison to stand trial for illegal possession. He was found not guilty in 1968.

With fourteen armed robbery charges against him, Sutton pleaded guilty to two of them and the remaining twelve were dismissed. Sutton received two seven- to ten-year sentences which were to run concurrently.

For various reasons one robbery charge against Portee was dismissed. The court then proceeded to try him only on the narcotics charge and found this easier said than done. Portee had jumped bail and was among the missing. When Boykins was found not guilty on the possession charge, however, Portee's indictment was dismissed. It was ironic that Portee was out on the street and didn't even know about it.

Compared to the dubious accomplishments of Shirts Kendrick, Boykins, Sutton, and Portee were angels. The actions of Schwankert and Tartaglia had rid Newark of four hardcore criminals. Schwankert could have been cited for shooting a wanted man instead of chewed out but, just as justice had been ruled out in the death of Lester Long, Newark's emotional climate ruled out vindication for a good police officer.

Kendrick's death failed to disturb the black community, but because it was the third police killing of 1965's summer season it brought Mayor Addonizio to police headquarters and again raised the specter of a civilian review board. Nothing was further from Addonizio's mind. The administration had no intention of keeping the trigger-happy element of its police in check. In the comedy's finale, Addonizio again dragged out his Human Rights Commission for another performance. On September 15, he announced that the commission was split six to six on the review board issue. Addonizio, however, was ready and willing with a tactical alternative: charges of police brutality would henceforth be sent directly to the FBI and the Essex County prosecutor.

Up Against the Wall

One of the first cases to be so treated was that of Walter Mathis, a seventeen-year-old boy who was shot to death by an off-duty detective on Christmas Eve little more than three months later. It was fitting that the Mathis case should have been one of the first to test the new procedure as it embodied all the injustices prevalent in Newark's system of law and order, not the least of which was the willing complicity of the press in reporting the episode to the public:

> A 17-year-old youth was shot and killed yesterday by one of two off-duty detectives during a struggle with him and four other youths. The struggle followed a report of a mugging by the youths, police said.
>
> Police identified the dead youth as Walter Mathis of 77 Nairn Place.
>
> Arrested and charged with assault and battery and larceny were Jerome Mathis, 19, the dead youth's brother, also of 77 Nairn Place; Charles West, 18, of 137 Dewey Street; and Donnell McNeil, 18, of 72 Pierce Street.

Told of Robbery

> Detectives John Balogh and Thomas Belosky were in a tavern at 504 18th Avenue at 12:25 A.M. when a man ran in and said five youths had beaten and robbed a pedestrian nearby. The man, whose name was withheld, said he ran to the aid of the victim but was waved off at gunpoint by one of the youths. Police said the man pointed out the five youths as they ran off and reiterated to the detectives that one of the boys had a gun.
>
> Balogh, his badge pinned to his jacket, and Belosky, holding his badge in one hand, chased the youths with guns drawn. They caught the youths at South 11th Street and Springfield Avenue. Police said that when the detectives ordered the youths against the wall, several of them started to back up and then all five suddenly jumped the detectives.
>
> During the struggle, Balogh shot Walter Mathis in the left side. The youth was pronounced dead at the scene by a Newark City Hospital doctor.
>
> The victim of the alleged assault was identified as Andre Jaszcyszyn, 43, of 43 Pierce Street. He was detained in City Hospital for intoxication and a bruised right knee. Police said they found $143 in his pockets but he told them he had left home with $163.[2]

The tragedy began to unfold at the Sitch Ukrainian Club, a private bar across from Club 18 bar on 18th Avenue, with a twenty-five-year-old Ukrainian bartender, Henry Sawaryn, whose command of English was less than perfect. Sawaryn, a husky man near 200 pounds, as were the two detectives with whom he had often drunk, played a pivotal role in the affair. It was he who had run across the street into Club 18 to call out the two detectives and send them after the five boys—all because he believed a man had been mugged in front of the Ukrainian Club.

"Andre was a good customer," he related. "He wasn't in the club that night. He come up and knock on the door. I told him I was closing and I would take him home. Then I look out the window. They were all around him. Two held his arms around him and some of them were going through his pockets. I went out and one went inside his coat for a gun and point

[2] Newark *Sunday News* story written by Hy Kuperstein, December 26, 1965.

it at me. I went to the bar across the street for help. When we come out the five men were running down the street."

"I remember it was Christmas Eve and we were trying to find a party," Rodney Mayes, the seventeen-year-old who had fled the scene and was arrested the next day, told me. "We all knew one another but we weren't all close friends. We sort of happened on each other during the night. I remember we were walking along in the street and we saw this drunk—I think he was sitting there—in front of the Ukrainian Club. We went over and began 'jugging' with him, you know, making fun of him. I was leaning against a pole or something and I remember them jugging with the drunk. Somebody may have put their hands on him but nobody hurt him and certainly we didn't rob him. It only went on for a minute and then the bartender came out and told us to leave the drunk alone and get out of there. I don't remember if there were hard words between the bartender and us or not. We just walked away. You can see where we were when the detectives caught up with us that we weren't running or trying to get away. I was running track in high school at the time and if I robbed anybody I would have been gone, you know, nobody would have caught me. That part about me having a gun—that's so silly I don't want to even talk about it."

The fact that Andre, the drunk, was found with $143 on him bears out Mayes' story. Also, he sustained no injuries coming from any supposed attack.

Sawaryn said that the first time he had seen Andre was when the drunken man had knocked on the club's door. One female witness, a white woman, subsequently told me that Andre had been drinking inside the Ukrainian Club for at least ten hours, more than enough time to account for the "missing" twenty dollars. Sawaryn said Andre was a good customer, as he was, and he told the intoxicated man to wait outside so he could drive him home. However, two eyewitnesses told me they saw the bartender eject Andre from the club because it was midnight and he wanted to close. Sawaryn told me he didn't know his two detective friends were at Club 18 but he had just run into the bar for help. But Balogh himself since told me that he tried to get into the Ukrainian Club first around midnight but Sawaryn had told him he was closing. It was after this that Balogh and Belosky had walked across the street to Club 18, which Sawaryn must have known.

Sawaryn also said the "five men" were running away when he and the detectives came out of the bar. Balogh testified they were "walking fast." The fact that the boys were as close by as they were at the confrontation around the corner rules out any running on their part. If the youths had mugged anyone—as Mayes said—it is obvious they would have been long gone.

Further, the gun supposedly used to threaten Sawaryn was of the utmost importance. After a search of the three prisoners and the dead boy produced neither a gun nor any other weapon, the boy not in custody, Mayes, was charged with intent to use a deadly weapon and threatening the bartender's life, together with larceny. No gun was ever found. It is probable that the gun story materialized only after the shooting when police found themselves with no gun and five boys, one of whom was a corpse with a bullet wound—not in the left side, as reported—but in his *back*.

"Do something for him! Do something for him!!" the nineteen-year-old brother screamed, catching the falling body in his arms.

They dragged Jerome Mathis from the body and took him and the others to jail, with the exception of Mayes, who had run around the corner and escaped during the confusion. Police told Jerome his brother was taken to the hospital instead of the morgue.

"Three detectives came here at three o'clock Christmas morning," Mrs. Mathis, forty-six, remembered. "They told me Walter was shot running away and Jerome was in jail. I said no, that couldn't be true. Then they left."

The facts of the affair—no robbery, no gun, and no flight as far as the boys were concerned—pointed to a case of murder or manslaughter. Faced at best with a *prima facie* case of manslaughter against one of their own, Balogh, a nine-year veteran at the time, the police and prosecutor's office reacted characteristically: the police officers were charged with nothing; Mathis, McNeil, West, and Mayes were charged with larcency; and all except Mayes were charged with assault on the two detectives. In addition, Mayes was charged with the gun violations.

That four of the five youths had bad records lent itself to the credibility of the police version. The dead boy had spent nine months at Jamesburg Reformatory for breaking and entry. His older brother's record began in 1960 at the age of thirteen when he was with some boys who assaulted and extorted money from white juveniles. Later the same year, Jerome Mathis was caught for breaking into a parking meter and three years after he had a loitering arrest and another for atrocious assault. In July of 1964 he was convicted on a breaking and entry and he, too, was sent away, to Annandale Reformatory. The eighteen-year-old West had several breaking and entries in 1963 and one for robbery in 1965, which was dropped. McNeil, also eighteen, had a breaking-and-entry arrest in 1960 when he was thirteen years old and in 1963 he was found riding in a stolen car.

Mayes, seventeen, had been in trouble for purse snatching some time before, but otherwise had a clean record. A future college student, he seemed the best adjusted of the group. It is ironic that Mayes was picked out as the gun wielder but, as he was the only one who fled, the police had no choice.

The trial was supposed to begin in June of 1966 before Judge Leon W. Kapp, one of the two most bigoted judges in Essex County, but was postponed time and time again. The delay itself seemed to be part of "the system." Finally, early in 1968, *two years* after the killing, a jury found the boys innocent of the larceny charge and was unable to reach a verdict on the assault. Also, Mayes was cleared of all charges relating to the imaginary gun.

"Judge Kapp got so mad when he heard the verdict he walked off the bench and left the jury standing there," Mrs. Mathis recalled. "The jury was out six hours and when Kapp heard the verdict not guilty he just walked away."

With this particular case everyone seemed to be most zealous, including the prosecutor's office, which proceeded to retry the four boys on the assault charge after yet another year had passed. This time, however, there was only one charge and it was impossible for the jury to cop out on the issue which was now rather apparent: four unarmed boys only one of whom weighed more than 150 pounds (Charlie West weighed 170) attacking two 200-pound detectives with drawn .38's. The jury deliberated for all of a half hour. Again, the verdict was not guilty.

"It's really a frightening thing," Mrs. Mathis said. "I've seen Balogh still riding around. There's a man with a gun who killed a boy and got away with it with the backing of the entire police department. I know he had to know somebody, a whole lot of people."

"It's bad when someone deprives a person of his rights," her fifty-five-year-old husband said. "This means the police can do anything to you and you can't do anything about it. I tried to press criminal charges against Balogh but the court wouldn't accept them."

Frustration of the parents was aggravated by what happened to Jerome Mathis, one of their remaining four sons and three daughters. After the tragic death of his brother and his being charged with two crimes, Jerome was never quite the same, according to Mr. and Mrs. Mathis. This condition was not helped when police arrested him for loitering a year after he witnessed his brother's killing. In September of 1967 he had his first narcotics arrest. Others followed and he was sent back to Annandale.

Still, the parents wouldn't quit. They had sat through the preliminary hearing and the grand jury proceeding. They lived with the trials through postponement after postponement and were there at the conclusion. Three years after their seventeen-year-old son had been shot to death by a Newark detective on the corner of Springfield Avenue and South 11th Street, four youths were completely exonerated of acts that had allegedly resulted in the

homicide. The game—as far as the police and prosecutor's office were concerned—was over. By this time few even remembered the dead boy's name,
no less details of the shooting. Again, the system.

As far as the parents were concerned, however, it was just beginning.
They pressed on with a civil suit charging the Newark Police Department
and John Balogh with the death of their son. The suit neared a finish without ever reaching court when the parents were offered a settlement of
$11,000. However, the dead boy had fathered an illegitimate son and the
judge hearing the matter directed that a large portion of the settlement
should go to the child. Mr. Mathis, also a Methodist minister, objected and
refused to close out the case, firing his lawyer and hiring attorney Nathan
Kurtz to represent the family. The litigation dragged on and provided a re-
evaluation of Walter Mathis' death, if only a private one ignored by the
press and completely unknown to the general public.

Throughout the years of trial testimony and depositions, the forty-year-
old Balogh's version of the shooting remained basically unchanged: "We
told them we were police officers and asked them to line up against the
wall. They wouldn't comply. Instead they kept kicking and swinging at us.
. . . They started swearing at us. . . . Then Walter grabbed my hand to
pull the gun out of my hand. The gun went off and the gun went up in the
air."

His testimony was backed up by his partner, Belosky, and two others
who could not be described as disinterested witnesses: another man who
had been with the two detectives inside Club 18 when they were called out
by Sawaryn and another off-duty policeman who happened to be passing by
in his car and saw the gun flash in the darkness. The account given by the
youths—that the Mathis boy had been shot with his hands against the
window and his back to the detectives—was substantiated by Lucie Borjis,
a Puerto Rican woman standing some fifteen feet away who had greeted
the passing youths, and by Thomas Savage, a colored man who also had
been passing in his car.

The strongest evidence, however, was mute: two morgue photographs of
Walter Mathis' body that showed a bullet wound in his back and the head
of a spent slug protruding from the top of his right shoulder. When looking
at them the police version of the shooting disintegrates. Under the tactics
that had been utilized by the prosecutor's office, however, these photographs had never been an issue.

At the tragedy's climax the five boys were in front of the glass window
at the corner of Springfield Avenue and South 11th Street, the two detectives facing them with drawn revolvers.

"Get up against the wall," Balogh shouted.

"Why? What did we do?" more than one of the startled youths asked.

"Shut up," Balogh said. "Up against the wall."

Four of the five turned as ordered and placed their hands above them against the window, Jerome and Walter Mathis on the far left and Rodney Mayes, who was too shocked to turn around on the right near the corner of the building. Walter, a thin, 140-pound boy who had a stammering impediment, was so frightened he never had time to ask what it was all about.

"All the others were facing the wall but all I had to do was take a step backwards and my back was against it," Mayes related. "I saw it all. Personally, I don't believe he meant to shoot. It happened so fast, none of us had done anything. There was no reason for him to shoot, that's why I believe he didn't mean it."

Balogh's .38 went off a few feet from Walter Mathis' back. The slug entered the lower portion of his left shoulder and ripped diagonally up through his skinny body, finally emerging on the top of his right shoulder. Mathis cried out and slid down the wall—as Balogh dropped his gun in shock.

John Balogh is a short, beefy man with a balding head and the face of a bulldog. His temperament can range from gentleness to flashes of hot anger and back to gentleness in a matter of seconds. Basically, he appears to be a good-natured if hard-bitten man. He grew up, married, and raised four children while living for forty years on Morris Avenue in the heart of the Central Ward ghetto.

"I can't figure it out," he told me. "Nobody ever tries to back the boys in blue. You got cops and cops and cops walking the street and when they get hurt nobody ever tries to do anything for them. My nose was busted once when I got run over by a car. A guy at City Hospital hit me in the head with an iron chair when I was a guard there and knocked my teeth out. I never collected a dime. Let somebody get hurt when he's getting arrested and you can bet there'll be fifteen civil liberties organizations yelling about it. I don't see anybody trying to help the cop when he gets hurt."

Did Balogh know that the man lying in front of the Ukrainian Club was merely drunk?

"He was laying out there on the sidewalk unconscious. Later on they found out he was drunk. How the hell could I know he was drunk?"

Was Balogh's gun cocked when the boys were against the window?

"I have doubts. It was brought out so much about whether the gun was cocked or not. Questions were asked. It puts doubts in your mind. It could have been cocked but I didn't think it was."

Had Balogh been drinking?

It was Christmas Eve, and several people told me that Balogh was a hard drinker. Mrs. Mathis subsequently told me that she had heard a superior admonish, "God damn it, Balogh, you're always drinking and causing trouble!"

While the case dragged on the parents continued to write letters to such officials as Police Director Spina and Peter W. Rodino, Jr., the district congressman. This resulted only in frustration for Balogh.

"They had shot the boy and they didn't say nothin'," Mrs. Mathis said. "They didn't even send us a sympathy card or nothin'. We're just second-class citizens."

"I'm still mad," the detective said. "I'll never forget that I had to go before the grand jury twice. I had the FBI investigating me. I had the attorney general of New Jersey investigating me. I had two grand juries investigating me. I was the one on trial for murder. No police officer I ever heard of had to go before the grand jury twice. Police officers are second-class citizens."

The letters of Mr. and Mrs. Mathis also inspired communication between local officials and others in Washington, who took note of the case. As with other "alleged" brutality cases in Newark, everyone seemed to be investigating.

In a return letter to Rodino a full year after the shooting (before the boys were cleared of all charges) Spina wrote:

> This incident [Walter Mathis' death] was investigated thoroughly by Deputy Chief Floyd Harle, commanding our inspection division. Essex County Prosecutor Brendan Byrne also investigated this unfortunate event.
>
> The facts were submitted by the prosecutor before the 1965 term of the Essex County grand jury. The case against Detective John Balogh, who actually fired the shot, was dismissed. Jerome Mathis, the brother of Walter, was indicted for assault and battery on Detective Balogh. Charlie West and Donnell McNeil were indicted for assault and battery on Detective Belosky.
>
> As a result of our investigation, it is my understanding now that Special Agent Howard Rice of the FBI has reopened this case for further investigation.
>
> From all the evidence that has been produced up to the present time, it is the opinion of the prosecutor and our inspection division that this tragic homicide was legally justifiable.

Howard Rice resigned from the FBI some time after the riot that hit Newark two years later. "Don't forget," he told me, "responsibility for moving on a case lies with the Justice Department in Washington, not us. We just go right down the line, presenting the facts, as is. The next move is up to them."

Hoodwinked Again

The lack of that "next move" is a suitable ending for the investigation into the death of Walter Mathis, and also for a study of events that had nurtured a riot. The concern of a black family living in Newark inspired nothing but official assertions that *everything* that could be done was being done. Actually, *nothing* was accomplished. The efforts of the Mathis family resulted in many letters, much investigation—and no justice. The Mathis homicide was probably the most investigated brutality case in Newark's history, and the result speaks for itself.

The family was far from alone. From September of 1965 to the riot, six other cases were sent to the FBI and nothing more was heard about any of them. When community leaders went to find out why, they were enlightened.

"To our utter amazement, and contrary to what the mayor had promised," said George Richardson, an Essex County assemblyman, "we were informed that the FBI had no jurisdiction in police brutality cases and can take no action unless a federal statute is violated. Since even murder is not classified as a federal offense, this gave the police a rather wide latitude of action. The black community concluded that it had been hoodwinked again."

5

CARETAKERS OF THE WHOREHOUSE

You Can Make a Million Bucks As Mayor of Newark

Nowhere are the ashes of the Newark riot thicker than at the city's administrative roots, those scattered by the mayor's office and the police department. Both have been, to put it mildly, infiltrated by the influence of organized crime. What began in the 1930's—Mafia kingpins leaving New York City to set up headquarters in Jersey City and Newark—soon developed into the phenomenon of institutionalized crime. That the Mafia, in a real sense, actually ran Newark can not be denied. At the highest echelons, they still control gambling in the city. They control the flow of narcotics. And they control the numbers game. This is no different than in most big cities, but what made Newark unique is that the Mafia also controlled the mayor's office, main facets of the administrative government, and also enjoyed a candid relationship—a euphemism—with the Newark Police Department.

Untroubled by the Democratic regime in Trenton—with Governor Hughes and Attorney General Sills both under mob control, according to the words of Mafiosi recorded by the FBI [3]—the Mafia through local political affiliations and boundless generosity made inroads into the Newark city administration. Old friendships with Mayor Addonizio and Police Director Spina that went back many years did not hurt their cause.

Newark's particular brand of corrupt politics goes back to 1949 when the city operated under a city commission form of government, and lovable Ralph Villani was elected mayor. Villani was the first of Italian heritage to be so honored. He was also the first mayor of Italian heritage to be accused

---

[3] Governor Hughes was nicknamed "Two Buckets" Hughes by the mob because of his political training which wouldn't allow being pinned down to direct answers.

by a grand jury of taking part in a shakedown racket four years later when he was turned out. Unfortunately, the amiable gentleman could not be prosecuted because of a statute of limitations. That the electorate didn't learn by this lesson was obvious from the election of a fourteen-year congressman, Hugh Addonizio, as mayor in 1962. Addonizio, a paunchy but otherwise honest-looking individual, was the second Italian to be elected mayor of Newark and the second Italian to be ass-deep in corruption.

"The only reason I came back to Newark is because I wanted to help a city in trouble and because I wanted to be closer to my family," Hughie later explained.

However, to an accomplice in extortion Addonizio had a different explanation: "There's no money in being a congressman but you can make a million bucks as mayor of Newark."

The way had been well paved for Addonizio's homecoming by Mafia bribery, threats, and job promises, which were used to get him elected and to have Dominick Spina, his diligent campaign worker, appointed as police director. Thus did Newark become an open city for criminal activity.

The biggest threat posed to Addonizio's election, as it happened, was from Michael Bontempo, then City Council president and another outstanding example of Italian civic virtue. The incumbent, Mayor Leo P. Carlin, a wily politician, promised Bontempo Police Director Joseph Weldon's job if he would enter the mayoralty race, thereby splitting the Italian vote. Bontempo reported to Mafia kingpin Angelo "Ray" DeCarlo of his intention to run. He also said he would drop out if the fix could be made with Governor Hughes to have him appointed director of motor vehicles, a reward for his presence of mind. Instead, Bontempo had to settle for $5,000 and promise of a job licking stickers at a Newark motor vehicle inspection station, should he ever be in need.

As campaign workers the Mafia's head men were diligent, at least as far as fund raising was concerned. Anthony "Tony Bananas" Caponigro contributed $5,000 toward Addonizio's election, Anthony "Tony Boy" Boiardo a whopping $10,000, Ham Dolasio $5,000, DeCarlo another $5,000, and three others $5,000 apiece.

Even before Addonizio had been elected Spina went to him—according to FBI recorded tapes—and tried to get Hughie to allow organized gambling in the city, should he become mayor. Addonizio denied the request. If Addonizio's avarice wasn't fully developed then, he quickly made up for lost time. As mayor, Addonizio soon learned what fun municipal government in a decaying city could be when he began selling everything at City Hall except the building. As one Mafia chieftain put it: "The guy's [Addonizio] taking $400, $500 for little jobs."

Addonizio and Tony Boiardo had grown up together in the same neighborhood and, long-time friends, their seemingly divergent occupations soon became mutually beneficial.

No sooner had Addonizio settled into the mayor's chair than Boiardo and his lieutenants set up a phony supply company and began shaking down contractors doing business with the city for 10 percent of their contracts. The middle man running the "company," whose address was actually a vacant lot, sent phony bills to the victimized contractors and, after payment checks were deposited in a bank, the money was withdrawn and returned to Boiardo. A good slice of the action then went to Addonizio and eventually a host of city officials, including eight of nine members of the City Council. By the time they were through, Boiardo, Addonizio and company had milked more than $1.4 million in kickbacks. What else they managed to collect must be left to the imagination.

In addition, soon after the election, Spina began pestering Ray DeCarlo to have Addonizio appoint him as police director, a situation that came to pass and made the picture complete. Thus did Newark become a sanctuary for organized gambling, which enterprise financed the heavy narcotic traffic and other Mafia hobbies.

Spina, a career police officer who would work his way up to deputy chief, had married into the well-to-do family of contractor Joseph Nesto. Authorities believed that Spina's sister-in-law, who gave the same home address as the police director, was involved in the operation of a gambling enterprise out of the Office Lounge Tavern in the East Ward. They also believed that her helpers were Angelo Ferrante and one of his sons, Daniel Ferrante. Another son, Police Captain Rocco Ferrante, the apple of Spina's eye, was marked by the police director to succeed him. Accordingly, Rocco was named by Spina to head—of all things—the intelligence division of the Newark police, whose function it was to keep track of gambling and vice violations.

Rocco, a likable, brawny individual not renowned for his thinking capacity, was also Addonizio's bodyguard, an arrangement that helped the right hand know what the left was doing. The Nesto family was thus in the best political position it had enjoyed since 1945, when Ralph Villani, then a city commissioner, had helped it to a $100,000 construction contract. A grand jury later chastised Villani in this affair for failing to "protect the interests" of the city.

Serving during the post-riot period, a further tribute to the intelligence of Newark's electorate, was a group of councilmen whose intelligence and integrity were open to question. Still hanging around was Villani, and their choice of the oldtimer to serve as council president both in 1962 and 1966 is indicative of their level of so-called thought.

From the city's highest executive office, to the City Council, to most administration offices, the corruption spread, reaching even the office of corporation counsel, whose job was to make the dirty work look legal. When the Hughes Report stated that *everything* was for sale at City Hall it was not merely using a figure of speech. The Mafia controlled the unions working on city projects, city officials awarded contracts to friends like Boiardo, who also shared in shakedowns of other contractors. Sometimes the victimized contractors got even by charging for work never performed. The drugged electorate paid the bills, possibly the most permissive captive citizenry in the history of this country.

The situation become so routine that the Mafia no longer had to remain under cover. Tony Boy Boiardo was listed as a "salesman" for Valentine Electric Company, a modest little enterprise that opened its doors fully funded in 1958. Aided by the greatest salesman since Jesus Christ, the company prospered. In ten years it became the largest electrical contractor in the area. Valentine was awarded half the contracts of the Newark Housing Authority and was soon doing better than $5 million annually. The city's other electrical outfits regarded many city jobs as "locked up" with few if any even bothering to submit bids. What was locked up was Newark—lock, stock and barrel—in the hands of the Mafia, and Valentine's star salesman was regarded by insiders as "the real boss of Newark."

Throughout this period, Addonizio was enjoying himself on many luxurious vacations in Puerto Rico and Florida for which he never paid a cent. Newark's mayor gambled frequently, often losing heavily, also without paying. In effect, Hughie could vacation and gamble when he pleased with his "many, many good friends" picking up the tabs.

Once Spina was named police director the morale of the department started to decline, largely because of his personal handling of crucial assignments to the detective division, one method utilized by corrupt law enforcement officers to negate the effectiveness of their own agencies. Although assignment as a detective amounts to a promotion—a $300-annual-salary increase and added prestige—no examination was required when the assignment system was instituted in 1955. Spina's predecessor, Joseph Weldon, established evaluation criteria when he took over in 1958. Evaluation under Weldon, who had a reputation for honesty, consisted of a written examination, a rating system, and recommendations of deputy chiefs.

Spina replaced this system with his personal choices. Men made the team for being good police officers, or avid spies in department politics and in the black community. Fondness for spaghetti was not a handicap. With incentive redefined, the department morale nosedived. Its members grouped as supporters or opponents of Spina. The anti-Spina faction included a group that backed Deputy Chief John Redden, the only police official with the leadership, character, and understanding of the city's problems to reverse the losses of the Spina regime.

The Single Continuously Lawless Element

"A large segment of the Negro people," the Hughes Report stated, "are convinced that the single continuously lawless element operating in the community is the police force itself, and its callous disregard for human rights."

White people may never know the bitterness and frustration that set in when a law enforcement agency outdoes criminals in lawlessness. In crying foul at the words of the Hughes Report, Spina, Imperiale and the PBA only tainted their own credibility. If anything, the report was only frosting on the cake.

The ghetto's streets are crime-infested, a way of life individual police officers routinely take advantage of. Frequent gambling parties, after-hours liquor spots, dope pushers, and hustlers are easy marks for shakedowns. Some police rationalize that if criminal activities can't be curtailed—as they can't be under the circumstances—then they can at least be used for personal gain. The cancer of lawlessness eating through the ghetto touches and finally infects all who come in contact with it. The necessary surgery of effective prosecution would cut away a large chunk of the police department itself. "The real money starts up around the top," one former officer told me. "The money patrolmen pick up is little stuff."

Once the lower police echelons realize that organized crime is licensed, they cut themselves in. Taking a cut from such rackets as numbers, the police form a virtual partnership. They are controlled from the upper echelons by assignments and the money is passed upward.

Many black policemen in Newark are hated in the ghetto not for serving the power structure but because they victimize their own people and often operate brutally in the process. Although there are only approximately 230 blacks on the force (which has an authorized quota of 1,512 and is currently at least 200 short), many of them are accomplished thieves. Black officers, particularly detectives, know the numbers carriers, junkies, and pushers on sight, and use their knowledge to shake them down. For a pusher, a payoff of a few hundred dollars is well spent if it prevents being fingerprinted and photographed.

White police start with an information disadvantage in the ghetto, but they quickly learn the knack of shakedowns and payoffs, known in the trade as "juice." Once in the ghetto, where the opportunities are so plentiful, white officers are seldom anxious to leave, particularly ranking officers who can take their cut while sitting behind a desk.

"There are some policemen that are interested in this sort of thing," Assemblyman Richardson testified before the Hughes Commission, referring to graft, payoffs, extortion. "Despite all the dangers of being involved in this all-black community, you couldn't run some of the white officers away from there. In my estimation, that is the reason why Captain Williams has not been assigned to one of those Negro precincts, because of obvious pressures from other people that have certain influences in the city."

What's the Sense of Letting Them Up?

Whether corruption spread from the city administration to the police department or vice versa is an interesting but moot question. Corruption in each has grown apace, increasing at about the same rate that whites retreated from the decaying city. Thus non-whites were not only cheated of political control while gaining numerical superiority. They were also forced to watch as leeches sucked the city's blood.

Since the city administration and the police were virtual partners in illicit activity, neither was about to blow the whistle on the other. Each looked the other way, and was aided in this endeavor by the legal guardians of the city —the prosecutor's office and the magistrates sitting in municipal court.

The 1965 deaths of Long, Rich, Kendrick, and Mathis were killings which became political in that the city's government shielded its police hirelings and preserved a philosophy of white domination. The city administration, through its Human Rights Commission, jumped to the aid of the police after the Long and Kendrick shootings. Even the medical examiner's office played this role in the Rich slaying. The police angrily attacked every call for a civilian review board, and the administration covertly backed them. The Mathis killing was so one-sided that it appeared the police were caught until the prosecutor's office came to the rescue, charging all the youths involved with crimes while ignoring the real culprits.

Despite the claims of the Imperiales, Giulianos, and Heffernans, police brutality is part of the everyday life of the ghetto, reaching print in most cases only when death or serious injury results. Police knew that the administration and its corrupt politicians would support them no matter how flagrant their violations and they sensed that public opinion was also in their favor. A little brutality, it was felt, would keep "them" in their place—the natural counterpart of white political dominance.

The arrest of Richard Owens, Jr., on the afternoon of January 13, 1967, is a case in point.

Owens, a husky thirty-two-year-old black, had come home from work to find no supper cooking, his infant son sleeping, and his common-law wife, Eva Getter, preparing to walk out on him after fourteen months. A slapping-screaming episode followed, the kind that comes over the police radio every night as a 555, "boy friend-girl friend fight." Owens told his twenty-year-old woman she could go, but he was damned if he was going to let her walk off with his six-week-old son. She became hysterical and left to phone the police.

"Most of these colored girls want some white cops to come out there and beat up the boy friends," one Newark officer explained. "They just want the guy beaten up and then they're happy."

Fifteen minutes later Officers Richard Schmaltz and Ronald Yscamp rang the doorbell. Owens, preparing to take a shower and thinking it was his returning wife, called out from the bathroom for her to come in. There was another ring. This time Owens put his shirt back on and went to the door. He opened it and looked into the faces of two police officers. Owens asked what they wanted. They asked him what the problem was. They also said they wanted to come in. Owens asked them if they had a search warrant. The two officers said they didn't—and Owens shut the door in their faces. The crime had been committed.

The two police pounded on the door and rang the doorbell until Owens opened it again. According to the police, they again asked Owens what the problem was. Owens said they called him a "black motherfucker."

Both sides agree that Owens tried to close the door several more times— but Officer Yscamp's foot kept it from closing. According to the police, Owens began punching at them. According to Owens, both officers shoved against the door, forcing it open and driving him backward into the living room where he fell against a coffee table, breaking it. Both officers rushed into the apartment. Officer Schmaltz rapped Owens over the head with a heavy flashlight while Yscamp held him around the neck. They handcuffed Owens. Schmaltz went to phone for reinforcements while Yscamp sat on the unconscious man's back. When Yscamp got off him, the awakened Owens walked into the bedroom, returning with his baby son. Yscamp began screaming at Owens to put the baby down. Eventually Schmaltz returned and both officers and the mother, who had been standing in the hallway, pulled and bent Owens' fingers to get the baby from his handcuffed hands. Owens gave the baby to Miss Getter, who ran out of the apartment while the two officers beat Owens unconscious.

Only this struggle over the baby gave credence to police testimony that concern for the child had *prompted* their entry into the apartment. Actually the police were never told that the baby was in any danger.

A claw or "wrist-breaker" digging into his flesh as he sat in a living-room chair stirred Owens into consciousness. Other police had arrived, and for the first time he was told that he was under arrest. A policeman, he said, kicked him in the neck and burned his right eyelash with a cigarette. The handcuffed prisoner was transported to the fifth precinct station where he realized that his knee was bleeding. He also began to vomit blood. Owens asked for some water and was handed a paper cup from a garbage can. The can was placed between his legs so that he could vomit into it—which he did, for an hour and a half.

Sergeant Jim Sellers, a veteran with a reputation for humaneness, cleaned Owens' knee and ordered the prisoner taken to City Hospital where the wound was stitched. Owens continued to vomit blood so profusely at the hospital that he had to be X-rayed standing up. Shortly after he lapsed into a coma with a brain concussion and the police had a hot one on their hands.

Eleven days later, in his hospital bed, Owens learned that he was charged with assaults on both Schmaltz and Yscamp and resisting arrest. Even if the prosecution could manage to draw twelve citizens from suburban Essex County who would be inclined to believe that Owens had been surly and had attacked both armed police officers, they would still, unfortunately, be apprised of Owens' hospital records. In addition, statements of both policemen and Miss Getter provided no link between the forceful entry and the later struggle over the baby. Further, the mother now insisted that she had not seen either policeman struck and that Owens loved the baby and wouldn't hurt it.

Doubtful of its chances before a jury, the prosecution simply *eliminated* that possibility. Charges against Owens were reduced from felonies to misdemeanors by prosecuting him under the Disorderly Persons Act. This tactic placed the decision in the more dependable hands of municipal court. The prosecutor added a fourth charge—accusing Owens of assaulting his own child—and it was no coincidence that Chief Magistrate James Del Mauro, one of Mayor Addonizio's corrupt cohorts, was to hear the case.

Del Mauro summed up the case with a statement based on prosecution allegations rather than testimony:

> The state produced as part of its case two Newark patrolmen, Richard Schmaltz and Ronald Yscamp. Both testified that on the date of the alleged incident, they were in uniform and responded to a complaint of a family dispute at 755 Clinton Avenue, Newark, New Jersey, at approximately 5:17 P.M. and were met upon arrival at said apartment building by Eva Getter, who informed them that she had been involved in an argument with her husband, and that he had struck her and locked her out of the apartment; that he had further refused to give her not only her clothing, but her baby, and *she further stated that she was in fear of what would happen to said child.*[4]

Since Owens' attorney, Morton Stavis, had brought a civil suit against the police, Newark's chief magistrate had no recourse but to retaliate by finding Owens guilty on all charges. The defendant was sentenced to six months for assaulting Schmaltz, three months for the assault on Yscamp,

[4] Author's italics.

six months for resisting arrest and another six months for assaulting the baby—in effect, a twenty-one-month sentence since they were to run consecutively. But to bring the unpleasant matter to a close—and placate the defendant and Stavis—Del Mauro suspended the sentences and placed him on probation for three years, during which time he would pay a one-dollar fine weekly.

Stavis refused to be appeased. From appeals in county court and through the higher New Jersey courts, he carried the fight to the U.S. Supreme Court. He lost every time, including the civil suit.

"What was on trial," said Stavis, "was not Owens' assault on two police officers but a *'mean nigger'* who had told two white policemen he didn't want them in his home. Second, no matter what Owens had done, he was unarmed and they had come damn close to killing him. Third, the conduct of the prosecutor had systematically and purposefully deprived Owens of his constitutional right to a trial by jury. These are the types of things we never really get a chance to talk about in a court room—we always have to play the game in left field."

Even while Owens was on trial for assaulting his child, the baby was being cared for at the home of his sister, where Owens had wanted him all along. As Stavis suggested, the real issues were never allowed to surface in court.

Newark police habitually use more force than is necessary to make arrests. They usually outnumber the person arrested, identified as "the attacker" in police reports, and unlike their victims are armed. "What's the sense of letting them up after you knock them down?" one officer put it. "When you put them down, keep them down, right?"

Police use unlawful violence against the powerless as a psychological tool to deter crime and establish status. The ghetto's vicious hoodlums deserve no better than they get, but this brutal attitude eventually becomes a habitual response to ghetto residents at the least challenge or rebuff, as shown in the Owens affair. A riot pushed this disdain to a frightful extreme: the running felons of yesterday had become merged in the minds of police with faceless, innocent human beings who just happened to get in the way.

The Owens case is also typical of police brutality in its legal aspects. Many municipal court magistrates are political *hacks* who depend on capricious councilmen for their jobs, and police testimony—however incredible —is invariably sprinkled with holy water and accepted as gospel.

Twenty to thirty Newark police officers have brought on many of the city's crises and have cost the taxpayers hundreds of thousands of dollars. Yet if they were dismissed the whole structure would be threatened. They depended on each other, the police, the municipal administration, and the influence of the Mafia—comrades in corruption. The corruption at City Hall resulted in a situation in which no police officer, not even the black ones, could be disciplined for brutality if the victim was not white. Brutality in this instance includes virtual *murder*.

If You Don't Pay Them, You Can't Operate

Spina's involvement in organized gambling and the corrupt dealings of Addonizio and others within the administration have been well documented by FBI recording devices. Their connections with Mafia kingpins Simone "Sam the Plumber" DeCavalcante, Ray DeCarlo, Gerardo "Jerry" Catena, Ruggiero "Richie the Boot" Boiardo, and his son, Tony Boy, are now a matter of record.

"You know Hughie Addonizio got hold of me," Tony Boy Boiardo told DeCavalcante and DeCarlo in early 1963. "He said, 'Look, tell DeCarlo that the FBI knows about Irving Berlin.' I'll tell you how much the FBI knows about Irving Berlin. This kid Vic [Pisauro] turned himself in. The prosecutor [Brendan Byrne] told the FBI that he's one of my boys and that I made him give himself up to the director [Spina]."

Boiardo was referring to the killing of bartender James Del Grosso at the West Side Tavern on South Orange Avenue earlier in 1963, an event that brought to light two Mafia factions within the city, as well as the pride that Boiardo took in controlling his men. One faction belonged to the Boiardos and the other included Angelo Bruno and one of his lieutenants, Carmine Battaglia, who had set up gambling in the tavern.

Pisauro, one of Boiardo's men, visited the tavern with Miss Patricia Fiore, who had known Del Grosso. Early in the morning, Del Grosso made advances to her and she rebuffed him. In the ensuing fight, he was killed by a blow over the head and his body was punctured by numerous stab wounds. Because it was in his territory, according to the tape, Battaglia "went around screaming about it." Though there were no known witnesses to the fight, police had teletypes out for Miss Fiore and Pisauro. Shortly thereafter, Boiardo told Pisauro and the girl to go to Spina and give themselves up, which they did.

"The FBI went to see Byrne and asked about this Pisauro—about how come he gave himself up," Boiardo said. "Byrne told them, 'We had Carmine Battaglia in here and told him if we don't get this man here—' Byrne said, 'We had him affiliated with Carmine but we found out we were wrong. This is Tony Boy's man.' "

On October 30 a jury acquitted both Pisauro and Miss Fiore of the Del Grosso murder, justifying Boiardo's faith in law and order.

Another portion of the FBI tape related the conversation of Boiardo, DeCavalcante, and DeCarlo on a 14th Street gambling operation of Ham Dolasco:

BOIARDO: You know Dick Spina asked me, "Why don't you and Ray [DeCarlo] get together and open up?" I said, "What is there to open up?"

DeCAVALCANTE: You know, Tony, thirty or thirty-five years ago if an ___ was even seen talking to a cop they looked to hit him the next day. They figured he must be doing business with the cop.

DeCARLO: Today if you don't meet them and pay them you can't operate.

BOIARDO: The only guy I handle is Dick Spina. Gino [Farina] and them guys handle the rest of the law. About seven or eight years ago I used to handle them all.

DeCAVALCANTE: Did you ever see the way Ham operates on Fourteenth Street?

DeCARLO: For five thousand dollars Ham and Tony [Anthony "Bananas" Caponigro, another Essex County chieftain] thought they bought a license.

DeCAVALCANTE: This was before the five thousand dollars.

DeCARLO: They walk into precincts and everything. You can't have a man and be seen with him. He's no good to you then.

DeCAVALCANTE: And how long do you think it will take the federal men to find out?

As long as it took to play the tapes—and they've been playing them for seven years now.

A Lack of Confidence

Organized gambling is Newark's biggest business. Estimates based on evidence seized by agencies other than the Newark police, in two raids alone, show the extensive activity in the city. One raid conducted in the second precinct in early 1966 showed that a lottery operation limited to one quarter of Newark brought in a weekly take of $130,000 collected by some 400 writers. The yearly take from this single operation amounted to $6.7 million. Experts have projected that the yearly take for the entire city approaches $27 million, a figure that does not include the lucrative take of bookmaking and gambling parties. Widely known organized gambling figures come and go in Newark with impunity while trafficking in the illicit business.

So broad is the license to operate that lottery pick-up men make little effort to conceal their activity. One man was arrested making pick-ups totaling $7,000 in lottery play on a busy corner in the Fourth Precinct.

Evidence of a law enforcement breakdown in the city is ample and clear. The total of lottery and bookmaking raids in 1965 was 142. In 1966 the number dropped to eighty-five and in 1967 to forty-eight. During this period gambling activity was rapidly increasing. If the Newark police were reluctant to make raids, the prosecutor's detectives were willing, with embarrassing results to the police. One raid by the prosecutor's men in 1965 resulted in the transfer of the entire fifth precinct's plainclothes squad to other duties, and on December 4, after a further series of prosecutor raids, Mayor Addonizio angrily abolished plainclothes gambling squads in all precincts. The prosecutor's men were doing a job and Hughie figured they didn't need any help.

The prosecutor's detectives said that when they told the Newark police of proposed raids, they arrived to find they were playing cops and robbers with themselves. The gambling operations had suddenly vanished. It is no surprise that the prosecutor's office then kept any information it uncovered on gambling activity to itself. Likewise, after the FBI tapes, neither were the federal people anxious to communicate with either the Newark police or the city administration on such criminal matters.

Four Essex County grand jury presentments between 1961 and 1965 had asserted police corruption and police reacted by continuing business as usual.

The April 1965 presentment charged political interference with the police department and lack of enforcement of Newark gambling laws, and drew attention to open activity of Harry "Tip" Rosen, a public relations man for People's Express. This local trucking company is jointly owned by Jerry Catena, Mafia chief of Newark, and Ralph Dameo, who in November of 1967 threw a banquet for newly appointed Police Captain Rocco Ferrante, Spina's right-hand man. Rosen also happened to be public relations man for the Newark Police Department, a combination of roles that seems practical but one which the grand jury found unsettling. Instead of being rewarded for efficiency, Rosen was fired. The presentment observed the following:

> We have a lack of confidence in the Newark Police Department's enthusiasm for a crackdown on the underworld. Nowhere has our attention been focused on any policy statement by the police department vigorously attacking organized crime. . . .
> There are things which to us, as laymen, are disturbing. They include: A) Political considerations seem to override all else in the assignment of officers to plainclothes and gambling details. We refer to the testimony Director Dominick A. Spina stated, that he makes the decisions regarding the transfers of personnel and he uses his own standards, particularly in regard to appointments to rank of plainclothesman and detective.
> All of this has been weighed in the light of Mayor Hugh J. Addonizio's testimony, which indicated that he has made recommendations for appointments and transfers of various individuals to positions in the police depart-

ment, and in many instances these were grounded in political motivations. . . .

B) Commanders have little say regarding the composition of their own divisions or squads in a sensitive field of gambling enforcement.

As a result of their probe, the grand jury recommended:

That transfers and assignments, as distinguished from raises in grades provided by Civil Service, should be made on the basis of merit and the good of the service. They should not be made through personal, political, or private motivations.

Despite this recommendation, Spina's private promotion system remained unchanged. Deputy Chief Eugene O'Neill said that within a month of taking command of the bureau of investigation in March 1968 he analyzed his men's productivity in raids and arrests. He then recommended that fifteen to twenty detectives and five lieutenants—almost half the men assigned to him—be transferred out of the division. Spina *never took action* on the recommendation. It might have been too costly. One Mafia figure said on FBI tapes he was paying $12,000 monthly for police protection.

A second presentment in December of 1965 again noted flagrant gambling violations and Spina reacted quickly to the new attack, tossing out a few slices of bologna for the public appetite. He labeled the presentment "vicious" and challenged Prosecutor Byrne to show him any organized gambling in Newark, a thoughtless move even in the name of expediency. Within forty-eight hours Byrne raided two apartments and charged fifteen people with operating a lottery.

There Wasn't Anything About a Car That He Didn't Know

The November 1966 indictment of most of the auto squad of the Newark Police Department on fifteen counts charging misconduct in office, extortion, and conspiracy furnishes an illustration of the flagrancy with which police may operate. Lieutenant Elmer Goodwin, the squad head, and Detectives Michael Kerr, Richard Serra, John Quinn, Walter McKenna, and George Diamond were brought to an end by their greed—and because they underestimated a foxy car thief, one John Hall.

"I worked closely with Hall for months and came to know him very well," Assistant County Prosecutor Martin Holleran said of the expert car thief. "I wouldn't trust him as far as I could throw a building, but I admired him. He was very personable and extremely intelligent. I thought of him as a kind of genius. There wasn't anything about a car he didn't know and nothing he couldn't do."

In 1965 Hall, then thirty-one, was operating a stolen car ring in Newark with a skill that would have brought him success in many a lawful endeavor, though it might have cramped his style. Hall purchased wrecks from junkyards, from which he salvaged all usable parts. Next he removed all traces of identification numbers from locks, chassis, body, and doorposts. Hall then transferred these identification numbers to stolen cars, using the ownership papers that had come with the legitimate purchase of the wrecks, and sold them as used cars.

In December, Hall's garage on South Orange Avenue was raided. Police demanded $5,000 to cover up evidence seized in the raid and, four days later, Hall paid it. With this stroke of good fortune, the six detectives enjoyed a plentiful Christmas. They returned to demand money a second time, and a third. Hall eventually figured the hell with this and moved his ring out of the city. By such unorthodox methods did the detectives rid Newark of illegal activity.

Eight months later Hall reopened operations in Newark in a Third Street garage run by a cohort, Shane O'Neil, twenty-four, who supplied stolen cars for the operation. And who should drop by to inspect the fire permit but Detectives Kerr and Serra? They were happier to see O'Neil than he was to see them. O'Neil spent the night in jail with the advice that his boss should contact the detectives. Later that month in a restaurant that Hall owned, O'Neil watched his boss turn over $2,000 to Lieutenant Goodwin, accompanied by Detective Quinn. Afterward Goodwin made a phone call, then told Hall: "Everything is taken care of. Don't worry about it." Hall and O'Neil were then allowed to pick up evidence that had been collected in the last raid.

Undismayed by the greed of the police, Hall opened still another garage, this one on South 12th Street, and continued to ply his chosen trade. Meanwhile, Lieutenant Goodwin became ill and, unfortunately for the other squad members, was replaced by an honest man. Lieutenant Eugene Buerle, the new squad leader, raided Hall's garage with aid of Messrs. Serra, Kerr, and Diamond, all old acquaintances as far as Hall and O'Neil were concerned. Three days later Hall called Quinn at police headquarters and Quinn advised him on how to *avoid prosecution*. The call was taped— not by police, but by Hall, who had just paid out another $2,000, was fed up, and probably felt a noose tightening around his neck.

It is probable that Hall was more shocked on hearing that Lieutenant Buerle was honest than Buerle was on finding out half his men weren't. The lieutenant's consternation might be imagined. Here he had just taken over a squad and one of his first major decisions was either to turn in his own men as criminals or to take the noose off Hall. The record shows that Buerle wasn't about to deviate from his duty, hard as it was. But John Hall, true to his style, wasn't going to give anyone a choice in the matter. He might have felt cramped but not so the detectives, who, even at this stage of the game, obviously considered themselves unreachable. Hall went so far as to tape other conversations with McKenna and Diamond, who were also ready with "inside" advice on how Hall could beat the rap.

At the conclusion of the mess there was Hall, car thief extraordinaire, straddled on the one side by the genuine efforts of Lieutenant Buerle to convict him and on the other by six police detectives who wanted him to get off so their extortion might continue. Even if the police officers weren't prosecuted, Hall would have naturally sung his brains out on the witness stand in his own trial anyway, and the tapes would have made his charges difficult to make light of. The situation was such that the police officers had put themselves into a position where they *had* to be prosecuted.

During Hall's trial Anthony Blasi, McKenna's lawyer, concluded his opening remarks to the jury by walking over to Hall, poking a finger at the bowed head of the star prosecution witness and, turning to the jurors for maximum effect, declaimed: "Thief! Thief! Thief!"

There is no record of laughter in the official court transcript.

Hall's tapes nailed down the case. The jury interrupted its deliberating at one point to hear some of them again. Even with this evidence, however, faith in the police died slowly and it took ten hours to reach a verdict. Goodwin had died of cancer, but the five others were convicted of conspiracy and misconduct in office, and four of the five were also convicted of extortion.

Hall's nerve had gotten him out of a tight one. Several stolen car indictments against him were still pending but because he incriminated himself while testifying it was doubtful that he would ever be tried for them. An old stolen car case, however, returned Hall to the custody of New York for parole violation.

She Was Supposed to Sell the Stuff

Nowhere is Newark's *malaise* more obvious than in the black junkies who roam its streets. They are responsible for the great majority of major crimes—burglaries, robberies, muggings, and murders—overwhelmingly committed against their own people, who sleep with two and three locks on their doors.

Once the pushers had to go into New York City for supplies of raw heroin, which they cut with quinine and packaged in small glassine packets or "decks." They were then distributed, often in broad daylight, on the ghetto's streets at five dollars per deck. By 1968, however, the dealers no longer had to make the trip as Newark had its own base of supply. During that year the narcotics traffic shot upward. Virtually flooded by the supply, the price in the ghetto dropped to three decks for ten dollars. Addicts and small pushers, readily visible in the street and hanging out in bars, were the only ones who seemed to get arrested. The big pushers went untouched. Law enforcement authorities seemed more concerned with manipulating the flow of narcotics than with eradicating it.

"One time I was in this girl's apartment and this dude comes in, you know, and drops a bag down," one pusher told me. "I didn't think nothing about it till I found out the bag was full of heroin and the guy was a vice squad cop. She was supposed to sell the stuff for him."

I'm Gonna Clean This Fucking Place Out

A bar-room brawl in the early hours of November 25, 1967, busted up the Chez Charles, then a Mafia-owned tavern on First Street. The fight lasted only a few minutes, but the tavern, scene of numerous other fights and a later murder, eventually lost its license and the police officers involved lost their jobs.

According to testimony at their trial, the action began at 1:30 A.M. when Nicholas Falco, an off-duty detective, perhaps inspired by the playing of Rasputin and His Mad Monks or by holiday zest, announced: "I'm gonna clean this fucking place out." He then proceeded to do so, with some help from others, including Newark police who were never identified. Two patrolmen answering the disturbance call—William Provost, Martinez's former partner, and James Caffrey—played the incident down in their reports. According to a member of the prosecutor's office, a waitress trampled during the fracas, however, had been hospitalized. The officers visited the twenty-five-year-old woman at the hospital and advised or asked her to forget about it. They also attempted to have hospital records falsified as to her injuries.

In December the Chez Charles was the scene of another brawl, and a police inspector received an anonymous call at home advising him to look more closely into the previous disturbance. He began to collect information. Two girls who had been in the club signed statements that Falco had been in the November brawl. Subsequently both suffered memory lapses and were unable to identify him. The president of the corporation owning the club, whose partner was an ex-convict listing ownership under his wife's name, signed an affidavit that he had paid Falco $600 to keep the thing quiet. Subsequently he also suffered an amnesia attack. Falco was never formally accused of taking a bribe, and the matter of three police officers writing false reports—hardly unusual for Newark police—appeared to be an internal matter to be settled within the department.

Surprisingly, however, possibly because someone wanted them off the police force, Falco, Provost, and Caffrey were charged with six counts of neglect of duty and conspiracy to violate criminal law. Eighteen months later they came to trial. Falco testified that he had been at the bar but left before any fight began. In fact, he said, he had been on his way to a Chinese restaurant in North Arlington at the time, apparently seeking Wonton soup. It took the jury six hours to say otherwise. The three were convicted and parted company with the Newark Police Department. Spectators included several well-tailored gentlemen in dark glasses who sat impassively through the five-day trial as though they were watching submarine races.

It Is a Very Large Business

The polarization that pervaded post-riot Newark included the police department, though here it was limited to a low murmur. On one side was the fifty-seven-year-old Spina and on the other, Deputy Chief Redden, who since 1962 had been watching with growing disgust as Addonizio and Spina helped turn Newark into a corrupt whorehouse. For the forty-eight-year-old Redden, the riot had been the last straw and his Irish anger flared. He called city officials bastards to their faces. He told them he'd testify before a grand jury and before the Hughes Commission.

While public attention was drawn to the evil black man, LeRoi Jones, and the ranting of Imperiale in the North Ward, the real struggle in post-riot Newark was a silent one. Few understood that, as far as Spina and organized crime were concerned, John Redden was the most dangerous man in Newark.

Police Chief Oliver Kelly went on terminal leave before his retirement on December 29, 1968, leaving the position open to one of three deputy chiefs, Anthony Barres, Eugene O'Neill, and Redden. Ordinarily the New Jersey Civil Service Commission would have scheduled a promotion exam, but the commission was not notified of the vacancy until after Kelly had left. Spina had five other deputy chiefs appointed after Kelly's departure, hoping that they would be at their new posts a year before an exam for the chief's position was held, thus fulfilling eligibility requirements.

In December of 1967 Spina said he had asked the commission to hold exams as early as possible in 1968. The director of classification for the Newark office, however, said he had received no such communication. Spina then said he had not asked for the exam because he wanted to choose from a "wider field" than the men then eligible. More accurately, he wanted to avoid appointing Redden, who had finished *first* on the list in the last two exams.

Newark's flagrant gambling activity, particularly because of Redden's testimony, was aired in the Hughes Report: "Based on my own experience, based on the statement—the public statement—of a man such as former Assistant Attorney General [John] Bergin, I would say that it was very prevalent," Redden testified. "It is a very large business." Redden further pointed out the assigning of personnel for "political reasons."

Badly stung by the Hughes Report, Mayor Addonizio ordered a special gambling squad into existence shortly afterward to save face and imprudently placed Redden in command. Between March and mid-April, the nine-man unit made twenty-two arrests and confiscated $15,370 in lottery play, two shotguns, six pistols, and $10,000 in stolen merchandise. They also confiscated $16,389 in cash. In six weeks the squad had collected more cash than the entire police department had in the previous three years. In one of their most successful forays on March 15, Redden's squad raided Frisco's Luncheonette. They arrested five men and confiscated a paper bag that contained $6,934 in cash, $498 worth of lottery play, some medicine, an apple, and—now what do we have here?—twelve tickets to Mayor Addonizio's birthday party.

Redden said his squad had also uncovered evidence of widespread loan-sharking in the city and that several big raids were being planned. They were never carried out. The end of the special gambling squad was first announced informally during a preliminary court hearing when a widely known professional gambler told squad members that there would be "changes" within a week. There were changes within a week. While the squad was out on a raid, a teletype order from Spina disbanded the group—much to the surprise of Addonizio, who had never been informed.

Spina said the men on the squad were needed elsewhere because of "a manpower shortage" but squad members told a different story:

"The number of arrests could have been tripled, but we had trouble getting search warrants."

"We were stepping on too many toes."

"We were getting close to the big people."

Addonizio was vacationing at Miami Beach when he heard of the disbanding of a squad he had ordered. "Spina discussed it with me before I left," the mayor stated. "He said they hadn't produced anything." Commenting on Redden's loan shark discoveries, he said, "Redden should take it up with Director Spina. I'm sure Director Spina is just as interested in arresting gamblers as he is."

Addonizio may have been joking but Essex County Prosecutor Joseph P. Lordi, who had succeeded Byrne, wasn't. The day following Spina's abolition of the gambling squad, Lordi said he would call for a special grand jury to investigate what was going on in Newark. The real question was, what wasn't going on.

6

TOM HAYDEN AND THE SEEDS OF RIOT

How Hard Can They Afford to Try?

In March following the riot, Tom Hayden, who had departed the city at least a month before, returned to Newark for a brief stopover. He was staying on the second floor at 631 Hunterdon Street with his girl friend, Connie Brown. Even as he left the house and walked up Hunterdon, police downtown were concocting evidence to support their theory that Hayden was the one man mainly responsible for the Newark riot.

A little after three in the afternoon he walked out of the ghetto that he knew so well and across the Clinton Avenue intersection to the other side of the street. Inside K's Restaurant a few doors up the block, Hayden took off his overcoat and sat down on one of the wooden chairs facing the front door. He pulled it close to one of the tables and leaned forward on his arms. "Mrs. K, a cup of coffee, please," he said with a familiarity that showed he had been in the restaurant many times before.

Hayden was a thin, medium-sized man. His hair and eyes were dark and there were pit marks on both cheeks, the result of childhood acne. He had traveled far in his twenty-eight years and, as his scuffed shoes, ripped shirt cuff, brown sports jacket missing a button, and worn trousers signified, the pay for a revolutionary may have been less than the Newark police insinuated.

Outside on the streets of black Newark, in the ghetto where he had lived for the past four and a half years, were the people and the section of the city that Hayden knew best. "This is where we started organizing," he said with mock seriousness. "You will notice the remarkable transformation that has taken place. . . . Nothing changes on the outside. It looks the same, the shell is the same, but the things that are ticking inside these people—they're new."

Hayden's book, *Rebellion in Newark,* written and published hastily only weeks after the riot, analyzed events from the perspective of a New Left revolutionary. The book likened activity during the riot to a vicious military suppression and painted an uncomplimentary picture of Newark's police:

> Dominated by the Italians who run Newark's politics, tainted by alleged underworld connections, including a token number of about 250 blacks among its 1,400 members (all of them in subordinated positions), the police department seems to many Negroes to be an armed agency defending the privileges of the city's shrinking white community.

Rebellion in Newark, the work of a revolutionary, had as a sequel the Hughes Report, an investigative work sanctioned if not blessed by constituted authority. In many ways they complemented one another in their portrayal of the riot, raising serious questions about how and why the victims had been killed. Now, eight months after, the beaten streets still bore scars of the riot, while the prosecutor's office and homicide personnel downtown were preparing a defense against *Rebellion in Newark* rather than genuinely seeking the answers. No one knew this better than Hayden.

"I think the prosecutor's office has been working a lot harder on some of the riot deaths since the Hughes Report," he said. "Justice can't be given by any report, though. Grand jury indictments for some of those involved in the homicides would be more like it. What I question is, just how hard can they afford to try? Right now they've got police detectives investigating other police officers and you know how that will come out." Hayden smiled. "At first the police department tried to discredit my book. They visited some of the people mentioned in it and tried to get them to sue me."

Hayden smiled again and drank some coffee. "One person they talked to was a woman I had never even met before. I got her name from a story in *The New York Times.* If the police would spend less time investigating me and more time investigating themselves, the city would be better off. In each of the riot homicides there has to be some action. If the police can get away with shooting people down on the street in cold blood, they'll do it again."

Going Through the Struggle Together

Hayden, one of the founders of Students for a Democratic Society, came to Newark with other young members in the summer of 1964 to found the Newark Community Union Project (NCUP). They aimed to put into practice the theory and method of participatory democracy and to organize ghetto people to take some control over their own and their children's lives—much to the dismay of the Newark police and even the suspicion of local residents.

"Our ultimate goal," wrote Eric Mann, a member of the group, "is to control the institutions in our community—not to substitute a local elite ⊃ for an alien one, but to provide a qualitative difference in the way these institutions are run."

Though Newark had been selected largely by chance, months of study could not have yielded a better-chosen location for their efforts. The ghetto, though it held the majority of Newark's residents, was essentially powerless. The atmosphere was stagnant, exactly as the city administration wanted. "To us," Mann wrote in *Liberation* magazine, "a ghetto is not a bad place to live because its residents are all Negroes or because most of them are poor. What makes a ghetto despicable—and what keeps it that way—is that the people in it have no control over the decisions that affect their lives. Store owners, welfare officials, school administrators, police, landlords and city officials are usually unresponsive to the desires of ghetto people. In fact, most often they exercise their power directly counter to the aspirations of the people in the ghetto."

Hugh Addonizio, formerly a fourteen-year congressman with a liberal voting record, became mayor of Newark in 1962 with heavy black support. Politicians like George Richardson believed the black community had supported him with the understanding that the new mayor would appoint blacks to responsible positions, where they would get the experience necessary should a black mayor be elected. However, with a political machine geared for white dominance and greased by corruption, that could only prove a vain hope. The disillusionment in the black community was expanded by CORE's civil rights drive in 1963 and the feeling of unrest grew steadily through 1964 and 1965, despite Addonizio's re-election and the election of thirty-three-year-old Calvin West, a Negro, to a councilman-at-large post.

West, youngest man on the council, joined another Negro, fifty-three-year-old Irvine Turner, who had first been elected central ward councilman in 1954 and had been slipping into senility ever since. Turner, who had set a goal of becoming Newark's first black mayor, was the chief Negro liaison between the ghetto and the city administration or, as LeRoi Jones put it, the "house nigger." John O'Shea, writing in the *Atlantic Monthly* of November 1965, characterized the councilman's style:

> Turner, who controls about 17,000 votes, practices a personal, bread-and-butter kind of politics in the classic tradition of the American ward boss of the nineteenth century. He boasts that he feeds more Negroes every week than the Newark welfare department. . . . Each morning the lines of supplicants queue outside his High Street home, and few are turned away

without something, even if only a promise. Turner also controls dozens of patronage jobs paying thousands of dollars annually.

The councilman's methods of keeping people in check were sometimes vicious. According to reporters for Newark's daily newspapers, Turner, who worked for several Negro weeklies, would copy down names from the police blotter of persons involved in unsavory incidents for possible later use against them.

The younger West's tactics, on the other hand, were far more sophisticated. His chief asset was his close personal association with Addonizio. Also, both his wife and sister had been appointed to City Hall jobs. As Turner's health failed, West was steadily gaining in influence, and he became the Addonizio machine's choice for Newark's first black mayor should the election of a non-white be inevitable.

Such was the state of black leadership in the ghetto that in a poll taken by the Hughes Commission after the riot, Turner topped the list and West was not far behind.

Hayden, who had thought the Clinton Hill area to be a mixed neighborhood, arrived to find a hardcore black ghetto controlled by such "house niggers" as Turner and West. He and his group of about seven began by walking the dirty streets, ringing doorbells and asking residents to join their project. "It was very rough going," Hayden recalled. "As we went along we refined our thinking. We still believed in participatory democracy but it was clear that people could not be held by an idea alone. Nor could we organize around a block—people change residences too fast and they didn't have much of a commitment to where they lived. Most of those who worked, worked outside of the ghetto. We finally saw that only the organizing experience itself, going through the struggle together, was enough to unify the people."

Bob Curvin of CORE had become active in the city in 1963 and a new unrest had been noticed by officials. That July—a year before Hayden's arrival—there had been five days of demonstrations at Barringer High School protesting all-white construction crews. These demonstrations ended when Mayor Addonizio, then in his first term, formed an organization of civil rights, business and labor leaders to conduct an apprentice program for the building trades. Elements of the ghetto were slowly becoming aroused, and in this widening trickle of discontent the NCUP people first wet their feet.

They picked tenements and demanded action against slum landlords, distributed leaflets against police brutality during the Lester Long controversy, argued in neighborhoods and in the Office of Economic Opportunity in Washington for participation of the poor in Newark's "War on Poverty." NCUP-allied people also held most of the staff positions in a neighborhood play street program, struggling with the community relations program of the Newark police for control. They worked gingerly and at arm's length with the United Freedom Ticket of George Richardson. The politicians prudently maintained some distance from the "radicals" and NCUP was suspicious of electoral politics anyway, feeling that it produced leaders who monopolized contacts, knowledge and decisions, imposed solutions from above and tended to reduce movements to a body of followers.

For exactly that reason—his reluctance to be named a leader—Hayden deliberately arrived late on the day NCUP people were in Deputy Mayor Paul Reilly's office, arguing for a traffic light.

The traffic light demonstrations made little news even in the city, but they were bringing the administration considerable irritation.

"I remember arresting Hayden at the corner of Badger and Avon when they were demonstrating for a traffic light," recalled Sergeant Sellers of the Fifth Precinct. "This was in the summer of 1965, a year after he came into the city. There were at least fifty people there, even women pushing baby carriages. It had the makings of a very bad situation what with people coming home from work and the demonstrators planning to walk right into the streets. So I went up to Hayden and I told him if those people went into the street I'd arrest him because he was leading them. You know what he said? 'You wouldn't dare.' They went anyway and I arrested about twelve of them. A police inspector was there and he told me, 'You've got the makings of a riot here; why make waves?' I told him, 'Waves, hell!' They were breaking the law and needed arresting. Hayden knew damn well the city couldn't put up a traffic light there or anywhere else, even if they wanted to. A survey has to be made and sent to the motor vehicle people in Trenton. Then they make their own traffic survey. It takes a long time to get a traffic light, it's not something you can do overnight by marching into a street."

Hayden wrote of the traffic light demonstrations in *Partisan Review* in 1966:

> I used to think such issues were "superficial," they didn't deal with "real problems," etc., but I've felt my thinking shift bit by bit this year. I had to learn that *real* children are killed, all the time. That families are worried about their *real* children. What the city fails to do about "minor" ills which by its own laws it should correct, is a measure of the callousness of the officials. That the people accommodate, by their silence at least, to the city's failure on such small matters, is a measure of how deeply they feel the futility of changing anything. Most people I talked to see the traffic problem, not on the basis of narrow self-interest, but as part of a system so abrasive that it cannot implement its own laws without militant pressure. The 20 I'm working with see it as a departure point for a community movement and a way to wrest something real from City Hall.

On the first day of the traffic light demonstrations, six Negro members of the Irvine Turner Association were standing at the corner awaiting the picketers as they arrived. They cornered the NCUP people and attempted to talk them out of being "fooled by whites and outside agitators." Turner, who, as the head "house nigger," was expected to control such anti-administration activity, felt threatened by the new black attitude creeping into Newark.

As disenchantment with the Addonizio regime grew, blacks who had been appointed to figurehead posts began quitting in disgust or were rendered powerless. One example was Al Black, who had been named chairman of the Human Rights Commission in 1966 because he seemed softspoken and unlikely to make waves. Not only did Black embarrass the administration with his report on the wretched conditions at City Hospital but his brutality hearings after the riot were unprecedented for an administration appointee. Black had to go. Three "administration men" were subsequently appointed to replace Black's supporters on the commission and the group then elected an ineffectual Negro to replace Black as chairman.

Blood Will Run Down the Streets of Newark

The proposed relocation of the New Jersey College of Medicine and Dentistry, an issue that arose in early 1967, had all the aspects of a game between the city administration and the college's board of trustees. The medical school trustees, reluctant to move to Newark at all, began with a demand of 150 acres before they would seriously consider the city. Testifying before the Hughes Commission, Donald Malafronte, administrative assistant to and spokesman for Mayor Addonizio, explained the administration's counter-move:

> We got a copy of the report and said, "We've been undone here." We all sat down with a map and looked around at the area we wanted to go into, which was Fairmount Urban Renewal Project. It worked out to 20 acres; if we pushed it, 30 acres; which we felt was more than sufficient for a medical school, still do. It was clear we were hung on their 150 acres as a stipulation, but we did have this rather glowing account of all the advantages of Newark. So we thought we would surprise them in this and we drew 185 acres which we considered to be the worst slum area. It included Fairmount and surrounding areas, which was clearly in need of urban renewal, and we were going to proceed with the renewal in any case for that area.
>
> We asked for a special meeting with them and at the meeting we confronted them with our offer of 185 acres. At that same meeting they had arranged to release their report and 150 acres, so we were at an impasse.

Their report which said Newark is a wonderful place, but we need 150 acres and, therefore, we can't come—they were confronted with Newark's counter-offer of 185 acres. What excuse do you have? This is when the battle joined. It became unclear. We, I think, in our hearts always felt they were using 150 acres to get out of Newark. We felt in the end they would come down to 20 or 30 acres in Fairmount, or in a battle we might have to give up some more acreage. We never felt they would ask for 185. We felt it was a ploy on their part.

Late in 1966 the medical school trustees agreed to come to Newark on the offer of 150 acres, but they had another ploy ready. The city was to give up 50 acres immediately and to produce the other 100 acres on demand after eighteeen months' notice. The trustees, however, asked not for cleared land, but for 50 acres *still covered* with buildings and people.

To us [Malafronte testified] this was a slap in the face. It was our opinion they were attempting to get out of the situation in which they found themselves, which was an aroused public demand they come to Newark. . . . What they wanted was across the street from cleared land. This, to us, was insanity and enraging because they knew this was not an urban renewal area.

They knew it—and so did the people who ran Newark. Yet in March the city pushed through the legislative authorization for condemnation proceedings on the property the trustees had chosen. The poor, pawns in this game of move and counter-move, were expected to pack up and find themselves another smelly, rotting tenement as they had so many times in the past. Contrary to what black leaders believed, only 3,500 would be displaced and most of them wanted to move anyway. Their leaders, however, enlarged the issue. All the beatings and cries for justice that had been laughed at, all the unjustified shootings, the rats and roaches, the leaking roofs, and the stinking toilets that wouldn't flush—they had all come together in a single issue with which everyone in ghetto Newark could identify. This was too massive and blatant an example of "nigger removal" for blacks to live with.

The Hughes Report, noting the mobility of Newark's shifting black population, suggested another reason why they were kept on the move:

The mobility of the Negro population also inhibits its political effectiveness. Albert Black, chairman of the Human Rights Commission, said in a staff interview that, if 30,000 Negroes were registered in a voting drive, 10,000 of them would be unregistered three years later because they had moved. This reduces their strength at the polls.

To the Central Ward blacks the medical school clearance represented an impending storm which would drown many of the powerless. But to those sheltered in City Hall the first bolts of lightning went unnoticed.

As the city prepared for public blight hearings in a setting of growing opposition, Colonel Hassan of the Blackman's Volunteer Army of Liberation appeared in Newark just as mysteriously as he would depart shortly before the riot. Colonel Hassan—actually a forty-two-year-old wig salesman from Washington whose real name was Albert Roy Osborne—had a showy manner, distinguished graying hair under a black beret and an outstanding gift of gab. The colonel called for an April 28 protest rally against the medical school. Newark police toured the ghetto displaying copies of Hassan's arrest record to discourage attendance but, in a manifestation of health, Bob Curvin, Kenneth Gibson, who had run unsuccessfully for mayor in 1966, George Richardson and other respected black leaders appeared at the rally with black nationalists.

The first of the Planning Board's blight hearings—held solely to fulfill federal aid requirements—opened on May 22 and was abbreviated when one of Colonel Hassan's lieutenants overturned the stenograph machine and the colonel himself tore up the tape. Subsequent public hearings exhibited only violent rhetoric, but community spokesmen left no doubt of their anger.

James Walker, an associate director of the small business division of Union Community Corporation, announced that if the medical school were built instead of new housing, "blood will run down the streets of Newark —your blood and my blood."

James Kennedy, assistant organizer for UCC's Area Board Two, was even more explicit:

> And when you approve this blighted area, we are going to go there and lie in front of those bulldozers a little. There is not one ounce of doubt in my mind that you will not build your medical school. The Lord help you, little white boys, because I will whip the hell out of anyone I can get my hands on. It is sure going to do my heart good to see you with that great, big 150-acre school and not a damn soul in it because they are going to be too scared. We couldn't find anybody on this Planning Board who lives in the Central Ward, so my advice to you is to stay the hell away from us and we will stay the hell away from you.

During the June 13 session, Richardson discovered that police were taping the proceedings in a side room. Spina defended the taping on the grounds that it could be used as court evidence against persons arrested for misconduct. "There was no secrecy involved," he claimed. Then he added, "We don't have to tell anyone what we're doing."

The Blood Will Be on Your Hands

The blacks who attended the blight hearings sensed that the administration had turned off its hearing aid. The dispute over a Board of Education secretary appointment, developing at the same time, only reinforced that perception.

When it became known that Arnold Hess, the board's secretary, planned to resign, the NAACP proposed that Wilbur Parker, city budget director and the first black in the state to become a certified public accountant, be appointed to replace him. The position had always been free of politics and had always gone to a competent man. It also carried responsibility, and the appointment of the more qualified Parker, it was felt, might help reverse the administration's deteriorating relationship with the black community. The motive behind the Hess resignation, however, was the administration's plan to appoint Councilman James T. Callaghan, a member of its extortion ring, a former labor hack and one of the more dim-witted members of the governing body—possibly one of the most unqualified men in Newark. The black community drew together to support Parker. "The Negro community is in turmoil over this injustice," Fred Means, president of the Negro Educators of America, said. "If immediate steps are not taken, Newark might become another Watts."

The June 26 meeting of the Board of Education began at 5:00 P.M. and lasted past 3:00 A.M. in a torrent of emotion. Harry Wheeler, a teacher and community spokesman, told the board that the appointment of Callaghan "is going to be the catalyst for blood running in the streets of Newark like there has never been anywhere else in America."

"The people all over this city are saying that if they do," Wheeler continued, "if they [the Addonizio gang] usurp power after we have lived up to the rules of the game, then we have no other choice than to move to take the situation in our hands. And I simply want to say to you that your actions tomorrow night will make you the instrumentality for the worst holocaust that this nation has ever seen, and I am not going to beg with you or plead with you as previous speakers have done. I am simply going to say to you that the blood will be on your hands."

Seventy community speakers spoke during the tumultuous hearing—which ended predictably with a decision that Hess would remain in the job for another year.

"The only issue I've seen Negroes get truly excited and concerned about was Parker-Callaghan," said James Threatt, director of the Human Rights Commission.

"When people lost faith in these legitimate efforts, I think the culmination of the defeats is what brought about the riots we had in the city," Richardson said.

The crowds of black people who attended the medical school and Board of Education hearings were mostly homeowners and concerned citizens, not participants in the riot that followed. Ghetto troublemakers and militants found that an inaccessible administration had created fertile ground for their work. Out on the street were the hoodlums, junkies, and hardened criminals who were the main participants in the riot. Yet the homeowners, revolutionaries, and looters were thrust together by the insensitivity of those in power. Black people felt no responsibility for what followed and their leaders urged them on. This led to the atmosphere during the riot that Governor Hughes characterized as "laughing at a funeral."

These simple facts were lost on the conservative element of society who could easily be convinced that "left-wing radicals" and "rabble-rousers" had created, sustained, propagandized, and eventually exploited both the medical school and Parker-Callaghan controversies. Any rational evaluation was certainly lost on the Newark police, who were now attempting to substantiate their explanation of the riot: Communist instigation. But the young NCUP activists and black nationals weren't responsible for Newark's disgusting living conditions or the issues which made the ghetto explode in anger. If there was a real conspiracy to provoke a riot, its plotters were easy to find. They were sitting in City Hall stealing.

An Attempt to Disrupt the Greedy Status Quo

"These people in Newark see a subversive as anyone who threatens their power structure," Hayden said in K's Restaurant, finishing his coffee. "They tack 'communist' onto the end of their definition—that's for their public relations. Anybody who doesn't think like they do is a communist. I don't think they know what a communist is. People like Spina live in a small universe. They don't understand how other people see the world, the dynamics of change. What they call crime is a way of life in the ghetto, something they keep a way of life by their actions, part of their system of oppression. What they call communist is nothing more than an attempt to disrupt the greedy status quo, to offset that system of oppression and make them realize there are human beings here."

A first effort at finding Hayden had ended at 227 Jelliff Avenue, a shabby house with a sagging porch just a few blocks away. A knock at the door was unanswered and a piece of paper tacked to it explained why:

Warrant of Removal Notice to Vacate to: Thomas Hayden. You are hereby notified your apartment must be vacated by Thursday, January 4, 1968, under the above court order. Failing to comply with this demand you will be dispossessed without further notice. Constable, Essex County District Court.

A few blocks from the house was a field full of withered weeds, decorated by a bare basketball hoop. It had taken Hayden's group two years to get that recreation facility, an unceasing effort matched by the city's effort to get rid of Hayden.

"The landlord was a Puerto Rican who couldn't speak English," Hayden said, ordering another cup of coffee. "I let a Puerto Rican family move in after I had already left the house. I don't think the landlord even knew about it. Anyway, I went back to the house when I returned from a trip to Asia and talked with the family. They told me the landlord told them, 'The previous tenants were communists and the government said I had to get rid of them.' "

In January Hayden returned briefly to Newark after a trip to Hanoi where he arranged the release of three American servicemen by the Viet Cong. The National Liberation Front had chosen him to receive the prisoners who were being released as a gesture of friendship to the American peace movement.

A second chance to meet Hayden was missed when he appeared before the grand jury hearing testimony on riot homicides. The New Left activist, represented by attorney Leonard Weinglass of Newark, testified for three hours before the special jury. At a press conference following his testimony, Hayden charged that the grand jury couldn't conduct a fair investigation into the riot deaths and suggested that evidence be submitted to an independent tribunal of citizens without ties to law enforcement officers. Hayden also accused the police of intimidating potential witnesses and of destroying their tape recordings of police radio calls during the disturbance. In addition, he told reporters that a federal investigator had indirectly informed him that he was on a list in the Newark Police Department of people "to get"—which was why our meeting in this restaurant had gone on long enough.

"One other thing," Hayden said, putting on his raincoat. "I was told by sources close to the top, near the governor's office, that Hughes knew Newark officials didn't believe Moran was shot by a sniper. [Fire Captain Michael Moran, killed by gunfire on July 15, 1967.] They let that go, they didn't say anything about that. It was very uncertain who had killed Moran, but saying a sniper did it was expedient at the time."

His handshake was strong. Hayden walked out the door and across Clinton Avenue, back into the ghetto he had come from where he had worked for so long. Between him and the Newark power structure were miles of sickness, poverty, and wasted lives. Between him and the police department were those bodies now eight months dead but still without any explanation.

7

THE BATTLE OF NORTH 14TH STREET

You Know How They Talk

At 5:11 P.M., Friday, July 7, just five days before the Newark riot began, an East Orange patrol car pulled up to 91 North 14th Street in response to a girl's call which had come into headquarters a few minutes earlier:

"Would you please send a police car to 91 North 14th Street, East Orange side. Pick up a Sherieff—he should be picked up and locked up."

"Why do you want us to pick him up?"

"Well—he is a Muslim and you know how they talk. The address is 91 North 14th Street and his name is Sherieff."

Sherieff is the Muslim name of Edward Chisone, who lived on the first floor. Ronald Washington, also a Black Muslim, lived on the second floor at the North 14th Street address, an ordinary two-family house sitting among a string of rundown houses on the East Orange side of Newark's city line.

"My arrival time was 5:11 P.M., shortly before car number eight," Patrolman Ralph Gruendel reported. "In the time elapsing before their arrival, I sat in my car and was insulted a number of times. I was called a 'white devil,' 'Satan,' 'skunk who dwelt on this earth,' my time was coming and I was meant to burn. Also that I was a person who wanted to rule. The orator also spoke out to the neighbors that they shouldn't be oppressed by people like myself."

When police approached the small group of Black Muslims standing around the front porch, they were told that the only woman in the house was Washington's wife and she certainly hadn't called for the police. They were also told that the call couldn't have come from the house since there was no working telephone and, since the police had no search warrant, they could not enter.

"They explained to me they had received a call and it was their job to come," the twenty-seven-year-old Washington told me. "There was no anger, no heated words and they left."

Five hours after the first incident, at 10:07 P.M., two more East Orange police cars responded to a minor traffic accident at North 14th Street. A black officer, John Harrison, parked directly in front of the Muslim house while investigating the accident.

"The group of men then formed on the front steps of that house and they began yelling insults at Patrolman Lago and myself," he reported. "They called Patrolman Lago a 'white devil' and me a 'tool.' Ignoring these insults and waiting for the tow truck which came and took the damaged car, I finished the accident report in headquarters."

East Orange police received another call at 12:50 A.M. "As in the first call, it was a female in quest of police," Detective Sergeant Ramsey Scott's report reads. "The female would not identify herself other than to state she lived either at 91 North 14th Street or in the immediate area. She inferred this by stating she would be standing on her porch and that she would meet the police when they arrived. She insisted that the group of Muslims were throwing stones at her home and also at passing cars and were also using loud and profane language. She stated she would sign a complaint. Radio cars were dispatched at 12:54 A.M. Patrolman John Harrison, realizing that the group was probably the same as he had been menaced by earlier in the evening, notified the other cars not to go directly in front of the house but to let him approach the group alone. He believed that he being a Negro would not create an incident. The other cars sat by as Patrolman Harrison approached the house. No female came forward either from number 91 or any of the neighboring homes to make her complaint."

Patrolman Harrison, who according to Scott had not been insulted but "menaced," picked up the narrative: "I went and asked the spokesman [Washington] who was there, about the disturbance call made by a woman. He stated that the only woman in the house was his wife and that they had no phone. I went back to my car and some of the men came to me and milled around my car stating that I was wrong to help the white man, etc. I instructed the radio cars to pull out of the area, which they did."

Detective Scott's report continues the narrative, relating Harrison's experience with an added theatrical tinge.

"The officer returned to his vehicle and as he got into it another car drove up and six or seven males jumped from it and surrounded his vehicle. They were all attired in 'karate' type uniforms."

Arriving in said auto were five Muslims from Newark—William Manik Jasper, Otis Hardy, Dennis Sims, Edward Walker, and Belton Williams—who had gotten out of a car in the normal manner. All the men had shaved heads, as did the Muslims they were joining, and none wore karate robes.

After Patrolman Harrison left, another policeman showed up at a scene that was growing uneasy. East Orange Detective Ted Nealy, also black, stated: "I was patrolling in car 33 on North 14th Street and I observed that a group of men were now on the sidewalk as well as on the porch of 91 North 14th Street. I stopped my car and got out and walked up to the men. There was no doubt that these men were Black Muslims. At this time, there were no other known police officers at the scene. I did not exchange a word with these men but started walking back to car 33."

According to later police reports, the Black Muslims were anxious to start a fight and were calling headquarters to bait them. If those men on the porch had been taking notes, however, their records would have contained legitimate cause for alarm.

First, two police cars came and the police were told they were not needed. Then two more patrol cars parked near the house investigating a routine accident. Two and a half hours later three more patrol cars were back again on much the same business as seven hours before. No one emerged to complain about rock throwing and again no woman came out to make a complaint. Next, yet another policeman pulled up, got out of his car, and walked over to the house. He scrutinized them for a few minutes without a word and then left as he had come.

If the police thought the Muslims' activity was suspicious, what could the Muslims have been thinking about the police? To their knowledge there had been no phoned complaints and they were being harassed.

To the police, all Black Muslims are criminals. Since many converts were first exposed to the faith in prison, the sect's membership does include *many* ex-convicts—not *all*. Sincere conversion necessitated abandonment of a criminal past, and most members feel compelled to lead their brothers and sisters to a new way of life.

Six of the North 14th St. Muslims had been arrested before, for petty offenses in almost every case.[5] Only one of eleven men had been convicted of a felony.

[5] The criminal records of Black Muslims are more an indication of the nature of police activity in the ghetto and how it helps create hardcore criminals than a reflection on the character of the men involved. Ronald Washington had been arrested three times, once in 1958 for "investigation" for gun possession, after which he was released, and again later that year for loitering, for which he was fined twenty-five dollars. The third arrest—seven years before the North 14th Street incident and five years before he became a Muslim—was for larceny.

William Turner had two previous arrests: failure to report for Army induction—routine for Muslims who are conscientious objectors—and assault and battery on a police officer in June of 1967, which couldn't have been serious since the matter was dropped.

Edward Walker had seven previous arrests beginning in 1959. Walker, a juvenile at

The group, which police claimed was "creating an incident," hadn't moved and wasn't even aware of what was happening. However, they must have sensed trouble and should have broken up. But flair, pride and an ill-advised sense of security because they were on private property led them to continue their prayer meeting at the house where it had been held in previous weeks without incident.

"When the cars returned to service from the 12:54 A.M. call," Detective Scott's report continues, "Sergeant Frank Fehn requested Patrolman Harrison to meet him several blocks from the trouble area so that he could assess the situation. Unknown to the sergeant and the other officers, the Newark police had arrived at the scene in response to a request of this department. Evidently, the East Orange cars *had left*[6] the area prior to the arrival of the Newark cars and therefore Newark was faced with the same situation that our cars had met."

If Scott meant that the Muslims were still there, that much is correct. It is strange, however, that the aid of the Newark police had been summoned to an area so dangerous that the East Orange police they were supposed to assist had driven off before they arrived.

Scott continues: "The first Newark car to arrive was that of Patrolmen Thomas Tretola and Frank Irwin. These two officers observed a group of colored males acting boisterous and causing a disturbance on the Newark side of North 14th Street at William Street. They told the group to move on and in response were told by the group to get out of their radio car

---

the time, was arrested for *resisting arrest*—a unique charge—and then for assault and battery and resisting arrest. Walker was fined ten dollars in each instance. With such an obvious tendency to violent behavior, Walker must have been watched particularly carefully. Within a four-month period in 1960 he was arrested on four different occasions, each time charged with carrying a concealed weapon. Concealed weapons in the ghetto include everything from an ordinary pocket knife to a can-opener. Such weapons have a history of materializing. Walker was sent to reformatories on each arrest and had kept out of the way of the police for six years. He was arrested again in 1966, this time charged with shoplifting, which matter was dropped.

Jack Cogman had one prior arrest that had come seven years before. In March of 1960 he was charged with being "an inmate of a disorderly house." The matter was subsequently dropped.

William Malik Jasper was twenty years old when first arrested for a narcotic violation. From then on he was marked, falling into the usual harassment and surveillance difficulties—failure to have an identification card and violations of probation arrests. Three motor vehicle violations were also on his record. Then in May of 1967, his head struck the blackjack of a black Newark detective and he was charged with assaulting the officer. This matter has never been disposed of.

Belton Williams was convicted of murder in 1956, when he was nineteen, and sent to Jamesburg Reformatory. He escaped and was subsequently returned. In May 1960, Williams was sentenced to five to seven years for armed robbery. He also had two motor vehicle arrests in 1967 and another robbery charge in April of the same year, which was dropped. If there is one Black Muslim in Newark who is continually harassed, it is Belton Williams. Nevertheless, from all appearances he is completely rehabilitated.

6 Author's italics.

and make them. The two Newark patrolmen immediately called their headquarters for assistance as their car was surrounded by this group of men and other men who came from the porch of 91 North 14th Street. The Newark dispatcher also called East Orange and asked where our cars were and of course advised they be sent back as their men were being harassed."

And where were the East Orange cars? At 1:03 A.M. they were "back in service," a police phrase meaning assignment completed. There were no disturbances and no citizens making complaints, only a small crowd of youths and the Black Muslims meeting on private property. A disturbance around Club Drewsie—the corner tavern on the other side of the street from the Muslim house—had resulted in a small crowd and, according to the report, arriving Newark police were being harassed not only by this group but also by the Muslims who supposedly had joined the crowd.

This was one of many erroneous assertions about the event which, rather than supplying factual information, created a mirage of what police claimed had happened.

"Some of the brothers arrived around the time of the tavern incident," Washington told me. "When the first Newark police arrived I heard one of them shouting, 'Get off the corner, get off the corner.' There was a crowd there and the four brothers were down around there. The police were coming about something that had nothing to do with us, a fight around the tavern or something. They drew their guns and chased the crowd. Then they followed the brothers over to my porch and one of them said to the other, 'I'm going to call for assistance.' Call for assistance? For what? I couldn't understand what he was talking about."

The Newark police had noticed the Muslims sitting on the porch. Instead of leaving as the East Orange police had done, they were ready to tangle with a group they hated.

Car after car arrived and the scene on North 14th Street became reminiscent of the police raid on the Muslim's South Orange Avenue mosque two years before.[7] Near 1:00 A.M. there were between thirty and forty

[7] Throughout the early 1960's, during the militant phase of the Black Muslim movement, the Newark police had undergone difficulties with a criminal element operating within the sect but outside of its Newark mosque. This led police to regard all Black Muslims as potential criminals, though the great majority were law-abiding citizens. This response reached its height on December 17, 1965 when a team of five Black Muslims held up the Robert Treat Savings and Loan Association on Clinton Avenue, shooting a policeman in the back and escaping with $8,700, which was never recovered. Mayor Addonizio and his chauffeur happened into the escape route, gave chase and were fired upon.

A few hours after the robbery, at 12:30 P.M., thirty members of the bandit squad, equipped with bullet-proof vests and submachine guns, descended upon Muhammad's Mosque on South Orange Avenue. They surrounded it, set up roadblocks, broke the

Newark police on hand, mostly members of the crime prevention unit, complete with paddy wagons and emergency trucks with searchlights. Shortly afterward there were also twelve East Orange cars. Throughout my investigation of the disturbance, if there was one set police phrase it was, "We wanted to prevent any incident." Any such claim is nonsense. The Newark police came with riot gear, including helmets and shotguns and—to prevent incidents—screaming sirens. Any claim that the police acted without calculation is refuted by the personal appearance of Director Spina, who left before the blood started to flow.

What Are We Going to Charge Them With?

It had begun with two anonymous phone calls which police believed were made by the Muslims to cause a confrontation. Actually, the phone calls came from William Turner's eighteen-year-old sister, who was an epileptic and mentally disturbed after the death of their mother shortly before. East Orange police arrived and, correctly assessing the situation and not wanting a confrontation, left. Then the Newark police, called in to assist prematurely, beefed up their strength to near forty men in a show of force—the standard Newark response that made a disturbance inevitable—and were calling on the East Orange police for additional help. Eventually hundreds of neighborhood people thronged the area as a mob of police formed in front of 91 North 14th Street. The police believed that the Muslims had planned it this way while the Muslims gazed in disbelief at the scene before them.

"There were people coming out of the laundromat on the corner to see what was going on," Ronald Washington recalled. "There were people coming out of the tavern. And there were more people coming out of the other stores and houses. By that time there were so many police I couldn't count them. 'Pay strict attention to what you see happen here,' I told the crowd. Then I began to pray out loud in Arabic and other brothers did the same. The police said we were chanting. I couldn't understand what they wanted. My wife was seven months pregnant and my three children were upstairs sleeping. Saying we were trying to start a riot to me is incredible."

---

plateglass door, shot and broke up the prayer house. Its terrified occupants—three women and five children in a Muslim day nursery—surrendered meekly. No evidence was ever found to link the robbery with the mosque.

Two Black Muslims were later arrested and convicted for the armed robbery. Judge Kapp sentenced Alvin Dickens, thirty-one, to a minimum of forty-three years, and James Washington, twenty-four, to forty-four years. The patrolman who was shot, William Maver, still has partial paralysis of both legs and has since been promoted to lieutenant.

Captain Daniel Fausto of the East Orange police arrived and—the Newark police having no business there anyway—assumed control of the combined forces.

"They weren't yelling obscenities, Muslims don't use obscenities or any profanity," Fausto said long after the event, *contradicting all* of the police reports. "Myself and Sergeant Fehn approached them on the porch there and I stood right at the bottom of the steps. I said something like, 'Well, fellas, how about keeping it down. Nobody's looking for trouble, how about a little peace and quiet?' They started chanting again. Then I said something like, 'Okay, you're going,' or something like that. I never told them they were under arrest with those words, not that I can remember. It happened sort of fast, I don't remember whether I said they were under arrest or not. I grabbed one of them by the arm and he pulled me up the steps. He went up and I went up after him. Next thing I knew I was thrown off the porch to the side by the small picket fence there and I was knocked out for a few seconds. Next I remembered everyone fighting all over the front and other officers rushing into the house.

"I never called on the Newark police for assistance, that's something I had to say," Fausto continued. "I remember Detective Nealy grabbed me and tried to get me out of the area but I wanted to remain at the scene. I was near the center walk and someone came running out of the house and I grabbed him and he hit me in the eye and that's when it busted open. I don't know which one did it but I was told Sims did it."

Within a few feet of Fausto before the fight broke out was Ronald Jones, a seventeen-year-old Black Muslim from the neighborhood who had been drawn to the house by the sirens.

"The officer said they had received a phone call and there was a peace disturbance and then a man on the porch said that there would be peace and quiet," Jones said. "The man on the porch then shushed the people. Then the police officer said that everyone on the porch is under arrest. Two policemen up front grabbed two men and the two men resisted. Then all the policemen that were close by moved in with force. Everyone was fighting and I ran inside the house looking for a place to hide. Finally I went into the bathroom upstairs. Mrs. Washington was in there with her children and two other fellas. They jumped out of the window into the alley and got away. I jumped after them. When I landed there was police in the alley and one of them hit me with a nightstick. More policemen ran into the alley—I think about six of them—and they hit me with their sticks. Then they handcuffed me and took me out to the street. They laid me down in the street with the others."

The youthful Dennis Sims, who didn't have a mark on him when he was arrested, had also been beaten and placed in the street with his hands handcuffed behind him. One by one, the Muslims were beaten with nightsticks that broke over their skulls and were dragged outside where police continued to beat them. Then twenty-two-year-old Roy Bell came out of the tavern and saw the bleeding men lying in the street.

"Bell is the only one I really remember," Fausto recalled. "I remember him vividly. He was the only one with hair on his head, he wasn't a Muslim. He appeared cheerful when I saw him. Bell came up to Sergeant Fehn as the prisoners were being put in the street. 'What's going on?' he said. Fehn told him to move on—I guess he was pretty gruff about it— and Bell jumped him from behind. He threw Fehn across the trunk of a car and began to pummel him. I grabbed Bell from behind but for some reason I couldn't reach his head with my blackjack, he was a pretty big fella. I hit him on the back as hard as I could—look, I bent my black-jack—but he didn't seem to even notice it. Then I called over a colored detective from Newark and he hit Bell over the head with his nightstick. Bell said something like, 'All right, I give, you got me.' Bell went down. I couldn't understand what made Bell get involved, he didn't even know any of the Muslims."

Roy Bell explained his actions during the Muslims' trial:

"I was looking over there and I heard glass breaking. I heard women hollering. And it seemed to me there were children hollering and I got emotionally upset and tears was in my eyes when I look and saw the way they were treating these people."

Chisone, twenty-three, had been standing near the bottom step when the two police officers first approached the porch.

"What you've got to remember is, it happened so fast and no one could tell what everyone else was doing, everyone was separate," he related. "When he told us to be quiet I said, 'yes, sir,' and turned to go back up the steps. Really, what would you have done? The police talking about all that shouting is silly. I had a wife who was nine months pregnant and two children and a home. The last thing I wanted was any trouble. I don't know who hit me but I got hit right away in the back of the head when I turned around and I didn't see anything. I fell to my left away from the steps and two brothers grabbed my arms and pulled me back up the porch. I went upstairs and got a towel and started to wipe the blood off my face and at the same time I was talking to my wife. 'The children are downstairs!' she shouted. I said, 'Wait here and I'll go downstairs and get them.' I started to, but the police were coming up the stairs. They came running into the kitchen and one of them bumped into my wife and knocked her down. I ran right out of the room—I was still trying to keep away from that fighting thing. They saw all the other people around the bedroom and they were too busy clunking them to chase me."

Chisone hid upstairs with William Jasper for a few minutes and then attempted to go down by the front stairs. He collided with Patrolman Tretola on the way up and rolled down the stairs where he was beaten and handcuffed and placed in the street. Jasper and Turner, among the last to be arrested, were treated similarly.

Washington had been standing on top of the porch when the police approached, well to the rear of most of the group. There is no doubt in his mind that after Fausto put his hand on one of the Muslims, a policeman behind the captain said "Get 'em" and the battle began. Chisone and some onlookers corroborated this, as did Mrs. Washington who was watching from an upstairs window when Chisone was hit. Washington had also run into the house at the first onslaught.

"I had no desire to die," he said. "I ran upstairs at the very beginning to get my wife and children. I got the children out of bed and put them into the bathroom with my wife. All the lights were off. By this time the police had climbed up the back stairs. I went into the bedroom and closed the door. The door flew off the hinges into the room and the first policeman went to club me and I grabbed his arm. We swung around and fell on the bed. I fell on top of him. Another officer standing in back of me started beating me on back of my head. When I came to, a policeman had his hand on my chest feeling for a heartbeat—he thought he had killed me. My wife heard one of them say, 'What are we going to charge them with?' Another answered, 'I don't know, we'll find something.' "

A Puddle of Blood in the Street

As the beaten prisoners were being dragged out, the crowd outside was still growing and becoming more angry by the minute.

"Then the police all went upstairs," a next-door neighbor said, "and I heard glass breaking and scuffling and the sound of little children crying. I heard one boy land in the alleyway between the houses and some policemen jump on him and start beating on him. My brother found some pieces of the nightsticks that they used."

"They were beating them all the way out to the street," another neighbor remembered. "One by one they brought the others downstairs and threw them into the street. I saw various policemen hit and kick the men who were lying on the street. This happened fifteen or twenty times."

Mrs. Lillian Williams, a resident a few doors up the block, was standing outside as the prisoners were brought out.

"I saw one individual [Washington] who said, 'Praise to Allah' with his face to the ground," she said. "His hands were handcuffed behind him and his head was bleeding. 'Shut up, motherfucker,' one of the cops said to him and beat him with his nightstick until he was quiet."

"There was a large puddle of blood where the men had been lying in the street," another resident said. "The police came to my house asking for water and a mop to clean it up but I didn't give them anything."

"I saw one boy being beaten by four policemen," Mrs. Wadell Green recalled. "The man who lived next door at 89 North 14th Street ran downstairs—he didn't have his shoes on—and he said, 'What are you trying to do to him?' An officer then says, 'He was trying to kill me,' and the man answers, 'How can he with his hands handcuffed like that?' Then they threw them all into the paddy wagon."

"Three Negro police officers came to my house and asked for a mop and water to clean the blood off the street," David Holden remembered. "We refused to give them the mop and water. I saw police officers cleaning up blood in front of the house on the sidewalk. The next day, Mayor Kelly and his wife came to the neighborhood, and Mayor Kelly[8] spoke with Mary Turner and me. I told the mayor what I saw and he told me, among other things, that he was going to look into the situation and asked me not to put anything into the newspapers."

"I saw policemen standing on the balustrade around the porch breaking in the windows," another nearby resident said. "I could hear a terrible series of sounds inside as glass broke and things were thrown around inside."

The arrested Muslims were first taken to the East Orange jail where they were forced to run a gauntlet of police nightsticks before reaching their cells. They were then transported to East Orange General Hospital where their bleeding injuries were treated. All the prisoners received numerous stitches in their heads and eyes, except for Otis Hardy, whose only notable injury had come when a cell door was slammed on his arm. Roy Bell had lost a lot of blood and passed out after being stitched. He was wheeled up to the X-ray department. Ronald Washington was stitched and then returned to jail with a broken hand. After being released on $1,500 bail, he returned to the hospital where his arm was put in a cast, but he was denied admittance because he had no hospital insurance. After relatives spoke for him, Washington was admitted and remained three and a half days in a bed.

Also hospitalized was William Jasper, who had several lacerations on his face and head which needed stitching. He was also X-rayed for a

---

[8] The investigation of East Orange Mayor James W. Kelly Jr. must have been particularly discreet, since no word of it ever became available. It also resulted in an exoneration of all police activities, since no action was taken against any officer. In fact, except for his word given here to Holden there is no sign it ever occurred.

possible fractured skull and treated for a painful abdominal injury that came when he had been—as Fausto described it—"kicked in the balls."

With the morning light on North 14th Street, a scene emerged that might have been left by a professional wrecking crew. Doors were broken from hinges, windows smashed, furniture broken and thrown all over the rooms. Glasses and dishes were smashed, drawers removed and overturned with their contents strewn on the floor. Food from refrigerators was strewn about. There were blood smears on the walls. Departing officers of the law had even boarded up the building's entrance in a departing *coup de grâce*. They had totally ransacked the house and—probably to their great surprise—had been unable to find a single weapon. This was also to their regret, considering the condition of their prisoners, which would take some explaining.

All things considered, the conduct of the police matched the ferocity of a rampaging band of barbarians. It was to their credit, however, that a last vestige of civilized training prevented them from putting the building to the torch.

8

A MAN NAMED SMITH

This Baby Is Mine

Eight months after the Newark riot, John William Smith was back at the spot where it all began. He was much the same as he had been then, but without any chance of ever driving a taxicab again in the city. The man said to have sparked a riot stood five feet seven and weighed 145 pounds, five pounds less than he had. His ribs had healed. If there were any psychological scars, they weren't showing. At the intersection of South 7th Street and 15th Avenue, he pointed to the other side of the street where, sometime after nine o'clock Wednesday night—five days after the Black Muslim incident—the cab driver had been arrested by two Newark patrolmen. The result of that act included the shooting deaths of twenty-three people, $1,967,140 in building damage, $8,284,060 in goods lost in burned and looted stores, and the arrest of 1,510 people.

"I can still remember very clearly what happened that night," Smith told me. "I had a lady passenger and came up behind this police interceptor which was double-parked at this intersection. I blinked my lights from low to high beam and cut around like I always do. Well, they signaled me to stop by tapping their horn and I pulled over to the curb on the other side of the intersection. They pulled alongside me and asked for my credentials. They said I had 'popped' the intersection, that I had run through without having right of way. I told them that—at the time I thought they meant I had crossed the intersection in the wrong lane—that they were standing still and I had made a normal pass. 'No, no, we were moving,' they said, so I could see they wanted to play games and then I guess I said the wrong thing.

"Go ahead and do what you want to do," I told them. I just wanted them to give me the ticket and get it over with, but I guess now it had the opposite effect. One of the officers jumped out of the police car and said I was under arrest. He told the woman passenger to 'get the hell out.' We waited there for another police car to take care of the cab and then we drove to the Fourth Precinct which was about a two-minute drive away. Then one of the officers, the same one who had gotten out of the police car before, turned around in the front seat and he used his stick on me. The cop who was driving told the other one who was hitting me to stop. 'No, no, this baby is mine,' the one who was using the stick said. When we got to the precinct I couldn't walk because he had also kicked me in the groin, and they started to drag me across the pavement.

" 'You don't have to drag him like that,' somebody called out. I heard somebody else yell, 'At least you can carry him.' Well, they carried me the rest of the way but once we got to the door they threw me in. There were at least six or eight policemen there who began hitting and kicking at me. They took me to a cell and beat on me some more until I thought it would never stop. They held my head over the toilet and one of them threw water on me from the bowl all over my head. Another one hit me on the head with a gun butt and I was also hit with a blunt instrument in the side. Finally they just left me lying there."

Smith's hair was bushy and he had a thick mustache. He was wearing a brown suede jacket and a neat cardigan sweater over a gray work shirt. Smith, a handsome man looking younger than his forty years, spoke quietly.

The intersection where we stood was like countless others in ghetto Newark—kids in the street, long rows of cars lined up at both curbs, littered gutters, and flimsy tenements—a fitting place to light the fuse that ran clear to the fourth precinct and set off a battery of explosions.

The setting was right but the character wrong. The image of a shouting cab driver, a toothpick stuck in his mouth, ripping down Springfield Avenue, might be a handy explanation for what happened here, but Smith had been miscast. Always a lonely, rootless man, the riot had not changed his quiet and elusive character and its aftermath left an articulate man given to long lapses of thoughtful silence.

"You want a justification, something to explain what happened," Smith told me. "There is no justification. I may have assisted the police in jumping to a hasty conclusion, that's all. They have a thing for any Muslim and my hair is bushy. They probably thought I was a Muslim. People here do not communicate at all with the community. I didn't start a riot. I was just a victim of circumstances. It could have happened to anybody."

Once in the precinct house, Smith was charged with assault and battery on both officers, resisting arrest and using loud and offensive language. He was also given traffic citations for following too closely, failure to drive in the right lane, and—after some checking—driving with a revoked license.

"I spent that night in a cell," Smith related. "The next day I heard the people were out in the streets and there was shooting and killing. In a way,

I was proud of them that they wanted to protest a gross injustice, but at the same time I was sad they were getting hurt. Nothing good could come from it. It's something to have unarmed people getting shot down like that and when you are a direct part of it the influences are much more dynamic. It was like a bad dream: I was laying in a cell and outside people were getting shot and the city was exploding.

"I have no close friends," Smith went on, "I've always been alone. The people out there were perfect strangers to me but they were getting beaten and shot because of something that had happened to me. Right now I do feel a sense of responsibility for what happened.

"I'm still living at the Esquire Hotel on South Street but I'll be moving before too much longer. You know, I've always led a quiet life—I treasure my privacy. But since the trouble I've found that privacy is something you can't control. You have to make certain adjustments in relation to your privacy because you know life is an open book and almost all of everything you do doesn't belong to you alone anymore once you step into the limelight. I can't relax too well without privacy and I'm tired of being cooped up in that little hotel room. I'd like to do something constructive again, like playing the horn. That means a lot to me and now that I haven't been driving, it means a lot more. I attended the Harnett School of Music in New York for a year by days and drove the cab at night. I was trying to learn a little more about the horn when my teeth gave out and I couldn't play anymore. Dental work costs a lot of money and I was trying to save it when the incident happened. There are some nights when I just think about it, the indescribable pleasure of playing the horn. Once you get inside the instrument, you can have a beautiful time. My objectives haven't changed any, I still want to play the horn, to study and develop my mind as much as possible."

Smith rode with me to the R & R Bar on Jones Street, just a half block from where Springfield Avenue continues its crawl up the hill like a devouring monster. It seems no matter where you turn the street is there. Cornelius Murray was shot by Newark police on the afternoon of the riot's third day in front of this bar and, about the same time, Oscar Hill had been shot around the corner. Some fifteen hours before these men died, James Sanders, a teenager, had been blown away by a shotgun blast a short distance away on the other side of the street. Ex-cab driver John Smith passed these places and he didn't know. He knew that people had been killed, but he didn't know where. We sat down at a table inside the bar, which was almost empty at this time of the afternoon. Smith, not a drinker, took one after being prodded.

"I don't know what will happen to me," he said. "I still have to stand trial. It's the waiting that's the hardest part. I enjoy reading Oscar Wilde and I've read Ayn Rand's *The Fountainhead* and *Atlas Shrugged*. Howard Roark, the architect in *The Fountainhead,* not only fights against the system that runs people's lives, but wins. Reality is so different. I can't see a man winning like that. I've gone over to New York to attend some of Ayn Rand's lectures, but I can't buy her philosophy even if I do enjoy her writing. Her philosophy relates to systems and I've never been a part of any system. I've always thought for myself. I'm still going to do my own thinking. All my life it's been this way."

John W. Smith was born in Warthen, Georgia and moved to Salisbury, North Carolina, when very young. His father was a municipal worker there. Smith has two brothers and two sisters still living in North Carolina. He took up the trumpet at seventeen and spent a year at the North Carolina Agricultural and Technical College, now the University of Greensboro. Smith traveled after joining the Army in 1950, playing in Army bands at Fort Knox, Kentucky, and Fort Rucker, Alabama. He also played in the Philippines and Japan, and was awarded the combat infantryman's badge in Korea. After his discharge Smith came to Newark, played the trumpet in some ghetto bars and eventually just hacked, trying to save enough money to get his teeth fixed. Smith had been a cab driver for five years.

"Working is a means to an end," he said. "You must use it as a tool to attain the things in life that bring satisfaction."

The ex-cabbie had no wife, no woman, no children and no close friends. With disability payments from the state for injuries he had received in the beating, he had just enough to live on, yet he was far from bitter. Smith was an enigma because he wasn't embittered and because his name was John Smith—a man whose face had been on the cover of *Time* magazine and yet remained as anonymous as ever. Some time soon, he said, he would go to electrical school. Some time soon he'd read a book he'd always wanted to read. Some time soon he'd play the horn again. He passed through the culture of poverty using words like "interceptor" for police car, "credentials" instead of driver's license. In a world of his own, Smith could remain untouched by brutalizing ghetto life. In the search to find an explanation for the events of that July night, Smith offered no answers.

Still ahead for him was a trial for assault charges against the two policemen. He had already been found guilty of the traffic violations and sentenced to sixty days in jail two months after the riot, a verdict that co-counsel Harris David was appealing. Also facing him was a civil suit he had filed against the Newark Police Department for $700,000 and a countersuit the police had filed against him, charging slander. They were seeking $16.5 million, perhaps an indication of his innocence.

One aspect of Smith can be stated with certainty. He was a lousy cab driver. In November of 1966, nine months before the riot, the State Division of Motor Vehicles had sent a letter to 51 Hillside` Place, Smith's listed address, notifying the cab driver that he had accumulated twelve points from four driving violations and that his license was being revoked under New Jersey's point system. Up to that time, Smith had been involved in six auto accidents, five in 1965 and one more in 1966. The motor vehicle people failed to hear from Smith, who had moved from that address, but his name popped up regularly. He was involved in three more accidents between the time the notice was sent and the time the revocation took effect, but was not personally notified of the action against him. In February of 1967 he was in two more accidents and the revoked license still went undetected. Smith said he had never known his name was on the revoked list, which seems not only possible but likely. The license he carried appeared valid and wasn't due to expire until the end of July—which, because of a chance meeting with Newark patrolmen John DeSimone and Vito Pontrelli, was a long month.

Something They Had Heard Once Too Often

"Patrolman DeSimone and myself were on routine patrol duty at dusk on July twelfth when he observed a Safety Company cab close in behind the patrol car," Pontrelli recalled. "I was driving, headed west on Fifteenth Avenue. The taxi cab was alternatively braking and accelerating, with its high beam flicking on and off. It tail-gated our patrol car for almost a block. Then the cab shot around us at the intersection of Fifteenth Avenue and South Seventh Street and went approximately one block on the wrong side of the street up to about South Eighth Street and Fifteenth. We pursued the cab to South Ninth Street where we stopped it. DeSimone asked the driver for his license and registration and Smith responded with insults and curses. My partner then told Smith he was under arrest, and his reaction to that was opening the cab door, hitting DeSimone in the chest. Smith punched DeSimone in the face. I got out of the car and we struggled with Smith and finally got him into the back of our patrol car. We called for someone to take care of the taxi and started for the Fourth Precinct. Smith became violent again and began fighting with DeSimone, who was in the front passenger seat. He even hit me. I put my red light and siren on because I figured if it was going to go on like this, I'd better get down to the precinct fast. Smith and my partner were fighting almost all the way down South Tenth Street to the precinct. When we got there Smith refused to leave the car and after we pulled him out he refused to walk. So we each took an arm and began dragging him. We were met by another policeman and the three of us carried him into the precinct.

"Just before we went in, Smith became violent again," Pontrelli continued, "there were several people who saw us carrying him and some of them shouted to us, 'Take the handcuffs off him, stop beating him.' Smith wasn't handcuffed because we had all we could do to get him into the radio car at the scene of the arrest."

The statements of both police officers directly contradict that of Smith, but subsequent events are a matter of record. Soon after the cab driver had been carried into the rear door of the Fourth Precinct, rumors that he had been beaten to death were all over the ghetto. Smith's fellow cab drivers were spreading them. Communication was also speeded because so many people in the congested Hayes Homes had witnessed the prisoner's arrival. A crowd formed rapidly in front of the precinct and within fifteen minutes Bob Curvin and several other civil rights leaders arrived. Police Inspector Kenneth Melchior arrived quickly to meet with Curvin, who had already decided to send to Newark Legal Services for a lawyer. Curvin, a pivotal figure in the July drama, is an energetic and responsible leader respected both by blacks and by knowledgeable whites, if not by the Newark police.

"One of the arresting patrolmen came out of the police station and walked to his car parked in the driveway of the gas station to the right," Curvin said. "Some of the crowd moved toward him and someone asked the officer what had happened. He answered that Smith had punched him in the mouth or something like that, and this was something they had heard once too often. 'Oh bullshit' and 'You're crazy' they began shouting. I would say the mood was growing increasingly tense."

Meanwhile Inspector Melchior went over the police reports and discussed them with the two arresting officers. DeSimone's report stated that his trousers had been ripped in the struggle with Smith. But DeSimone stood before him, his trousers untorn. Melchior told the patrolman to correct the "error."

The crowd outside had grown to about seventy-five persons by 10:00 P.M. and was still growing. Some were anxious to enter the police station. "Don't wait to go in now," Mrs. Esta Williams, a community leader, shouted. "My husband was beaten in there two years ago. If we had gone in when they took him in it never would have happened." The group surged toward the station house but were told they couldn't all go in. After a brief wait, twelve were allowed to enter, including Curvin. After talking to DeSimone and Pontrelli, Inspector Melchior joined the twelve to discuss the situation further. Curvin told him they objected to the arrest of Smith and wanted to see the prisoner. Melchior agreed to allow four persons back into the cell block to see Smith. "Don't listen to what he says," they were told. "He's obviously upset and nervous, as you might expect."

Some unusual things had occurred. A police inspector had been on hand immediately to correct an obvious lie on a report and citizens were being allowed to view a victim of what was always described "alleged brutality" a few days later. Curvin and Mrs. Williams found Smith lying on a bench with his feet drawn up to his chest, moaning and in great pain. "He was laying there groaning and crying," Mrs. Williams said. "I went to the two arresting officers and asked them to roll up their pants legs to show me where Smith had kicked them, but they wouldn't."

"That part about the two officers being injured was the usual bull," Al Black, who was also on the scene, said. "They both looked like they had just stepped off a Hollywood movie stage. There wasn't a mark on them."

Several of the delegation took a look at Smith and quickly returned to ask Melchior why he hadn't been taken to a doctor. The inspector dispatched a lieutenant to take a look at Smith. He reported—as everyone already knew—that Smith needed medical attention. He was taken out of the precinct's rear door and driven by police car to Beth Israel Hospital. "Several cars followed the patrol car to the hospital because, frankly, no one trusted the police enough to let them take someone to a hospital, even in a situation like that," Curvin related. Hospital records show that Smith was treated for cuts on his head, an injured groin, a fractured rib and other injuries to his rib cage. He was then taken to police headquarters downtown and later held on $1,250 bail—$1,000 for the assault and another $250 for the traffic violations. Meanwhile, Patrolmen DeSimone and Pontrelli had reported to City Hospital "for treatment"—a routine Newark police operating procedure in such incidents.

As Smith was being taken to the hospital, Timothy Still, president of the Newark anti-poverty agency, Don Wendell, acting executive director of the agency, and Oliver Lofton, director of the Legal Services Project, arrived at the precinct building. By that time the crowd had grown to 250 people. "We don't want to talk about Smith," one woman shouted at Melchior. "We want to talk about what we see here happening every day, time and time again. If we are not going to do anything about what we can see from our windows happening in this neighborhood every day, *what the hell is it?*"

There was no answer to the woman's question. Inspector Melchior directed some dozen policemen, who partially dispersed the crowd without carrying nightsticks. More and more angry black people continued to arrive as the inspector went back inside to meet with a larger group of community people. Four police officers accompanied him but left when the residents objected to their presence. Off to one side of the room, Lofton, Still, Curvin, Wendell and James Walker, an official in a Newark manpower development program, participated in a meeting. It was decided to encourage the ever-increasing crowd to go home and return the next morning for a meeting and demonstration at City Hall.

"This was to me a bad decision," Curvin later said. "The crowd wasn't prepared to go home and there needed to be more concern about doing something with them that was constructive and allowed them to express their dissatisfaction with what happened."

While this meeting was in progress, the crowd outside became more tense and the scene changed to one of impending violence. Lofton, Still and Curvin rushed outside to try to calm them.

Shortly before midnight a Molotov cocktail burst into flame against the police station's wall and police, now with riot helmets and nightsticks, surrounded the building. There was still relative order but with the ring of police and the angry crowd face to face, yelling racial epithets at one another, all hell was threatening to break loose.

"We asked the inspector to give us an opportunity to talk to the people," Wendell said. "He asked us, would we guarantee that we could disperse the crowd? Nobody could guarantee that, and that crowd was in no mood for anything like that. We told him we couldn't. We would attempt to channelize this energy, get them down to City Hall for an all-night vigil. This was to get them out of the area."

Inspector Melchior agreed to give the community leaders fifteen minutes to dissipate the hate and resentment it had taken generations to accumulate. He handed the bullhorn to Curvin and removed the police back inside the Fourth Precinct. The three leaders attempted to form the throng into a march to City Hall. Some of the crowd joined in behind Tim Still and the others as they led the column, but it wasn't enough. Some youths in the throng began to throw rocks at the precinct house and, at 12:15 A.M. Thursday, some twenty-five policemen charged out of the old stone building clubbing everyone within reach. After this show of raw power, all the young kids began to throw rocks and anything else they could get their hands on, while in liquor stores around the corner on Belmont Avenue, the first looting broke out.

The riot in Newark had begun while, in a cell at police headquarters downtown, John Smith lay on a jail bed.

I Am Not Accepting a Complaint Against the Police

The single event that had triggered a riot was like many others, each side giving a version of what had happened, with the truth somewhere in between and no way to get at it. Only one thing was agreed on by both sides—a woman passenger had been in the cab at the time of Smith's arrest. She has never been found. We may never know exactly what happened that night, but some aspects of the incident are apparent.

Police contend that Smith answered a request for his driver's license with "insults and curses" because he knew he was driving with a revoked license, yet they described a pattern of erratic driving in full view of a patrol car that certainly didn't fit the normal pattern of one driving without a license. As a matter of fact, few would drive that way anytime with police present, particularly Smith, who had already been ticketed four times previously for minor offenses.

Police say the cab driver answered their announcement that he was under arrest by opening the cab door, striking DeSimone, and then punching him in the face. Smith weighed 150 pounds and was unarmed. Pontrelli weighed 200 pounds, DeSimone near 160 pounds, and both were armed with guns and nightsticks. Smith then supposedly battled both officers, who had difficulty getting him into the back of their patrol car. Smith was so violent that they were unable to handcuff him, yet they remained at the scene radioing for another patrol car to take the taxi in before starting for the Fourth Precinct. Once inside the police car, they said, Smith calmed down, but for the police to take a violent prisoner in custody without first searching him or putting the cuffs on violates all police procedure. Still, if the officers had been excited and nervous—a circumstance to which they do not admit—this could have been overlooked. Yet three other police cars arrived minutes later, and Smith still remained unhandcuffed and unsearched. This seems highly unlikely unless the arrest hadn't proceeded as DeSimone and Pontrelli had described it.

It is easy to imagine Smith as surly and excited when confronting two police officers. It strains the imagination to picture him attacking them physically. Smith's history can be searched in vain for an example of violent behavior, even an isolated incident, including four years of Army duty under ever-present authority. It is impossible to believe that suddenly, at age forty, he would assault not one but two armed police officers.

So we have a high-strung black cab driver and two Newark policemen hassling on a ghetto street. Police said they did only what was necessary to get him into the back of their patrol car, but no more. They also stated that their prisoner became "violent again" after being carried into the precinct building. If there is one place a man would be unlikely to become violent, it would be *inside* a police station, especially a black man inside the Fourth Precinct, which was notorious for its racism. There is no disbelieving Smith's beaten condition, since community leaders saw him immediately afterward. Was he beaten before he was taken inside, or after, or both? He said he was unable to walk, police said he just wouldn't. Witnesses outside the building watching the two officers drag Smith agreed with the cab driver. According to the police, Smith ended up in the condition he was found because of his continued resistance *inside* the police station, which is hard to believe. Smith claims he was beaten both before and after his arrival.

Smith was abandoned in a cell in need of medical attention. There is no indication when he would have received it if community people had not spoken up. Does allowing a suffering prisoner to lie in his cell fit into the behavior pattern of police officers who had utilized only reasonable force or those who had made sure an "uppity nigger" knew his place? Smith's hospital records point to the latter.

Wheels of justice turned quickly—but only against the luckless cab driver. Smith, his ribs wrapped in a six-inch-wide bandage, appeared in municipal court nine days later to file criminal complaints against patrolmen DeSimone and Pontrelli—as they had already filed against him. Chief Magistrate Del Mauro expressed the prevalent attitude in Newark's courts:

"In these times of stress, with all the havoc and destruction, a policeman killed, a fireman killed, more than twenty people killed and fifteen million dollars of damage, I am not accepting a complaint against the police. It was this particular man, if I recall from reading the papers, that originally caused the rioting when he was arrested and rumors swept throughout the colored community that he had been killed. He has been paroled. . . . He is alive and there is nothing wrong with him."

But there was something wrong with Smith, and something wrong with Newark—and one symptom of the sickness was sitting at the judge's bench.

I'm Still My Own Man

"I'm still an independent agent," John Smith said as we left the R & R Bar. "I run my life the way I see it. I've found that I communicate more with my people because of the tremendous sacrifices they've made. I'll try to widen my range of communication, but I'm still my own man. I'm predominantly self-motivated, nobody is running me. You couldn't pay me enough money to run out in the street like a wild man."

We walked to my car and no one, not the bartender, nor any of the men who had come into the bar while we were there, nor any of those passing on the street, knew who he was.

PART III

Gravemarkers by the Wayside

9

A THRILL OF PRIDE

**Once You Begin to Look at Problems as Problems,
They Become Problems**

In the early hours of Thursday morning, the liquor stores on Belmont
Avenue around the corner from the Fourth Precinct were ripped open with
yells and the crash of glass. Although the police said that they knew weeks
before that there would be trouble in Newark by the end of July, to say
the riot had caught them in disarray would be an understatement. Their
logistics were poor, their riot training and preparation nil. Throughout the
spring and summer the city had seethed on the brink of trouble, and orders
for restraint—deeply resented by many police officers—had been City
Hall's only preparation for the riot.

"Originally only the most aggressive, the boldest of guys would go in
but some others joined them," the respected Tim Still described the first
looting. "The radio cars were going back and forth and they saw them in
there. They saw them in there getting the whiskey and they just kept going.
They didn't try to stop. As a result of that, all the people saw that the cops
didn't care, so they went in, too. I think if the cops had moved in and did
something they may have been stoned but I think that would have been
the proper thing to do. A lot of stuff could have been avoided at this
point."
This mistake was compounded soon after in the daylight hours of Thursday. While his assistant, Don Malafronte, called Wednesday night "the
most serious incident Newark ever had," Mayor Addonizio looked the
other way and hoped it would just go away. Police Director Spina, standing
amidst the broken glass of the Fourth Precinct, seemed to hold similar
views. "The situation is normal," he said. "Put the windows in early in
the morning, get the place cleaned up. Just return it to normal and don't
treat it as a situation, because once you begin to look at problems as problems they become problems." There was a *problem* all right and of all the

113

ranking police officers Deputy Chief Redden seemed to know best what it was and what was going to happen. Early Thursday morning he ordered all men in his command on twelve-hour duty.

"I was almost certain there was going to be a large-scale disturbance the evening of the thirteenth," he said.

Mayor Addonizio insisted on regarding the events of Wednesday night as "isolated incidents" and hoped nothing more would happen. Even as he went through the meaningless chores of the day, young people up on the hill were preparing their answer to years of deprivation—firebombs and piles of rocks, just enough of each for the Newark police to claim later that the riot had been well planned. A meeting with black leaders—Bob Curvin, Earl Harris, a former Essex County official, schoolteacher Harry Wheeler, George Richardson, and Duke Moore, board member of UCC— was held Thursday afternoon.

"To say it was an isolated incident, I think, was the most tragic mistake that was made following Wednesday night," Curvin said later. "In fact, one of the reasons that I felt so terribly frustrated on Thursday afternoon when I went to that meeting was to hear the mayor speak as though it was all over."

From this meeting came three demands: that DeSimone and Pontrelli be suspended, that a special panel investigate the Wednesday night disorder and that Lieutenant Eddie Williams, the only black ranking officer on the force, be promoted to captain. According to Earl Harris, Addonizio wanted forty-eight hours to consider the demands. Malafronte, speaking *for* the mayor as he often did, said that Addonizio agreed to transfer the two policemen to administrative duties, agreed to the panel and promised that Williams would be made a captain, at the cost of also promoting four white lieutenants ahead of him on the civil service list.

If there was an air of complacency around City Hall, it quickly evaporated with the appearance of leaflets in the Central Ward: STOP POLICE BRUTALITY, COME OUT AND JOIN US AT THE MASS RALLY TONIGHT, 7:30 P.M., FOURTH PRECINCT.

The leaflets, printed at UCC's Area Board Two and distributed by some of Hayden's NCUP people, were at best a belated attempt to channel the ghetto's frustration and anger, but probably were also an effort to start at least enough trouble to let the administration know that the ghetto wasn't going to take much more from the police. Afterward they would be used as evidence that the riot had been instigated. The leafleting and picketing, as well as the meeting in Addonizio's office, were actually meaningless. The riot was going to happen anyway. "Regardless of what the mayor did, regardless of what civil rights leaders did, regardless of what planners of the demonstration did—the riot was going to happen," Hayden wrote. "The authorities had been indifferent to the community's demand for justice; now the community was going to be indifferent to the authorities' demand for order."

At 4:45 P.M., Police Director Spina finally appeared to sense how serious the situation was and ordered 500 police to be available that night, with provision for emergency recall of off-duty men, extension of duty tours, and detectives in uniform.

By 6:30 P.M. there were ten pickets in front of the precinct building— Jesse Allen, James Kennedy, and Derek Winans, all of Area Board Two, among them. An hour later, the line had grown much larger and some 300 community people stood across the avenue by the side of the Hayes projects when James Threatt arrived to announce Addonizio's promotion promise for Williams—an announcement greeted with a barrage of rocks, bottles, and pieces of wood and metal. It lasted for a quarter of an hour. Then more than forty club-wielding police in riot helmets charged out of the station house. The riot's second night had begun.

Police who hadn't been permitted to stop it the night before now couldn't stop it. The riot spread rapidly with roving bands of youths breaking and tearing, ripping stores to pieces as many community people moved in to pick them clean. By nine o'clock Springfield Avenue, a short distance away, was a mass of black people indulging in a form of shopping hitherto only for the wealthy. What they couldn't carry away was hauled out in wagons, baby carriages, cars, and trucks. For the first time in their lives, there was no restriction on selection and everything was within their price range. New furniture was carried into the rundown tenements and the old sofas, chairs, and mattresses soon lined the street. No trick contracts, no installment plans, first come, first served. Cars with tow lines ripped the iron gratings from store windows and junkies cleaned out every drug store in the ghetto. Police "areas of containment" became wider as the fever spread. The rioters settled for the shopping areas around Elizabeth Avenue on the south, Central Avenue in the north and, in the center of the city, Clinton and Springfield Avenues. The people seized control of their ghetto which, if only for a matter of hours, became *theirs* in fact.

Few shots were fired as businesses were looted and ransacked. Seven blocks of Clinton Avenue—from Jelliff to Osborne Terrace—became a nighttime Easter Parade. After midnight there was a short period of relative calm. "By twelve-thirty," Spina said, "it appeared to me that perhaps we had won and that the violence was over."

The police director was incorrect in more ways than one. It was just the beginning and so far it was the ghetto people who had won. The violence in the coming days would be their punishment.

As if in response to the remarks of Spina and Addonizio—who also thought the city "had turned the corner"—more people flocked into the streets. The longer they looted with impunity, the more serious the situation became as others yielded to the temptation. And for women who had been unable to clothe decently their three or four kids only a day before, it was a considerable temptation. Those in the streets who had been losers all their lives were finding that a riot could be fun—while those in power pondered a situation which had already gone too far. Even as they lost precious time, the State Police—who had put themselves on standby alert the night before—waited for a call for assistance.

By 9:00 P.M. Thursday, Deputy Chief Redden had returned from a tour of the area with one simple expletive: "We need help." Not being the police director, Redden could afford the opinion that the police had allowed the situation to get far out of hand. At midnight, Addonizio had discussed the situation with Spina and, according to Malafronte, the mayor accepted Spina's assessment that state help was unnecessary. The State Police log contains this entry for the period just before midnight:

> Presently, bands of eight to 15 people traveling on foot and in cars, looting and starting fires. Four policemen injured, four new areas have broken out in the past 15 minutes. There is still no organization within the Newark Police Department. All available transportation in use. The Fourth Precinct appears to be running its own show. There are no barricades. No requests for State Police from Director Spina.

At 1:30 A.M., Spina directed Redden to call the State Police to alert them of the mutual assistance pact—something they were already well aware of. Redden, in a daring move that arose from his own assessment of the situation, delivered quite another message: "The director has told me to call you and to have the State Police come in." Redden was told to wait for a return call from Trenton headquarters. When it came ten minutes later, Redden repeated his unauthorized call for assistance. In another ten minutes Spina received a call that apparently informed him of Redden's move. Irritated, Spina ordered the deputy chief to cancel his request and to tell the State Police instead to "stand by"—which they had been doing since Wednesday night.

Spina and Addonizio met again at 2:00 A.M. to discuss the situation. According to Addonizio, Spina still believed no aid was necessary, but the mayor convinced him to call for help at once. In Spina's version, it was Addonizio who didn't want the State Police to come in. Spina said he called the mayor at 2:30 A.M. to tell him the State Police would be needed and Addonizio told him that the crowds would disperse at daybreak and reinforcements wouldn't be needed. Spina said he called the mayor yet again at 3:00 A.M., strongly advising that Addonizio request Governor Hughes to dispatch both the State Police and the National Guard.

Undisputed fact, however, is that the governor was awakened at 2:20 A.M. by a phone call from Mayor Addonizio who, in Hughes's words, "was quite upset and insisted on the deployment of State Police and National Guardsmen to the maximum extent possible. He told me that a riot was out of control."

Who was conveniently forgetting his words and decisions of Thursday night? It doesn't much matter.

The Whole Town Is Gone

When Colonel Kelly of the State Police arrived at City Hall at 3:00 A.M. Friday to meet with Addonizio, the riot was still spreading rapidly. Kelly asked Addonizio what the situation was. "It's all gone, the whole town is gone," the mayor replied. Kelly asked about some problem areas. "It is all over," Addonizio stated. Kelly then asked if the mayor had any idea of who the instigators or troublemakers were or what the State Police should look for. "I don't know," Addonizio sighed.

Two and a half hours later, the first state troopers began to arrive. At seven o'clock the National Guard rolled into the city in trucks, their apprehension at facing what they understood to be raging black savages lessened somewhat by support shouted by white residents: "Go kill them niggers."

First guard detachments camped at City Stadium on Bloomfield Avenue, well outside of the riot area, and state troopers were assigned to various areas in the city as they arrived. Within hours there were nine battalions of guardsmen—4,000 men—and 475 troopers joining the majority of Newark's 1,300-man police force and the city's housing patrolmen. A five-hour meeting at Roseville Armory determined a strategy and a chain of command: Colonel Kelly would have supreme authority over both his own State Police and the National Guard, though General Cantwell—his military pride at stake—did not concur. Together, the occupation forces would be led by the two officers who knew Newark and its people the least. Spina would command only his police force. Addonizio would be allowed to watch.

"During the whole course of this thing," Addonizio said later, "I was sort of left out of a lot of things that were going on and this is my city and I have to stay after all the people pull out."

As joint operations commenced it soon became clear that the situation would become worse instead of better. The three law-enforcement bodies were on different radio frequencies and couldn't communicate. Spina, who knew what should be done and possessed the background, couldn't lead. Addonizio, who could have offered meaningful help, was so numb he was useless. Colonel Kelly even had to dig up maps of the city for himself.

Not only had the city administration and the Newark police failed to prepare for their own control of the city, but they had also made it impossible for anyone else to do so. On June 7—only one month before—a high-level meeting between state and Newark law enforcement officials had been held to discuss the possible responses in case of a civil disorder. High on the agenda had been a communications system.

"The line between the jungle and the law," said Governor Hughes in Newark, his fingers tightly gripping a cigarette, "might as well be drawn here as any place in America."

Out went the military forces—nervous and afraid of blacks—with .30 caliber M-1s and Reising .45-caliber automatic rifles, marching with Hughes's war declaration. That he and his dismal attorney general, Sills, had allowed that jungle to flourish, did not deter him from blaming the great majority of that jungle's residents who were innocent of everything but having to live there.

By noon Friday a plan had been agreed upon to place blockades at 137 intersections, one string to go down the Hawthorne Avenue hill on the southern fringe of the riot area where the Moss boy would be shot to death. Other outposts were to be set up along Central Avenue. A minimum of three guardsmen were assigned to each barricade and by 2:20 P.M. they were stationed at their posts. Soon after, insulting harassment and beatings by them began. Inside the riot area jeeps and trucks with other guardsmen and troopers were on never-ending patrol, aided by police cars. Slowly but steadily the looting diminished. There had been twenty-six arrests that first Wednesday night and thirty-four more on Thursday. As the looting subsided, gunfire became more and more intense. Before Friday only one sniping incident had been reported but soon reports of sniping—a great many of them false—began to flood police headquarters. The Sears Roebuck store on Elizabeth Avenue had been looted of twenty-four rifles and this circumstance probably resulted in a great many false alarms. With a communications system which was all but non-existent, with the unfamiliarity of the troopers and guardsmen with the area, and with the guard's complete inexperience, the situation was chaotic.

Up to this time the main streets of the ghetto had been made a shambles, but there had been no homicides. By daylight Friday three had been shot to death—Mrs. Rose Abraham, forty-five, mother of five; James Sanders, Jr., sixteen; and Tedock Bell, Jr., twenty-eight, father of four. Neither Mrs. Abraham nor Bell was a looter and the boy was shotgunned in the back running from a liquor store.

There were 906 arrests on Friday, and by afternoon Colonel Kelly felt that most looting was under control and crowds were being contained. By this time seven more had been shot to death—Isaac Harrison, seventy-two, father of nine; Robert Lee Martin, twenty-two; Detective Fred Toto, thirty-three, father of three; Cornelius Murray, Jr., twenty-nine, father of three; Rufus Council, Jr., thirty-five, father of two; Oscar Hill, fifty, father to six children, one unborn at the time of his death; and Leroy Boyd, thirty-seven, father of two. One was a police officer and *none* of the others were involved in criminal activity.

Early Friday evening the looting was under control and the National Guard had 173 roadblocks up, sealing off the ravaged area. At the cost of Toto's life and the lives of nine black people—eight of them innocent of any wrongdoing—a riot was under control.

A Kind of Resentment

By Saturday fourteen square miles of the riot area had been sealed off by the National Guard and controlled by state and Newark police. Patrols spent much of the day clearing rooftops of debris so that it could not be hurled at passing troops and in time the entire area was in the complete control of law enforcement personnel. The power had changed hands as one riot had ended and another was just beginning.

More community people were being stopped and harassed. Some were humiliated, others beaten. After Eddie Moss had been shot at a National Guard checkpoint on Hawthorne, two more were killed Friday night: Richard Taliaferro, twenty-five, father of one, and Albert Mercier, Jr., twenty. Both were caught looting. Both were shot in the back. Before 3:00 P.M. Saturday another looter, Billy Furr, twenty-five, was shotgunned in the back on Avon Avenue. These killings plus the state troopers' wild shooting on Beacon Street and other incidents were occurring in full view of the black community. Police were also breaking into homes. Innocent people were being punished for a riot over which they had no control.

"Our patrols ran into a kind of resistance," Colonel Kelly said Saturday, "a kind of resentment."

What could he have expected?

At six o'clock Saturday evening two columns of National Guardsmen and state troopers were directing mass fire at the Hayes projects at the corner of Springfield Avenue and Hunterdon Street, large caliber bullets splattering against the bricks, sparking and showering the area with splinters of metal and stone. Mrs. Spellman was shot at this time. Several residents witnessing the shooting from an apartment across the avenue on Hunterdon watched with alarm as the troopers turned and began firing in their direction. Mrs. Gainer was hit a few doors down the block. A short distance away on Bergen Street where the same thing was happening, Mrs. Brown was slaughtered.

Thus far the dead—with the exception of Toto—were unarmed blacks who had been executed for petty crimes, or innocent men, women and children who were slaughtered, some in their own homes. The "line" Governor Hughes had spoken of to separate the jungle from the law had indeed been drawn but, the question was, who was on which side?

Two more were shot to death Saturday night: Raymond Hawk, twenty-four, father of one, and forty-one-year-old Fire Captain Michael Moran, father of seven, including one unborn child. Despite far-fetched descriptions of his death by the police, Hawk, too, was most likely innocent of criminal activity.

That same night, black stores on Springfield Avenue were shot up by state troopers and Newark police. The latter made sure to make a similar visit to Earl Harris' restaurant to repay him for his active participation in community affairs.

Harris, a member of the county governing body from 1963 to 1966 and an unsuccessful city council candidate in the South Ward in 1966, was—like Curvin, Richardson, and Harry Wheeler—concerned about the administration's callousness, corruption, and brutality. This, as far as the Newark police were concerned, made him an instigator. The forty-five-year-old Harris, active in the medical school and Parker-Callaghan controversies, had been refurnishing a store on Elizabeth Avenue to ready it for an August opening. When he bought the place it was a vacant, dirty building. Harris spent six months putting in an air conditioner, refrigerator, grill, steel paneling, shelving, and fixtures. Police emptied as many as seventy-five rounds of shotgun and revolver ammunition into the restaurant and, as not another store in the area was touched, their visit had been a special one. Left at the scene were shotgun casings and the recollection of a Puerto Rican woman living across the street. She had looked out of her apartment window while police were shooting up the restaurant. "Get your head in there, or we'll blow your brains out," a policeman shouted at her.

Through Oliver Lofton, the liaison between the black community and the occupation forces, Governor Hughes heard of the unfortunate accident to Harris' restaurant and sent a car to bring him to Roseville Armory. Harris, a medium-sized man with steel-cold eyes, distinctive graying hair and an even temperament, remembers the incident: "That lying son-of-a-bitch Hughes told me he was going to see to it that I would be compensated for the damage. They had done seven thousand dollars worth of damage. I took his personal word that I would be compensated."

Earl Harris must have been a special case, as both Colonel Kelly and General Cantwell visited the restaurant to count bullet holes. They looked, they had tape recordings of eyewitnesses made and Harris never heard from any of them—except through newspaper stories in which Kelly and Cantwell declared their men chaste of any unlawful actions in Newark.

By Sunday morning the riot was over, by any standard, but the troops remained, still patrolling the streets. Food was becoming a major problem, yet most black people were afraid to step outside of their homes—testimony to the occupation's effectiveness. With grocery stores either unable or unwilling to open their doors, the National Guard, in its only humanitarian act during the occupation, distributed emergency food. During the day, Hughes announced he would offer executive clemency to any person accused of nonviolent plundering in return for information leading to the arrest and conviction of a sniper. His offer had no takers.

After five o'clock Sunday afternoon, Janes Rutledge, Jr. was caught looting on Bergen Street. His body had so many shotgun and revolver bullet holes that the death of the youth became the first rallying cry for justice in post-riot Newark. During the day, black leaders continually called for the removal of the troopers and guardsmen but their pleas went unanswered. "It was the feeling of the Negro leaders that the augmentation of city police by the State Police and National Guard created and intensified the unrest," Spina stated. About midnight Sunday, Attorney General Sills and Major Eugene Olaff of the State Police discussed the possibility that continuing patrols within the riot area might be *stimulating* sniper fire. Shortly after, just before 1:00 A.M. Monday, the Pugh boy was shot by a guardsman in front of his home on 15th Avenue.

On Monday food stores, restaurants, banks and public utilities opened again and at three o'clock Governor Hughes lifted all other emergency restrictions with only bars and taverns still remaining closed. During the course of the disorders, members of the Newark Fire Department had been nothing short of heroic. It was they who took the brunt of the ghetto's anger. In addition to 64 false alarms, they fought and controlled 250 fires, 13 of them considered serious. Many times they had come under sniper fire. Nearly all these fires were in business establishments as most arsonists stayed clear of buildings where their people lived.

By mid-afternoon the occupation forces who were being heralded as having saved the city by putting down a riot began to withdraw.

"I think probably a day earlier we could have started to remove the patrols off the streets and then eventually have taken the ribbon from around the area and things of that sort so that we could have phased out in a more gradual stage than we did," General Cantwell said.

"I have a feeling, too, that when we removed the National Guard from the scene there came a feeling amongst the populace that things were going to be all right again," Spina said.

The riot claimed its twenty-third homicide victim late that night, twenty-year-old Raymond Gilmer, father of four, including an unborn child. Newark police put a bullet through the back of his head as he ran from a reportedly stolen car. Things might be all right again but they would never be quite the same.

The throb and drudgery of ghetto life returned slowly in the weeks that followed as people in black Newark and elsewhere read the wide variety of public information that follows a major catastrophe.

There were the words of Governor Hughes:

"I felt a thrill of pride in the way our State Police and National Guard have conducted themselves."

And then there were the meticulous counters who announced that these same state troopers and guardsmen had fired 13,319 rounds of ammunition to keep the peace.

10

RUN, BILLY, RUN FOR YOUR LIFE

If the Cops Show Up, Run Like Hell

"I met Billy Furr at the corner of Avon and Livingston when he barged into my conversation with a Black Muslim who called himself Haking X," Dale Wittner wrote in the July 24, 1967, issue of *Life* magazine.

Haking was predicting that the riot would go on "until every white man's building in Newark is burned," but Billy disagreed.

"We ain't riotin' agains' all you whites. We're riotin' agains' police brutality, like that cab driver they beat up the other night," Billy declared. "That stuff goes on all the time. When the police treat us like people 'stead of treatin' us like animals, then the riots will stop."

With that he turned away from me and went with his friends in search of cold beer, which he knew he could not buy legally because of the curfew.

Photographer Bud Lee and I came on Billy again later—a block farther down Avon at Mack Liquors. He and his friends were looting the store, which already had been broken into the day before. They loaded all the beer they could carry into car trunks and handed it out to passersby. When he noticed me, Billy thrust a can in my hand.

"Have a beer on me," he said. "But if the cops show up get rid of it and run like hell."

William Furr, who would soon get a chance to put his advice into action, used to work at the Fisher Bakery on Belmont Avenue, a few blocks away from where he met the magazine reporter. An improbable looter, he was born and lived his entire life in a neat two-story home on a corner of Hollywood Avenue in Montclair, an upper-middle-class black residential area. Furr was an only child and, though his father died when he was a child, he lived with his mother and grandparents in a stable family. When Furr was nineteen years old he went to work in Fisher's maintenance department where his grandfather, who had been with the bakery for forty-two years, was foreman. After Furr married, his wife also lived with the family in the Hollywood Avenue home. In the winter of 1966, after Furr had been at the bakery for more than five years, Fisher's shut down and both he and his grandfather were out of a job. Furr began collecting unemployment and looked for another job. Friday about noon, he left for the unemployment office in Newark—which was then in its second day of riot—and his people never saw him again. Furr eventually ended up with some friends at Mack Liquors on a sunny, calm Saturday afternoon and began cleaning out the beer other looters had left behind. The store, at least, would survive.

"Oh, business is good," a clerk inside Mack Liquors said six months later. "We opened up again about two months after the riots. I wasn't here during the trouble but it really must have been something." The clerk was stacking cases of beer behind the counter, somewhat like the twenty-four-year-old Furr and his friends had been doing. Dale Wittner and photographer Bud Lee must have been standing just outside on the sidewalk, which was now being washed down by a cold winter rain. Wittner, who didn't say whether or not he finished drinking his can of beer, continued his narrative in *Life* with the arrival of a Newark police car:

> . . . a city police car skidded to a halt directly in front of Mack Liquors. There had been no warning—it had raced in with its siren silent. This was the first sign of police authority on the block in more than an hour, except for a young Newark police trainee who had sipped beer and watched the looting with me. In an instant the shotguns that bristled from the cruiser's windows shattered the relative calm. The sudden explosions, rather than clearing the streets, sent mothers screaming out to pull children to safety. Apartment windows that had been empty were now full of dark faces, each of them in danger of being shot.
>
> For the looters caught in the store there was no place to run. They simply fell to the floor or froze in their tracks, hands above their heads. But Billy was standing outside with a six-pack in his left hand. He ran.

If You Have a Gun, Use It

"Addonizio ordered me not to shoot," Spina testified before the Hughes Commission. "I don't know where anybody got the idea that they couldn't shoot their guns. I was quite mystified. I heard a lot of shooting going on because I was in the area and I didn't see any of our men shooting back. Then around six or seven hours after a lot of this firing was going on some of the superior officers were coming to me and saying, 'Do you think it is okay to shoot? When are we supposed to shoot?' The first couple of days that they asked me the question I didn't pay any attention to them and wondered why they even asked me."

To clear the matter up, Spina then gave a vague order over the police radio: "If you have a gun, whether it is a shoulder weapon or whether it is a hand gun, use it."

The police director told the Hughes commissioners he issued this directive in accordance with departmental regulations ordering a man *not to use* firearms unless he was absolutely sure a high misdemeanor—which included larceny or looting—was being committed. Spina also told the commission he *never intended* that people be shot down for looting. Unfortunately, this had been one directive the police director didn't give his men.

Sometime after 8:00 P.M. Thursday—approximately four hours *before* the first homicide—Deputy Chief Redden clarified the situation over the police radio with a precise directive: "Firearms may be used when your own or another's life is in danger and no other means are available to defend yourself or apprehend an offender."

This order, a duplication of standard police regulations, remained in force for the police until the end of the disorders according to Redden, who again had shown he was one of the few superior officers with presence of mind. A look at the autopsy reports on the homicide victims raises the same apprehensions as those felt by the Hughes commissioners and clearly shows that Redden's order was ignored. Instead, after a two-day buildup of anger and resentment by the police, individual officers correctly assumed they would never be held accountable for their actions and used Spina's directive—"If you have a gun, use it"—as a veritable hunting license.

Shotgun Wound of Back

A twelve-year-old boy named Joey Bass, Jr., had been one of the kids playing nearby when exploding shotguns signaled the arrival of the police. An hour earlier he had been home shining shoes with his older brother but his friends had called him out to play. Eventually, Joey Bass ended up at the corner of Livingston and Avon, some seventy yards from Mack Liquors where Billy Furr began his race for life. Furr ran past the magazine reporter, his shirt open and blowing about him as he went down the block . . . 123 Avon passed by in a second . . . 119 . . . 117 . . . run, Furr, run. Drop that six-pack and run for your life! Billy Furr did run—straight toward the Bass boy whom nobody had told to get down.

He raced past me down Avon. I was barely 30 feet away from a yellow-helmeted officer with a shotgun pointed toward my head. "Get down," he screamed. I fell hard to the sidewalk just as a blast from the weapon exploded over me and the officer shouted an order to halt. But apparently Billy kept running behind me. From the ground I looked up into the sweating face of the policeman as he squinted down the long barrel. I prayed he wouldn't shoot. He pulled the trigger. Tiny pieces of the spent shell fluttered down on me as blue uniform trousers of the Newark Police Department flashed past toward Billy lying on the ground.

Contrary to police regulations, there had been no attempt to apprehend Billy Furr. Neither was there any effort to halt his flight by hitting him in

the legs—an easy shot at that distance. And what Furr was shot with pre-
cluded his survival. Rather than the birdshot shotgun ammunition ordinarily
used by most departments during civil disturbances, the Newark police were
using high velocity Double 0, the most powerful ammunition in ordinary
use. These green shells contain either nine or twelve slugs—each one-third
of an inch in diameter—that are far more than what the press usually
describes as "pellets" when they enter a victim's body. At close range a
shotgun firing Double 0 is as deadly a weapon as any devised by the genius
of man, as Furr's morgue photographs show. One blast containing nine
slugs had been aimed at the fleeing man with marksmanlike results, six of
them ripping into his back. Two slugs went completely through Furr's body
and another came out his right eye. Police supplied no ballistic report on the
three slugs remaining in his body, none being necessary with such an open
and shut case. Billy Furr's "race" for life was fixed.

The concern of the Hughes Commission over the Furr autopsy report
supplied by police—"Homicide by shooting, shotgun wound of back"—
would have been intensified had it known the details routinely evaded by
those few words.

Billy Furr had made it to 111 Avon Avenue. A group of neighborhood
boys pointed out the exact place in front of the tenement's stone steps
where he had gone down. A photograph in *Life* shows a can of beer lying
at Furr's feet, a warning for all black people who would steal. Another
photograph on the magazine's cover shows Joey Bass lying under a ONE
WAY street sign, his eyes staring at nothing in particular as though he never
knew what hit him. The Bass boy's faded blue jeans are worn to threads
around the knees, his dirty sneakers are only half laced, his blood is leaking onto the sidewalk. Two of the shotgun slugs that had missed the running
Furr had gone twenty yards farther down the block and had also given Joey
Bass a dose of law and order.

Already people were screaming obscenities from the windows and bottles
arched from a rooftop. More gunfire cleared the windows for a moment,
but they quickly filled again. "Call an ambulance," a policeman yelled back
to the car. Up the street the officer who had shot Billy stood over him, the
shotgun resting in the crook of his arm. Billy's blood poured onto the dirty
sidewalk. Then a girl was beside him sobbing and ignoring the order to "get
the hell out of here."

"I'm his girl friend. Help him. Please do something. God, don't let him
die," she pleaded.

Back at the corner of Livingston there was more shooting as a line of
police reinforcements arrived with an ambulance. I ran toward the crowd
being held back at gun point on the corner. In the center, blood streaming
from his neck, lay little Joey Bass, Jr. Two pellets from the same shotgun
blast that killed Billy had struck Joey in the neck and thigh. Around his
form surged about fifty sobbing men and women, trying to break through

the small ring of police. Nearby two other youngsters cried quietly on the curb. The people who wanted to help were clubbed away with rifle and shotgun butts. Their frantic efforts kept the police too busy to help the boy, who we all thought was dying. One Negro appeared to try to snatch the pistol from an officer's holster. He was knocked to the pavement. I watched as Joey was put in the ambulance and rushed off to the hospital. I walked back towards Billy's lifeless body. The girl was still kneeling beside it. She would not believe he was dead and ambulance attendants had to pull her away before they could cover Billy Furr.

"Oh, Joey, yeah, I remember him," a fourteen-year-old boy named Kim recalled down the block from Mack Liquors. "He was the boy right next to me in the hospital. I got kicked in the stomach playing football and Joey was right in the same hospital room with me. Come'n home with me if you want and talk to my mother. She saw Joey, she may know more."

Kim, his brothers and sisters and his mother lived a few doors up the block from the shooting. He led me back into one of the rotting tenements. When he opened the door a small television set gave the room its only light. Dolores, Kim's mother, lay on a couch covered by a blanket. "When Kim went to the hospital, Joey Bass was in the bed right next to him," the mother said. "Did Joey ever say anything? You know, every time I'd see him, he'd never say nothing. He looked like he was in a trance. The last I went to the hospital was the only time he ever talked. Joey asked me to bring him an airplane the next time I came, but my boy went home and I never saw Joey again. I don't know what happened to him after that."

The official police report on the death of William Furr read: "Observed looting and shot while fleeing, either by a sniper or by the police." Furr's pretty widow and his mother came to one of Al Black's Human Rights Commission meetings in the ghetto. The mother, for one, didn't think it was right how her son died. Two civil suits were filed in behalf of Furr's mother, Mrs. Joyce Furr, one against the Newark Police Department and the other against the Metropolitan Life Insurance Company for refusing to pay accidental death benefits. The former was still pending after three and a half years and the suit against the insurance company was successful in what could be termed a precedent-setting case.

"Say hello to Joey for me," Kim's mother had said. "Say hello if you find him." Joey Bass, who had come north from Swainsboro, Georgia, six months before the riot with his parents, two sisters and six brothers, had disappeared back into Newark's sprawling ghetto after four and half months in City Hospital. Outside the dingy tenement a cold miserable rain was still coming down, washing off the sidewalk where Billy Furr had paid the price of law and order and Joey Bass had picked up the change.

11

THE BLACK KILLERS

You Better Get Out of Newark

Eyvind Chandler and his friends were drunk shortly before 7 A.M. that Friday, yelling and "acting like niggers" as the riot's worst violence and destruction swept through the ghetto. Now a winter chill replaced that summer heat and the shabby buildings of Fairmount Avenue huddled together at the corner of Fairmount and South Orange Avenues where Chandler shot a mother of seven children.

At the time of the shooting, the thirty-three-year-old Chandler stood at 246 Fairmount, a few houses from the corner. The porch on which Mrs. Jessie Mae Jones sat is across the street and some forty yards down the block. All the porches on this part of the block are more than twelve feet high. Chalk scribblings and crayon drawings mark 255 Fairmount, where the thirty-one-year-old woman sat. "She got shot right here," one of the neighborhood kids said, pointing to the porch's doorway. "Then she staggered inside and fell in front of those steps." The creaking wood steps are painted orange except where feet have worn away the paint. Some of that wear comes from the seven children of Mrs. Jones and her husband, all of them now long gone.

Jessie Mae Jones was born in Quitman, Georgia, and spent her childhood near Fort Pierce, Florida. She was married at sixteen and came to Newark in 1956.

Chandler was born in Oxford, North Carolina, one of thirteen children. He was graduated from the segregated Joe Toler High School, had a year of college and, as had his brothers and sisters before him, left the farmland for the north. Chandler lived in Jersey City for fifteen years, where three of his sisters had married and settled. Through this period he was employed as a printing press operator at various plants, working out of Local 300, AFL-CIO. Two older brothers lived in nearby Newark, where Chandler moved in 1965. He remained unmarried and lived alone most of the time on Camden Street, a block from Fairmount.

As a southern product transplanted into an urban jungle, Chandler had a surprising record. He had never been arrested and his work record was excellent. His forty-six-year-old sister, Mrs. Tazzie Simmons of Jersey City, called him by his nickname, "Ivy."

"Ivy was in the choir here at the Monumental Baptist Church and he was an usher, too," she related. "Then he started to drink and he never did that before and he started to smoke and he never did that before, either. I told him he better go back to church and stop all that; I was always more a mother than a sister, I'm a mother to all of them. Ivy told me when he was small I could tell him what to do but he was grown now and I couldn't tell him anymore. I think he stayed away from seeing me because I would always be after him. 'You better get out of Newark,' I told him. 'That's a bad place to live.' Every Sunday now I go out to Rahway Prison to visit him."

In Newark, Chandler was doing day work, taking painting and carpentry jobs and tending bar. Mrs. Jones was working as a nurses' aide at a nursing home outside the city.

"The riot drove the cabs and buses off the streets," Dolores, her fifteen-year-old daughter, remembered. "She walked all the way home. It took two hours but she didn't seem to mind. She was so busy watching people stealing and burning. That night there was so much going on we couldn't sleep, so my mother and sister, Constance, sat out here on the porch until dawn. At six-thirty in the morning the neighborhood seemed quiet. Then a gray Cadillac driven by a white man moved up the street and it happened."

Chandler recalled his movements that night for the police:

On Thursday night when it was really going on I met a gang of looters and rioters on Bergen Street and Fifteenth Avenue. I didn't know these guys but they were looking for someone to join them and one of the guys had about three or four guns and I had been drinking and I was feeling pretty good and he gave me a gun so I joined them. We all came down to the Blue Star Lounge on the corner of Fifteenth and Camden and everybody started tearing the place down and some of them went inside. I stayed outside with some of the others and they started taking whiskey out and they were giving it to the people around there and then we all left there and went to South Orange Avenue and Camden Street. We went and then we hit the whiskey store across the street there on the corner and after that broke down the people started in there and carrying whiskey out and stuff out and then we went to Sixth Street and South Orange Avenue and over there the police were coming down South Orange Avenue and when we saw the police we all started running like flies all different ways.

This was after midnight, so we couldn't go no farther, we couldn't fight the cops and we all went different ways. Then I met some other fellows up around South Orange and Fairmount and we got off the avenue there and we all sat around having a party drinking whiskey. Then around four o'clock in the morning we started throwing rocks and bottles at everybody passing in cars. So then about 6:00 A.M. I was right by 246 Fairmount Avenue and this Cadillac was passing and they were throwing rocks at the car and when the car got about in the center of the block he stopped and he fired a shot. I don't know who or where he was firing at and so when he fired, I pulled the gun out that I had in my belt and when I pulled it out it went off and the shot hit the sidewalk or the street and ricocheted and hit me in my left ankle. So then I fired down the street toward the car.

Chandler's shot was wild. It missed the white man who had gotten out of his Cadillac and who hadn't fired at anyone (an incorrect portion of Chandler's story). It also missed the car. It hit Mrs. Jones in the abdomen as she sat on her porch.

"I screamed at the man who had fired the shot," Dolores said. "Then a friend of his ran over and told me my mother had only been grazed and she would be all right, but she died on the way to the hospital. Two days later I was walking to the grocery store and I saw the man who had fired the shot. I ran home and told my father and he drove me back to the store. He told some policemen who were riding there in a police car and they arrested the man."

"Nobody could believe it when Ivy was arrested," his sister related. "That's the first time he was ever in any trouble like that. When they took his driver's license away he couldn't get around anymore and I think that had a lot to do with the way he acted. He used to drive down to Baltimore to visit the family there and all over. I think he was in with bad company, that Newark is a bad place."

Charges of Sniping Were a Lot of Malarkey

It was men like Chandler who accounted for what came to be popularly termed "snipers" in Newark during the riot, though one would never know it from the exaggerated press and magazine reports. What was at most a meager and disorganized response to wild gunfire on the part of the occupation forces was subsequently blown out of all proportion. The image of a black man, his head wrapped in a scarf, peering down the barrel of a Mauser from a tenement window is based on colorful imagination rather than truth. This image was given false credence in the July 28 issue of *Life* magazine, which contained both a photograph of a supposed sniper and a story, "In a Grim City, a Secret Meeting with the Snipers," both of which were fabrications.

Colonel Hassan, gone but not allowing himself to be forgotten, entered into Newark's post-riot confusion via his *Blackman's Defender News-*

letter. He wrote that the man who had posed as a sniper was his lieutenant and that "a dingy, dimly lit room above an alleyway" described as the meeting place in the *Life* article was really "a first-floor rear room overlooking a rubbish- and refuse-littered backyard."

To get the record straight: first, the sniper photograph in *Life* had no connection with the story, which was written several days later, according to its author, *Life* senior editor Russell Sackett, no matter what may have been implied by the wording and format. Second, Sackett told me he had seen no weapons during his visit and hadn't identified the group he talked with as "a sniper organization"—a phrase later edited into the copy to accompany the photograph. Sackett said he knew neither the man portrayed as the sniper nor the apartment where the photograph was taken—and neither did Colonel Hassan. The colonel was referring in his newsletter to the meeting place Sackett had visited, not realizing that the camera work and writing had been completely separate entities. Sackett declined to divulge the meeting's location to me—as he did to the Newark police when they visited *Life*—but said that Colonel Hassan's name was plastered on the walls. This makes the location an easy matter as there was only one such place, Hassan's ghetto headquarters. It also explains why Hassan described what he thought was the photo locale.

Another of the colonel's allegations is more serious: "Five hundred dollars was paid to the fabricated sniper organization for permitting the taking of pictures and the interview by Sackett in *Life* magazine." In its riot report the state PBA commission noted that it "invited the magazine to clarify the situation but the invitation was refused." (It failed to mention that the Newark police were actually negotiating payment with the colonel for his version of who started the Newark riot.) *Life* denied the allegations.

A far more important issue than whether a magazine paid for fabricated photographs, however, is that there was no organized group of snipers operating in Newark during July of 1967, nor has there been any since. There is irony even in this: not only weren't there organized snipers but the situation was so one-sided and leadership in the ghetto so splintered that Newark's so-called militants couldn't even produce a passable facsimile.

Some of the anger and resentment of black men from treatment at the hands of the occupation forces led to shots at the invaders with pistols and revolvers. According to National Guard reports, this gunfire was "deliberately or otherwise inaccurate."

It was a little of each. Ghetto residents were fearful of killing white men because they were unable to shoot with impunity and then leave the area, something that didn't concern the law enforcement officers. Most of the gunfire came from people without organization who lived at or near where they fired from. The occupation forces lacked communication and one shot fired from a tenement might be reported as "sniper fire" half a dozen times as it reverberated a mile or more through the city, giving a false indication of organized resistance.

Police cite gunfire directed at firehouses in the ghetto as proof of organized sniping. Yet it has been documented that the rioters did not set fires which would burn black people out of their homes. The gunfire directed at firehouses came from men who wanted a safe target, one that represented the power structure but was unarmed.

Telephone callers, some with radios monitoring police radios, falsely reported snipers in the area to police, hoping the area would be cleared for the community's safety and for further looting. This was the product of a few people with know-how rather than any organized planning.

The only bona fide snipers in the city were police sniper teams with high-powered rifles and telescopic sights posted on rooftops during the riot's third day. Not one of them reported so much as *a single sniper* and they were taken off. "As a matter of fact," Spina reported to the Hughes Commission, "down in the Springfield Avenue area it was so bad that, in my opinion, guardsmen were firing upon police and police were firing back at them. . . . I don't really believe there was as much sniping as we thought. We have since compiled statistics indicating that there were seventy-nine specified instances of sniping."

"The charges of widespread sniping," said Tim Still, "were a lot of malarkey used as justification to shoot the people and homes."

Both Colonel Kelly and Major Olaff felt there was a pattern to the gunshots reported as sniping, but they were both strangers to the city.

"There was no pattern really, the sniping that went on made no sense at all," said Spina, by far the better oriented authority. "I think a lot of the reports of snipers were due to the, I hate to use the word, trigger-happy guardsmen, who were firing at noises and firing indiscriminately sometimes, it appeared to me, and I was out in the field at all times."

Unfortunately the police director was less candid when it came to the behavior of his own men.

The Toto Shooting

Though more than 6,000 law-enforcement personnel were easy targets on the city's streets, even for a b-b gun, only five policemen were wounded by gunfire—at least one of them shot accidently by a fellow officer—and two white men were killed, Toto and Moran.

Detective Toto was shot on Friday afternoon near the corner of Broome and Mercer Streets, a short distance from Springfield Avenue at the side of the Scudder projects. An hour earlier, police had opened fire at a crowd of innocent people standing in front of the projects. They killed a seventy-two-year-old man and wounded his son, killed another man, and a little girl on an upper floor of the projects lost an eye. At least three angry men returned the fire with handguns from the upper stories and Toto was hit.

I'm Not a Violent Person

A quizzical look behind Howard Edwards' eyeglasses lit up his boyish face. After reading of his deadly activity during the riot, seeing the man face to face could only prompt the thought, *this* is Howard Edwards? So it was the dangerous culprit. Not only had the long search through Staten Island been successful, but Edwards appeared tame enough to talk with.

"I was just glad to get out of Newark," he recalled. "I'm lucky to be alive. Shit, they sure messed me up behind a lot of nonsense."

The unassuming, slightly built man had reached his twenty-fourth birthday and, after his Newark experience, Edwards had occasion to feel lucky. He recalled that the sight of Goethals Bridge stretching out ahead of him on the trip home was one of the most welcome sights he had ever remembered seeing. Indeed, there were times when Edwards thought he'd never make it.

"They kept me in solitary confinement in what they told me was *death row* for seventeen days," he related. "I was scared, I didn't know what the hell was happening."

Edwards was luckier than Fire Captain Moran, who was hit by a .30 caliber bullet during the riot's fourth night and died shortly thereafter on the way to Presbyterian Hospital. Mike Moran was heavy-set, standing five feet eleven and weighing more than 200 pounds. He was as gentle as he was big, spending some of his off-duty time doing chores for the Little Sisters of the Poor, a charity mission around the corner from Fire House Eleven on Central Avenue. He left his wife, Ann, and seven children, the last born after his death.

The five-foot-eight Edwards is as unlikely a villain in physique as in demeanor, weighing 125 pounds after a good meal. Outside of his Newark visit, the most exciting thing Edwards ever did was go horseback riding once. He also received a speeding ticket at one time during his uneventful life. Fate once again—as with John Smith, LeRoi Jones, the Black Muslims of North 14th Street and even Eyvind Chandler—had miscast Edwards in the role of the ruthless black man, this time, no less, with a machine gun.

A woman's voice over a telephone, pleading and promising a good time, brought Howard Edwards into riot-torn Newark. "Her name was Lossie," Edwards related. "She works out at Willowbrook State School where I

work. She said, 'Come'n over, the riot's over.' She said she had a girl friend
for my brother, Walter—he was home on leave from the Air Force—and
we could slip on in with no trouble."

Walter Edwards, twenty, drove into Newark and Howard took over once
they had come off Route 1 down the McCarter Highway ramp. "When I
went over to see her before, she had brought me from work," he said.
"Now I didn't know where the hell I was but I thought if I was driving
I could find the street. I wound up on Central Avenue. The first guardsman
I came to, I stopped and asked him where Montgomery Street was. He was
real nice and explained, 'You go up the hill and turn left,' like that. He
didn't say a word about warning me or nothing, everything was all right.

"There was a steady string of guardsmen all along Central Avenue, every
forty or fifty feet were two or three standing there," Edwards continued. "I
was driving real slow and the next guardsman I came to said, 'Stop, you son
of a bitch' or 'Stop, motherfucker,' one of the two, and he lowered his gun
in my face. I don't know why, maybe it was his attitude, calling me names
like that . . . really, I was just afraid of getting arrested. I just got this car
two weeks before, you know, and I didn't have any registration for it. The
car cost fifty dollars and I just switched the plates from my old car and I
didn't want to go to jail for a stupid thing like that. When he said 'Halt' I
stepped down on the gas and pulled way. They opened up from the back
and side and all over. Bullets busted through the windows. My brother and
I ducked down on the seat and I kept driving up the hill. After that I was
afraid to stop and kept right on going, I must have driven about eight blocks
up the avenue and at every intersection they were shooting at us, steady
shooting. Don't ask me how I got all the way up the hill. Finally they shot
the two rear tires off and the car stopped. I just sat there shaking. My
brother jumped out the car and started running towards the right. 'Wait for
me,' I yelled to him but he was gone. I ran in the same direction until I
couldn't run no more and I hid behind a bush. When I stopped running, I
noticed the blood on my shoulder and arm and I thought I was gonna pass
out, shit like that."

Edwards' black 1957 Chevrolet, now bullet riddled and windowless, had
come to a halt near Fire House Eleven at 9th Street, not far from the last
of the National Guard checkpoints. In its flight the auto had passed 500
Central Avenue, a large factory building where Mike Moran would be hit
less than half an hour later. Bullets fired from down the avenue behind the
fleeing car had hit a sprinkler pipe inside the factory, setting off an alarm
at the firehouse which summoned the fire captain to his death. Edwards'
arrival had also been well heralded at the firehouse itself, with other .30
caliber bullets thudding into that building. Firemen inside doused the lights
and hit the floor—believing that they were under attack from a band of
snipers.

It was mainly through the misinformation of these firemen that the death of Moran was settled on the skinny shoulders of Howard Edwards, at least as far as the mass media were concerned. On September 10, over three and a quarter million readers of the New York *Sunday News* had an opportunity to read an account of the fire captain's death entitled "The Murder of Mike Moran." If Edwards' account of his adventure lacks drama and daring, the newspaper version makes up for it:

> "At 10 P.M.," says Melody [Fire Captain Thomas J. Melody] "we heard the gun. It was an automatic weapon—I'm sure it was a tommygun. Bullets sprayed all around—they were shooting right at the firehouse. We put out the lights, slammed down the big door of the garage, and hit the floor." The men of both fire companies lay tense in the darkness as slugs bounced off the brick front and against the sidewalk. Then they heard another gun speak up. "That was a National Guardsman named O'Shea. The gun shooting at us was being fired from a moving car that somehow had broken through a roadblock. O'Shea fired back." There were two Negroes in the car and, says Melody, "I don't know why they weren't hit. O'Shea shot out their entire windshield. The car spun around and came to a stop near the firehouse and the two men jumped out. O'Shea took off after them. He caught one [Howard Edwards, supposedly] but he wasn't the one with the gun. That one got away. He ran a block down to the rear of the St. Rose of Lima [Home for the Aged] yard and shot the gun off around them."
>
> At 10:13 P.M. the firehouse received an alarm, not a regular alarm but a private job, an ADT. The ADT alarm was linked to a sprinkler system in the factory at 500 Central Avenue. When the system, normally activated by fire, began sprinkling, the alarm went into the firehouse. . . . Engine 11 had no trouble getting to its destination. The factory from which the ADT alarm had come in was only a short block, maybe only a hundred feet, from the firehouse, but on the opposite side of Central Avenue. . . . As his men rolled out the hose, Mike looked over the building. There was neither smoke nor flame. But it wasn't a false alarm. False alarms are turned in from street boxes. The sprinkler system had turned in this baby. It later developed that what activated the system was a sniper's bullet which ripped into one of the sprinkler's pipes. But the firemen didn't know that. As far as they were concerned, the factory contained a fire not yet visible. . . . A 30-foot ladder was raised and the firemen swung it so that they banged the window with it. They banged it twice and the glass gave way.

As Moran stood at the foot of the ladder more shots broke out. He was hit in the left side by a shot that hit the building wall and ricocheted. A guardsman standing near him was wounded less seriously. Moran was facing the building so the shots had to come from the left—from down the street where the string of roadblocks were. It is extremely probable that the guns which had come so close to taking Edwards' head off were the same weapons responsible for Mike Moran's death, Hayden's information at K's Restaurant proving correct at long last. And while the "snipers" received an abundance of exaggerated publicity, nothing more, strangely enough, was heard of Howard Edwards.

As it turned out, the dangerous militant was spotted by some guardsmen passing in a jeep—not by O'Shea—and taken prisoner. He was walked back to the firehouse.

"One of the cops handcuffed me behind my back and started cursing me," Edwards recalled. "He called me a 'black nigger' and he said he was gonna kill me and I was the motherfucker that had killed the fireman. Then he took his gun and hit me on the head and knocked me down. He kicked me in the face. You can see I still have a knot on my forehead where he hit me with the gun. 'I didn't kill nobody, I came here to see somebody,' I told him. 'I'm not a violent person.' He told me, 'You're a lying motherfucker.' Then he said to the other cop, 'Let's kill the rotten son of a bitch.' Another cop started kicking me in the leg at the police station. I was interrogated there for a while and I told them everything. Then they took me to the hospital where they took some pellets out of my shoulder and then they took me to the jail. They finally told me I was charged with murder. 'Murder, what?' I said, 'I didn't kill anybody.' Then they told me I was a material witness in the murder. I didn't know what they were talking about."

The longer the firemen's story went uncontradicted, the more ferocious became the assault on the firehouse and the more cunning and vicious was Howard Edwards. To this day they still believe Edwards machine-gunned the front of the building and had something to do with Mike Moran's death. Fire Captain Melody admitted to me that he hadn't seen gunfire coming from Edwards' car or anywhere else for that matter, except for the heroic work of Guardsman O'Shea. Melody became angry when told he had been wrong, as might be expected, and responded: "Well, tell me this. Then why were the guardsmen shooting at the car?" The fire captain would get better replies if he directed his question to Emerson Moss or Ozell Brown.

In more detached circumstances, one look at the ferocious countenance of Edwards would be enough to convince most anyone he was telling the truth, particularly with his insistent babbling of innocence. Besides, his story was so absurd—the idea of coming into a riot-torn city to see a girl—it had to be true. Police talked to the girl friend and, after she verified Edwards' account, they were stuck with an alleged machine-gunning maniac who wouldn't kill a mouse. Police believed his story even to the extent they never bothered to pick up his brother, yet Howard Edwards, an innocent man who had nearly been killed and his car shot up, was held for seventeen days in jail on the ludicrous charge he was a material witness in a murder. There was no urgency about capturing Walter Edwards, the man supposed to have actually committed the murder. Thus, with the complicity of the police and courts, Edwards' innocence was overlooked.

At the time, Newark was enveloped in the fiction that black snipers had killed Moran, which offered a good—and desperately needed—public relations crutch in the post-riot city when considering what the occupation had really been like. Police allowed the false reports regarding Moran's death to stand uncontradicted and *never even announced* Edwards' release or the facts of the case. Nor did any newspaper make any kind of an effort to find the truth. Two months after the shooting, and one month after Edwards was home again on Staten Island, the New York *Sunday News* published its erroneous account, further burying the truth.

Information on Moran's death was so one-sided that even Tom Hayden had taken it at face value, though not without raising some interesting questions:

> There is one further figure in the Moran story: a material witness. At about 10 P.M., approximately 25 minutes before the death of Moran, Caufield [Fire Director John P. Caufield] related, a car with New York plates drove past Moran's fire station and machine-gunned the front entrance. The driver lost control of the car and smashed into a hydrant by a driveway. Two Negro men fled the car; one was captured one block away by the National Guard, the other was wounded, but apparently not captured, by another guardsman. Moments later Caufield arrived and went with Moran to the nearby fire, where Moran was killed. The [New York *Daily*] *News* quoted police as identifying the man captured by the guardsmen as Howard J. Edwards, 23, of Staten Island; considered as a material witness as to the shooting and charged wtih violating curfew, he was held in lieu of $100,000 bail (the highest charged anyone). The [Newark] *Star-Ledger* reported also that Edwards was held, and added that "he was arrested in a car not far from the Central Avenue building where Moran was killed. The time of the arrest was shortly after the shooting." The police believe Moran's killer was in the car with Edwards. In one story we are told the two Negro men fled the car, in another story we find that one remained and was arrested. In one story we are told that the unarrested Negro man was wounded, in another that he got from the point of the wreckage to the scene of the supposed fire in time to shoot Moran and a guardsman, then still could not be found and arrested. In one story we are told the police believe this unknown, wounded Negro to be the killer, while in another story Director Caufield himself acknowledged that "we couldn't see where the bullets were coming from."

Does this incredible maze of statements seem more believable than the idea that police were firing on themselves and could very well have killed Captain Moran? There were, in fact, some reporters at the scene of the Moran shooting who felt the shots were coming from the police. Certain papers, the *Washington Post* for example, decided to leave unanswered the question of who killed the fire captain. Not so state and local officials. In carrying the myth to 2500 angry firemen at Mike Moran's funeral, they intensified the suspicions and fears of a crucial part of the white community.

Hayden, without even knowing the facts of Edwards' arrest, was on the right track. The silence of investigating officials regarding Moran's death was deafening. Hayden may have been fishing, but if he had substituted "guardsmen" for "police," he would have hit on the truth, according to no less an expert than Howard Edwards himself.

"I didn't think he got killed by a sniper the way they hushed everything up," he said. "That's the way it seemed to me. They were charging me with the fireman's murder and every time I asked them a question, they wouldn't even answer me."

Walter Edwards got out of the area without being shot and hitched a ride back to Staten Island that night. He learned later that his brother was all right, then left for an aunt's home in Gastonia, North Carolina, where he completed his month's leave and returned to California.

Early in August, Howard Edwards was taken from his solitary-confinement cell at the Essex county jail on Newark Street to municipal court. When he had been arrested, scores were there staring at him. Photographers kept a safe distance while capturing for posterity the man who had challenged the entire National Guard with a machine gun. Even television cameras had been on hand. Now, however, there were no onlookers. Edwards was quietly charged with violating the city curfew as hundreds of others had been, convicted, and told to tiptoe back to Staten Island.

"They told me where my car was," Edwards remembered, "they said they had it in storage and I would have to pay twenty-five or thirty dollars to get it out. My girl friend went over to see it when I was in jail and she told me the tires were shot off, it had no windows and there were half-inch holes in the roof. She said with all the bullet holes it was sort of ruined. I told them to keep the car. Then they told me I'd have to go back to the jail for my wristwatch and money. All I wanted was to get out of Newark. Shit, I told them to keep that too."

12

THE TRAGIC DEATH OF ISAAC HARRISON, THE SILENT DEATH OF HOMER MOSELY

They Were Still Firing at Ground Level

"There was me," the stocky man said, "there was my brothers, Bussy and Horace, and there was my father. We were standing here in front of the projects with a crowd of people when the three police cars turned the corner from Springfield Avenue." Virgil Harrison went on, his voice never changing tone, "They just got out of the cars and started shooting. There weren't any looters running around us, that was bullshit. All that was going on over on Springfield Avenue. At first I thought they were firing blanks 'cause they were shooting directly into the crowd."

"It was a matter of seconds," the man next to Virgil Harrison, Willis "Bussy" Harrison, said. "They pulled up, got out of their cars and started firing. There was no warning, nothing. I didn't hear any of that nonsense about looters and snipers until we got back from the hospital."

The Harrison brothers, Virgil, thirty-two, and Bussy, thirty-five, were standing exactly where they had been then, just thirty-five yards from where the police opened fire. A round scar on Virgil Harrison's right forearm marked the spot where a .38-caliber bullet ripped through it and he walked with a limp that went with another scar on the side of his left knee. "When we saw they were really shooting at us, we went for the entrance there," he continued. "My father got hit then. I thought he had just fell because everyone was pushing, so I picked him up and I was helping him up the steps when I got shot in the arm. When I got by the door, I got shot in the knee and I went down. Somebody pulled me in the doorway. My father was already in there, he was bleeding badly and moaning. They were still shooting at the building outside."

"I tried to make a tourniquet with my handkerchief for Virgil's arm but the blood was streaming out so fast it didn't do any good," Bussy Harrison said. "It just got soggy with blood and slipped off. The only way we would get out of the building was to take our undershirts off and wave them like flags."

Virgil Harrison lived on 7th Avenue at the time of the shooting and later moved into a Scudder Homes project a block away on Howard Street, on the thirteenth floor of one of Newark's main high-rise, brick prisons. Two of his brothers also lived there, and the group had been walking out of the project when the police opened fire. Ike Harrison, Jr., thirty-four, the brother who hadn't been home at the time of the shooting, lived with his wife, their teenage daughter and his father, seventy-two-year-old Isaac "Uncle Daddy" Harrison, who had been born in Jamaica and lived in New Jersey for half a century. Isaac Harrison settled in Burlington in the southern portion of the state until 1943 and then brought his family to Newark where he sweated in iron foundries around the city and raised nine children. After they had grown, the old man lived with his wife, Evelyn, at the senior citizens' project on nearby Lincoln Street. After her death in February, he went to live on the tenth floor of the projects with Ike, his eldest son.

"After my mother died he just putted around," Bussy Harrison said. "There was a senior citizens' recreation place and he'd go over there to play pinochle. He always would be stopping by, he liked to be around his family."

Bussy Harrison, his wife, Ann, and their five children lived in another of the Scudder projects on Broome Street on the fifth floor.

"They were just standing there watching what was going on over on the avenue, as people will do," Mrs. Harrison said, pointing from the window. "There were men and women, even children down there. The police weren't shooting at looters. It was surprising to me they'd even say they were shooting at snipers and looters after what happened. It was such a bad thing, what they did, I get angry even talking about it. They said on the bullhorn for everybody to get out of the building after the shooting. I had five kids in here and, you know, with kids you get excited worrying about them. We went out the far exit and a bullet smashed the glass above one of the kids' heads. I pulled my children back and we went over to my brother-in-law's house and they'd never get me to come out of there. If they were going to shoot us, they'd have to shoot us in our own homes."

No matter how many months had passed or from what angle the corner was viewed, it was still just thirty-five yards from 60 Broome Street, the first Scudder project on the corner of Broome and Mercer where the Harrisons had been shot down, out into the street where the three police cars had pulled up. Officer Homer Mosely, forty-two, a black patrolman in car 108, had been one of them. From behind their cars the small group of police looked at the crowd of people standing on the cement walkway not as curious spectators but as black people, the enemy. Anger and frustration took hold of the police and they opened fire. The warm air was pocked with the popping sound of .38 caliber revolvers and shotguns firing Double O ammunition. A continuing barrage ricocheted off the brick walls behind the crowd and fell to the ground like bird droppings. Those in the crowd didn't believe the police were firing live shells—until they heard the slugs chipping at the bricks. Sounds of gunfire were then mixed with the screams and shouts of frightened human beings, a hideous mixture that reverberated through the thirteen-story cement canyons of the Scudder projects.

They screamed and ran. And with these moving targets several Newark police officers who had been firing into the walls dropped their aim and continued firing. This episode was dealt with sympathetically in the Kerner Report but with one serious error.

The report stated:

> As the police arrived three of the looters cut directly in front of the group of spectators. The police fired at the looters. Bullets plowed into the spectators.

The Kerner commissioners got this faulty information from initial police reports. Eventually, supposed snipers replaced looters as having precipitated police gunfire for obvious reasons. First, there weren't any looters in that immediate area. And, second, the looters would have had to be running past the innocent bystanders for a full ten to fifteen minutes, which is as silly as it sounds. Inexplicably, people were being shot down at ground level as police fired at phantom snipers.

"We were under fire, I would say, for approximately ten minutes by the Newark police," Horace Morris, Isaac Harrison's forty-year-old stepson, said. "They said they were looking for a sniper on the roof or the upper floors of the building but they were still firing at ground-level range."

Morris, an articulate man who was an associate director of the Washington, D.C., Urban League, had been attending a National Urban League conference in New York at the time of the riot and had stopped to visit his family before returning to Washington. The group of men—Bussy, Virgil and Isaac Harrison and Morris—had been walking to Bussy Harrison's car, parked nearby on the corner, when the shooting began. For him the message was the same one teacher John Thomas had given at the Human Rights Commission meeting not far away.

"Once I had an opportunity to collect my senses," he said later, "and really evaluate and think this thing through, it came to me in stark reality that regardless of how far up the economic ladder any Negro goes, that there's still this oppressive thing of prejudice that he is subjected to by the white man here in America. And I realized that I was extremely fortunate not to be killed myself. And that even though I had played football for Syracuse, even though I was an elementary school principal who had educated white children, even though I work with white people in the Washington Urban League, even though there are white people that I consider close friends—that, as the boys say, when it gets down to the nitty-gritty, right down to where it really matters, you're still a Negro and you're still identified with every other Negro in America, be he in a ghetto or in a suburban neighborhood. You're still a brother."

His sons took Isaac Harrison to City Hospital. The white-haired old man had been hit with five Double O slugs, four in the chest and stomach and one in the arm. He died at 9:30 P.M. Virgil Harrison was also taken to City Hospital for treatment of his two gunshot wounds.

"I was there until Sunday, three days," he said. "They put a piece of adhesive tape on my arm, a piece of tape on my knee. I bled all night long. They took X-rays but I don't know what the hell happened, they said the shotgun slug wasn't in my knee. They told me all I needed was rest. After Sunday, I went to Presbyterian Hospital and they operated on the knee and took out the slug."

Virgil's father had been a long-time member of the Episcopalian Christ Church on Congress Street. His funeral was held downtown in Trinity Cathedral with Bishop Leland Stark, head of the Diocese of Newark, conducting the funeral service himself. All the Harrisons and their families, the hard-working guts and strength of Newark as their father had been before them, were there. Even Virgil, who came in a wheelchair with a doctor and nurse, attended the funeral. Steve Flanders and Robert Potts of CBS made lengthy interviews outside the cathedral with the sons, Flanders for radio while Potts taped a segment for television. Virgil Harrison returned to Presbyterian Hospital while the rest of the family accompanied the casket to Cedar Lane Cemetery in south Jersey. The old man was buried alongside his wife, as he had wished. Television coverage of the funeral was never shown. According to a CBS newsman, CBS had decided that in the post-riot climate such a segment as an old man's funeral would be too controversial.

Such decisions kept the public in almost total ignorance about the realities of the Newark riot. It was little wonder that the Hughes Report, and even the Kerner Report, were rejected in disbelief by the majority of New Jersey's white citizens.

Henry Franzoni, a Bloomfield attorney, also attended the funeral. Afterward, he began assembling bits of evidence and information about the shootings.

Police claimed that they were sent to the projects because of reported sniper fire and, after checking the area, had been fired on while returning to their cars. If this ever happened, it certainly wasn't at 4:00 P.M. when police opened fire on Isaac and Virgil Harrison and Robert Lee Martin, who had been shot by police near the same location a few minutes before the Harrisons. It was anger over these senseless shootings that prompted gunfire from the upper stories of the projects when police, returning to the scene an hour later, were fired upon. Detective Toto, standing near the same area where police had fired on the defenseless crowd, was hit in the chest by a .22 caliber bullet around 5:15 P.M. and fatally wounded. It was the same thirty-five yards—but now the bullets were being returned.

"I talked with at least fifteen eyewitnesses to the shooting," the thirty-five-year-old Franzoni said. "Not one of them saw Toto go down. His shooting occurred much later in the afternoon. Police tried to group the shootings together and blame the whole thing on snipers. If there is one thing they all agreed on, it was how they just couldn't believe the police were firing on them with live ammunition. They thought the police were shooting blanks."

Franzoni had no doubt of the veracity of such statements given to him by residents of the Scudder projects. In his office are paper bags containing spent Double O and revolver slugs they had picked up from the ground.

Investigation into the riot homicides was being carried on by private attorneys such as Franzoni and, theoretically at least, by Newark authorities. Only one of the groups took the job seriously, however. While homicide and the prosecutor's office personnel could be credited with an effort accomplishing little or nothing, men like Franzoni gathered what physical evidence they could. Nor was there any confidence in what the police would do, as evidenced by the slug taken from Virgil Harrison's knee. Not trusting police facilities, a hospital employee borrowed the slug and had it analyzed by a private source before returning it. This maneuver was prudent since police went a good deal beyond bungling and incompetence, misplacing bullets or being unable to come up with reliable ballistic information on slugs taken from the bodies of riot victims.

Police witnesses to killings were also rare, except in the most obvious cases in which certain policemen had to admit having been there. Policemen who had seen other policemen shoot down innocent people suffered lapses of memory and the prosecutor's office did not work overtime trying to find them. Ghetto witnesses were either dead or too far away to be able to identify individual officers.

Officer Mosely, whom Bussy Harrison had recognized among the police who were firing at them, was an exception.

"I used to tend bar over at Big Mike's Tavern on Bergen Street and I knew Mosely," he related. "When we finally were able to make them stop shooting and we got out of the building, I saw him there by one of the radio cars. He told me he was working the radio and had nothing to do with the shooting. Two weeks later I bumped into him at the tavern. He approached me to say how sorry he was that my father had been killed. He said how

there wasn't anything he could do, how his hands were tied. I asked him
who were some of the other police shooting there and he said he couldn't
remember, or wouldn't, I don't remember which."

Five months after the shooting, on the morning of Monday, January 22,
Franzoni was ready to approach the Essex County prosecutor's office to
offer information on Isaac Harrison's death. With him were Virgil and
Bussy Harrison, who had no faith in the outcome. Andrew Zazzali, Jr., in
charge of presenting information to the special grand jury investigating the
riot deaths, asked for the identity of the patrolman who had witnessed the
shooting and was told "Homer Mosely," which name he seemed to recognize. The assistant prosecutor left the room and returned a few minutes
later to announce that Mosely *had died* the night before.

To this day nothing will convince the Harrisons that Mosely did not
meet with foul play.

"How he died, it was a real Dick Tracy thing, I'll tell you that," the
older brother said. "I saw him over at Big Mike's many times and I know
he would have to identify the other cops. It was very convenient for the
police department that he died, I'll tell you that. I went over to the funeral
home where he was at to see him, to make sure he was the one. He never
had any heart condition, I'm sure of that."

"As far as I'm concerned," Franzoni told me, "the prosecutor's investigation was little more than an attempt to whitewash the entire situation. Zazzali acted like he wanted someone to drop all the information right into
his lap before he'd do anything. For one thing, I gave him a list of eyewitnesses who had seen the shooting and they were never even contacted.
Mosely's death should be investigated. One thing I'm sure of, if they
thought one cop would be able to identify a half-dozen others who had shot
wildly into a crowd, his life wouldn't be worth a plugged nickel."

Tell Mommy I'll Be Right Back

Homer Mosely, Sr., had been a police officer in Newark for eight years
working out of the Fourth Precinct building, where the riot began. He had
come to the city twenty-eight years before from Jacksonville, Florida.
Mosely was an Army veteran of World War II and worked for a Newark
engineering firm and attended a photography school before joining the
police force. His wife, Mrs. Mary Elizabeth Mosely, is head clerk at one of
the city's downtown department stores. Together they raised two sons and
two daughters. The family had moved into an attractive home on White
Terrace, a short residential street running off Clinton Place in the South
Ward, fifteen years before.

"He'd come home from working in the riot very tired," his forty-four-year-old widow recalled. "He told me he saw people getting hurt and shot for nothing, for no reason at all. Homer said he didn't want to go out in it again."

Mosely was described by those who knew and worked with him as a warm man with a big heart which, until Sunday morning, January 21, was in excellent working order. At forty-two years of age, Mosely was strong as a bull at 170 pounds, a light drinker and smoker. According to his doctor, he had an ulcer but was otherwise in top physical condition.

"I had to work overtime that Saturday or I would have been home," Mrs. Mosely said. "We were supposed to go out that night. Around five he got a phone call and left the house in a hurry. He told my daughter, 'Tell Mommy I'll be right back,' and he went out the door. That's the last time we ever heard from him. He would stay out all night sometimes, but he'd always call home and let me know where he was. He would always call home, but this time he didn't. At nine o'clock the next night his two police partners came to the house and told me Homer had died from a heart attack. I asked them to tell me how it happened and they wouldn't tell me. 'It can't hurt me because I know about where he goes and it can't hurt Homer, so tell me the truth,' I told them. I told them I knew about where he died but they still wouldn't tell me anything. Both of them were crying.

"I always thought when a person died mysteriously like that there would be a coroner's inquest," Mrs. Mosely continued. "Homer always told me he didn't want anyone cutting him open after he was dead so I didn't ask for an autopsy but I thought there would be an inquest. Now I'm sorry there wasn't an autopsy. I kept telling his so-called friends, 'Why do you have to hush everything?' I don't know whether they're afraid to face me or what it is but I've always had the feeling something's fishy. 'Those friends you're going around with are not really your friends,' I told Homer, 'be careful.' I told him that four months before he died."

According to his brief obituary—the only published report of his death—Mosely "died Sunday while visiting friends at 25 Gold Street." This particular house is notorious as a virtual police clubhouse offering white and black prostitutes, gambling and liquor. Mosely was one of many Newark officers—both white and black—who frequently stopped in. The woman who runs the house told me that Mosely was there that Sunday morning, became sick and died, when, actually, the police officer had slept there that night. His death certificate was just as abrupt. Cause of death was listed as "occlusive coronary arteriosclerosis," which means Mosely's heart stopped beating. This conclusion, though medically accurate, does not take into account the fact that Mosely had been ill for at least twelve hours before his wife was notified and when she finally was, it was only to identify a corpse at the city morgue.

Whatever went on inside 25 Gold Street that Saturday night and Sunday has been private knowledge for those involved.

Mrs. Mosely is a strong woman who understood her soft-hearted husband and was familiar with his comings and goings. Any effort to protect her from learning the details of his death had only an opposite result, a feeling of apprehension that has stayed with her. "We were married for twenty-three years," she said. "It's not right to just hand me a death certificate and tell me my husband is dead."

Two more blacks—an old man and a policeman—had gone to their deaths in Newark wrapped in shrouds woven of official lies.

13

SLAUGHTER ON CUSTER AVENUE

I Never Should Have Taken Him Out of Bordentown

"Could I help it if the kid was killed in my place?" thirty-two-year-old Joe Campisi, owner of the former Jo Rae's Music Room, asked. "I didn't ask him to rob me. After it was over I started to get threatening phone calls. At first I told the guys who called to go fuck themselves but after a while I said the hell with it and sold the place."

SIMPSON'S LOUNGE, a new blue neon sign, had replaced the old one but that was the only noticeable change at the corner of Bergen Street and Custer Avenue. The bar adjoins several party rooms to the right rear and a liquor store to the left where nineteen-year-old James Rutledge, Jr., was caught looting during the riot. He was shot to death with the outrageous details of his death swept under the official carpet. For some in black Newark, LeRoi Jones among them, Rutledge is remembered as "the kid who got shot thirty-nine times." The memories of the three younger boys who were hiding in the bar when Rutledge was shot are haunted by the reverberating shotgun blasts which splattered the wall with their friend's remains.

Robert "Poochie" Hatcher was fourteen years old at the time, Dennis Hughes was thirteen and Brian Gary was fifteen. The first two come from middle-class homes in Newark's residential Weequahic section, while the Gary boy lived on Chadwick Avenue around the corner from the bar. Everyone except Brian Gary had been in the poolroom on Jones Street less than an hour before the shooting. Rutledge laughed as he lost what little money he had playing pool.

"We came home on the bus," Poochie Hatcher related. "Jimmy got off the bus at West Kinney Street with another boy who was with us. He was betting us a dollar he could beat the bus home. He started running alongside the bus but he fell behind and we couldn't see him anymore. The other boy quit and we never saw him but Jimmy ran all the way to Custer and Bergen where we got off."

It was a warm Sunday afternoon with disturbances in the city almost completely over and a shuttered bar offered excitement worth looking into. This was particularly true when Brian Gary, a friend of the three boys, could be seen through a side window, moving about stealing cases of beer. The Gary boy had already twice visited the Essex County Youth House for similar activity. Poochie Hatcher had been in trouble once before, while Dennis Hughes had managed to keep his record clean.

Earlier in the riot, Jo Rae's had been looted of its liquor and the windows were covered with plywood. Brian Gary had dislodged the covering on a side window to get inside and he was soon joined by Rutledge, Hatcher, and Hughes. Minutes later, police arrived at the scene. What transpired was reported in the *Washington Post* of July 24, as written from the accounts of the three boys:

> James W. Rutledge, Jr., was 14 when his father walked out and left his mother with 12 children. They moved to Trenton, New Jersey, and the family lived on welfare. Last year, his father took Jimmy out of Bordentown Reformatory, where he was serving a sentence for car theft, and brought him to live with him in Newark. On the morning of Sunday, July 16, Jimmy, who was 19, left the house of a friend to recover some food that Rutledge's companions said he had looted earlier. They saw him alive for the last time on Bergen Street at noon. At 5:25 P.M. according to a police report, Rutledge and three companions entered Jo Rae's Music Room, a boarded up store on the corner of Bergen and Custer Streets. "Rutledge threw a knife at a policeman when ordered to surrender and was shot by police while trying to escape," the police report said. According to witnesses, the four young men were about to leave the music shop when Jimmy said, "Run the cops." All of them tried to hide. Nine state troopers came through a hole in the window. One trooper told Rutledge to "get off the floor" and the young man came out from where he was hiding and said, "Don't shoot. I'll serve my time in jail." The troopers frisked him. Rutledge turned and said, "I will come peacefully." At that point, the witnesses continued, a trooper shot him from three feet away. As Jimmy fell to the floor, the same trooper shot him four more times. Then another trooper said: "This nigger ain't dead yet." The trooper who did the shooting reloaded his rifle and shot Rutledge's body about eight more times. A police cameraman entered and a trooper suggested that a knife be placed in Jimmy's hand, the witness said. The police finally decided to put a pair of scissors in his hand, the witness said. He also heard the flash bulb go off three or four times. The other young men were arrested as they emerged from the store. Orlando K. Perry, director of the Perry Funeral Home, said he counted 39 rifle wounds when he prepared the body for burial last Tuesday. Four of them were in the skull. At the funeral on Saturday, an usher handed Jimmy's father a rose. But he turned away and walked to the cemetery roadway and threw the flower to the ground. "I should never have taken him out of Bordentown," he said.

As the police—two Newark officers and two state troopers—entered the bar, Rutledge ran to the left into the liquor store where he hid behind a counter. The three boys scampered to the right, hiding in the party rooms. Just as they couldn't have helped hearing what transpired in the liquor store, it was a physical impossibility for them to have seen anything. The three boys, however, were determined that the police be made to pay for their friend's death. The affidavit of the Hughes boy[1] appears in *Rebellion in Newark,* a circumstance which was used by the prosecutor's office in the attempt to discredit Tom Hayden:

> The two troopers . . . looked at each other. Then one trooper who had a rifle shot Jimmy from about three feet away. . . . While Jimmy lay on the floor, the same trooper started to shoot Jimmy some more with the rifle. As he fired . . . he yelled, "Die, you dirty bastard, die you dirty nigger, die, die. . . ." At this point a Newark policeman walked in and asked what happened. I saw the troopers look at each other and smile. . . .
>
> The trooper who shot Jimmy remained . . . took a knife out of his own pocket and put it in Jimmy's hand.
>
> Shortly after three men came in with a stretcher. One said, "They really laid some lead on his ass." . . . He asked the state trooper what happened. The trooper said, "He came at me with a knife." . . .
>
> [We remained where we were] . . . for about fifteen minutes, then I got up and walked to the window and knocked a board down. [Poochie Hatcher] and [Brian Gary] came over to the window and two National Guardsmen came to the window and said, "Come out or we are going to start shooting." . . .
>
> A National Guardsman said, "What do you want us to do, kill all you Negroes?" I saw a Newark policeman say: "We are going to do it anyway, we might as well take care of these three now." I saw the Newark policeman go over to [Poochie Hatcher], point a pistol at his head and say: "How do you feel?" Then he started laughing. . . .

The three boys lied to the *Washington Post* reporters and to the Legal Services Project people who took their affidavits. They also lied to the FBI which, because of the gruesome appearance of Rutledge's corpse, made the shooting the object of a late but intense investigation. Then they finished by lying to me, even though repeatedly told that any lies would only damage the integrity of anything written on Rutledge, whose death, God knows, never needed fabrication to make it worse than it was.

Errors in the *Washington Post* story and the affidavit are too numerous to detail, but there weren't nine state troopers, no rifles, no scissors, or police photographer, and, as Joe Campisi told me, the knife found near

[1] The affidavit, on page 52, was certainly that of the Hughes boy but not identified as such. Also, names of the boys were left blank but here have been filled in.

the body had been used to cut lemons and was left on a counter inside the bar.

Who the Hell Are They to Ride Away from Something Like That?

Orlando Perry, a thirty-four-year-old black undertaker, entered the controversy when he picked up Rutledge's corpse from a funeral home used as a morgue facility. "Now I know a bullet hole when I see one," the mild-mannered man said. "I've been looking at them since I was fourteen. I'm not in a position to speak for anyone but myself. I'm not qualified to make an official announcement or anything like that, but I know what I saw. When I said there were thirty-nine bullet holes, there were thirty-nine bullet holes."

After receiving permission from the dead boy's mother, Mrs. Lassiephine Rutledge, who still lived in Trenton, photographs were taken of the body. Unfortunately, by the time the photographer arrived at Perry's, the undertaker had already proceeded with the embalming. This is a process which includes cleaning out the body and head cavities, particularly necessary with the messy condition of Rutledge's corpse. Perry had proceeded to do just that, re-opening the body along the cuts that had been made during the autopsy and placing a portion of the bullet-punctured skull taken from the back of Rutledge's head into the body cavity, as some undertakers do. The photographs were taken innocently enough but then used deviously. Leaflets were soon being spread over the ghetto showing Rutledge's opened corpse as grim testimony to what had been done to him.

In his estimation of bullet holes, Perry was mistaken only in that he was unfamiliar with what Double O shotgun ammunition could do at close range. A sense of outrage while removing twisted pieces of lead from the corpse had evidently overcome his sense of practicality. State troopers were not prone to waste ammunition shooting "a nigger" thirty-nine times. Even so, Perry's error was understandable under circumstances that make the Rutledge shooting the most shocking homicide in the history of Newark.

Rutledge, tall and rather slim, was hit by four, possibly five shotgun blasts that ripped between thirty and thirty-five slugs into his back from less than five yards. Twenty-two of these slugs passed completely through his body. He was also hit by four .38-caliber bullets, also in the back, three of these also passing completely through his body. Two more .38s hit him in the right arm. Six other .38-caliber bullets were neatly placed in the rear of his skull. Actually, Rutledge was shot only sixteen or seventeen times in all, accounting for some forty-two holes in his body. His routine morgue photographs are worse than the propaganda leaflets, truth in this particular instance being worse than fiction. Rutledge was not shot thirty-nine times, he only *looked* that way.

Such carnage had left Campisi with a shot-up liquor store, a gory scene he cleaned up before any homicide detectives or the FBI got there. There were two puddles of blood, the good-natured Campisi remembered, one where the body was found behind the narrow eighteen-foot counter on the right and another near the counter's other end. The bar owner related how the FBI had been mystified by this second puddle, but a recollection of Sergeant Sellers, the first ranking officer to reach the scene, explains it.

"The body was first placed on a rubber sheet," he said. "Because of the cramped space, we had to lift the body over the counter and when it tilted, some blood spilled out."

FBI investigators went over the store every day for weeks digging out bullets and shotgun slugs from the shelves and woodwork. They were wasting their time. Any inquiry into the death of Rutledge was announced for public relations, not justice. Joe Campisi's private investigation was only philosophical but accomplished just about as much. "I've thought about the shooting a thousand times but what good does it do to think?" he said. "That's the way it is. What happened, happened and that's it. They did what they did. Like they say, you can't fight city hall."

According to police reports, the first radio message of a break and entry at Jo Rae's came in at 5:05 P.M. Word of a probable D.O.A. (dead on arrival) came at 5:12 P.M., bringing Sergeant Sellers to the scene. The forty-seven-year-old Sellers remembers vividly what he found.

"One Newark officer who was part of the shooting was by the window at the side of the bar where the boys had entered," the twenty-year police veteran stated. "This was the one who said Rutledge had thrown the knife. The body was next door in the liquor store through the passageway off the bar. He was laying face down with his feet towards the Bergen Street wall. It was dark in there but I had my flashlight and there was a large quantity of blood. He had been shot many times. There was a butcher knife lying a few inches from his right hand. I was only in there for five minutes but like I told the FBI when they investigated, it looked to me like an overkill. There were definitely excessive bullet holes. There were holes on the walls around the body and also traces of blood from bullets that had gone through the body.

"The state troopers involved in the shooting were pulling away when I arrived," Sellers continued. "They were riding up Bergen Street. As I said before, when I found out there had been a homicide, I was angry. Had I known then they were involved, I would have had them remain at the scene even if I had to arrest them. It may have been a riot but this was still a homicide. That's something you just don't ride away from. But there they were . . . hop on a horse, riding into the sunset—just like the old westerns, you know? Who the hell are they to ride away from something like that?"

It Was That Kind of a Thing

The ghetto had the distorted tales of the three boys and photographs of what appeared to be a mutilated corpse. Police were disadvantaged in what propaganda they could come up with. They managed, none the less, to do the shooting justice. According to first police reports, "Rutledge threw a knife at a policeman when ordered to surrender and was shot by police while trying to escape." Shortly after the fusillade, the two Newark officers from whom this report came left the scene shaken, leaving the two state troopers. The knife probably was placed next to the body at this time. The troopers then left the scene, a violation of procedure but prudent under the circumstances, and were never able to confer with the Newark officers as to exactly *what* Rutledge had been doing to bring about such a death.

In testimony before the grand jury, the first explanation of the shooting was changed to "they observed a man rise from behind the counter holding a knife in a raised position." Rutledge's refusal "to surrender" had been lost in the translation and his attempt to escape was also omitted, perhaps as a matter of practicality. A study of the scene shows he would have been running into a solid wall. Other testimony by the four involved police officers was similarly contradictory. Such an offering as a nineteen-year-old frightened kid threatening four policemen carrying shotguns and .38s boggles the imagination. Rutledge had gone down in a burst of gunfire which had riddled his back, the officers testified, as they had protected themselves from a vicious knife attack. Here was a skinny kid who had been hit with a tremendous force driving more than twenty lead slugs completely through his body and just enough imagination had been summoned to leave the knife inches from his fingertips.

Only one Newark police officer cared to recall the scene inside the tavern. "As far as I know nobody said anything inside the bar," the twenty-eight-year-old policeman said. "I was either the first or second into the liquor store and the two state troopers were behind us. A shadowy figure was behind the counter and I fired wild. . . . I could have hit my partner for all I knew. I'm not sure how many times I fired, I was like a scared animal. I've never talked to the state troopers, either then or since. They could give me a traffic ticket for all I know and I'd never remember them. The FBI asked me, 'How many times did you fire?' I told them, 'You tell me, I don't know. I fired anywhere up to six bullets because I know I didn't reload.' The grand jury asked me what the others were doing. 'I can only account for what I did,' I told them. 'You don't know too much,' they told me. I told them I had told them all I could. Let them ask the others if they want to know what they did, I can only speak for myself. I didn't say I ever saw anybody attacking, I just opened fire. I don't believe I saw any knife in the tavern, I just walked outside and went across the street to phone for an ambulance. I answered for what I did and it's all over. I stick to my job so when I go home I can forget about it. If the others want to take graft and pay-offs, let them. Me, they pay me a salary and I make out on it. I'm not greedy, I don't get myself involved in anything so once I leave the job I can forget about it. . . . Just for the hell of it I'm going back to look at the place some time, just for memory's sake."

Under the circumstances prevailing in post-riot Newark, it was unlikely that anything would come to homicide investigations by the prosecutor's office, but with U.S. Attorney Satz and the FBI working on the investigation of Rutledge's death, there was some basis for hope.

That hope would not be fulfilled.

"There were four men involved in the shooting," Satz stated. "Each one says the other three did the shooting. It was that kind of a thing."

"I don't want to sensationalize the case," Satz was told. "I just want to find out the truth of what happened inside that bar."

"I think it needs sensationalizing," the U.S. Attorney replied. "All we have now is four defendants and no witnesses."

Satz also had a corpse with 42 holes in it, 6 of them in the back of the skull, and yet the U.S. Attorney's office did nothing.

PART IV

Planting the New Crop

14

BANISHMENT OF THE TRANSGRESSORS

Is It Conceivable Men in Blue Would Commit Such an Outrageous Act?

The trial of LeRoi Jones for carrying concealed weapons was held outside of Essex County in Morristown where the playwright thought he might have a better chance at, to use the euphemism, "a fair shake."

"There weren't any guns," Jones added to his previous statements on his arrest. "I don't keep guns. And I certainly wouldn't be so stupid as to carry guns into the middle of a riot." LeRoi, who had made a blunder just being where the police could get their loving hands on him, was begging the question. The critical point was whether or not the guns police said they had found in the camper bus had been fired.

Jones was dressed in a dashike and played his role to the hilt. "You got a hundred white people here," he shouted at a panel of potential jurors. "They're not my peers, they're my oppressors." LeRoi then attempted to walk out of the courtroom but was instead escorted to the county jail. He labeled the legal proceedings "a kangaroo court" and interjected at least one obscene word, "shit," to be precise. Jones also insisted on arguing with Essex County Judge Leon W. Kapp, who didn't appreciate his wisdom being questioned quite so overtly and who, as it turned out, was saving his ire for one onslaught at the trial's conclusion. Five arresting officers swore they didn't know who Jones was at the time of the arrest and that the two guns were found in the van. It seemed that no one knew who Jones was, even two witnesses who testified for the defense.

These witnesses, a husband and wife who had been standing on their porch at the time, were unable to identify the playwright by name. They had seen, however, police officers encircling a man dressed in a dashike who then disappeared from view. From other movements of the police and some screams—coming from LeRoi no doubt—they felt that someone was being beaten. Another defense witness, a neighbor who lived near The Spirit House on Sterling Street, had happened along at the time of the arrest, he testified, and distinctly heard LeRoi interrogating one of the police:

"Why don't you stop hitting me with that stick?"

The reply, said the witness, had been another rap, this one on LeRoi's head.

Yet another defense witness, a woman who had viewed the arrest from a window in her second-floor apartment, remembered a prisoner being kicked by one of the throng of police officers.

Medical testimony corroborated that Jones had suffered a nasty cut on his head and another on his lip. Also, McCray had a cut head and a broken arm. All of which was routine as far as Newark police-community relations were concerned and quite beside the point. It was Jones *who was on trial,* not the police.

Naturally enough, Jones and his two companions were found guilty as charged on the testimony of the five police officers, which was—despite Judge Kapp's later thoughts on the subject—not particularly reliable. This was substantiated by the officers themselves, who also testified that no one had beaten or even struck Mr. Jones. How, then, had he gotten that messy cut on his head that had bloodied his dashike? And who had broken McCray's arm? Jones had been injured, police said, by a bottle that had flown mysteriously through the air, coming from they knew not where. The second question they didn't even bother to answer.

Judge Kapp told the jury that the police were "the shields against violence and lawless acts," and then, referring to Jones's claim that he had been framed with the police planting the guns, asked the jury: "Did they appear to you to be evilly disposed and wicked men who would resort to such calumny? Is it conceivable that these five men in blue would confer and agree together to commit such an unconscionable, outrageous act? In the final analysis, ladies and gentlemen, what interest did these officers have at the time of the arrest other than to restore law and order under extremely hazardous conditions?"

In his clearly prejudicial charge, Judge Kapp even got to the testimony in Jones's defense, asking the jury if it wasn't introduced "merely in an attempt to contradict and discredit the testimony offered by the officers."

This final push to the jury shortened the time it took them to reach a verdict. It deliberated all of one hour.

LeRoi Jones can be bad enough himself at times, but he certainly brings out the worst in other people. First, he had goaded peace-loving officers of the law into beating him to a pulp and, not stopping there, here he was enticing a decent, God-fearing judge into railroading him to prison. The playwright was lucky to have escaped with his poetry, but Kapp would even get around to that, too—in another chapter of LeRoi's march up Calvary.

The sentencing of LeRoi Jones took place back home in Newark in January and was the final push to the playwright's crown of thorns. Before sentence was passed, Jones's lawyer, Irvin Booker, asked Judge Kapp for leniency. Booker noted that Jones had four natural children and two step-children. The black lawyer also said his client couldn't pay a large fine and nothing would be gained by incarcerating him, which was certainly not the feeling of the Newark police. At one point Booker also said that Jones regretted his acts—while his client sat slumped in a chair, shaking his head no. Asked if he had anything to say before sentencing, Jones was game to the bitter end: "I don't agree with Mr. Booker. I don't think this is a righteous court." Then with his homework behind him and a Greenwich Village literary magazine before him on the bench, Judge Kapp let fly. If LeRoi insisted in his cantankerous way of being a critic of Judge Kapp's courtroom procedure, then the judge would reciprocate by reviewing some of LeRoi's poetry. The man in black robes had the right audience—LeRoi Jones, bearded and scowling, bushy haired, and arrogant as ever, plus a gallery well laced with fans—but the wrong place for a poetry reading, particularly verse written by Jones, who seems to have a fixation on the word "shit." Judge Kapp, reading from the *Evergreen Review,* circum-navigated this problem by tactfully introducing "blank" for all the nasty words:

BLACK PEOPLE

What about that bad short you saw last week
　　on Frelinghuysen, or those stoves and
refrigerators, record players, shotguns,
　　in Sears, Bamberger's, Klein's, Hahnes',
Chase, and the smaller joosh
　　enterprises? What about that bad jewelry, on
Washington Street, and
　　those couple of shops on Springfield? You
know how to get it, you can
　　get it, no money down, no money never,
money don't grow on trees no
　　way, only whitey's got it, makes it with a
machine, to control you
　　you can't steal nothin from a white man, he's
already stole it he owes
　　you everything you want, even his life. All the
stores will open if you
　　will say the magic words. The magic words
are: Up against the wall mother fucker this is a
　　stick up! Or: Smash the

window at night (these are magic actions)
    smash the windows daytime,
anytime, together, lets smash the window
    drag the shit from in there.
No money down. No time to pay.
    Just take what you want. The magic dance
in the street. Run up and down Broad
    Street, niggers, take the shit you want.
Take their lives if need be, but
    get what you want what you need. Dance
up and down the streets, turn all the music up,
    run through the streets with music, beautiful
radios on Market Street, they are brought here
    especially for you. Our brothers
are moving all over, smashing at jellywhite
    faces. We must make our own
World, man, our own world, and we can not
    do this unless the white man is dead.
Let's get together and kill him my
    man, let's get to gather the fruit
of the sun, let's make a world we want black
    children to grow and learn in
do not let your children when they grow
    look in your face and curse you by pitying your tomish ways.

Judge Kapp read a second poem for good measure, then commented: "This diabolical prescription to commit murder and to steal and plunder . . . causes one to suspect that you were a participant in formulating a plot to ignite the spark . . . to burn the city of Newark. . . . It is my considered opinion that you are sick and require medical attention. . . ."

"Not as sick as you are," said Jones, breaking into what was meant to be a soliloquy.

". . . Your talents have been misdirected," Judge Kapp carried on. "You have the ability to make a wholesome contribution to ameliorate existing tensions. . . . Instead we find that you are in the vanguard of a group of extreme radicals who advocate the destruction . . ."

"The destruction of unrighteousness!" shot in Jones, making it a duet.

Kapp's gavel smashed down and Jones, sentenced to an additional thirty days for contempt of court, was led away.

The liberals leaped to the playwright's defense like he had become a helpless, dangling participle—as indeed he had:

"This season it's LeRoi Jones who gets ten times the average jail sentence for his part in the Newark disturbances," wrote Murray Kempton in the New York *Post*. "The charge: being caught with a .32 caliber pistol and imperiling the peace of a city into which the National Guard had fired 10,414 rounds of automatic ammunition that weekend. His actual crime, judging from the court's emphasis at sentence time: offensive poetry."

"LeRoi Jones got the toughest sentence to come out of the Newark riot because he writes lousy poetry," Jimmy Breslin announced on ABC television.

"The sentence is clearly a violation of Jones's right to free speech," said Henry di Suvero, executive director of the New Jersey American Civil Liberties Union. "Judge Kapp is punishing Jones not because of what he is charged with, but because of who he is and what he is."

No matter, Jones may have been free of mind but his body was soon en route to Trenton State Prison. The playwright stayed long enough for them to shave off his beard and give him a haircut. He appeared clean-shaven back in Newark a few days later, free on $25,000 bail—a sum LeRoi termed a ransom. Jones waited while Raymond Brown, prominent New Jersey attorney, appealed the conviction of the playwright and his two companions. It would be a long wait.

What Crime Had They Done?

Compared to the cantankerous Jones, the North 14th Street Black Muslims were models of gentlemanly deportment—but the "justice" afforded them was even worse. Under ordinary circumstances it would have been difficult to make honest identifications of individual prisoners but with the darkness, confusion, and bloody condition of many of them, the task was impossible. Police found themselves with eleven prisoners—ten of whom had been badly beaten—yet participating officers were unable to make any identifications, with the exceptions of Roy Bell and, supposedly, William Jasper. Nor were they sure what the defendants could be charged with. One portion of Detective Scott's report could be taken as truth: "*. . . due to the numbers involved and the fact that all had their heads shaved and were dressed somewhat similarly, personal identification as to who did what is an impossibility with the exception of William Jasper, he being identified by Ptl. Henry Martinez of the Newark Police as having been the man who first struck Capt. Fausto.*"

Giving credence to Scott's report, Fausto visited the office of Assistant Prosecutor Michael Riccardelli, who was to present the matter to the grand jury, and admitted he couldn't identify *any* of the defendants (with the exception of Bell). The captain also said that he wanted the matter dropped. With the prisoners injured as they were this was an impossibility, as Fausto quickly found out. Riccardelli said he let the other police officers "make up their own minds about identifications." They did.

By August 24, when the prisoners were indicted on charges of assaulting police, the officers exhibited a convenient recovery from what must have been temporary amnesia. Jasper, who had been hiding inside the house with Turner and Chisone, was charged with assaulting Fausto and Newark officers Tretola and Martinez. Chisone was charged with assaulting Martinez in the alley after leaping from the second-floor window—when he had actually been arrested after falling down the stairs. Sims was charged with an assault on Fausto, even though the East Orange captain admitted while in the prosecutor's office (and later on to me) that he couldn't identify anyone who had assaulted him.

Roy Bell, the one man who was identifiable, was charged with assaulting Sergeant Fehn. All of the remaining defendants were charged with assaulting various police officers, with the exception of Hardy, who was charged with aiding and abetting in the assaults, and seventeen-year-old Ronald Jones, who had already been acquitted in juvenile court.

Once again, the memory of Newark policemen had healed faster than the wounds of their victims.

For the convenience of the court—and easier identification of the defendants—two trials were scheduled. Those Muslims said to have been arrested outside the house came to trial first, while those arrested inside waited in the wings. Defending all but two Muslims in the first trial and all the defendants in the second was Thomas Kelly, Orange attorney who was assigned the case by the Public Defender. Under the circumstances—the post-riot climate and the unsavory reputations given the Black Muslims by the mass media—it was a less than thankless assignment. Long after the second lawyer bowed out, the thirty-eight-year-old Kelly continued to live with the battle of North 14th Street.

Bell, Chisone, and Sims were found guilty early in February 1968, in the courtroom of Superior Court Judge Joseph S. Lyons. Otis Hardy, a big man who was described as making more than his share of noise on the porch, was declared innocent of aiding and abetting the assaults. William Jasper, who testified he was inside the house during the fighting—the only place he could have been, even according to honest police witnesses—went unbelieved by the all-white jury. The twenty-eight-year-old man was found guilty of separate assaults on Fausto and Tretola, thanks largely to the testimony of Henry Martinez. Jasper was found innocent of assaulting Martinez himself, evidently as the jurors felt the Newark officer just *had* to be wrong about something. A neutral observer would have to agree that Martinez's testimony approached clairvoyance.

At the end of the month the remaining Black Muslims—except for Edward Walker, who failed to show up—and other police officers met again in Judge Lyons' courtroom to re-create their earlier meeting at 91 North 14th Street. If there is room for argument about the arrests outside the building because of the supposed initiating assaults on Fausto and Fehn, there can be none with the disgrace that went on inside. With no announcement of arrest or anything else, police broke down doors and clubbed men who were never given a chance to submit to arrest. Police then tore the house apart. Of the two groups, the wrong one was on trial.

"What were these men being apprehended for in their own home?" Tom Kelly asked the all-white jury in his summation. "What crime had they done and what damage had they suffered compared to the damage suffered by the police? . . . The police in this particular instance manifestly abused the power given them by the state when they invaded this house and when they beat these men within that bedroom and then in the street and then in the police station and then have the audacity of turning around and charging these men with assaulting police officers."

For those twelve contented residents of spacious homes surrounded by green lawns and bird baths that is white, surburban Essex County, Kelly's pertinent questions must have sounded like so much Greek. It took the jurors four hours this time, though, an improvement over the first trial. Black animals lost out to the men in blue once again—guilty to a man. The eight convicted Black Muslims were scheduled for sentencing on April 3.

With twelve judges sitting in the Essex County court system, it was no coincidence that Superior Court Judge James R. Giuliano, the assignment judge, had assigned the LeRoi Jones case to Judge Kapp and the Black Muslim affair to Judge Lyons, the two judges in the county who have never been accused of impartiality. Some attorneys regarded both men as being out-and-out bigots. Such assignments went along nicely with the anti-black post-riot climate.

"What is funny, if they just wanted to arrest us all they had to do was say that and we would have gone along meekly and humbly," Chisone mused after his trial. "No one wants to get his head busted. But I don't think they just wanted to arrest us, they came down there to do something else and I admit it, they sure put a hurtin' on us. The trial was really something, the things the police said. This was the first time I had ever been arrested and the first time I saw a trial other than on Perry Mason and it knocked me out. Some of the things they were saying were unbelievable. This is the type people we have to deal with. I didn't think police would say things like that under oath but I've learned to accept that along with everything else."

Ronald Washington was more bitter in his assessment.

"They looked at us and saw something different they didn't understand," he told me. "They saw something ten times bigger than what we were. They were scared and they hated us. They are what we called them, white devils, and they acted like white devils."

Of all those arrested at the battle of North 14th Street only William Malik Jasper had been unable to make bail. He remained behind bars from July 8 through the trial eight months later and then stayed in jail until the April sentencing. It is ironic that the man who had suffered the most physical punishment—with the possible exception of Washington—was still behind bars and had even been convicted of assaulting two police officers.

Jasper had lived with Edward Walker in the rear of his small restaurant, the "How To Eat To Live Shop." They lived in a worn, three-story brick tenement about seven blocks from the county courthouse. The building has a small mud backyard that ends at a wire fence. Surrounding the tenement is a scene reminiscent of the aftermath of a bombing run—piles of rubble from razed buildings, deserted houses and mounds of earth, all standing in dreary desolation.

With Jasper in jail, Walker was alone with plenty of time to think. "He came down to the court for the first trial when it was my turn," Chisone recalled. "I guess he wanted to see what he could expect. Walker wouldn't even talk about what happened on North Fourteenth Street, he just didn't want to hear anything about it. He would say things like, 'They were a hundred percent wrong as far as I'm concerned,' and 'They were wrong what they did,' and 'Now they want to put me in jail,' stuff like that. You couldn't say anything to him. As the trial went on he told me he was thinking of not coming in but what could I tell him? I accepted it but I couldn't tell him to accept it too. He had to make his own decision."

As the first trial ended with the expected results, Walker was still making up his mind. The week before the beginning of the second trial found Walker still thinking it over. On the first day of the second trial, Walker failed to show. Sheriff's deputies went up the hill those seven blocks to bring him in. They found food cooking on the kitchen stove and the rear door standing open—it had taken a rap on the door for Walker to make up his mind. Footprints in the mud outside pointed in the direction of the rear fence, over which Edward Walker had fled in search of a system of justice he could understand—and another breakfast. He would find only the latter.

Sentencing of the Muslims, postponed by the murder of Martin Luther King, was carried out a week later on April 9. Edward Chisone, Ronald Washington, Belton Williams, Jack Cogman, William Turner, and Roy Bell were all sentenced to eighteen months in prison. Dennis Sims, a juvenile, was given an indeterminate sentence and William Jasper received two to three years on one assault conviction and three to five on the second. Assault on a police officer carries a maximum sentence of seven years. Considering the absurdity of the charges and the overall mockery of justice prevalent throughout the trial, Judge Lyons chose to be lenient.

Tom Kelly immediately set about appealing the convictions and getting the men released on bail, a routine procedure which was complicated by Judge Lyons, who refused to grant bail. There was, the good judge said, no appealable issue. Kelly went to Judge Victor S. Kilkenny of the Superior Court's Appellate Division who, at a loss to explain Lyons' action, set bail for the convicted Muslims. Getting them out of jail, however, was another problem since bondsmen were reluctant to arrange bail for convicted defendants unless someone of means assumed financial responsibility if they went over the hill. Eventually, Kelly himself signed a $1,000 bond for Cogman. Miss Hazel Rollins, friend and co-counsel on the appeal brief, signed for Chisone, and Walter S. Thomas, an insurance broker, signed for Washington. The parents of Turner and Williams signed for their sons and within a month these five prisoners were released. Only Roy Bell was still a resident at Caldwell's Essex County Penitentiary.

Sims was sent to Yardville Reformatory and then moved to Bordentown Reformatory to serve his sentence. Jasper, who had been in jail since his arrest, was sent to Trenton State Prison to begin serving the first of two terms which were to run consecutively—a parting gift from Judge Lyons.

For his efforts on behalf of the Muslims, Tom Kelly captured the esteem of at least one member of Judge Lyons' courtroom. "I see you're running around to get those boogies out in the street," one of Lyons' court clerks cheerfully told him.

Kelly's appeal brief dealt with the issue of identification, as admitted in Scott's report, and the failure of Judge Lyons to mention the issue of self-defense in his charge to the jury.

"Everybody was going to do something for the Black Muslims, all the great liberals," Kelly said. "They were appalled, they were going to do this and that and they were going to get justice. The big-time lawyers came into the case and backed out so fast it made you dizzy. Everybody was going to do something and nobody did a damn thing, not a one. Please never call me a liberal. They're all full of shit. Even the Muslims. I sent a letter to Elijah Muhammad in Chicago asking him to sign for them and he wrote me back telling me to go through the local mosque, Brother Shabazz.[1] The guy came down to the trial but when I asked him to sign

---

[1] The honorable Elijah Muhammad may or may not have returned Kelly's letter, the leader of the Black Muslim movement having died sometime around 1968—one of the best kept secrets of modern times. It is well known, however, to inner circles. "But I read in *Muhammad Speaks* that he's speaking in Chicago this weekend," I said

for the men so I could get them out of jail, he said he couldn't do this and he couldn't do that. He's full of shit, too. The guy drives a Cadillac a block long. Everybody was going to do something for the Muslims and they're all full of shit. Walker had the right idea; I hope the hell he went to Mongolia and they never find him."

You Went Out on the Street with a Gun

Eyvind Chandler was behind bars for the death of Mrs. Jones. Upon his arrest, Chandler gave police a detailed confession of his act of wild shooting. The thankless job of providing his defense then fell to John J. Francis, Jr., who also was assigned by the Public Defender's office.

Quite inexplicably—to almost everyone but Essex County Judge Melvin P. Antell—Chandler was charged with murder, the premeditated killing of a human being. Chandler was suddenly on trial for his life and his attorney felt justice's bite along with the prisoner. In an unusual move, Francis asked for a bill of particulars regarding Chandler's indictment and found that no witnesses to the shooting had even testified before the grand jury which had indicted his client. The thirty-four-year-old attorney had the indictment thrown out. This success, however, was short-lived. Chandler was re-indicted a few days later.

"I couldn't understand it," the soft-spoken Francis said. "For me as an attorney it had always been a clearcut case of manslaughter. Before the trial I discussed a plea to a charge of manslaughter with the prosecutor's office. Then I conferred with Chandler and offered a plea of guilty to the charge of manslaughter to the prosecutor's office with his agreement. This was acceptable to them. Then with both of us agreeing, Judge Antell refused to accept this plea and Chandler went on trial for murder. The prosecution's chief witness, Dolores Jones, Mrs. Jones's daughter, testified that Chandler had never aimed the gun at her mother or even at the man in the car, whom we were never able to find. There were four or five other eye-

---

to Kamiel Wadud, leader of Orthodox Muslims in Newark. "The only way they'll have Elijah there is if they wheel him in his coffin," Wadud responded with his characteristic laugh. It is to the interest of the few who know of his death—the CIA and FBI among them—that the sole sustaining force behind the nationalist Black Muslim movement be "kept alive" for reasons, ironically enough, of national security. The Black Muslim movement in this country is a strange mixture of bona fide spiritual rehabilitation, an economic hustle with mosques all over the country contributing to considerable stored wealth, and a network of informers paid by the federal government to keep tabs on criminal elements within the nation's ghettos. Malcolm X, who started within the movement to become its strongest leader, realized its true nature and broke away to become a grave danger to the movement's existence, a situation rectified by his assassination in Harlem's Audubon Ballroom on February 21, 1965. Malcolm, now recognized for his greatness, was gunned down by Black Muslim stooges with the full knowledge, if not the financial support, of the federal government.

witnesses and none of them testified that Chandler had aimed or had even pointed the gun at Mrs. Jones. After the prosecution had presented its case, I again offered a plea of guilty to manslaughter and the prosecution again said they were willing to accept. But Judge Antell still refused to accept it. The prosecution waived the death penalty but in Judge Antell's charge to the jury he even included a full recitation of the jury's function with respect to the dealth penalty despite the Supreme Court's admonition that it should never have been included in the jury charge in such a case. After all this—thank God—the jury brought in a verdict of manslaughter."

"Well, the jury in its wisdom called the offense manslaughter," Judge Antell told the convicted man at the April 23 sentencing. "I have no choice but to accept their verdict. Naturally, I want you to know that had the verdict been murder, I would have taken it as my solemn obligation to sentence you to thirty years in jail."

Obviously, Judge Antell disagreed with the verdict. The judge, regarded as one of the more liberal in the county, was acting out of character. He appeared to have been influenced by the chaos and death of the riot—but in the wrong way. Doubtlessly Judge Antell's harsh treatment of Chandler had been affected by his sense of responsibility to impose justice in the tragic death of an innocent woman. No one in Judge Antell's legal vicinity had similar feelings about Mrs. Abraham, Mrs. Spellman, Mrs. Gainer or Mrs. Brown, all of whom had been killed by white men.

"You went out on the street with a gun," the judge said to Chandler. "There is only one use for a gun. You want to kill somebody or maim somebody."

Twice, while imposing sentence, Antell said the defendant had "fired through a crowd of people," a statement unsupported by fact. According to the eyewitnesses and the defendant's own confession, Chandler had fired in the direction of the car, *not at* Mrs. Jones or anywhere near any crowd. Further—and more important—Judge Antell's reference to Chandler's intent directly contradicted the trial testimony. Nevertheless, with a possible maximum sentence of ten years, Judge Antell sent Chandler to Trenton State Prison for eight to ten years, at last fulfilling the fate of the only man in the Newark riot to be charged with murder.

"Just a few lines to say hello and many thanks for your service during my trial," Chandler wrote to Francis from cell 240. "I know that you worked many hours on my case. I can't express what I mean in words, but if I ever get free again I will show you how much I appreciate your work in other ways."

The Newark lawyer, appealing only the severity of the sentence, summed up his case in an excellent brief: "More impressive than the background of the Newark riots or the sentencing judge's lingering conception that the jury should have found the defendant guilty of first or second degree murder, was this individual defendant's right to be judged on his own background and character. Eyvind Chandler had never been arrested prior to this time, let alone convicted of a crime. His post-arrest probation record was good. He had finished high school, had a good work record, came from a family with good work habits and could, at the time sentence was imposed, have been gainfully employed."

From Many Blows from Many Directions

John Smith's trial for assault began in late March before Judge Lyons, another "coincidence." By the time all the testimony had been taken five days later, the hapless ex-cab driver was as good as convicted, even as Judge Lyons primed the jury before their deliberation. The issue was a simple one of credibility, Lyons told the jurors—sounding somewhat like Judge Kapp—with the case hinging on whether they believed Smith's version of his arrest or that given by the two police officers. It took the all-white jury six hours to make up its mind.

DeSimone and Pontrelli both testified that Smith's cab had passed them at a high rate of speed and they had pursued it past 9th Street, finally stopping it when Officer Pontrelli tapped on his horn. "I told him to take it easy, to watch his language," Officer DeSimone testified. "He continued so I got out, pointed a finger at him and placed him under arrest for using loud and offensive language." Both policemen said they hadn't used a nightstick on Smith. In other respects, their testimony only repeated their original statements: at no time had Smith been beaten. Two defense witnesses who had been near the Fourth Precinct when the patrol car arrived added sharply contrasting testimony.

"Please don't kill me, please don't kill me," cafeteria cook Herman Dawkins quoted Smith as yelling as the two officers pulled up near the police station. "Nigger, you can get up—you can get up," Dawkins further quoted the police as saying to Smith when the car had stopped.

Miss Ann Thomas, the other witness who had been standing near Dawkins at the time, testified she heard Smith complain of his head aching and of his inability to get out of the car. She testified she had heard Smith yelling even after he had been "thrown into the door of precinct headquarters." Both witnesses testified that Smith was being beaten with a nightstick by the policeman sitting in the passenger's seat but reduced their credibility by not agreeing how many times they had seen the officer swing. And then there was Dawkins' statement that he had seen Smith in the rear seat being beaten. Actually, he later admitted, all he had *seen* was the flailing club. Such minor points must have unsettled the minds of the jurors, who apparently reached a conclusion that not only was Dawkins incorrect as to how many times DeSimone had swung, but the police officer must have been thumping dust out of his back seat.

Defense Attorney Oliver Lofton did score some points, however, in his cross-examination of the two officers. Both DeSimone and Pontrelli admitted they *hadn't even attempted* to handcuff their prisoner or search him. And, even stranger, they supposedly pursued the "speeding taxicab" almost two blocks without using their siren or red dome light.

If the testimony of police and of defense witnesses was at odds, there was no such problem with testimony as to the physical condition of the combatants. Officer Pontrelli suffered a scraped right knee and some "bruises," while DeSimone underwent treatment for a superficial "laceration" of his lower lip and a "bruise" on his chest. John Smith, the defendant charged with having assaulted two policemen, had a hole in his head and numerous bruises over his body, a groin injury which might have been caused—a doctor testified—by a kick or blow from a nightstick, a fractured rib and other damage to his rib cage, all coming "from many blows from many directions."

Smith, in the folds of an old story, being unraveled at his expense, testified in his own behalf—but only in a manner of speaking.

"You knew you would be in difficulty when the policemen asked for your license," stated Assistant Prosecutor Paul T. Murphy.

"Such a condition existed, but I didn't know about the revocation," Smith responded.

"Isn't that the reason you struck the driver?" asked Murphy.

"Know any more jokes?" replied Smith, drawing Judge Lyons' ire.

In the style of LeRoi Jones, Smith also made a nuisance of himself by referring to DeSimone as "little smarty-pants" and his experience inside the fourth precinct as a "little sadistic party." Smith's humor was unappreciated but, nevertheless, closer to the truth than much of the trial's testimony.

From the beginning it appeared that both stories—that of the cab driver and the police—had been colored to suit their respective needs. But testimony on Smith's physical condition could be totally believed: never had the overkill been more blatant. This particular guilty verdict was not only unjust, but inexplicable as well. Smith was found guilty of assaulting DeSimone but not of Pontrelli who, according to medical testimony, had sustained more "bruises" than his partner.

Smith, the last of the riot personalities to be sentenced, appeared before Judge Lyons on May 15. The occasion was highlighted by Lofton's plea for leniency and for a suspended sentence—which fell on deaf ears. "Smith has taken on the psychological responsibility for the riot deaths and has been in a psychological prison for the last ten months," the respected attorney told Judge Lyons.

The articulate Lofton was playing the game by the rules of the hometown team and resorting to rhetoric that might please the old judge's ears. Lofton—one of the coordinators of an unsuccessful drive to place the Newark Police Department in receivership—could well have supplied Lyons with quite another message: Smith had been brutally beaten, his trial was a farce, racist police had taken the occasion of a riot to maim and shoot innocent people, and Lyons himself was a bigoted old man who had no business sitting on that or any other bench.

Lyons sentenced Smith to a two- to three-year prison term. Smith, his hands cuffed behind his back, was led away despite a further entreaty by Lofton that execution of sentence be delayed until he had opportunity to appeal. Like Kelly, Lofton had to try in a higher court with a plea for Smith's release, pending appeal of the conviction. The prosecutor's office then asked the ludicrously high figure of $10,000 bail. Superior Court Judge Edward Gaulkin reduced it to $5,000, still high enough to keep the prosecutor's office happy, and Smith was released nine days later.

The appeal brief was painstaking and lengthy, citing ninety-six cases. It was also noteworthy in that it was sent directly to the Supreme Court of New Jersey and challenged judicial prerequisites as well as certain aspects of the trial. Its essential thrust was the obvious truth that the petit and grand jury systems that had indicted and convicted Smith—as well as all others arrested during the riot—were so constitutionally defective that justice was impossible. The appeal, written by Carl Broege of the Legal Services Project, explained in words and statistics what everyone visiting the Essex County Courthouse already knew: seemingly endless streams of black defendants and white jurors. The United States Constitution, wrote Broege, guaranteed Smith "due process and equal protection rights to an impartial jury representing a cross-section of the community."

The system had excluded Smith's neighbors who were more familiar with police conduct and credibility. Their common knowledge was unimaginable to the jurors he wound up with: an assistant manager for Mutual Benefit Life Insurance, a housewife whose husband was a research analyst—and others equally distant.

All told, fifty-four prospective jurors had been called to fill Smith's jury and only three of them were black. These three were eliminated as a matter of course. "The plain inference," wrote Broege in great understatement, "is the prosecutor determined that, since the defendant was black, it was necessary, as a tactical measure, to remove all black people from the jury."

Broege, a law student at the time the brief was written and now an attorney, used exhaustive research compiled by Dr. Walter Dick of Rutgers University to show that while blacks represented 25 percent of the county's population, they constituted an average of only 6 percent on grand juries. With their juries packed with super-patriots from the Kiwanis, Lions, and Rotary Clubs, the county system was a force for a form of law and order but hardly for justice. It represented "arbitrary picking" rather than random sampling.

> It has been said by many, that the civil disorders with which this case is so tragically connected were to a large extent fermented by the lack of faith of black citizens in the society in which they are living and that this lack of faith is part and parcel with a lack of confidence in the administration of justice whenever the machinery of the courts touches the lives of Negroes. Long ago cases like *Strauder v. West Virginia* held out the Fourteenth Amendment to the United States Constitution as a promise to all citizens, black and white together, that government would treat them as perfect equals. America has too many times reneged on this promise.

While Broege chose his words discreetly, such had not been the case with Governor Hughes following his arrival in riot-torn Newark, as the law student noted in his brief. "New Jersey will show its abhorrence of these criminal activities, and society will protect itself by fair, speedy and *retributive justice,*" Broege quoted Hughes as saying. "Governor Hughes called for rigid prosecution," he continued. "Governor Hughes brought the authority of his office to bear upon the passions of prospective jurors at a time when events alone were enough to create a high pitch of hysteria and prejudice in the city of Newark."

In addition, Broege cited more than thirty cases in contending that the grand and petit juries which had indicted and convicted Smith were unconstitutional. He also cited ten more cases contending that Judge Lyons had made a reversible error after DeSimone and Pontrelli had enjoyed a lunch chat together during the trial. Despite the court's sequestration order, DeSimone, who had testified during the morning session, did discuss with Pontrelli questions he had been asked during Lofton's cross-examination. DeSimone later admitted this from the witness stand. Yet, the motion for a mistrial had been denied.

Finally, the appeal brief dealt with the jury's obvious "cop-out" verdict, finding Smith guilty of assaulting DeSimone but not Pontrelli. "Either the officers' testimony is credible or it is not," Broege wrote. "If it was not credible enough to convict as to Pontrelli, it could not have been credible enough to convict as to DeSimone."

Some Call It Justice

By the time litigation of the riot's black culprits was filed away the credibility of the Newark police had been slightly tarnished, as perjury will do. If there are two occupational groups that can be expected to lie with abandon on the witness stand, they are hardened criminals and experienced police officers. The former lie habitually to protect themselves while the latter do it with equal finesse, largely as a matter of convenience. Prosecutors such as Zazzali in the Jones trial, Murphy, who prosecuted Smith, and Riccardelli and George Franconero, who were both involved in the North 14th Street mess, must know what the police are doing, but look the other way as a matter of practicality. Judges, too, know, but they have reappointments to worry about, especially the political hacks who act as magistrates in the city's municipal courts.

Such permissiveness, of course, only encourages further transgressions to the point where police feel free to say just about anything under oath. Just as no white policeman will ever be punished for murder in Newark, as Hayden said, neither is it likely that any will even face a charge of perjury. As the black majority grows and the mood becomes angrier, so the acceptance of lies becomes part of everyday life. The white population calls it justice, but non-whites have other words to describe it.

Once a police officer looks the other way on a numbers runner and sticks out his hand, a chain reaction begins, setting off far more serious deviations. What would seem to be minor transgressions of duty are stepping stones to total corruption. Likewise the acceptance of straight-faced prevarication leads directly to perjury. There are no such animals as "minor corruption" or "little lies" in this vein, since both evolve into predatory monsters. They are almost never a matter of isolated instances. A police officer who accepts a five-dollar bribe will shortly be in the market for as much "juice" as he can get his hands on. In much the same way, an officer who lies to his sergeant will eventually lie to anyone. The sergeant usually can't afford to care because he is a bigger liar.

Violence perpetrated on ghetto people is condoned by police superiors, if not by overt action then at least by silence. Lies on a witness stand soon follow. Thus, corruption and the breakdown of discipline lead to brutality and police savagery, and eventually arrive at perjury. The Newark Police Department has gone unchecked for so long there is no telling how much it has corrupted itself.

He Couldn't Have Had Anything to Do with a Riot

A few months after his release, John Smith left the Esquire Hotel on South Street, an area off South Broad Street with heavy heroin and prostitution traffic, and moved to more respectable quarters on Clinton Avenue. On July 13, the first anniversary of the Newark riot, an anonymous man with a trumpet and a supply of books checked into the Hotel Riviera, a large brick building standing on the corner of Clinton and High Street. During the ensuing three months, he went to a dentist and had caps put on his teeth. On October 10 the man checked out, leaving a forwarding address: John W. Smith, 616 Marsh, Salisbury, North Carolina. The hotel manager had to use this information but once. On or about December 3, a letter from the New Jersey Division of Motor Vehicles addressed to a John W. Smith arrived at the hotel after his departure. It notified the addressee that he was eligible to apply for a driver's license since his period of revocation had elapsed.

For some reason, the hotel manager was able to recall this guest out of hundreds who had since come and gone. "He seemed to be interested in literature," he remembered. "At least he had quite a number of books in his room. He also had a musical instrument of some kind. I'm sure you are mistaken, though, he couldn't have had anything to do with a riot. You must have the *wrong* Smith."

15

TARZAN AND THE BLACK WITCH DOCTOR

Give 'em Hell, Tony

Handbills urging Nutley's white citizens to "Support Law and Order" had been distributed by kids along the small Newark suburb's streets. They flushed out some 300 men, women, and children who now stood elbow-to-elbow in the Riviera Tavern's parking lot on a warm spring night, waiting to hear what "the niggers" were doing in nearby Newark. In the aftermath of destruction and senseless killing of blacks, came the seemingly inevitable white response.

It was a small crowd by Anthony Imperiale's standards, but they were his kind of people—a mixture of poor and middle class, the paunchy and the robust, the frightened and the brainwashed who didn't understand who the real enemy was. Imperiale, president of Newark's North Ward Citizens Committee, arrived a half-hour late, at 8:30 P.M. He was neatly dressed in an iridescent brown suit and a black turtleneck. The 230-pound man climbed on a table with a microphone and what the crowd lacked in size, they made up in enthusiasm.

"Give 'em hell, Tony," an old man shouted. *"Give 'em hell."* That he would—with no coaxing necessary. Innocently ignorant of the bullet-scarred projects and the splintered wood of Jo Rae's Music Room, Imperiale now carried his law and order rallying cry to a bar parking lot. In front of him were his people, even less informed than he was and as anxious to hear the angry words as citizen Imperiale was to deliver them. Black animals just seven miles away had run wild and burned Newark. Now these people were taking a night off from TV, gathering in a bar parking lot for a lesson from a teacher whose mouth was open but whose eyes were closed.

Imperiale was spreading the word to the fearful "left out" people who had decided they had been ignored long enough. Black Newark was busy just trying to stay alive while its wild kids stuck needles in their arms and stole everything not nailed down and here was Imperiale, telling ghost stories to white children.

"I didn't see any flags in the city of Newark lowered to half-mast when Governor Lurleen Wallace died," he began. "Why not, when they could do it for that Martin Luther *Coon*?" Lusty cheers. "When is it gonna stop?" Imperiale cried. "Everybody says, *'Don't bother 'em now, leave 'em alone and they'll calm down.'* Well, it took riots that burned down half of a town before we learned." With more cheers the voice became more excited, carrying its listeners with it. The momentum was rolling: the lost people were finding themselves and a spokesman.

Imperiale's group had only 200 dues-paying members, but thousands of sympathizers among the ward's 43,000 predominantly Italian residents. They were the same people who had marched in support of Patrolman Martinez after the Lester Long killing and they had been down at City Hall screaming for police dogs after the riot. The Bergen *Record* took note of them in a February 15, 1968, story:

> NEWARK—Angry militants within the white community, many skilled in the use of firearms, judo and karate, are banding together here to meet the threat of Negro riots this summer. They estimate their strength at 1,550, claim to own an armored car and a helicopter, patrol the streets in cars called "Jungle Cruisers," urge the use of dogs by police and vow they are ready to defend themselves.
>
> Saying the Negroes are rumored to be planning an Easter Sunday knife attack on white women and children, group leader Anthony Imperiale, a five-seven, 230-pound karate expert, declared: "If anyone does that around here and if I catch him, I will personally send his head home without his body."
>
> All members of the group, called the North Ward Citizens Committee, are encouraged to own guns and are trained in their use. The group plans to picket, counterpicket and apply political pressure applied by other minority groups. To bolster police patrols, the Citizens Committee's Jungle Cruisers—so called because the area is referred to as "the jungle"—reportedly patrol the neighborhood nightly between nine and midnight. A native of the North Ward, Imperiale attended Webster Street School and Boys Vocational High School. He says he served in the Marines from 1949 to 1953, became a staff sergeant and was honorably discharged. Now 37 and married, he is the father of four children. Besides teaching karate and judo, he is part owner of a small construction business. Asked if there was a central cache of arms, Imperiale hesitated, cast his eyes down and said no. It was the only time that Imperiale balked at answering a question or failed to look directly at the person to whom he was speaking.
>
> As a parting gesture, he issued a warning to the Negro community. Talking about alleged rumors of Negro plots to kill police and white families, he said: "That's one of the oldest commie tricks, to instill fear. They're

making a mistake. It's only making people more angry: if it's supposed to be a warning to us, then let this be a warning to them. Don't come into the North Ward and try anything."

Such melodramatic nonsense swelled the Imperiale crusade, turning it into a reality just big enough to be picked up by the mass media, which found Imperiale an interesting subject. Imperiale was on his way to a dubious notoriety: a chunky, balding man waving a rifle in front of TV cameras and urging others to do likewise in a garble of "dems" and "dose" that would improve with exposure but would never approach the finesse of a LeRoi Jones.

They Want to Know If You Love Them

Jones's voice carried a pleading ring that matched the wounded look in his dark eyes and carried out over an audience of at least a thousand blacks.

"Newark is a black city," he told them. "White people leave after five o'clock and they leave you with fallen-down buildings, rats and garbage. They give you liquor, heroin, and hair-straighteners and then they want to know if you love them." His brown arms came from beneath the colorful dashike and the hands gripped the podium's outer edge. The man was sweating, big drops running down his face.

"What we have that we love we make for ourselves, things we value are black things," Jones cried out. "The white man hasn't given you anything since he brought you here." His brow furrowed and his voice rose. He leaned forward with both elbows and arms cradling the podium and the voice pleaded. "We were brought here as slaves and to be slaves and do the white people's work. They brought you here and now they tell you you're free. You'll never be free without power—black power is the control of our own lives. This is the power we're asking for, the power to declare war, the power to be men even if it is alien to the wishes of the white people, even if they do not like it. If you would only come together and unite they wouldn't bother you. Black people here are slaves because they like being slaves. You must like it or you wouldn't let it continue."

The black throng echoed its approval, filling South Side High School's large auditorium with a dull roar. While the people in Imperiale's parking lot cursed an illusory enemy, those from Jones's ghetto groped toward a real identity. From poet-playwright to bloodied victim of the riot, LeRoi Jones now thrashed with a straw broom against the wall of Newark's corrupt political machine. This was basically what he had prophesied for himself in 1963:

LeRoi Jones: born October 7, 1934 in the dumb industrial complex of Newark, New Jersey, the son of Coyette L. Jones, a postal supervisor, and

Ann L. R. Jones, a social worker. Went to school in Newark in guise of skinny, prim middle-class Negro, i.e., lower middle-class American, but drifted about the Third Ward slum to meet junkies, whores, drugs, general dissolution and thus protect myself against the shabbiness of "black bourgeois" projected social progress. Went to Rutgers, Howard, New School, Columbia. Secured to phenomenology and religion. All of this interrupted by the air force, where I served as a weather-gunner and read a great deal.[2] Began to publish after release. Then began the magazine *Yugen* and Totem Press. Married a middle-class Jewish lady as protection against Bohemia, produced in quick succession two beautiful mulatto girls. Writing nonfiction books and teaching at New School. Aspirant political agitator with a tapped phone.

After three more years of wandering in the wilderness of junkies and whores, Jones moved closer to his aspiration. In the Harlem of 1966, lovable LeRoi could see it all clearly: "It's simple, Harlem as an independent state with its own laws—black laws—and its own culture—black culture. It will be the only future in this country—the black future. If any whites should still be around, they might be allowed to wander through the black world as tired, placid tourists."

The dream for Harlem became the playwright's quest for Newark.

Following the riot and his harsh prison sentence, Jones had that much more fuel for his furnace, which was now going at full blast. In January the Afro-American Club invited Mrs. Sylvia Jones to speak at a Central High School meeting and Mr. Jones abruptly substituted. LeRoi, who can be curt with his explanations, mumbled, "My wife has a throat ache." He then told his audience: "The white man has made us slaves, starved us, beaten us, taken our women, made us live like pigs and caused us to suffer as no animal should."

A similar appearance by the playwright at Intermediate School 201 in Harlem a short time before when one of his plays was presented, had caused an earlier stir. The subtle message of the play—which contained such immortal lines as "Whitey! Whitey! Who should we lynch! Whitey! Whitey!"—was too much for three teachers who walked out during the performance. One of them asked for reassignment to another school.

It was subsequently learned that Jones had been appointed chairman of an advisory committee at the Robert Treat Elementary School in Newark, his job being to advise the school's administration on expenditure of $79,-697 in federal funds allotted for special education programs for deprived children. The Board of Education's reaction to this might be imagined. One member called for suspension of whoever had been responsible for

---

[2] After serving two years in the Air Force, Jones was given a general discharge because of what was termed a fraudulent application. The playwright had neglected to mention membership in the Civil Rights Congress, an organization then listed as subversive by the U.S. Attorney General.

Jones's hiring. That individual honestly responded that he had been instructed to hire "people with interest in the school attendance area." As
would be seen later, few had more interest in school attendance than LeRoi
Jones.

If the Board of Education lacked appreciation for the playwright's gratis
appearance, colleges were ready to pay for his services—but only once.

In February, Jones and his theatrical troupe traveled to the Madison
campus of Fairleigh Dickinson University where they made an entrance
some seventy minutes late. LeRoi explained he had "experienced car
trouble." A welcoming committee, however, was still on hand: a tight
police guard around the gymnasium, stage, and campus and a dozen uniformed police, State Police plainclothesmen and both the Florham Park
and Madison police chiefs. Speaking before some 200 interested students,
Jones cut his talk to ten minutes and included his standard theme: "Newark
is a ghetto because white people control it. They live in Short Hills, Par-
sippany, and Madison, come in and take the money out." This was followed by a twenty-minute satirical skit, *Home on the Range,* after which
Jones was through for the night. After his valid comments on the white
suburbs of Newark, Jones did his part to reverse the economic drain. He
returned to the city with $750 of the university's money as his fee.

"With cops all over the place," Jones quipped, "they must think we were
coming to steal the place."

Unity was the only message at the South Side High School rally in Newark, the first held by the United Brothers, a new political group backed by
Jones. Maulana Ron Karenga of "US," Los Angeles-based black nationalist group, called generally for blacks to "think, talk, act and love black,"
and Jones made a direct plea for support and participation in a June political convention to select black candidates for two councilman-at-large
seats in the November election. Looking beyond the convention—Newark's
first such gathering and a beginning of true political awareness—Jones
hoped to unite the city's non-whites behind a single black candidate for
the mayoralty election to be held in May of 1970. He proceeded along
those lines, deriding Newark's two Negro councilmen, the aging Turner
and the amiable West. LeRoi also had some kind words for his favorite
newspaper, calling for a boycott of the Newark *Evening News* and promising to start his own paper, *Black Newark.*

Newark's blacks didn't need any newspaper to understand distrust and
hate, having had much experience of both. Imperiale made matters worse.
While his own gatherings were, at best, out-and-out racist demonstrations
followed by beer and pretzels, Imperiale found it his duty to send a telegram to the Human Rights Commission complaining of the "racist meet-

ing" at the high school—before the event had even begun. The cheerful message was read to the packed auditorium, further assuring the audience of the clarity of Imperiale's vision.

He Said I Was a Diamond in d'Rough

Anthony Imperiale, youngest of a family of nine, also spent his childhood in Newark, though in another part of town than did LeRoi Jones. When he was thirteen, police found his father, a nightshift worker at a button factory, murdered and floating in the Passaic River with forty-eight cents in his pocket. Three years later Tony, who described himself as a "rebellious little bastard," dropped out of high school and went to work in a garment factory. From there he enlisted in the Marines, where he remained for a few years as a disciplinary problem. Hardly an example of law and order in those days, he was discharged—according to a federal dossier— "under conditions other than honorable." After the Marine experience, Tony became a welder in a factory where things went relatively smoothly for two years until—according to Imperiale—he punched another worker.

"In fact," said Tony proudly, "if it wasn't for my friends who pulled me off, I think I'da busted his ribs."

As his next endeavor, Imperiale answered a newspaper ad and entered the "fund raising field." Here, in a position more to his liking, he commanded a four-man crew collecting old clothing for a firm that had contracts with various charitable organizations. "Wit'in eight mont's I was being tutored in English on request of the owner," Tony said. "He said I was a diamond in d'rough. Wit'in one year I was his t'ird in command. I handled hirin', firin' and payroll."

As a traveling troubleshooter for the firm, Imperiale visited out-of-town drops and, in his own quaint way, resolved labor difficulties with a finesse marking him for bigger and better things. In Nyack, for example, Imperiale looked in on a dispute between workers and a crew chief and, when challenged, utilized his diplomacy and knowhow. "He went home to his wife wit' two black eyes and a fractured nose," said Tony. "I then resumed hearin' de grievances." However, company checks began to bounce as high as the disrespectful crew chief and Imperiale's firm folded.

Undaunted, Imperiale rented a storeroom for twenty-five dollars a month and went into business for himself, selling used clothing to New York exporters for shipment to Italy and Algeria. Unfortunately, he had forgotten to purchase a license and was soon out of business. Next came a stint as a Pinkerton plant guard where—according to Imperiale—he wore his uniform with such aplomb that he was soon promoted to undercover work.

But another argument soon moved Tony to a more lucrative field of police work, a private detective bureau in West Orange that specialized in divorce work. Here Imperiale learned more sophisticated techniques of law enforcement. Accompanied by two photographers, Imperiale's job was to break into motel rooms occupied by unfaithful spouses. Tony soon learned never to trust a disrobed woman.

"Dis one guy was a bruiser," he recalled. "He knocked da shit outa our two photographers, den he looked at me and said, 'And you, squirt, I'm gonna bend yuh like a pretzel.' I didn't feature dat. I resorted to my judo and karate. So after I beat the shit outa *him* dis woman plowed me on d'head wit' a lamp. I don't know what kept me alive, but I put my hand in her face and pushed her on d'bed and told her I'd break her up like her boy friend if she ever tried dat again."

In his renditions, Tony has never lost a fight. Nevertheless, this form of police work eventually lost its allure and Tony spent the next few years aimlessly drifting back and forth among a variety of jobs, including selling fish in a supermarket, driving a bus and truck, another fling at detective work, construction labor, running his own delicatessen, building summer patios, and overseeing a karate school, all with varying degrees of success. Imperiale's bus driving career ended abruptly one day during a heavy rainstorm when he suggested to his riders that they adjourn to a nearby tavern for some refreshment. The delicatessen venture ended after a burglary when Tony discovered he had bought pilferage instead of burglary insurance.

Sometime during all this Imperiale—to his credit—had four sons, managed to get a high school equivalency diploma, and perfected his judo and karate enough to obtain black belt status, an effective publicity gimmick. During this time, Tony also made numerous applications to bona fide law-enforcement agencies. He was rejected each time.

Imperiale also developed a familiarity with the terms "nigger" and "coon" that did wonders for his popularity. Soon the leader of a small but growing group of God-fearing citizens, punks and do-gooders, Imperiale made his first notable appearance in post-riot Newark by "testifying" before the PBA riot hearings. He related how he and about forty of his neighbors had armed themselves during the riot—the reasoning behind such an act being far-fetched since the rioting was far away. Certainly, there was no disturbance in the North Ward that would justify men walking around with shotguns and rifles.

Not stopping there, Imperiale firmly established his organization's flair for bravado and thrilled his young admirers by also relating how his group had engaged in several "gunfights" with rioters in the area, including one in which he said several of the enemy had been shot.

An honest effort to understand the man made a trip with him into the Springfield Avenue ghetto a necessity, first, to see if he had nerve enough to come with me and, second, to establish if there was any insight behind the man's beliefs—which by this time had turned some white communities into armed camps. By 1:00 A.M. smoke and black men, pretty black girls in blond wigs and dark-skinned foxes had turned this bar on the avenue into a wild, shadowy Saturday night thing. Imperiale ordered scotch on the rocks, his favorite drink.

"I grew up with them, I played with them and I ate with them," he offered.

"And loved their women, too?" he was asked.

"I'd be lying if I said no," the beefy man replied. "Negroes visit my home all the time. There are a few families on the other side of the street."

Once we had entered the bar—one of the nastiest in black Newark—the first question was answered. There was nothing wrong with Imperiale's nerve. Back at his home on Summer Avenue, we had left his wife, Louise, and two executive leaders of the North Ward Citizens Committee, Dom De-Anthony, thirty-nine, and Rick Couzzi, fifty-six. She told her husband not to go, while the other two acted as if I had been sent to lure their leader down into the strip so he would get his head busted. "Well, if you're gonna die," Imperiale told me on the ride down, "you're gonna die."

The first thing to understand about Tony Imperiale is his total ignorance of what had actually taken place during the riot and his lack of interest in finding out. When informed of several viewpoints which ran contrary to his own, Imperiale's response was positive. "Every gun has its own ballistics," he said. "They should check every gun and find out who killed those people."

"If they find out a policeman was guilty of murder or manslaughter, would you arrest him?"

"I sure would," he responded.

Al Black had the same view, as does any man who believes in justice. Yet these two men—Imperiale and the chairman of the Human Rights Commission—had argued at a city council meeting about police dogs in the ghetto and were supposed to represent the opposite extremes of every issue. Black believed that Imperiale hated black people and Imperiale thought Black just wanted to run over white people. Nothing would convince them otherwise, and relaxed conversation in such a setting as this was out of the question for them.

"If making Eddie Williams captain of the Fourth Precinct gives all the colored people in Newark something to look up to and improves the situation, then I'm for it," Imperiale said—another topic he and Black agreed on. While Black didn't think much of Mayor Addonizio, Imperiale thought even less. "Nobody liked the way Addonizio reacted after the riot," he said. Imperiale also believed a sniper had killed Fire Captain Moran because that's what he had been told. Now, after being informed of another view, Imperiale showed signs of growing consciousness. He said that Governor Hughes had done wrong letting people believe something that was highly questionable. Al Black had the same view.

"All we want is unity," Imperiale said. "Black and white, colored neighbors helping white neighbors, unity in our community." This was a message that had failed to emerge from the North Ward leader's previous appearances. Imperiale also exhibited some common sense. He really didn't believe that nonsense about an Easter Sunday knife attack, his group had only 200 hardcore members, there was no stockpile of weapons, and for the eight rifles and shotguns in his home there was ammunition for only three of them.

"I think the K-9 corps would be a good thing for Newark," Imperiale persisted.

"Look around you at all the brown faces," he was told. "Mention dogs and they think they're back in Alabama. They see hate and after that they won't listen to anybody. It's an emotional thing, a symbol. If you want to talk about other constructive things, you can't start with a word that means hate."

"What difference would a civilian review board make?" Imperiale said later. "That's a lotta crap."

"Don't you see that if the colored community had some hope of meaningful redress they wouldn't have to resort to violence over a thing like the Smith beating?"

"Maybe you're right," he replied. "We'll put the dog issue aside. I don't think the police review board is a good thing but we'll put these things aside and talk. I'd like to talk to Al Black and anyone else who wants to better the community."

"That would be a good idea," he was told.

"Maybe something can come from this," Imperiale said.

Upon reading of the Imperiale group in the *Record* story, I had been skeptical that it was as menacing as presented. My naivete led to hope that the tense situation in Newark would be lessened if Imperiale were acquainted with some accurate information. The meeting became a must. I felt he would come to the strip with me, if for no other reason than vanity, since in effect I was daring him. This was the only part of the notion that proved correct and all that came of the trip was an article in the Elizabeth *Daily Journal*.

The *Record*'s story had made him appear a blood-spitting vigilante and mine depicted him as a misunderstood moderate willing to listen to reason. In a comic touch, Imperiale threatened to sue both newspapers.

The North Ward Citizens Commitee continued to base its appeal on misinformation, fear, and emotional hang-ups. One indication of those attitudes occurred at the Imperiale home while talking to DeAnthony and Couzzi before we left for the strip. DeAnthony related how he had been on Market Street in downtown Newark with his teenage daughter and had left her alone for a few minutes.

"Go ahead, tell him what happened to you," he urged her.

"A colored man winked at me," she said.

DeAnthony didn't want to know about the shameful way Italian boys from his neighborhood treated black girls, a treatment that if reversed would be enough to start a race riot. Couzzi, a founding father of the North Ward Citizens Committee and basically a good-natured man, exhibited a store of erroneous knowledge that explained where the committee got some of its misinformation. "Oh, come on, Ron, you know where Hayden gets his money," he said. Having dismissed Tom Hayden in one sentence, he next examined John Smith, passing the word that the cab driver had been paid by the communists to attack the two policemen.

Imperiale represents the dichotomy between the personal man and the public image, the good guy next door and the raving demagogue telling a crowd what it wants to hear. Tony is a nice enough guy who went through thirty-seven anonymous years until he happened to see himself on television and went hairy in the roar of the crowd. With notoriety came the expected affectations: Man Tan, a toupee, flashy dress, a Cadillac. His single message was as consistent as was Jones's, the rousing talk at Nutley as good an example as any. "You've been fortunate not to have been hit by a riot yet," Imperiale told the crowd, pushing improbability to the limit. "You know that the enforcement of law is what the taxpayer depends upon. This is how we feel safe. This is that one thin line between us—law and order, the boys in blue."

Politically, Imperiale was a Goldwater man in 1964 and later a staunch supporter of George Wallace. John Behringer, the state Ku Klux Klan Grand Dragon, claimed he had inducted the North Ward leader into the Klan at a West Caldwell ceremony in April of 1967.

Imperiale said he wanted peace, yet he helped spread the Easter attack nonsense. He wanted unity and security for his own people, yet he sent the telegram to the Human Rights Commission which invited trouble. He called for responsible black leadership, yet he publicly denounced Martin Luther King during his March visit to Newark. The discrepancy between what the man said in candid conversations and what he caused to happen can't be reconciled. In the final analysis, Imperiale's main contribution to Newark's peace was major, though unusual: he kept control of his own group. Within months, this one man had helped turn Newark into a polarized city. Calling for law and order, Imperiale created an unprecedented climate for violence. In the process, he made himself a political force.

We Are Fighting for the Power to Define Our Lives

Post-riot Newark had evolved into a vocal confrontation between Imperiale's followers and those of Jones, a confrontation which was threatening to become violent. LeRoi Jones, the leader without community support, and Tony Imperiale, who had a throng of shouting supporters but no knowledge with which to lead them, were pushed to the forefront.

Their match-up was a natural for the mass media: Jones, the bearded thirty-four-year-old black poet and playwright, a Muslim; Imperiale, the thirty-seven-year-old karate instructor and ex-Marine, a Catholic. One slightly built with eloquent hands and dark, wounded eyes; the other a barrel of flesh with "Death Before Dishonor" and "Louise and Tony" tattoos decorating his beefy arms. One an intellectual who studied Frantz Fanon's *The Wretched of the Earth,* the other a man without insight or proportion, who attached great importance to the philosophical utterances of George Wallace.

"Essentially what we are fighting for is the power to define our lives," Jones stated. "Newark is a city where black people are in the majority and we mean to be masters of our own space."

"We are very disturbed with conditions and the way the riots were handled," said Imperiale. "We must untie the hands of the police department and restore full authority and law enforcement."

Imperiale hated the junkies and hoodlums, while Jones despised the heroin and those who sold it because it perverted his people. Rather than blaming a racist society that created the drug problem, the city administration that nurtured it, and the police department that exploited it, Imperiale wanted to punish its victims. Jones wanted control of the ghetto by blacks to re-educate the people while Imperiale, who could see no farther ahead than his shoes, wanted to put them all in jail. Jones looked to meaningful change while Imperiale swatted at flies, ignoring the disease giving them birth. Jones had been turned into a bloodied martyr by the Newark police and took upon himself the task of unifying black Newark. Imperiale turned himself into the neighborhood hero, charging off on what amounted to his own moral crusade.

But it was the Italians who controlled a corrupt, racist police department, directed a city administration with corruption so long entrenched that it defied grand juries and who made up the Mafia hierarchy pouring heroin into the city. If Tony Imperiale had dedicated himself to moral reform, he had chosen the right locality but the wrong people to begin with.

"A Bunch of Commie Animals"

It was only Imperiale's welcoming committee for the New Jersey American Civil Liberties Union's 1968 annual membership meeting that saved the event from mediocrity. At least thirty-eight pickets—including about a dozen off-duty police officers—braved cigarette butts and cups of water dropped on them by disrespectful hotel guests while they trudged the sidewalk in front of the Military Park Hotel in downtown Newark with messages of law and order.

In 1965 after the Long shooting, James Farmer had marched to Military Park for a civilian review board. Shootings, beatings, and finally a riot had followed and Governor Hughes's commissioners recommended a review board with the same result: off-duty police marching with intimidating .38s. Now as ACLU members prepared to discuss the Hughes Report, law and order advocates were marching again at the site where it had begun three years before. The man who had prompted that crisis—Henry Martinez, now a good friend of Imperiale—was on hand once again.

The ACLU people arriving for their meeting were greeted by placards reading ACLU ARE FINKS, N.J. RIOT REPORT STINKS, and SUPPORT LAW AND ORDER. The demonstrators belonged to the North Ward organization and a group called Women's Organization for the Return of Law and Decency (WORLD), which consisted largely of policemen's wives and female relatives of the former group.

Another of the placards was UNTIE POLICEMEN'S HANDS, and—even the staunchest Imperiale supporters would have to admit—the events of Saturday, April 20, fulfilled this entreaty beyond wildest expectations. "We've tired of the ACLU coming into Newark and trying to run our city," said Imperiale. "This jazz about police brutality is nonsense. The ACLU is a bunch of commie animals."

The experience of Ronald Kurtenbach, twenty-six-year-old conscientious objector who was serving his alternative service at Bethany Baptist Church in Newark, prefaced the day's events. Kurtenbach, one of those gentle rarities who should be preserved in a glass bottle, is one who insists that the evils of the world can be eased by meaningful communication. While walking past the picket line, he became engaged in conversation with its members and ultimately with Imperiale himself, a rather large man in a white turtleneck sweater, he remembered. Imperiale told Kurtenbach that looters should be shot and the church worker naturally replied he didn't think so, calling into play Imperiale's tactics when at his wit's end. He grabbed Kurtenbach by the collar and, dragging him to the corner, threatened to push him into a sewer. A plainclothes police officer,

one of Imperiale's supporters, showed Kurtenbach a badge and told him to
get out of the area or *he* would be arrested—for loitering.

At 11:45 A.M., Mrs. Rita D'Joseph, the ACLU's education director,
approached the hotel entrance with a box of paraphernalia to be used at
the meeting. The pickets hurled insults but she entered the hotel without
physical incident. On her second trip from the car with additional material,
however, she was pushed and kicked in the shin, hard enough to draw
blood. The police, stricken with sunblindness, saw nothing.

Inside the hotel, Mrs. D'Joseph wiped the blood from her leg and
composed herself. She then called Henry di Suvero, the state ACLU
executive director. Di Suvero and L. Walter Finch, a state ACLU board
member, found Mrs. D'Joseph inside the lobby. She related that she had
pointed out one of those who had assaulted her to a police sergeant, but
he had done nothing. The trio found the sergeant in the hotel foyer and
di Suvero told him they wanted to press charges against the man Mrs.
D'Joseph had identified.

Finch and di Suvero went to the front steps where Mrs. D'Joseph
pointed out the picket who had kicked her—a man described as about
five feet eight, with sunken teeth, a two-day growth of beard and who
appeared to be tipsy, drifting in and out of the picket line. The ACLU
executive again approached the sergeant, again telling him he had identified
the man who had assaulted Mrs. D'Joseph. The sergeant said again that
everything was under control and that the suspect was being watched.
Di Suvero, getting an inkling of what was happening, walked toward what
appeared to be a newspaper photographer standing on the curb.

"We want to press countercharges, we want to press countercharges,"
Imperiale began to yell, and the pickets picked it up. Ignoring the clamor,
di Suvero asked Joseph Bruno, who had been hired by Imperiale to take
photos, if he worked for the Newark *News*. "I don't work for that commie
paper," Bruno, a rather intense individual, replied. "You say we pushed
your women, we don't push women," Imperiale shouted at di Suvero,
joining the pair. The North Ward leader continued to shake his fist and
shout, "You pushed our women, you were pushing a pregnant woman,
everybody here saw it."

"He pushed a pregnant woman," the pickets began chanting, *"he's a
communist, he's a faggot."*

Di Suvero and Finch walked away and stood with their backs to the
hotel wall, facing the walking pickets. "I don't give a damn who hears
me, whether these cops hear me or not," shouted Imperiale, following
them and pointing a finger in di Suvero's face. "Whether they lock me
up, whether I go to jail or not, you're not going to get away with pushing
our women around."

In chorus, the pickets picked up this newest chant, *"the faggot pushed a pregnant woman.*" Di Suvero was then pushed backward against the hotel wall by a female picketer, whose identity he wasn't sure of. The next thing the ACLU leader realized, a hefty picketer, Miss Marie Di-Bernardo, WORLD's treasurer, was shouting that *she* had been assaulted. Donald Mangione—husband of WORLD president Lucille Mangione, a WORLD "adviser" himself, Miss DiBernardo's brother-in-law and also an off-duty Newark policeman, all rolled into one—gallantly stepped from the picket line and placed di Suvero under arrest. The slightly built ACLU leader put up quite a struggle—according to Mangione—which brought Joseph Tunnero, another off-duty policeman and Mangione's partner, into the "fray."

With the two police officers on either side of di Suvero, propelling him toward a police car, Imperiale then struck a blow for law and order. Quickly and with the finesse of a karate expert he punched di Suvero—in the genitals. Police at the scene also failed to notice Imperiale's *coup de grâce,* but his God-fearing, family-loving, commie-hating, law-abiding, peaceful citizens screamed with delight.

"He's a faggot," one yelled.

"What's he bending over for?" a woman shouted. "He's got nothing there!"

The thirty-two-year-old di Suvero was taken to the third precinct and booked. He was charged with assault and battery on Miss DiBernardo, resisting arrest and using loud and profane language. After he was taken to a cell, two police officers separately approached him and asked if he was Italian. Di Suvero replied that he was, to which one responded, "You better not say it too loud around here." As di Suvero was being transported to headquarters downtown for fingerprinting and photographing, the two officers who were taking him received some kindly advice from their sergeant: "I don't want no trouble. No detours or any funny stuff. Do you understand? I want him brought right up there."

Bail for di Suvero, a Harvard Law School graduate, a member of two state bars, and a family man with three children, was set by Municipal Judge Aaron Narol inexplicably at $1,000. After his release five hours later, di Suvero learned of a fourth charge, threatening a police officer. Four days later Mangione and Miss DiBernardo went to a doctor to be treated for "wounds" suffered during the struggle. The ACLU filed a federal suit six days after di Suvero's arrest against Imperiale and the Newark Police Department, charging a conspiracy between Imperiale's organization and the police and asking the federal district court to restrain the illegal activities of the Imperiale group. At eight o'clock that night Mangione added a fifth charge, assault on a police officer—namely himself.

This charge, and the only other indictable offense against di Suvero, threatening the life of a police officer, were subsequently dismissed by the grand jury.

After the jurors had listened to Mangione's bizarre testimony on his "wounds," which an assistant prosecutor personally described to me as being "suspicious," it was the least the jurors could do. Another charge against di Suvero, using loud and profane language, a misdemeanor, was also dismissed. This left the ACLU leader with but two remaining charges, simple assault on Miss DiBernardo and resisting arrest, which were subsequently tried in municipal court.

The di Suvero trial lasted seven days. Photographs taken by Bruno were subpoenaed by the court and proved to be embarrassing for the police. Henry Martinez, whose testimony at the Muslims' trial had been incredible, told me he had merely been "driving by the hotel" when he happened on the picketing. A photograph showed him clutching a placard. Another prosecution witness was Ronald Gasperinetti, the most notorious police officer in Newark. He also testified he had not been picketing—but another photograph showed him holding a placard inscribed, UNTIE POLICE HANDS, in his case a joke.

Then there was Officer Tunnero, who had testified previously in a federal hearing that he hadn't been picketing. He, too, was shown in a photo grasping a placard. Tunnero's reason for being at the hotel was also humorous. It seems, the police officer testified, Mangione's wife and two children were marching in the picket line and he was there to aid his partner in looking after them.

"I came to bring water and food or help if the baby cries," Tunnero explained.

"I see," said Len Weinglass, attorney for di Suvero, "you came to bring *milk for the kiddies.*"

As interesting as the legal proceedings were, there was also extracurricular activity. While the trial was in progress, Mangione and Tunnero came upon Ronald Kurtenbach again, this time talking with Mangione's twelve-year-old son in front of the policeman's home. Kurtenbach was arrested for failing to obey an order to move on. Apparently unaware of the young man's religious affiliations, the police officers even charged him with possession of a four-inch knife that had mysteriously materialized. For Mangione in particular, the arrest of di Suvero was the highlight of his four-year police career, and at times it appeared that he was going off the deep end. On several occasions he interrupted courtroom proceedings to shout out some thought of his own and, after some damaging defense testimony, Mangione actually threatened the witness outside the courtroom.

"I think we've witnessed here," Weinglass said in his summation, "an unfortunate spectacle of police officers—and I say this advisedly—committing perjury in an attempt to cover up an illegal action which they took on the streets of the city."

Judge William H. Walls, possibly the most proficient judge sitting in municipal court, agreed. He described the testimony of prosecution witnesses as "improbable," "inconsistent," and "colored by that type of self-interest which the courts have recognized as removing a witness from the category of the disinterested." Judge Walls acquitted di Suvero.

By the trial's conclusion, however, the verdict was overshadowed by the clear view that had emerged of Imperiale and his group, many of them bona fide police officers who sincerely believed themselves the saviors of white Newark. They felt justified no matter what their actions. Another observation was that although LeRoi Jones, John Smith, and the Black Muslims could be railroaded into prison terms on perjured testimony, such could not be the case for a prominent white attorney.

Riots Are Much More than Anti-Social Protest

By this time the confrontation in post-riot Newark was complete. LeRoi Jones was heralded only by his inflammatory poetry and plays which were more than enough to damn him, even in the eyes of middle-class blacks. Imperiale, on the other hand, came with a grass-roots organization the playwright could only dream of duplicating. One would come to political power while the other would seem limited to exhorting his people in the wilderness.

"Riots are much more than anti-social behavior," Tom Hayden had written. "Riots must be viewed both as a new stage in the development of Negro protest against racism and as a logical outgrowth of the failure of the whole society to support racial equality. A riot represents people making history."

So they did make history, putting Newark on the map. Ironically, with Hayden now long gone to other battlefields, the seeds of discontent and political self-realization Hayden and his NCUP people had hoped to plant in the sprawling ghetto were now being fertilized by Imperiale's rhetoric and were growing in the white wards.

16

FIRE AND FAIRY TALES

Can We Use the Shotguns?

Hoodlums began setting fires in broad daylight and the still-scarred city staggered toward sundown in the smell of burning tenements. Martin Luther King had been murdered and on April 9, the day of his burial more than 800 miles away in Atlanta, the city of Newark was burning. A first blaze started up at 2:30 P.M. at Bergen Street and Springfield Avenue, westerly winds drifting heavy, acrid smoke down the avenue past boarded-up stores which had never recovered from the riot, past ever-moving patrol cars with shotguns protruding from their windows, past scores of hard-looking black kids who came together in little groups that eventually swelled into throngs. They were Newark's children, one out of every three high school students a dropout and four out of every ten teenagers unemployed. They came mean and angry from their ghettos within Newark's twenty-three square miles—a quarter of it taken up by Newark Airport, Port Newark and uninhabitable marshlands—which give Newark the highest population density of any major city in the country.

Beaten black people who had survived into middle age stood on the sidewalks watching their ghettos burn as their children gathered in restless gangs. Hardcore hoodlums started their fires and disappeared, reappearing blocks away in another burst of flames as the black youths of Newark—disinherited members of a crumbling city and products of a culture of poverty who embraced crime as a way of life—took to the cobblestone avenue in their own wake for a non-violent man who actually meant little to them. Martin Luther King had visited Newark only a week before, meeting the city's Negro ministers who were now touring the streets in police cars with loudspeakers urging restraint. King had come for donations for his poor people's march on Washington and some of those same ministers now rode through the ghetto with "I have a dream" recordings hanging heavy in the hot air, a message designed to keep Newark sane but which would only infuriate people more. Those hearing the words "Great God Almighty, free at last" could only spit in disgust. With the death of a man of peace had come the ultimate crisis for Newark, to burn or not to burn. The reluctance to use the firebomb that had marked the 1967 riot was gone. The riot's shameful bloodshed and its callous aftermath had produced a more vicious and violent brand of hoodlum.

Drifting through these clusters of wild young kids were new entries in the drama, Orthodox Muslims in red tarbooshes who spoke calmly and with poise. Ghetto products they were but their demeanor was that of noblemen who had traced their ancestry back to the Hamitic tribes. They were followers of the prophet Muhammad and the assassinated Malcolm X, brown-skinned men who smiled at insipid terms like Negro and Afro-American.

As more fires broke out, the Muslims walked among the crowds of teen-agers as peacemakers urging restraint, adding their voices to an experiment to save the city. The Greater Newark Chamber of Commerce was paying 500 young UCC workers five bucks a head to circulate through the ghetto calling for calm and many potential looters found themselves wearing black peacemaker armbands instead.

At 6:00 P.M. there was a meeting at UCC headquarters on Branford Place off the downtown area. Willie Wright, then UCC vice president and a vocal militant who headed his own Afro-American Association, took one look at the police shotguns and angrily walked out. LeRoi Jones, the only other man in the city who could be called a real live black militant, stayed and even recorded tapes telling the kids to stay off the streets. But regardless of what anyone did, mobs of angry kids were forming in the Central and South Wards as they had the year before.

By 9:00 P.M., where Prince and Mercer Streets come into Springfield Avenue, there was a horde of 300 brown sullen faces all around me, standing on a street pockmarked with asphalt where the cobblestones had worn out. Across the way the prison of the Scudder projects reached into the sky, recalling Isaac Harrison's shooting. Mayor Addonizio and several of his bull-like bodyguards appeared on the sidewalk, the mayor taking a chastising from several of the hoodlums who crowded around him.

"Why didn't you go to the King funeral?" a kid with a ragged hat asked.

"We sent our representatives," Addonizio replied.

Only two hours before he had visited the North Ward Citizens Committee headquarters—riding up to find Tony Imperiale standing in front with a rifle in his hands. The mayor of Newark shouted and argued with a nobody who had risen to notoriety by holding a rifle and shouting in front of a TV camera. Imperiale told the mayor that he couldn't search the place because he didn't have a warrant. Imperiale also said he was going to call his lawyer. Now Addonizio was facing the insults of hoodlums, talking softly and looking at his shoes, looking anywhere so he wouldn't have to meet those mean eyes.

"We didn't hear Newark mentioned on TV during the funeral," one of the mean faces said. Addonizio tried to explain while his bodyguards scanned the crowd and moved closer.

"All right, break it up," Dominick Spina shouted from the curb where he was standing, five yards away from me. Every few minutes Spina called out for the kids to get out of the street and they moved not an inch, scores of gaunt faces, now smiling, now sullen. The more the UCC kids with bullhorns and the Muslims advised them to go home, the more youths flocked to the teeming avenue. Councilman Irvine Turner pulled up in his green Cadillac. Councilman Calvin West's voice was drowned out.

"Do whatever he tells you," Spina said to his men, nodding to Kamiel Wadud, the bearded leader of the Muslims.

"Ten guys set those fires up on Springfield Avenue and they're gone and they want you to go out on the streets to get shot," Wadud shouted. "That's the trick and you're falling for it."

At 10:00 P.M. in the middle of the cobblestone avenue an anonymous youth in a gold and maroon jacket held up his arms and led the mob away toward downtown Newark. The supposed leaders were ignored by those who didn't want to be led. The angry horde surged down the cobblestone hill.

"Let 'em go, let 'em go!" the police radio blared. "Do not disperse them . . . keep on the move . . . do not stop your cars."

They marched down the sloping avenue in the middle of the street— young, wild and unreached by anyone, heading for Newark's main business section. Step by step, calls over the police radio marked their progress, adding the last ingredient to Newark's crisis, an addition that would either save the city or turn it into a virtual blood bath.

"Can we use the shotguns?" a voice asked at 10:10 P.M.

"How about the shotguns?" another police car radioed.

"Knock that off," an officer commanded. "Do not use any shotguns!"

"Some of the kids in the group have guns! They have guns!" another officer shouted a few minutes later.

"Who has guns?" the officer replied. "They don't have any guns."

"There they go! There they go!" another voice baited.

"They're not going anywhere, they're not doing anything," the officer responded. "Knock that off!"

Newark's fate, as always, rested in the hands of the police department. As anonymous policemen called for permission to use shotguns on unarmed teenagers, their officers kept them in check. The more insulting some of the juveniles became, the better most of the police took it. Reactions had changed since the riot. Black kids who had talked freely with reporters and passersby now disdained whites and seemed to lack interest in whether they lived or died. And police officers who had treated blacks with aggressive hostility during the riot now remained cool.

"Tell the guys to keep calm, keep them calm and we can beat this," called out the voice of Inspector Richard Murphy. Officers like Murphy helped prevent major destruction and wholesale bloodshed in the city.

Once reaching the downtown area the moving horde split into small groups with the same leaderless energy that had brought them together. Police and youth feinted and bluffed downtown as Tim Still and ministers pleaded with the kids to go home while, far up the hill in the ghetto, it was beginning.

"Springfield and Charlton, they're looting Richie's Pawn Shop!"

"Five eighteen Bergen, they're breaking in!"

At Avon and Livingston—where Billy Furr died—and on 17th and 15th Avenues more fires sent gray clouds drifting across the sky, filtering into the orange glow over the smoldering city. By dawn more than 195 fires—twenty of them serious—had broken out, leaving more than 600 ghetto people homeless. The kids ripped at the scabs of already wounded Newark, bringing fresh blood. To be there was an incredible experience—watching as they pushed forward while the city choked in smoke and tear gas, breaking through plate glass windows and throwing debris into the street. Once again Springfield and Clinton Avenues were lined with furniture and broken glass, looking like disaster areas. Iron window gratings were bent by straining human hands and twisted into ugly contortions. Plywood soon replaced store windows which lay strewn over the sidewalks like pieces of an unsolvable puzzle. Police had no sooner secured one store and left when the juveniles attacked again, ripping off the covering and beginning the looting all over again. Without using sirens, police cars raced from store to store and over it all rang the constant clamor of burglar alarms, clanging on and on into the morning daylight—death knells for more white businesses in the stricken city. More than fifty stores were looted, some of them cleaned out. Seventy-one persons were arrested during the action, fifty-two of them adults. Forty-seven were charged with looting and twelve with arson.

"We were able to contain any outbursts in a limited area," Addonizio said. "If we had handled it any other way, the situation would have exploded into a riot."

The city's experience had taught the administration some aspects of riot control—though little else.

Can You Tell Me What to Do?

Two liquor stores stood at the intersection of Avon and Bergen, Sid's Tavern on the southeast corner and Avon Liquors on the other side of the street. Both had been broken into earlier and at 2:20 A.M. groups of young adults and juveniles waited all around me on the north side of Bergen to get at them again. One youngster threw a garbage can through the window of Avon Liquors, another picked up a piece of wood and smashed what was left of the glass. Three or four others climbed in and out of the window, running off down Bergen Street with fifths of liquor cradled in their arms. Police soon arrived and secured the building—but as soon as they left it began again. By the time a car carrying Mr. and Mrs. Samuel Weissman pulled up in front of their store at 2:50 A.M., there was little left inside worth saving.

"This is the second time, I have no insurance," the old man moaned. He walked through the broken glass, rubble, bottles of beer, and wine strewn over the floor. "They took my cash register, they took my cash register," Weissman went on, wringing his hands. "They took it last summer, this is the second time. How could they do this?" Standing by a smashed showcase was his wife, an elderly woman with shaky hands and a quivering voice. She looked at me with pleading eyes and asked, "Can you tell me what to do? Please tell me what to do."

Two looters were apprehended coming out of the store and police caught a fifteen-year-old boy inside. They stood there in the broken glass and debris on the same street corner, a fifteen-year-old kid and an old woman who wanted someone to tell her what she should do. The kid would never be anything but what Newark had made him and the woman lived far away where it was white and safe. Police just told the kid to go home but he stood there with the others on the littered street as an answer to the crying woman's question.

LeRoi and I Don't Love Each Other

On the day of King's murder an effort to lessen racial tension resulted in an unusual meeting in Spina's office. Present were Al Black and Spina, Malafronte, the mayor's right-hand man, Curvin, now director of a Rutgers University community action program, LeRoi Jones and some associates, and Imperiale with two of his organization's officers. There were also two new figures: John Rees, a forty-three-year-old Briton whose stay in Newark would be brief but interesting, and Kamiel Wadud, the impressive Sunni Muslim with the shaggy black beard who was mainly responsible for dragging Jones to the meeting. For Curvin, who had a far different style, Wadud's men in red tarbooshes were puzzling, but Wadud had been able to work with some success with Spina.

Heated words were exchanged between Curvin and Imperiale and then between Jones and the North Ward leader before Wadud imposed himself—surprisingly for those unfamiliar with him—by telling people to calm down. The meeting suddenly became more productive, and led to further meetings. In what for him was a burst of revelation, Imperiale suddenly realized that Jones didn't want Newark burned down.

This initial meeting was followed up eight days later by a second rendezvous, this one in Rees's office in The Hallmark House, a luxury apartment building on Broad Street across from City Hall. Showing up were Jones and a few of his people and Imperiale, accompanied this time by some of his cadres attired in their World War II surplus, and, of course, John Rees, an amiable gentleman with an English accent and a man of many roles. As it turned out, the meetings were the brainchild of Rees, who functioned as a sort of self-employed traveling salesman of police public relations, but who, as far as Wadud was concerned, was actually a CIA man. The bearded one was also on hand and he and Rees had laid enough groundwork that it was unlikely a brawl would wreck the place. Indeed, by this time Jones and Imperiale were calling each other LeRoi and Tony.

"LeRoi and I don't love each other," Imperiale understated, "but we respect each other."

On such a benign note fairy tales might spring to life. The occasion became even more bizarre when Newark Police Captain Charles Kinney, head of the Newark Police Department's subversive squad, joined the dynamic duo later in the evening. Something strange was afoot.

What transpired in the office of John Rees—a dress rehearsal for a radio show to be taped in the early morning at the CBS studios in New York—was only for those of warm heart and weak mind. The realities of the Hughes Report and the Kerner Report were being replaced with hints of intrigues, international conspiracies, Maoists, and the sinister Thomas Hayden. Highlight of the four-hour parley came when Jones developed a yen for a green salad and Imperiale directed two of his scouts to fetch it— perhaps the city's first example of black power.

Close to 2:00 A.M. the group broke camp and headed for the city and its date with destiny to explain all of Newark's past difficulties and show the Newark police as saviors of the city. If CBS had been too faint of heart to inform the public of Isaac Harrison's last moments, it was ready to record the comradely embrace of Imperiale, Jones, and the Newark police.

The half-hour show was fed to the public that next afternoon, with some surprising answers coming to light from even more surprising questions.

There were certainly scores of hanging questions about the riot still to be answered.

Had a corrupt administration, a graft-infested police department and disgusting living conditions pushed Newark over the precipice? Had the police chosen an incredibly stupid time to beat John Smith and the Black Muslims? Would a police review board have eased conditions leading to the riot and would immediate action on Smith's beating have stopped it? Who killed Isaac Harrison? Why had Billy Furr been shot down? Why did Eddie Moss have to die? Mrs. Spellman? Mrs. Gainer? Mrs. Brown? Michael Pugh? What had happened to all the investigations of the shootings and brutalities during the occupation? Had anything been done for relatives of the dead? Was anything forthcoming? Had anything happened in the city between the riot and Dr. King's murder to provide half a reason why those kids shouldn't have been mad enough to burn the city to the ground?

Alas, there wasn't time for such foolish trivia. What was needed was a topic of universal interest and one which needed no background information: communists. Captain Kinney, Imperiale, and Jones together blamed all of Newark's troubles—the riot as well as the recent fires—on "white-led, so-called radical groups" and "communists and the Trotskyite persons." The last offering was from Imperiale who, if he ever saw a "Trotskyite," wouldn't know whether to pet it, take it home for supper, or give it a karate chop.

LeRoi Jones, an expert on "white communists," at least, started the whitewash:

> Recently, in the recent developments, sort of situation in Newark, the unrest caused by Dr. King's death, we found that a lot of the turmoil and a lot of the, in general, the kind of riotous situation has been caused by instigators, people who really have no interest in the community except to cause riotous conditions. We, the Black Nationals in Newark, believe that we can gain power in Newark through political means, and there are white-led, so-called radical groups, leftist groups, that are exploiting the people's desire for power, the black people's legitimate desire for power, exploiting it and actually using the black people as a kind of shock troops to further their own designs. . . . We know that there have been a lot of professionals working in the communities—a lot of white people working in our communities to do things that were not beneficial to black people.

> STEVE FLANDERS, CBS announcer: I think I'll turn now to Captain Charles Kinney of the detective division of the Newark Police Department, who, I think, can throw some more light on this situation.

> KINNEY: Well, yes . . . I find myself in agreement with LeRoi Jones . . . to the extent that there are groups in our city, there are groups

in our city who are desirous of having a riot, who are desirous of changing not only the form of government in the city of Newark, but are desirous of changing the form of government in the United States of America. Any strife that they can cause, any trouble they can make between the black and white community is a means to their end. . . . I have prepared a full report and I am accusing the New Left, and in particular the Students for a Democratic Society of Newark. They operate as the Newark Community Union Project, and this group has come to our city and they've been active in our city some four years and they've been very, very active in fomenting the trouble that we've had in the city of Newark, using black men and using white men to take care of their own particular needs. . . . In Newark, the leader is a man named Thomas Hayden.

FLANDERS: Mr. Tony Imperiale, do you feel this is a dangerous situation? I saw you nodding your head when Captain Kinney mentioned Tom Hayden and he mentioned this group. What is your viewpoint on this?

IMPERIALE: Well, first of all, from the time that our organization had formed, we immediately, our own people, began investigating as to what we could do to find out what caused some of the riots here in the city of Newark. It seemed at that time that everybody was sweeping the dirt under the rugs, blaming everybody but where it was supposed to go. And we believed that the communists who have no interest in the city of Newark, except to cause a destruction on behalf of possibly Moscow or Peking, came in here and helped out on these riots.

Now, we were interested in Thomas Hayden also because we had picked up certain information as to his activities. When we found this Students for a Democratic Society, we had our own people who posed as college students attend many of the meetings.

JACK CAVANAUGH, CBS announcer: Captain, how about these alleged conspirators again? You say they are leftists. Were there communists involved here? Were they Chinese Communists, Russian Communists?

KINNEY: Well, again, though there are distinctions between them and some periodicals make great distinctions between them, they are communist-led, whether they're pro-Peiping or pro-Moscow. Some of this information that is coming and that's being used is coming right from Peiping, as a matter of fact, and it's coming from China by way of Canada, as a matter of fact, and this information is being used by these people and we're the target for today.

FLANDERS: Mr. LeRoi Jones, why do you think Newark was chosen as a target by these groups?

JONES: Well, I don't know. Newark is a bad place. It's a bad ghetto and there was, I think, a leadership vacuum caused by, you know, establishment Negroes, Toms, on one hand, and a kind of a despair and a kind of a sloth and despair, on another hand, and this is the kind of vacuum that these kind of fantasy revolutionaries like to slide into and utilize for their own ends.

CAVANAUGH (to Imperiale): Are you convinced that these outside agitators that Captain Kinney speaks of, if it hadn't been for them, there would have been no trouble in Newark last summer?

IMPERIALE: I honestly believe that, because I think they played a major part. Now, we've had Negro ghettos since I was a boy. We never had revolutions like this. Somebody had to come in and spark it. You can't tell me that black people did this on their own, because they never did it before. And this is why, more and more, as we get into the evidence, I'm firmly convinced that it was outside agitation that caused this riot.

CAVANAUGH: Mr. Jones, do you feel the same way?

Yes, Mr. Jones, how about that? Do you feel the same way? LeRoi, doubtlessly awed by Imperiale's intellect and grasp on history, groped his way forward.

JONES: Well, I don't feel totally the same way. I say that there's a lot—to a large extent there's a lot of frustration, you know, in the ghetto, like—well, you don't have what you had before, before you got television. You know black people can see all your goods, all your property now, all your stuff that they want. . . . they couldn't see it on radio.

CAVANAUGH: But you think it would have been quiet in Newark if it hadn't been for these outside agitators?

JONES: I don't think it would have been quiet, no. I mean the people are going to react to certain things, because they react to certain things, you know. We've got a different generation going on.

There they were, captured together for the entertainment of a mass radio audience, but without benefit of accurate introductions: Charles Kinney, a captain in what was, perhaps, the most corrupt police department in the country; Anthony Imperiale, a ruffian who had made—according to his federal dossier—thirteen unsuccessful applications to become a policeman; and LeRoi Jones, a talented playwright with a psychic hatred of whites—a real, live black militant who had just been housebroken.

IMPERIALE: I'll agree to sit down with any American, if it's going to mean peace in the city of Newark and prevent bloodshed. But the police director called us in. He wanted to talk with us. And after a good first hour of hostility, of airing, of clearing the air, we got to find out that we're just all Americans concerned with our people and for our lives.

God bless you, Tony. After this immortal drivel stored forever in the archives of CBS, the sarcastic humor of Jones seemed out of place.

FLANDERS: There are those who would question your motivation, Mr. Jones. There is one question I think we have to raise to bring this into context, and this question is, you have been convicted of an incident, crime, last summer, and being under sentence now, there are those who would question your motivation in cooperating or coming out publicly in this fashion. Is there anything to this? Is there any substance to this?

JONES: You mean was I promised something for doing it?

FLANDERS: Precisely.

JONES: Well, I told you before that they promised to make me a Secretary of State, and so when you see that happen, you know that's what it was.

Having flushed out the real villains, the show would have been incomplete without setting the record straight with a few swipes at the Hughes and Kerner Reports. A volley from Kinney was followed by Imperiale:

I for one, along with the captain, go along on his reply to the president's report. I don't think that the governor's report was just. I think that the governor was looking for a way out. He called it a criminal insurrection when it came about. A criminal insurrection it was. And then later on, when he has this committee to investigate, he retracts "criminal insurrection." [3] I think that the governor's report was tarnished and was entered with unclean hands before it got off. So in my personal opinion and in the opinion of some of the people in our ward we disregard it.

As far as the president's report, again I have to agree with the captain, because it contradicted itself, where it said that certain outsiders came in, which could have been communists and the Klan, and fomented these riots. And as long as you have contradiction and they come up with excuses that we don't have facilities to conduct a proper investigation, then I don't think that the investigation should have been printed, because it discredited our police department and it discredited a lot of other things, and I'm not in agreement with either of the reports.

Had Jones forgotten that scar on his head, "the kid who got shot thirty-nine times," police and guardsmen emptying broadsides into creaking tenements, that two-and-a-half to three-year sentence he was facing—or was he just remembering the last? The Kerner and Hughes Reports had both been written with integrity and honesty in the face of anticipated resentment. To deny them would deny the people Jones said he cared so much about, those people up on the hill. And it would also be a denial of those honest enough to make their suffering a matter of record. Jones had gone through most of the show sitting in his chair mouthing nonsense but in

---

[3] On Friday morning, July 14, at the Roseville Armory, Governor Hughes described the disturbances in Newark as a "criminal insurrection." Later on he termed it a "riot," perhaps after being advised that many Newark businesses lacked coverage in their insurance policies for "insurrections." According to his press secretary and regardless of what Imperiale had to say, the governor did not alter these statements or retract them.

the last few minutes he dropped his script, salvaging some of his self-respect:

> Well, what can I say about those reports? Those things are, you know—we knew those things that those reports said, like, my father, grandfather could tell you about that stuff. You know, they've been saying those things a long time. It's just that now somebody, white men, want to make it official.
>
> I will say one thing about law and order, though. I think that if you are going to start with the law-and-order bit, you ought to start by respecting, you know, your president and your governor's commission reports, you know. You can start there, you know.
>
> IMPERIALE: LeRoi, that was a bad thing to say, because you know what I'm referring to, about respecting presidents. You certainly didn't in one of your speeches. That's hypocritical now.
>
> FLANDERS: Well, on this minor note of irritation, I want to thank you all. . . .

That "minor note of irritation" struck to the very heart of the issue. If Jones and Imperiale could not agree on the behavior of police officers in the past, what would be their basis of agreement for the future?

He Probably Did It to Save His Ass

Anyone with the least knowledge of the Newark riot and its children, those wild leaderless kids, would react to Kinney's "theories" of pro-Peking communists with the amusement they deserved. These people in authority just wouldn't quit. The Newark police and city administration not only wanted to behave just as they pleased but, as in the beatings of the Muslims, they didn't want the public to be aware of it. They didn't want to give the perpetual losers *anything*. Newark would spare no effort to wipe its public image clean at the expense of Hayden or the communists or anyone else that could be utilized as a scapegoat. The CBS show was but a warm-up for Captain Kinney, who got better with time.

As for Jones, the playwright had shown another of his faces and escaped from the shabby affair with little more than a black eye—which looked well under his crown of thorns. By this time it was well-known LeRoi was a glutton for punishment, anyway. He had left the white intellectuals, giving up fame and fortune, sneered at the liberal activists, cursed anything white and made fun of the Toms, so why shouldn't he sell a few of them down the river? He was doing it after all for his beloved Newark, black Newark. Trouble was, many thought he was doing it for himself. An excellent article by Stephen Schneck in *Ramparts* magazine strongly insinuated there had been a deal between Jones and the Newark authorities whereby the playwright could look forward to something resembling justice rather than two and a half years.

Hayden put it more bluntly: "He probably did it to save his ass." Reached at the *Ramparts* office in San Francisco by CBS after the show, Hayden replied to the charges in a manner more befitting a family network. He just laughed quietly when told what he really was supposed to have been doing for the previous eight months, little of which he had even spent in Newark. "It must be a joke," he said, then added, "people are being misled in the traditional way."

Jones knew full well that cooperation couldn't hurt him in Newark, where almost anything could be fixed, but there was more to it than met the eye. There was also more to John Rees and his efforts at achieving reconciliation than met the eye. Rees—who described himself as a "professional generalist" and "freelance consultant" doing much of his work with law enforcement agencies—had really come up with an idea.

Six days after the radio show, the firm Rees headed sent "A Preliminary Proposal for a Community Peace Patrol" to Washington for federal consideration. The proposed federally financed project would grant $12,000 each to Imperiale's North Ward Citizens Committee and to Jones's political group, the United Brothers, for their services. That was just the beginning. The entire project would come to over $743,740 to administer and outfit a community peace patrol made up of both groups with uniforms, helmets, cameras, walkie-talkie radios, tape recorders, and even their own patrol cars. Sizable funds for training of these patrols would go to National Goals, Inc., Rees's company. The togetherness of Jones and Imperiale was now somewhat clearer.

News of the proposal broke two months later when it bounced back from the Department of Justice and from Governor Hughes's office. Spina, who had signed his name to the plan, now had a change of heart. And it became clear that there were no deals to be had for Jones in Newark.

Newark Was Still Burning

As city officials had found that they could no longer depend on prosperous "nigger ministers" to control "their people," so they soon learned not to expect much better from "militants." LeRoi Jones was now a brother-in-arms with police, but Newark was still burning. Jones would be the first to laugh at the thought of *anyone's* controlling the compression chamber's children. If a wild breed of hoodlum was one by-product of the riot, inability to control him was a natural counterpart. There were more than eighty fires after the radio program, some the work of landlords who burned their own buildings to collect the insurance. The biggest blaze in the city's history wiped out a block and a half of the ghetto on April 20, leaving the Bergen Street–Avon Avenue area across from the boarded-up Avon Liquors looking like a disaster area. Thirty-four firetrap tenements lay in charred ruin and 600 more people were homeless. A total of 170 persons were arrested through the period of the fires, only 7 of them repeaters from the riot of eight months before.

The most unusual development of Newark's crisis following Dr. King's murder was, it goes without saying, never publicized. A new feeling of black pride had infiltrated the city's organized criminal activity. Angry numbers runners suddenly refused to work, calling for black bankers to handle their receipts. This unexpected rebellion ended quickly as phone calls instructed the runners they'd better get back to work before someone got hurt. Some of these calls came directly from the Newark Police Department.

I Only Want Law and Order

With this background of charred wood, Imperiale and Jones both turned to becoming youth advisers. The former appeared at Newark's predominantly white high schools and Jones spoke to and for black students who were boycotting classes at all eight of the city's high schools.

Imperiale's first effort was a ninety-minute address before a thousand screaming supporters at Barringer High School, lambasting Al Black, Governor Hughes, Martin Luther King, Mayor Addonizio, Oliver Lofton, Earl Warren, the Newark Board of Education, the ACLU, and the Newark *Evening News*. He followed this with a three-hour rampage at Vailsburg High School, this time including his new friend, LeRoi Jones, in a harangue which eventually turned some of his audience into a bloodthirsty mob. Nine black youths, Seton Hall University students who had done nothing to provoke the crowd, were set upon by Imperiale's listeners, some of them heaving bricks.

"The students moved toward us for security," said Father William Linder. "Imperiale's little gang was there—I know, because I've seen them in a number of other places. They circled us in a double row. It was organized, no doubt about it."

"Don't behave like animals," Sergeant Chester Popek shouted at the mob from the top of a police vehicle. "Do you really want a thousand against a handful?"

The crowd roared that it did. Only actions of Newark policemen, who formed a human wall around the college students and three priests and two nuns also under attack, prevented a literal massacre.

The North Ward leader's stirring rhetoric was interrupted by the concern of Governor Hughes over LeRoi Jones's efforts in the area of school attendance. Imperiale was not exactly helping black student attendance at the white schools either. Hughes was concerned that both men were contributing to the thorough polarization of the state's largest city, a polarization which now included the young.

Jones and Imperiale met with the governor during separate sessions in his Trenton office, in a four-hour session of night meetings which also included Spina, Addonizio, and other city officials. Hughes urged Jones and Imperiale to use whatever influence they might have to get pupils back into the schools and to cool the situation in Newark rather than inflame it. The governor charged that the North Ward Citizens Committee was in the mold of the brownshirts of Hitler's Nazi Germany, overlooking the group's free taxi service to nervous women, some of them virgins. The governor also said he would ask the state legislature to outlaw such vigilante groups—which he did, with the state senate passing an anti-vigilante bill in February of 1969.

Imperiale spoke to more than 1,500 persons at East Side High School the night following the Trenton meeting, telling the throng that he refused to disband his private army but, in deference to the governor, would have them divested of their army fatigue uniforms.

The vigilante told his audience that Governor Hughes asked him what he wanted and he replied, "I only want law and order." Imperiale, the biggest threat to law and order in the state, also told the wildly applauding crowd that he had turned down nine political jobs offered to shut him up. "I won't sell you out," he cried.

Imperiale, interested in more than law and order, planned to join the same power structure he had been deriding by running for councilman-at-large in the November election. Imperiale, a man with an aimless past, had hitched his wagon to the powerful vehicle of white fear. It was fused by the frustrations and ignorant prejudices of uneducated people like himself who were trapped in aging, over-taxed houses with no way to get out. "They say all Maddox did in Georgia was wield a pick handle and catapulted himself to the governor's chair," said Sam Raffaelo, Newark lawyer who introduced Imperiale to politics. "Tony can be mayor of Newark, he can be governor. Tony is sweeping the country, everybody's talking about him."

LeRoi Jones agreed only that Imperiale was "an authentic spokesman for his people," such as they were.

17

ASK ME NO QUESTIONS, I'LL TELL YOU NO LIES

A White Stokely Carmichael

"On occasion, Hayden came to class to teach, filthy and disheveled, wearing worn clothing and shoes, needing a haircut and shave," Captain Kinney related to the House Committee on Un-American Activities. "On several occasions he brought along Constance Brown, who was not a student, but who sat in on the classes."

The fifty-one-year-old Newark police captain, who was taking a political science course at the Newark campus of Rutgers University, had run into Hayden by coincidence and dutifully took note of all suspicious activity. The original teacher of the course, Dr. Abraham Yeselson, had been awarded a fellowship and therefore left the university before completion of the semester. He had turned his teaching duties over to Hayden, who—as far as Kinney was concerned—not only set a poor example for his students but even brought along his girl friend.

"When Hayden missed a class," Kinney went on, "his place as an instructor was in turn taken by his attorney, Leonard Weinglass."

Also, Kinney revealed that when Hayden returned from North Viet Nam with three released Army sergeants who had been captured during the war, he was met at the airport by Weinglass. Kinney described to the committee how Hayden and Weinglass joyously embraced. This, said Kinney, was a strange lawyer-client relationship.

Other facets of the New Left theorist's life were also scrutinized: Hayden had been editor of his high school's publication and hadn't had the proper respect for authority; he had been editor-in-chief of the University of Michigan's publication and had received a B.A. in 1961, after which he had gone to Atlanta as field secretary for SDS; he had married a Texas girl and was separated; he was involved in anti-war activity; and, of particular interest to Kinney, Hayden had been termed a "white Stokely Carmichael," bent on disruption of Newark.

Kinney had also uncovered that Hayden believed that UCC, Newark's anti-poverty organization, "emphasized social action as the keystone of the war on poverty but only a certain kind of constructive social action; this theory soft-pedals the idea of attacking power structures. Instead, the goal is to bring ghetto residents into the 'mainstream' of competitive society."

"Hayden, in other words," translated Kinney, "makes it clear he believes in destructive social action in attacking power structures, and is opposed to the idea of bringing ghetto residents into the mainstream of our society."

Kinney also noted that Hayden, together with Connie Brown and other NCUP people, had been arrested on April 1, 1967, while picketing a food store on Clinton Avenue. And Hayden's other cohort, Weinglass, had refused to testify before the PBA's private "investigation" of the riot.

And what had been Hayden's role in the riot? A devious one according to Kinney:

"On the evening of Thursday, July thirteen, Thomas Hayden—May I point out that the riots started on the night before, on July twelfth—on the evening of Thursday, July thirteenth, 1967, Thomas Hayden was with Leonard Weinglass in Weinglass' law office at forty-three Bleeker Street, Newark. The telephone rang and either Hayden or Weinglass answered it. A conversation ensued, and when the phone was put down either Hayden or Weinglass said to the other, 'It's started, let's go.' They left the office and were evidently referring to the rioting which had begun in the vicinity of the fourth police precinct."

Thus unfolded the Newark Police Department's second attempt to discredit Tom Hayden. The effort was a continuation of the city administration's strategy to find scapegoats for the riot after the Hughes Report. It was a revamped version of the Kinney-Imperiale-Jones burlesque, and was presented to an appreciative audience. Kinney's testimony began in Washington on April 23 and lasted two days. From the beginning it had more holes in it than Hayden's wardrobe.

The inspiration for Kinney's hostility to Hayden's appearance and girl friend is uncertain, as the captain failed to reveal what grade Hayden had given him on his report card. What had Hayden been teaching? It seems to have escaped Kinney's attention.

Kinney's insight into Hayden's theory of social action came neither from tapped phones nor undercover agents and was hardly clandestine. Hayden himself had written it in the November 1965 issue of *Liberation* magazine. Hayden also kept it no secret that the food store he was picketing systematically robbed the poor by raising prices on the day welfare checks arrived. The allegation that Weinglass had refused to testify disregarded that the PBA gatherings were an investigative sham and that the attorney had been joined in his refusal by Al Black and even by Mayor Addonizio.

As for the mysterious telephone call coming into Weinglass' office, Captain Kinney certainly had a flair for the dramatic. Actually the call had come on Wednesday night—not Thursday as Kinney said—and there was nothing suspicious about it. "The call came from someone in the community at the fourth precinct after Smith's arrest," Weinglass said. "They thought I might represent him. I don't know where they got that ridiculous quote from. They pestered my secretary but she said she never told them anything like that. When the call came, Tom and I were throwing a football around outside."

That Man Is Full of Shit

Other NCUP people under investigation were Jesse Allen, thirty-six, ghetto resident and full-time organizer, Robert Kramer and Norman Fruchter, both full-time organizers, Carol Glassman, Miss Brown's roommate, Corinna Fales, and Mrs. Terry Jefferson.

Miss Fales and Miss Glassman were described as young ladies who were "harassing the power structure" while Mrs. Jefferson, a black woman who served as NCUP office manager and treasurer, was able—Kinney pointedly noted—to endorse checks made out to cash, thus concealing distribution of monies. He apparently regarded this as of great import, though he didn't guess what this sinister possibility might mean. Kinney did report, however, that on February 11, 1949, nineteen years previously, Mrs. Jefferson had signed a petition for a Martha Stone, then head—according to Kinney—of the Communist Party in New Jersey.

Kramer and Fruchter were described as film directors heading a non-profit organization of underground film makers in New York. Their films were often distributed without charge to community groups.

"In a little more than two months," *The New York Times* of April 13, 1968, reported, "Camera News has completed and released nine 'news-reels.' The word is a slight euphemism because the films are not the generally bland, politically neutral (sic) films that once made up an important part of every movie theater's program. Instead, they are short, bold documentaries aggressively and unequivocally biased toward points of view favored by the left, old and new."

What Kinney saw that was subversive about people making films was never made clear, just as he forgot to include what the petition Mrs. Jefferson signed was all about. As a matter of fact, if there was one consistency throughout Kinney's presentation it was his failure to say what anything was about, except that it was "subversive."

For example, Kinney added that Fruchter had also been involved in picketing at the New York Board of Rabbis on April 9, 1964, demanding "excommunication" of Jewish slumlords. Praiseworthy as others may have found Fruchter's action, Kinney viewed it as subversive.

What led to suspicion of Allen, organizer of NCUP's Peoples Action Group, is that he "attended a meeting during the Newark riot of Negro leaders who issued a set of demands that they said must be fulfilled before the rioting could end." In Kinney's view this made him a subversive also.

After UCC had divided Newark's sprawling ghetto into local area boards, Kinney testified, the NCUP activists had completely "taken over" Area Boards Two and Three. From facilities at Area Board Two had come a steady flow of leaflets antagonistic to the city administration. Kinney didn't relate whether the reported "takeover" of Area Boards Two and Three had been accomplished by sleight-of-hand, a bloody coup, or by democratic procedure, which last was the case. Nor did he explain what poverty organizations were supposed to do with such raw power after seizing it, if not aiding the poor. Kinney's testimony on the mysterious "takeover" was certainly lost on Jesse Allen: "That man is full of shit," said Allen, "I don't think he knows what the hell he's talking about."

When the Clinton Hill ghetto erupted in a minor riot in May of 1969, Allen was in the forefront—though his role probably confused Captain Kinney. A community committee afterward commended the dangerous subversive for his "courageous and tireless efforts" to restore order, despite being "abused and buffeted" by hoodlums. "They were angry at him [Allen] because he said he didn't want to live in a city of anarchy," the executive director of UCC stated.

So far Kinney's report had failed to uncover any dangerous plots that NCUP might be preparing, but its tactics had not gone unnoticed: "NCUP members rise at public meetings to argue with officials and more often than not they dispute not only the grounds for the specific decision that is being made, but also the right of the official or the constituted authority to make that decision for the people whose lives will be affected by it." Questioning the authority of the white appointees and chosen house niggers to make such decisions was indeed subversive.

Closely allied to the NCUP people, Kinney testified, was Derek Winans, thirty-one, a paid consultant for UCC and a former *Wall Street Journal* reporter. Why would a wealthy 1962 *cum laude* graduate of Harvard and a member of one of Newark's founding families choose to live in a ghetto except for some suspicious reason? Winans had first made himself suspect by participating with Hayden in voter registration drives in Mississippi in 1963 and had returned to that lawless territory in support of James Meredith in 1966. His post-riot activities only heightened Kinney's suspicions: "Besides organizing a drive for food and medical suppies for the riot-torn sections of Newark, Winans' organization found time to call for a 'speedy grand jury investigation into the police action which precipitated the riots' and 'to support the establishment of a civilian review board in Newark.' " And if these devilish activities weren't enough, Winans had also written for *Ramparts* magazine, though once again the content of his writing went unnoted.

The lives of Albert Ray Osborne, alias Colonel Hassan, and John Smith were also examined for discovery of where each had gone astray. The colonel had a lengthy criminal record that included robbery, larceny, burglary, taking money on false pretenses, forgery, and passing bad checks. He had also left $2,000 in unpaid bills owed to Xerox and the telephone company when he hastily departed Washington for Newark. Kinney could not link the bad debts, however, to any international subversive conspiracy.

Smith's army record included two court-martials, Kinney said, though, as so frequently occurred in his report, their content went unspecified. Actually, Smith had been court-martialed only once, about 1952, in Kokura, Japan, for refusing to work with a group other than his own. A second court-martial was mistakenly affixed to his record, an error that plagues the John Smiths of the world.

Kinney, dazzling the group with his psychological insights, also said that Smith was a mentally troubled man who went through life with a fixation about "getting his teeth fixed" because a gap in his teeth prevented his playing the trumpet. His frustrations and instability had come to a head, Kinney said, at the time of his attack on Officers Pontrelli and DeSimone, about whom Kinney volunteered no psychiatric findings.

Four months after Kinney removed his posterior from HUAC's witness seat, John Smith did visit Dr. T. W. Jaker of Irvington, adjoining Newark, and had his teeth fixed.

Phil Hutchings of SNCC, a participant in the medical school and Parker-Callaghan controversies, had been a roommate of Stokely Carmichael at Howard University, Kinney testified. Hutchings had a hand in opening the Black Liberation Center in the South Orange Avenue ghetto that had become the headquarters for Colonel Hassan for a short time until, just before the riot, it burned down. Kinney mentioned the mysterious fire but overlooked the charge that the Newark police had been responsible.

James Walker, another name added to the still-unrevealed plot, had used threats and coercion in organizing the taxicab drivers after Smith's beating, Kinney said. He described Walker as an angry man who had been in "the forefront of every demonstration against constituted authority" in the city. In this case Kinney was correct. When considering what "constituted authority" amounted to in Newark, it could be understood why Mr. Walker was an angry man, very angry.

Kinney also noted that Morton Stavis, Newark attorney who was handling John Smith's civil suit against the police, as well as several other Newark police brutality suits, had appeared previously before HUAC on

February 28, 1956. When asked at that time whether he belonged to the Communist Party, Stavis refused to answer on grounds of the Fifth Amendment. Stavis was again being listed as a subversive because he acted on behalf of the defenseless ghetto in challenging the Newark police.

A detailed history of LeRoi Jones with a list of leftist organizations he had once been friendly toward and anti-Semitic leaflets he had been responsible for following the riot were also presented for scrutiny. Kinney also cited as incendiary a one-act play, *Arm Yourself or Harm Yourself,* written by Jones and produced three weeks after the riot at The Spirit House. Later in his testimony, however, Kinney welcomed LeRoi's tactical shift and cooperation with the Newark police. "It was a very happy occasion," Kinney told the representatives with a straight face, "for me to find myself in total agreement with LeRoi Jones."

Kinney also read into the Senate's record some of LeRoi's more juicy comments at the CBS gathering but conveniently neglected the playwright's revealing statements:

> FLANDERS: Mr. Jones, when you spoke a few moments ago about these white-led groups, were you aware at that time, or has this just come to your notice now, that Mr. Hayden was perhaps behind this?
>
> JONES: Well, I don't know. You know, I don't know the extent of any of their workings because to me they all seem interested in the same ends, and whether it's Tom Hayden—I don't know Tom Hayden, you know—but they seem to be interested in the same ends. That's manipulation of black people for reasons of their own.

Bob Curvin, a thorn in the side of the police since the Lester Long affair, also was listed among the conspirators. Kinney viewed Curvin's efforts to calm people at the fourth precinct after Smith's beating as an attempt to *start* a riot.

Kinney added a moment of conscious humor to his unintended comedy: "In my opinion, to give Robert Curvin a bullhorn to 'quiet a crowd,' is like giving an arsonist a book of matches and a can of gasoline."

Nevertheless, the commissioners of Governor Hughes had found Curvin well spoken and articulate, as would befit a man with two college degrees.

"Curvin has for years harped on the theme of police brutality, the creation of a civilian review board, the removal from office of Director Spina and other matters, most of which have focused on the Newark Police Department," Kinney testified.

Kinney testified to the continued post-riot activity of subversives by citing the fire that had wiped out a block and a half of the ghetto only days before his appearance. Shortly afterward, however, a young teenager further loused up Kinney's plot by admitting that he had set a fire which a strong wind had whipped into the huge blaze that followed.

I Saw the Motherfuckers Standing There

For the better part of two days, Kinney had plowed onward without interruption. Only once did his listeners raise questions. That occurred when Representative Albert W. Watson of South Carolina picked up a copy of the Kerner Report and commented:

"In reading the president's Civil Disorders Commission report, and I am sure you have read it yourself, at least part of it that related to Newark, some rather serious charges are made against the police. And I assume since you are a captain there, that you are knowledgeable, and especially as we think of the study you have made, that you are knowledgeable of what transpired. I would like to read just two paragraphs and ask for your comment in respect to this on page sixty-six of the report."

Representative Watson then read directly from the Kerner Report:

At 5:30 P.M. on Beacon Street W.F. told J.S., whose 1959 Pontiac he had taken to the station for inspection, that his front brake needed fixing. J.S., who had just returned from work, went to the car which was parked in the street, jacked up the front end, took the wheel off and got under the car.

The street was quiet. More than a dozen persons were sitting on porches, walking about, or shopping. None heard any shots. Suddenly several state troopers appeared at the corner of Springfield and Beacon. J.S. was startled by a shot clanging into the side of the garbage can next to his car. As he looked up he saw a state trooper with his rifle pointed at him. The next shot struck him in the right side.

At almost the same instant, K.G., standing on a porch, was struck in the right eye by a bullet. Both he and J.S. were critically injured.

The conversation that ensued, casting doubt on the integrity of the Kerner Report, was carried in newspapers around the country:

REPRESENTATIVE WATSON: Now from that I assume that this man was just innocently working on his car and not firing or anything and the police just walked up and shot that man. Do you know anything about this incident?

KINNEY: No, sir, I don't know anything about that particular incident. But we have encouraged people, if there are people in our community, though they shouldn't, that don't trust the Newark Police Department, they have the county prosecutor's office, they have the attorney general of the state of New Jersey to go to or the U.S. Attorney who is stationed in Newark. Certainly, there must be somebody under our form of government that these people would trust, I would hope.

WATSON: Personally, do you know anything about that particular incident that is listed here in the report?

KINNEY: No, sir, as far as I am concerned, that is a fabrication of somebody's mind.

WATSON: Have you noticed that before and, if so, have you checked into it to find out anything about it?

KINNEY: I have read this and we have checked—I and my associates have checked—and done everything we possibly could. But this type of information is almost impossible to check out.

WATSON: You certainly have no record of any such incident as that?

KINNEY: We do not.

REPRESENTATIVE WILLIAM M. TUCK of Virginia: (referring to the Kerner Report) Is there any basis of authority for making that statement?

WATSON: No basis at all, Mr. Chairman, this is commentary about various initials. You might be able to identify the initials, but certainly they are meaningless to me. It gives no authority. It just states as a fact that it (the shooting) happened. And you (to Kinney) are unaware of any such incident?

KINNEY: I am unaware of any such incident.

James Sneed, thirty-eight, the "J.S." of the Kerner Report (Chapter 2) still lives on Beacon Street, which, if Kinney ever wants to find it, is a one-block, one-way street connecting Springfield and South Orange Avenues. The same goes for Karl Green, a youth with a perpetually swollen right eye who was named "K.G." in the report and who lives on the other side of the street. In the Sneed case the Kerner Report was correct to every detail. In Green's case there was one error, the trooper's bullet hitting him by the side of his right eye and not *in* the eye itself.

Information as to whom the initials identified is readily available—despite Kinney's comments—from the chairman of the Newark Human Rights Commission, the Newark Legal Services Project, the Hughes Commission or the Kerner Commission representatives who had visited Newark. Even without such identification, Beacon Street being mentioned in the report, it would have been an easy task for police detectives to find James Sneed and Karl Green. This particular trip up Springfield Avenue, finding both men and substantiating beyond doubt the words of the Kerner Report, took me all of twenty minutes. It seemed everyone on the block had signed the petition describing the activity of the state troopers. Everybody on the block knew who and where Sneed and Green were. It is obvious that police were interested in investigating only those matters which might be useful to them.

James Sneed is a slight, harmless man. For the previous six years he had worked as a pipefitter in Harrison, a small city east of Newark across the

Passaic River. As was true also of Karl Green, Sneed had never heard of
Captain Kinney, didn't know he was included in the Kerner Report and
didn't even know what the Congressional Record was.

"I don't remember much after the trooper shot me," he told me.
"I stayed in the hospital two weeks the first time, then I came home.
After that I had to go back again when the wound got infected. I stayed
a little better than a week the second time. When I got shot there wasn't
but a couple of police standing there on the corner. The whole thing
didn't make me mad, no, I just wondered why they would shoot me when
I wasn't doing anything."

Across the street from Sneed's building a few doors to the left is a
three-story tenement with a small porch numbered 53 Beacon Street,
where Green was standing when shot. Sneed's car had been jacked up on
the west side of Beacon, near this porch at the time of the incident. The
eighteen-year-old Green lived with his mother and father, two sisters and
three brothers in a second-floor flat of the crumbling building next to
where he had been hit. After being released from City Hospital he had
gone to work for Newark's Department of Sanitation, a position he will be
allowed to remain at until the day he dies, if he performs to standards.

"I'd say I was in the hospital two to three weeks," he told me. "The
bullet hit me here near the edge of my right eyebrow and it went into
my head. It must have bounced off my skull and it was sticking out
underneath the skin. You can see where they cut it out on the front of
the eyebrow. I had a lot of terrible headaches and I went back to the
hospital and they gave me some medicine. I still get headaches and all I
can see out of the eye is light. I was laid up for quite some time, quite
some time. Sure, I saw the motherfuckers standing there but I wasn't doing
anything and I never thought they'd shoot. I was standing right there on
that porch talking to two friends and they were lined up across the street
near the corner. I seen the motherfuckers, they had on riding pants with
yellow stripes, like they were the fucking Canadian Mounties or something, all that motherfucking, fancy shit. God damn if I know why they
were shooting. Yeah, man, I get mad when I think about it. I got reason
to be mad."

Tell Us About That

Thirteen pages of the Kerner Report pertained to the Newark riot and
Kinney might well have felt apprehensive as Representative Watson prepared to read his second paragraph. Included on these pages were the
homicides of the two boys, Eddie Moss and Michael Pugh, the tragic

deaths of Isaac Harrison, Mrs. Spellman, Mrs. Gainer, and Mrs. Brown, and three other incidents—the Beacon Street shooting which had just been quoted, another wild shooting in which a three-year-old girl lost an eye, and the vengeful shooting at black-owned stores. Representative Watson—who had picked beforehand what portions he would read—chose to treat Kinney with kid gloves and turned to the last mentioned, obviously the least offensive of all the incidents.

> WATSON: We have another statement on page sixty-eight. I quote again from the commission report. "In order to protect his property, B.W.W., the owner of a Chinese laundry, had placed a sign saying SOUL BROTHER in his store window. Between 1:00 and 1:30 A.M., on Sunday, July 16, he, his mother, wife, and brother were watching television in the back room. The neighborhood had been quiet. Suddenly B.W.W. heard the sound of jeeps, then shots. Going to an upstairs window he was able to look out into the street. There he observed several jeeps, from which soldiers and state troopers were firing into stores that had SOUL BROTHER signs in the windows. During the course of the three nights, according to dozens of eye-witnesses, law enforcement officers shot into and smashed windows of businesses that contained signs indicating they were Negro-owned." Tell us about that.

> KINNEY: Well, sir, the accusation was made primarily that members of the New Jersey State Police and members of the National Guard committed these acts because they were not indigenous to our city and therefore were unknown. The New Jersey State Police and the New Jersey National Guard have made a thorough and complete investigation of these charges and they have received no substantiation whatsoever. No one can come forth to identify individuals. There is no backing for that particular statement to give it the weight that appears in that particular commission report.

Watson had not only chosen the least brutal incident but also one with which Kinney would have been most familiar. Not only did the Kerner Report publish the experience of "B.W.W." but New Jersey's Hughes Report had done it weeks before as well, identifying Bow Woo Wong's Chinese Laundry on South Orange Avenue. The Kerner Report did have one error in its account: Mr. Wong hadn't put a SOUL BROTHER sign in his store window but one of his black neighbors had written it on the glass for him.

Robert King, whose cleaning store window had also been broken (Chapter 2), had identified State Police cars 530, 535 and 491 as having been responsible. King's testimony is recorded in the Hughes Report—which was required reading for Captain Kinney—and the report substantiates that these police cars indeed were in the Newark ghetto during the riot.

Kinney's response to Representative Watson not only avoided this embarrassing information, but raised the State Police and National Guard phony investigations to the "thorough and complete" category.

There Must Be Somebody These People Can Trust

By the end of Kinney's two-day visit, it should have been obvious that his presentation was something less than truthful. Kinney had testified under oath. And while his lies should have been uncovered, they went uncontradicted. Wire services gave coast-to-coast publicity to the Newark police captain's statements without ever checking them. Even in Newark, the state's two largest newspapers continued in their dereliction, failing to identify the two shooting victims the Newark police said *didn't exist*. Thus, the press and the police had reached a new low in their virtual alliance. Formerly lying about innocent people who had been shot down, they now denied such people *even existed*. This perverted situation was compounded not only by the lethargic press but by the conclusions of Representative Tuck, which the press dutifully did report:

> I have always had the view—maybe it is not entertained by others—that the police have the right to use such force as is necessary to prevent violation of the law and to subjugate them and bring them into custody. I think much of the troubles we have had recently would have been spared us if police had used a little bit more of those nightsticks and a few bullets once in a while. That is the kind of law I was taught.

With all due respect to Representative Tuck, Newark *already had* this form of law and order. James Sneed and Karl Green couldn't even be given an honest admission of guilt by those who had wronged them, no less retribution. Both men could no more seek compensation from anonymous state troopers who had refused to identify themselves than Bow Woo Wong could claim damages when they were through shooting up his laundry. All three supposedly had been victims of *mysterious black phantoms* and were without legal redress. Captain Kinney himself emphasized the irony: "Certainly, there must be somebody under our form of government that these people would trust, I would hope."

It was Newark's form of government which had drawn Tom Hayden to the city in the first place.

Kinney's painstaking case added up to nothing. He and the two men assigned to him had been working on the subversive pitch since August, when Spina gave him the job. In a city virtually owned by organized crime, their efforts were directed at phantoms. The testimony of Kinney not only failed to reveal any conspiracy but, had his listeners been more perceptive, behavior cited by Kinney as being *subversive* would have pointed toward the riot's real villains.

"In Newark, certain individuals conspired, and are conspiring, to replace the leadership of the Newark Police Department," Kinney summed up for his listeners. "Other individuals conspired, and are conspiring, to turn out of office the present administration before its lawful term expires."

Kinney had unwittingly stated a truth. A group whose activity was shrouded in secrecy *was meeting* and in time it would attempt to "replace the leadership" of Dominick Spina and also "turn out of office" certain members of the administration before their lawful term expired. It would be impossible, however, even for Kinney, to arrest or charge with subversion members of a special Essex County grand jury investigating the corruption of Newark's municipal government.

18

NAILING THE LID ON A COFFIN

To Protect the Freedom of Our Society

"She's been dead more than a year now," Moise Abraham said. "She was sleeping that Thursday night and the gunfire woke her up about twelve-thirty. The other kids were inside but she went looking for our seventeen-year-old son. She stood on the sidewalk down the street there talking with a neighbor. There were looters around the corner on Springfield Avenue and when police cars arrived they ran down Blum Street. My wife became frightened and she ran, too."

Abraham was a large, heavy-set man, seemingly as gentle as he was big. Rose and he had been married in 1944 and had six children, the eldest married and the others still living with them. Since 1959 Abraham had worked for the city as a laborer. Rose also worked, as a domestic. With both parents holding down jobs their family was provided for. As the forty-four-year-old man sat on his front porch stoop and talked, he was some sixty yards from where his wife had been shot.

"I stood right on this porch and saw everything," Mrs. Shirley Banks, a next-door neighbor, recalled. "She was standing right down the block in front of that gray house talking with a woman on the porch when the police came around the corner chasing people." Mrs. Banks, a thirty-one-year-old woman in a white dress, pointed down the block. "You could hear the bullets . . . ping . . . ping . . . hitting off the cars. Mrs. Abraham started to run across the street. She got as far as the middle when she fell to her knees. She got up and made it to the other side of the street. Her son got to her then and helped her here. We didn't even know she had been shot."

"I said, 'What's that wet on her dress?' " Abraham said.

"Then she collapsed in front of the house," Mrs. Banks continued. "You could see the police easy, they had white helmets on . . . the cop that shot her leaned against that tree there [ten to fifteen yards from where Mrs. Abraham was hit] and aimed."

"I drove her to the hospital," Abraham went on. "The bullet hit her in the hip and drove up into her stomach. She died in twenty-four hours. She had to wait six hours to be operated on."

Moise Abraham's son, Moise, Jr., went into shock for several days after his mother's death and hadn't fully recovered. "He still can't talk," Abraham said. "He can talk some but sometimes he can't talk at all. He still goes to a doctor once a week. The bills are forty dollars a month and the Mount Carmel Guild is helping with them but I still can't afford it."

Mrs. Abraham's funeral cost $2,000. Her husband had a $700 insurance policy and he had to borrow $1,300 from a bank, a debt he was still paying off. Some time after the riot Abraham gave a photograph of his wife —the only one he had—to some black newsmen from New York City. Neighbors told him his wife's picture had been shown on television but Abraham himself never saw it. Neither did he see the photograph again. It was never returned and Abraham forgot where the men came from.

Mrs. Rose Abraham was the first of twenty-six people who died in Newark's riot. Her death was investigated by the eighth grand jury of the 1967 term, which was assigned the task of hearing testimony on all the riot deaths. Three of these were clearly from accidental causes: Mrs. Elizabeth Artis, sixty-eight, had become frightened by continued gunfire in the heart of the riot area and died of a heart attack; Mrs. Helen Campbell, forty, was killed in a collision with a fire truck on High Street; and Victor Louis Smith, twenty-two, was found dead in a hallway from an overdose of narcotics. The remaining twenty-two deaths were homicides.

For six months following the riot the prosecutor's office and its homicide detectives, with some initial help from homicide detectives of the Newark police, collected evidence and witnesses pertaining to these cases.

The city had allowed months to pass without telling Newark's black citizens how and why their wives and husbands, mothers, fathers, sons, and friends had died, more from official indifference than tardy judicial process. Because there had been no official word regarding irregularities in the deaths, white communities believed there *were none,* or they certainly would have heard about them by this time. Whites had been surprised and even offended by instances of "excessive force" reported in the Hughes and Kerner Reports. They would have been more shocked and less offended if made cognizant of exactly what "excessive force" meant. The controversial subject of how twenty black people had been shot to death was being given careful treatment. Thus far it had been official only that bodies had been picked up, had been carted to one of the city's three morgues, and that relatives of the deceased had eventually been notified to come in and identify a corpse.

Finally, on April 4, nine months after the riot, the holdover grand jury handed up its presentment to Superior Court Judge Giuliano. It listed twenty-five deaths—twenty-two homicides plus the three persons who had died from accidental causes—in chronological order. The one death left out, that of Mrs. Jones who had been shot by Eyvind Chandler, had been handled routinely by a previous grand jury. She had been the fourth to die and her death was not included in the numerical order.

Judge Giuliano immediately sealed the presentment and reviewed it in private, a timely decision considering the city's mood after King's murder. Only attorneys and reporters, however, were in suspense as to its contents. By this time, politicians could guess, and law enforcement personnel and the prosecutor's office well knew what the result would be. The only other group involved, those in the ghetto who had lived with the shootings, were too uneducated to expect anything. In fact, few of them knew what a grand jury was, or that any action on the riot dead should have taken place once the bodies had been hauled away. Their only schooling had been experience with the police.

The term "grand jury" has a ring of omniscience and purity which is often far from justified. At times a jury may be a political weapon, a gilded weathervane of the times, or even an instrument of ugly injustice. As Newark's attorneys well knew, a grand jury was comprised of twenty-three men and women who were assembled, given information and witnesses by the prosecutor's office, and then left to themselves to draw conclusions. Their evaluations, as often as not, would be influenced by those who had instructed them. That the jurors may have asked many specific questions regarding various aspects of the homicides—chiefly, whose hands had held the guns—does not mean there was an effort to furnish them with answers.

On April 23 the jury's presentment was made public. Its findings weren't much of a surprise in a city with Newark's background. First, the wording of the presentment's conclusion—*"in the final analysis, the responsibility for the loss of life and property that is the inevitable product of rioting and mass lawlessness cannot be placed upon those whose duty it is to enforce law and protect the freedom of our society"*—was more a direct reply to the Hughes Report than an explanation of homicides. Second, the presentment, contrary to its supposed intention, *raised far more questions* than it answered. Newark's press, however, reprinted the presentment's findings as given, without any questions, either then or since. Relatives of the deceased were thus given their only official reply more than *nine months later* in newspapers. As the first, last and only official word on how twenty-two humans had been shot to death, the presentment was a calculated, disgraceful travesty.

If It Runs, Shoot It

> Rose Abraham suffered a fatal bullet wound of the right hip. The bullet recovered from the victim's body had insufficient characteristics for identification or comparison with any known weapon. She was out looking for one of her children when she was shot by someone whose identity could not be determined. According to all witnesses including her husband the shooting occurred at Springfield Avenue and Blum Street at which time police were attempting to clear this area of looters. After the shooting, a neighbor drove her to the hospital under escort by Newark policemen.
>
> Due to insufficient evidence of any criminal misconduct the jury found no cause for indictment.

Police have never admitted responsibility for the death of Rose Abraham. From the words, "police were attempting to clear this area of looters" it is obvious that the jurors recognized that Mrs. Abraham was a victim of the police. But the jurors refused to make that recognition a matter of record.

From the outset, the grand jury's treatment of the homicides appeared to be merely a continuation of the police department's investigation of itself, including the insinuation—which will reappear throughout the document—that police were doing everything in their power to aid the victims, the opposite of the truth.

> James Sanders was fatally shot in the back by a Newark police officer who pursued him observing him and others burglarizing a liquor store at the corner of Springfield Avenue and Jones Street. Officers pursued him through a vacant lot where Sanders while running turned and threw a bottle at them. After he failed to comply with a command to halt, he was felled by a shotgun blast.
>
> Due to insufficient evidence of any criminal misconduct, the jury found no cause for indictment.

The little two-story house at 52 Beacon Street was almost as old as the ancient Phillip's Metropolitan C.M.E. Church which stood directly across the street. Its wooden floors were warped with age and the landlord was putting yet another coat of paint over the dirty walls on the second floor. The stone of the church gave it a look of permanence and its iron fence lent a dignity hopelessly out of place in the street life that now surrounded it. The church had been built for another world, one which had retreated and left the structure as a reminder of where James Sanders, Jr., used to live. His father and mother had lived at 52 Beacon Street with their eleven children for about three years, within yards of the homes of James Sneed and Karl Green. Since the riot and death of their eldest son, sixteen-year-old James, a fire had damaged the upstairs, explaining the repainting going on. An old woman sat downstairs in a living room cluttered with her meager belongings, waiting to move in and pay $125 per month, taking the place of the Sanders family which was long gone.

The Sanders boy was caught looting after 4:00 A.M. at Sampson's Liquors at 77 Jones Street, a block over at the Springfield Avenue intersection where Murray would be shot twelve hours later. The former owner, who was white, had sold the place after it had been cleaned out during the riot, but still owned another liquor store on Belmont Avenue. As police arrived, Sanders had crossed Jones Street and run down the east side of the street toward a vacant lot a block away where some planks had been removed from a fence, giving easy access to Beacon Street.

According to the grand jury, "Sanders while running turned and threw a bottle at them." The shotgun blast that followed hit the boy full in the back, blowing him away like a large rag doll. Morgue photographs again told the story of Double O ammunition Newark police were using in their shotguns. Seven of the nine slugs hit the boy in the back, three going right through his skinny body. The remaining four slugs were removed and placed in a paper bag which is still attached to his file in the medical examiner's office.

The body remained unidentified in the morgue for eight days while his parents wondered where he was. They had been to City Hospital but were told all bodies there had been identified. Several days later Mrs. Sanders heard on the radio that some bodies still weren't identified and she and her husband returned to the hospital. They were told their son's body may have been sent to either of the city's other two morgues.

"We went down to police headquarters then," Mrs. Sanders said at her new address on Peshine Avenue. "They showed my husband some pictures. He said James was all shot up. My husband went to another morgue to identify the body. He had to go because I blanked out."

Mrs. Sanders worked as a nurse's aide well outside of the city in Summit and looked much older than her thirty-six years. She had come to Newark with her father and stepmother from a small town near Richmond when she was seventeen. There were still ten children for her to worry about with James gone, a task she accomplished alone as well as she could.

"My husband hasn't been home for weeks," she said in a tired voice. "He stays away for weeks and months at a time. I don't know where he is—it's been like this since six years after we were married. The oldest girl hasn't been well. I don't know exactly what's wrong with her. They cut her in the stomach, something about her menstruation, something like that. James was my favorite in many ways, he was really a good boy. He hadn't started smoking yet and he never got into trouble like other boys his age. He was *retarded,* you know. He was always getting beaten up, little boys ten years old could beat him up. He wouldn't fight back, that was part of his retardation. I only had one picture of him but somebody stole it out of my wallet where I work and now I don't even have that."

Another section of the grand jury report deals with Richard Taliaferro:

Richard Taliaferro was fatally shot in the back by a police officer while fleeing from a burglarized liquor store. The officers ordered the victim to halt but instead Taliaferro and his companions fired hand weapons at them. One of the officers returned the fire with a shotgun. No weapon was found at the scene of the incident; however a large crowd had gathered around the victim before the police had an opportunity to reach him.

Due to insufficient evidence of any criminal misconduct, the jury found no cause for indictment.

Only police officers testified before the jury regarding the death of Taliaferro, shot on the sidewalk at 11:15 P.M. Friday not far from his home. The twenty-five-year-old Taliaferro had had difficulties as a juvenile but became a hard worker upon leaving school at the age of sixteen. He worked at Pechter's Bakery in Harrison and then at the A & P Bakery on Frelinghuysen Avenue in Newark. On Friday he returned home from work at 5:00 A.M. and went to bed. After getting up and eating, the excitement of the riot drew him outside. Just after 11:00 P.M., Taliaferro was with a group of people who began pulling at the grating covering the window of the WC Liquor Store at the corner of South 8th Street and 11th Avenue. I know of no witnesses who could say whether Taliaferro participated in the break or was merely standing with the crowd when the police arrived, but it made little difference.

"There were three cars," Darnell Jones, eighteen, said. "We were on the other side of the street just looking. They came in like they were gonna blow somebody's head off, they were shooting at everybody. They didn't yell nothing, they just started shooting."

Taliaferro ran across the avenue and up South 8th Street but before getting far he was hit with a shotgun blast. Although a big man—six feet two and 220 pounds—two of the four slugs passed through him. Nevertheless he continued to run, crossing the street and then sitting down on the front stoop of 86 South 8th Street.

"We were watching from here, a few houses down the block," Reggie Brown, seventeen, said. "He just sat there on the steps and leaned over. He leaned further and further and fell on the sidewalk. The cop who shot him stepped over the body and looked in the alley for somebody else. There wasn't no gun, nobody had guns but the police."

Taliaferro had four brothers and two sisters, all of them older. He had lived around the corner from where he was shot, with his father, Harry Taliaferro, sixty-seven; his mother, Elizabeth, seventy; a sister, her husband and three children; and another sister.

"He was such a nice boy," the old mother said, rocking in a rocking chair. "The boy worked all the time. He never did miss a day's work. He never did tell anybody when he got married. He was married, you know. Richard lived a few weeks with his wife and I guess things weren't working out so he came home again. He had a little girl, too. She's up in Syracuse and he used to send money up there."

"He didn't like anything loud or rough or anything like that," Frances, one of the sisters, said. "We don't know too much about how he died. We never received any notice or anything. We didn't see anything in the paper. He was born in City Hospital and he died there."

At the time of the shooting Taliaferro was due to report for Army induction. Two weeks later, on July 27, his family received a letter addressed to him from local board 19 in Newark: "You are directed to report to the local board AT ONCE." The last two words were in bright red.

The grand jury went on to Albert Mercier, Jr.:

> Albert Mercier, Jr., was fatally shot by a police officer as he was fleeing from the scene of a burglarized warehouse at Mulberry and Chestnut Streets. He was observed by the police and a civilian witness coming out of the alley behind the warehouse with a package in his arms. Upon seeing the police officers, he dropped the package and ran. The package contained merchandise from the warehouse. Another civilian witness observed the police officers running on Mulberry Street and firing at Mercier. The victim's father said that he had learned from a companion of his son at the time that the two had broken into and had entered the warehouse.
>
> Due to insufficient evidence of any criminal misconduct, the jury found no cause for indictment.

Albert Mercier, Sr., forty-seven, and his wife, Mrs. Gussie Mercier, forty-five, had come north from Lincolnton, Georgia, thirty years before. They had four daughters: Roberta, eighteen, and Rosemarie, fourteen, still at home and two others who were married. Through years of hard work, Mercier had managed to purchase two bars, the Cozy Corner in 1961 and the Babalu Club in 1965. This legacy was intended for Mercier's only son, Albert, Jr., who had graduated from East Side High School two years before. Those intentions were wiped out, along with the twenty-year-old youth, at 11:55 P.M. Friday not far from the Babalu Club on Mulberry Street, a dreary cobblestone street running through downtown Newark. The scene of Mercier's death was far from the riot area. He died because police behavior was becoming uglier as the riot persisted. Mercier was sentenced to death for a petty crime, as were other victims, and he was executed on the spot.

The youth, over six feet tall and heavyset, managed to squeeze through a 14-by-20 inch opening in a sliding door after he and a companion had kicked in the panel. Nothing inside W. W. Grainger, an electric motor company, was worth shooting a man over.

"When someone's running from you," his father said, "you know damn well they're afraid of you. I want to know why they had to kill him." A year later, Albert Mercier, Sr.—a gravel-voiced man who smoked three packs a day—was still grieved enough to retrace the steps again, as he had done many times before in his mind.

From the truck platform door the younger Mercier had run some twenty yards to reach the street, another fifteen to cross it and then down Mulberry Street's sidewalk some twenty-eight more yards where he was overtaken by a .38 caliber bullet that kept on going after it killed him. "That's my belief on the right hand of God," his father said. "They just killed him because they wanted to kill him. A month after the riot two cops came into my bar trying to sell stolen television sets—*stolen!* He wasn't doing no God damn other than what they were doing but nobody shot them."

> William Furr died of shotgun wounds in the back resulting from shots fired by two Newark patrolmen as he fled from a burglarized liquor store. The patrolmen had responded to a radio call indicating a break and entry at the location. Upon their arrival, they observed Furr leaving the liquor store with beer in his hands. He disregarded several orders by the police to halt and was felled by shotgun fire as he fled. A civilian testified that he had observed the shooting and that the police had fired one or more warning shots before firing the shots which killed Furr and wounded a young boy. This shooting was depicted dramatically in a weekly magazine published shortly after the incident. The photographer who had taken the pictures was subpoenaed but failed to appear.
>
> Due to insufficient evidence of any criminal misconduct, the jury found no cause for indictment.

On January 30, Bud Lee, the freelance photographer, returned from a *Life* assignment in Rome while staff reporter Dale Wittner was on a lengthy assignment in Hong Kong. Together they had captured the story of Avon Avenue, though only Lee was requested to appear before the jury. More than a year after Furr's death the photographer—a personable, sensitive man—re-created the Saturday afternoon scene for me with words as he had done before with photographs:

"The whole time we were in Newark we never saw what you would call a violent black man. Wherever we went they treated us very well. The only people I saw who were violent were the police. When we were out there on Avon Avenue with Billy no one was scared, there wasn't any danger. We were all drinking beer and talking. I didn't take a beer because I don't drink beer but that's the only reason. When the police came, Billy panicked and ran. I couldn't understand why, he was the only one who ran. It all happened so fast. Then when they shot I never believed they'd really shoot to hit him but there was the shot and he went down. He was alive for three or five minutes afterwards and he seemed to be in great anguish.

"I was standing right over him when he died," Lee continued. "It took him about five minutes to die and the police were so busy pushing the people back they didn't do anything for him. I remember we asked if they were going to do anything for him and a cop mumbled, 'The guy's better off dead.' I don't think he was being mean or anything, he said it matter-of-factly. He was really feeling sorry for Billy but he couldn't do anything for him, I think. To be honest, I didn't come to the grand jury because I didn't want to, really. I really felt that I had nothing to add to what the police saw. It happened so fast, I was so surprised when they shot him."

Manslaughter

The grand jury treated the three deaths at the Scudder projects:

Isaac Harrison, Robert Lee Martin, Frederick Toto. These three persons were all fatally wounded by gunfire at approximately the same time and at the same location in the sequence as set forth below. Isaac Harrison suffered fatal shotgun wounds in the left chest and abdomen as he was attempting to enter his son's car which was parked at the entrance of 62 Broome Street, commonly known as Scudder Homes project. Robert Lee Martin died of a fractured skull due to a fall caused or probably caused by bullet wounds in the right arm and back of the left shoulder, suffered while he was walking down Mercer Street between Broome and Howard Streets. Approximately 10 or 15 minutes after the shooting of Harrison and Martin, Newark Detective Frederick Toto was fatally wounded on the corner of Broome and Mercer Streets by a .22 caliber bullet which entered his left chest traveling in a downward path.

On the basis of the evidence presented the grand jury believes that these three deaths were closely related. At the time, extensive breaking, entering and larceny had been taking place in the vicinity of Springfield Avenue, Broome and Mercer Streets. A large crowd of people had gathered in front of the Scudder Homes project. Newark police responded to a radio call, checked the location, and upon return to their car they were met by sniper fire apparently coming from the project. The police retaliated by firing upon the project and it was at this time that Harrison and Martin were fatally shot and a young girl in an upper floor in the project was wounded. A Catholic priest from a local parish testified that he had administered to the needs of

Martin and Harrison. He was leaving the area when he heard gunfire resume and from a vantage point about a block away on Mercer Street observed puffs of gunsmoke from the upper floors of the project. It was at this time and possibly as a result of the renewed sniper fire that Detective Frederick Toto was fatally wounded.

Due to insufficient evidence of any criminal misconduct on the part of any identifiable individual, the jury found no cause for indictment in any of these three deaths.

As Hank Franzoni—attorney representing the Harrisons—had guessed, the jury's presentment on these homicides reflected an intention of the police to group them as closely as possible, thus explaining the deaths of Martin and Harrison as the result of counter-fire against snipers. Even so, the jury didn't explain why the supposed counter-fire had been at ground level. Few if any Scudder project residents testified before the jury. All three shootings were separate incidents. The twenty-two-year-old Martin was actually the first to be shot, his body lying on the sidewalk of Mercer Street before the Harrisons and Horace Morris began walking to their car. Toto was hit sometime later in the afternoon at that same location, a direct response to the other shootings.

Robert Lee Martin came north to Newark in 1966 with his parents, two younger sisters and an older brother after graduating from high school in Greenwood, Mississippi. Three sisters who had left home before the move had married and settled in Newark. Weldon Martin, the fifty-nine-year-old father, is a tall, thin man with deep lines in his light brown-skinned face. Ruby, his fifty-one-year-old wife, is a tired, dark-skinned woman, as shy as her husband is humble. "The three girls came to Newark before Robert Lee did," she said. "There was nothing for them in Greenwood, as the children got older they left. There was supposed to be jobs in Newark."

At the time he was shot, Martin was walking with his brother-in-law Herbert Price up Mercer Street from Springfield Avenue toward the project where Price lived. Both had worked the night before, Martin until 6:00 A.M. at his seventy-dollar-a-week janitor's job and Price until midnight. Martin had come to his brother-in-law's apartment after sleeping and he and Price were trying to buy groceries. The stores were so crowded they gave up and started back to Price's apartment. Both men were empty-handed. As they crossed Broome Street, walking on the right sidewalk, the twenty-four-year-old Price saw three police cars approaching them on Broome from the right.

These were not the three cars that turned onto Broome from the opposite direction shortly thereafter and opened fire on the projects. It is likely that these latter police cars were responding to shots fired at Martin, reported as "sniper activity."

Price also remembered seeing people crowded in front of the projects, further setting the scene for the Harrison shooting a few minutes later. Martin and Price continued walking about forty yards from the corner along the side of the project.

"I don't know where those cars went," Price said. "I just glanced back over my shoulder . . . like this . . . and I saw a police car in the intersection in back of me. Some of the police were standing with their guns up in the air. The police had yellow stripes on their pants. I don't know where the shots came from but they were the only police in back of us that I saw. I just glanced back, you know, and there in front of me part of Robert's head flew open and he went down. Part of his head just flew open before he hit the ground. I told that to the grand jury. He curled up on the sidewalk there where he fell and I panicked and ran through the project parking lot. I ran all the way to tell his mother and father that Robert had been shot."

Price had come to Newark three years before from a little town near Tallahassee, Florida, and had met and married Anna, Martin's oldest sister. He is a strong-looking muscular man with a sensitive nature. "I'll never forget Robert going down like that," he said. "I see it sometimes, you know. I never want to talk about it but if it can do some good, I do it. I told it all to the grand jury and I thought they'd say that Robert was innocent. We never knew they said anything. After it happened I got nervous, afraid to walk on the streets at night. I moved to Orange. Things weren't going right at work, either. You know Robert and I used to work for the same people. I couldn't concentrate too good, my nerves were bad. I'm better now, just a bit nervous. I went to see two doctors. Finally I had to leave that job and I got a driver's permit to get my license so I could get a better job."

Inconsistencies between Price's statements and the presentment require a closer look. One bullet had passed through Martin's right arm and another had hit him in back of his left shoulder. Dr. Albano's first listed cause of death, "homicide by assault with blunt instrument," can be attributed to haste, but there may have been a third bullet hitting Martin in the head, although such a wound did not show up in autopsy photos. Further, and more important, according to Dr. Albano's autopsy and records, the slug that had hit Martin in the back had made its way up into his neck where he found it just beneath the skin. The doctor said he had *turned this bullet over to the police* who then failed to include such information in their ballistic report or even to note that any bullet had been found.

Five more victims were dismissed as follows:

Eddie Moss was fatally shot in the right side of the head while riding with his family in an automobile. The father testified that he had run through two barricades between Elizabeth and Hawthorne Avenues. The National Guardsmen on duty in that area indicated that the automobile had crashed through their barricade, that when they approached the car, it accelerated and did not stop at their command to halt. As it sped away, the guardsmen fired two shots at the vehicle. They did not know that anyone had been hit because the vehicle never stopped, but sped down Elizabeth Avenue. The father stated that he was unaware that his son had been hit until he returned to his residence. No bullets were recovered nor is the family aware of the present location of the vehicle. Other incidents of gunfire occurred while the vehicle was en route to its destination; therefore the exact location of the fatal shooting is unknown.

Due to insufficient evidence of any criminal misconduct, the jury found no cause for indictment.

Michael Pugh was fatally wounded in the upper right thigh while emptying garbage in front of his home. No bullet was recovered. Some friends testified that they believed the shot had come from National Guardsmen stationed at the intersection of Bergen Street and 15th Avenue about a block away. The identity of any guardsmen in that area could not be determined. Shortly after the shooting, the victim's companions stated that they hailed officers in a passing car which transported the boy to the hospital. The identity of these officers is unknown, although State Police communications recorded at the time indicated that an unidentified State Police car did transport a young boy from that location to the hospital.

Due to insufficient evidence of any criminal misconduct, the jury found no cause for indictment.

Mrs. Eloise Spellman, Mrs. Hattie Gainer, Mrs. Rebecca Brown. Mrs. Spellman was fatally shot in the left side of the neck while standing in the window of her 10th-floor apartment in the Hayes Homes project on Hunterdon Street which is diagonally across from a firehouse located at the corner of Springfield Avenue and Hunterdon Street. Several witnesses testified to heavy fire by State Police and National Guardsmen directed at the upper floors of the project.

Mrs. Hattie Gainer was fatally wounded in the chest while she was in her second-floor apartment at 302 Hunterdon Street at about the same time that Mrs. Spellman was killed. Her daughter observed State Police in the area and immediately after the shooting the State Police entered her building investigating suspected sniper fire from the building.

Mrs. Rebecca Brown whose home was in the same general area as Mrs. Gainer's and Mrs. Spellman's was fatally wounded in the left abdomen by rifle fire at about the same time. A relative said that bullets had splintered the window frame of the window at which Mrs. Brown was standing. He stated that National Guardsmen had arrived in the area just before the shooting, had dismounted from their vehicles and had taken cover behind them. Then they commenced shooting at the surrounding buildings.

These three women were all innocent victims of shooting by State Police and National Guardsmen who had responded to the area because of reported sniper fire and at the request of the commanding officer of the firehouse located at the corner of Springfield Avenue and Hunterdon Street. He testified that there had been no police nor guardsmen in the area and that he had been obliged to take the fire company out of service because of persistent sniper fire in the area. The tapes of State Police communications indicate that there was sniper fire directed at the southerly side of the firehouse at this time. It was impossible to determine the identity of either State Police or National Guardsmen who fired weapons in the area.

Due to insufficient evidence of any criminal misconduct on the part of any identifiable individuals, the jury found no cause for indictment in any of these three deaths.

Nine months after the burials of Eddie Moss, Michael Pugh, Mrs. Spellman, Mrs. Gainer, and Mrs. Brown, a grand jury came close to attributing the deaths of all five to the National Guard and the State Police. But not the responsibility, which, the presentment states, *"rests squarely upon the shoulders of those who, for whatever purpose, incite and participate in riots and the flouting of law and order in complete disregard of the rights and well-being of the vast majority of our citizens."*

References to "our citizens" masks the truth that two separate societies are involved and that in the one in which the jurors live, state troopers and guardsmen are unlikely to be walking up the streets pumping .30 caliber bullets into occupied homes.

Further, the presentment's language sanctioned a singular view that an entire population—men, women, and children—was accountable for the unlawful acts of a minority. The inference was clear that the guilty included Eddie Moss's father, for taking his family out for hamburgers, Michael Pugh's mother, for telling her son to carry out the garbage, and Mrs. Brown, Mrs. Spellman, and Mrs. Gainer for being the same color as the rioters.

The Dead Attackers

Raymond Hawk died of a gunshot wound of the head which he received as he was running toward Newark police officers with an object which looked like a section of pipe or cable. The police responded in answer to a report of a burglary taking place at that location. There was evidence of forcible entry at the rear of the premises and a tire iron was found at the scene. The sworn statement of a civilian witness who did not testify was read to the jury.

Due to insufficient evidence of any criminal misconduct, the jury found no cause for indictment.

Raymond Hawk used to live in the Dayton Avenue projects on the fringe of Newark, nowhere near the riot area, yet around the corner from where the top of his head was taken off by a shotgun about 10:20 P.M. Saturday. "To me he was the best husband in the world," his twenty-two-year-old wife said. "He had a good job, we had all the things in the world to look forward to." The couple had a two-year-old son.

Hawk, twenty-four, had worked farther down Frelinghuysen Avenue at the J & R Clothing Company for eight years. After work on Friday he picked up Roberta, his wife, and drove to nearby Linden where they spent the night with her family to stay away from the rioting. Leaving his wife and son there, Hawk drove back to Newark, where he visited a brother-in-law, Nathan Peterson, in the projects where he used to live. Shortly past 10:00 P.M. Hawk's car was parked a short distance away on Frelinghuysen Avenue and he was walking past Sharpe's Drug Store when four or five police cars screeched to a halt. A subsequent shotgun blast took his life. Police testified that Hawk was a lookout for a group who were breaking into the rear of the drug store. They said Hawk attacked them with a tire iron as they responded to the burglary call. From this the grand jury deduced that Hawk had been involved in a burglary and had been shot in self-defense.

To this day, management personnel where Hawk had worked for so long react to his name like a plague, believing he died tainted with crime. Actually, the burglary in the rear of the drug store was the work of neighborhood juveniles who did no more than scratch up the door with a crowbar. A subsequent statement by Assistant Prosecutor Zazzali that Hawk *jumped from the roof* is also strange, since he sounded no alarm to his alleged accomplices. The boys in the rear ran as arriving police opened up with shotguns.

Only one person was apprehended at the scene, Raymond Peterson, Hawk's eighteen-year-old brother-in-law, who was walking home from a store further up the avenue at the time.

"They opened the doors and fell out before the cars even stopped," Peterson said. "They were just shooting away. I thought they were shooting blanks for a minute . . . pop, pop, pop . . . like that. Some slammed the doors and others just left them open. They were shooting like they were crazy. One of them said, 'God damn, I shot all those shells and didn't get a God damn one of them.' They frisked me and brought me around the building to where a body was laying on the sidewalk. One of the policemen asked me who the body was. It was laying on its back with blood all around the head and there was a hole straight through from one side to the other. I found out later it was my brother-in-law but I didn't recognize him then from his face. One of the policemen frisked the body and he said, 'He's clean.' There wasn't any pipe or anything there either. His eyes were open and fluttering back and forth and he was moaning and groaning.

" 'You sure you don't know him?' one of the cops said. He turned the body over with his foot as he was talking. Then one of them told me to lay down on the sidewalk next to the body. I laid there for about ten minutes. 'Call an ambulance,' one of the policemen said. Then he looked back at the body. . . . 'Never mind, call homicide,' he said. Two colored cops took me in. 'Damn shame the way they killed that man,' one of them said."

Raymond Peterson was taken to police headquarters downtown and charged with breaking and entering and violation of the curfew. The charges were later dropped.

> Raymond Gilmer was fatally shot in the back of the head by one of three shots by a Newark detective as he fled after disregarding an order to halt. Prior to the shooting, Gilmer had been observed by Newark police officers carrying a package out of a basement door at 744 Bergen Street. After the vehicle in which the police were riding made a U-turn, Gilmer was ordered to stop. Instead, he fired a shot which hit the left rear door of the police vehicle and fled in a Pontiac sedan. The police pursued with siren on and lights flashing to Clinton and Jelliff Avenues where Gilmer jumped from his car and attempted to flee. The Newark detective fired three shots, one of which struck Gilmer. A search of Gilmer's car, later proven to have been stolen, disclosed the presence of a .38 caliber revolver containing four live bullets and one spent cartridge which had been secreted under the left front seat. A civilian witness testified that he had heard the police siren and observed the shooting as described. After the shooting he and everyone else were ordered off the street. He also testified that all stores in the area were closed including a restaurant located at the corner of Clinton and Jelliff Avenues. A statement by an alleged eyewitness who did not testify because of his absence from the state, was read to the jury.
>
> Due to insufficient evidence of any criminal misconduct, the jury found no cause for indictment.

This account appears to be but a revamping of police reports (which had proven to be a lot less than accurate), and the presentment excluded or qualified statements from eyewitnesses who disagreed with police accounts. Arline's Foods, a restaurant on the corner of Clinton and Jelliff, *was* occupied at the time of Gilmer's death and several occupants witnessed the shooting. Lance Corporal John Richardson, home on leave from the Marines, was taking care of the small shop for his mother and was "the alleged eyewitness." Civilian witnesses who agreed with police accounts were identified as such while others were called "alleged" witnesses and their testimony ignored.

"The man got out of the passenger side of the car and ran," Richardson said. "A siren sounded only after the police car came around the corner. Without any warning a shot was fired from the patrol car. All the policemen got out of the car and one walked over to the body. He shined a flashlight on the wounded man and began to go through his pockets. There weren't any weapons, only a wallet. Afterwards all the policemen went back to the body and merely looked at the man who was still breathing heavily. No effort was made to call an ambulance—I called an ambulance myself. After the shooting a news car pulled up. They got the story of the policeman who had shot the man and took his picture. As they were going back to their car, I said, 'There were witnesses who saw it. Don't you want to get their side of the story?' They just got in their car and left and that was it."

Richardson said he watched police search the 1964 Pontiac Gilmer had reportedly stolen and that they found nothing. A bullet hole in a police car door was attributed to the dead man who, according to official police reports, had hidden a gun beneath the car seat and then ran from the car with a knife. This appears to have been another case of overkill in evidence. If Gilmer had fired on the police car it was unnecessary to say a knife was found near the body, there being reason enough to shoot. Finding a gun—if indeed they did find one—alleviated the situation. The knife claim then evaporated and by the time police testified before the grand jury it disappeared.

The twenty-year-old Gilmer ran thirty-six yards before a .38 caliber bullet hit him in back of the head and emerged from his forehead. "They left his brains out there by the side of the building," an area resident said. "They were there for weeks, flies and all."

It would seem that Raymond Gilmer—last to die in the Newark riot —had been in trouble from the beginning. One of ten children, he was reared by his sixty-seven-year-old grandmother, Mrs. Bessie Hopkins, in an ancient brick tenement at the corner of Ferry Street and Manufacture Place deep in the East Ward. His father, Luther, had left years before for St. Louis and never lived with the family. He had fathered only one of the other children.

Gilmer quit school in the tenth grade to take a low-paying job and was loading potato sacks on trains until a railroad strike caused him to be laid off. He had a juvenile record, including two trips to Jamesburg Reformatory and one to Annandale, all for car theft.

Gilmer's sweetheart, Sharon, had given birth to two of his children and stood by him while he was away. He stood by her and married the girl in 1965. They had one more child and at the time of her husband's death Sharon was eight months pregnant. They were living in an apartment at 776 Bergen Street, deep in the ghetto.

On Monday morning—when the riot was over—Gilmer left the house early, saying he was going to look for a bigger apartment. He ended up at his grandmother's, staying there until 3:20 P.M., when he returned to the Bergen Street apartment, next door to the laundromat basement where police said they first saw Gilmer near midnight. A few minutes later Mrs. Gilmer was a widow. Mrs. Hopkins was the first to hear of her grandson's death and phoned Sharon.

"I went to the hospital after the phone call," the nineteen-year-old widow recalled. "They wouldn't let me see him because I was pregnant. You know he was shot in the head. He was lying in a place near the emergency room. At first they were going to let me see him but they saw how big I was and they didn't want me to see him. I snuck back with my sister and I saw that it was him."

The baby, a boy, was born a month later.

Murder

Tedock Bell was fatally shot in the right chest while running from the corner of Magnolia and Bergen Streets where a store had been burglarized. Apparently he was shot by an unidentified Newark police officer who had called to him to halt. Witnesses indicated that Tedock Bell had been at the intersection with others who had turned back from that location leaving him in the area. One witness saw the shooting clearly from a nearby second-floor window and testified that she heard the police officer call "halt" before he fired his weapon. Bell continued to run to the corner of Fairview and Magnolia Streets where he fell.

Due to insufficient evidence of any criminal misconduct, the jury found no cause for indictment.

Hoffman's Market on the corner of Magnolia and Bergen Streets, the store Bell was wrongly accused of looting, was completely cleaned out during the riot and never opened its doors again. Exactly a year later it wore a mask of rusting iron grating on a face of rotting wood. No more penny candy, no more boxes of starch for pregnant black girls. The boarded-up old store was a depressing monument to twenty-eight-year-old Tedock Bell, Jr., who died four years after coming to Newark from North Carolina.

"I think it was wrong," Mildred Sparkman, Bell's twenty-six-year-old sister, said. "I wouldn't care so much if he was out doing something, that would be one thing. But he stayed home so he wouldn't get into anything. Then to have him get shot like that."

Bergen Street was dark and quiet in the early morning hours of the riot's second night as Bell, his mother, wife, and sister-in-law, Fannie Edwards, twenty-six, sat on their front stoop. Bell and Edna, his wife, had four children and lived in the second-floor front apartment, paying eighty-eight dollars a month for the four rooms. He earned $150 a week as a machinist in a plastics factory and also worked part time as a bartender. A short distance down the block on the other side of the street was Ben's Tavern where Bell worked on weekends. A block further on the opposite side was Hoffman's Market. Both had been totally cleaned out by looters, leaving nothing to be taken.

"About three-thirty Friday morning we walked down the block to see what had happened," Fannie Edwards said. Bell, Fannie Edwards and two other women walked down Bergen, crossed Magnolia, and stopped at the grocery store which had bare shelves and a wide-open front door. The other two women walked on, leaving Fannie Edwards and Bell standing in front of the building. Just then a police car came down the Magnolia Street hill and stopped at the store. A Newark policeman got out and stood by the side of the car. He fired his revolver into the hot night air. Bell stood by passively in front of the store a few yards away while Fannie Edwards ran farther up Bergen Street.

"Tedock told me, 'You shouldn't run because you weren't doing anything,' but I ran," she said. "The gun frightened me. When I came back Tedock was still standing in front of the store and I walked by. 'Where are you going?' he called to me. I told him I was scared and was going back home. I left him standing in front of the store and I walked back up the block and waited for him on the front steps. From there I could see him good, standing in front of the store."

Then another police car, this one with four or five Newark officers wearing riot helmets, came down Bergen from Springfield Avenue and passed by Fannie Edwards. She watched the car as it pulled up to the curb at the corner of Magnolia and Bergen. Bell was now standing just off the curb watching the approaching police car. One of the officers got out and approached Bell, taking out his revolver as he walked. Fannie Edwards was too far away to hear what the policeman was saying but she saw her brother-in-law suddenly run across Bergen and into Magnolia Street with the policeman—gun in hand—coming after him.

"I thought they were just trying to scare him," she said. "The policeman ran to the corner and pointed the gun. He fired three times. I didn't see any reason why the police would shoot."

Bell was from five to ten yards away when a .38 caliber bullet hit him, leaving a half-inch exit wound. He went down on the red bricks, then got up and continued running. The policeman who had shot Bell returned to his car and it turned the corner, coasting down the hill. From the intersection at Bergen the red bricks of Magnolia Street slope down a block to Fairview Avenue where Bell finally collapsed. The police car pulled up. They looked at Bell and correctly assumed he had drawn his last breath or was about to. "Take the man to the hospital, you shot him!" a neighbor called out, as others came to their windows and porches. One of the police made a motion with his hand telling them to go to hell and the car sped off into the darkness, making good its escape.

"He got as far as this sewer grating when he collapsed," Mrs. Sparkman said. A brother of a neighbor who was visiting from Georgia took Bell to City Hospital where, near 4:00 A.M., he was dead on arrival. "Damn," he said, "they ain't no different up here than they are down home."

Mrs. Sparkman was with Bell's mother, Mrs. Mary Bell, and Fannie Edwards when they went to the hospital the next afternoon. "At first they told us he was all right," Mrs. Sparkman said. "We asked to see him but they told us we couldn't right then. This went on for fifteen minutes. Then I went outside to a phone booth and called the information desk. They told me that Tedock had been dead since he had gotten there."

Dr. Albano reported that the hole in Bell's back was an *exit wound* and that he had been shot in the right chest. Either he turned before being shot, or the medical examiner's office made another error. The police officers present at the shooting never admitted it. His body was shipped home to Ayden, North Carolina, where he was born. "I just didn't want him buried here," his mother said.

Rufus Council died from a .38 caliber bullet wound in the head. The bullet was too badly distorted for identification purposes. He was one of a large crowd of people gathered on the north side of South Orange Avenue a short distance from Broome Street. Several witnesses testified that an unmarked car containing four police officers was driving north on Broome Street from the direction of Springfield Avenue to South Orange Avenue. This would have been a few minutes after the death of Detective Toto. The occupants of the car were observed to be shooting in the air and as the car turned into South Orange Avenue the officer sitting in the rear of the car behind the driver fired his pistol into the crowd which resulted in the death of Rufus Council. There was conflicting testimony as to whether the car's occupants were Newark police officers or State Police.

Due to insufficient evidence of any criminal misconduct on the part of any identifiable individual, the jury found no cause for indictment.

The smell of cooking barbecue from Roz's Restaurant drifted up the ghetto street past a rusted fire escape where Tommy Grasham had watched thirty-five-year-old Rufus Council, Jr., die. "He stayed here in the winter before the riot in the second-floor apartment with some other people," the fifteen-year-old boy said on the fire escape. "He wouldn't hurt nobody. He stayed there a couple of months and they all had to move because they didn't pay the rent. I don't know where he was staying when he was shot."

Council, a dark-skinned man of 150 pounds, had been born in North Carolina and came north years before, leaving behind two teenage children and a wife. The building on the corner, 1 Prince Street, was listed by the police as his last address. He was a neighborhood drifter who did odd jobs to survive and at the time of his death was working for a moving company.

Around 4:30 P.M. Friday, Council had a sandwich at Roz's and then stood on the avenue, joining a crowd watching police fire on the Scudder projects a few blocks away. Suddenly sirens wailed—announcing the Toto shooting—and police cars raced down Broome Street, some officers shooting into the air. Council broke from the group and went back to the safety of the restaurant, standing in the doorway. As an unmarked police car turned right onto the avenue, the officer in the rear seat behind the driver leveled his revolver. One witness said Council put his hands up and shook his head, telling the police not to shoot. A .38 caliber bullet struck him in the head and he dropped in front of the restaurant as the police sped off like gangsters.

"I saw it from the fire escape," Grasham said, pointing to the spot where Council went down. "The police car came up and the cop shot him out the car and kilt him. The bullet hit him in the head. He went back . . . like this . . . and fell on his back in front of the door. He laid there, I'd say, at least a half-hour. There was blood coming out of the left side of his forehead."

"I've seen him around here for seems like eight years," a man said. "He drank a lot but he never bothered anybody."

"Seems he had a wife down in North Carolina," another man said. "He just came back and forth between here and there for years."

"I liked the man," Mrs. Albartha Frazier, the new owner of the little restaurant, said. "I live across the street there. After he got shot I came out to see. I came over and saw him lying there. I took his pulse and he was dead."

From the sidewalk at 69 South Orange Avenue, Council took a short trip to the morgue in the basement of City Hospital. A call was made some time after to a little house on Deep Creek Road in the town of Fayetteville, North Carolina. His wife, Mrs. Susie Council, then found out that Rufus wouldn't make it home again on his own. Later another phone call from Fayetteville by Susie Council was put through to the Woody Funeral Home in Newark. She told the funeral home to pick up Rufus Council and send him home.

> Oscar Hill was fatally shot in the right chest. The autopsy revealed a lead bullet which was too badly distorted for identification purposes. There are no known witnesses to this shooting. He was employed at the Spring Manor Tavern, located on the east side of Jones Street near Springfield Avenue.

During the day he had visited the tavern, talked with fellow employees and was scheduled to report to work at 5:00 P.M. which he failed to do. His body was brought to the hospital by persons unknown.

Due to insufficient evidence of any criminal misconduct, the jury found no cause for indictment.

At the time of his death Oscar Hill, fifty, had lived with his common-law wife of nine years, Mrs. Alene Johnson, in a second-floor apartment at 497 Belmont Avenue. This is a brick building with a green wood front, one of a string of aging two- and three-story apartment buildings that make up the Belmont Avenue ghetto. Hill and Mrs. Johnson had five children, and all but one, a fourteen-year-old girl, were his, but he treated them all alike.

"I loved him very much," Mrs. Johnson said. "We were very close. He did his own washing and cooking and mopping for years. He did almost everything by himself. He used to help me with the diapers, he was a big help. I know I'll never find another one like him. I dream about him sometimes, he comes to me in my sleep. I live with that and I raise his kids because that's what he would have wanted."

Oscar Hill and his legal wife, Mrs. Agnes Hill, forty-eight, came to Newark from North Carolina in 1953 with her daughter, Bernice, now Mrs. Bernice Curry. They settled above the Howard Bar deep in the ghetto. Hill tended bar for years at another nearby bar, Maxie's, until it closed down, then worked at the Howard Bar. His wife left him sometime before 1957, leaving also her daughter. Hill raised the girl by himself and she loved him as much as a natural father.

After she married and moved away, Hill stayed on alone above the bar for ten years. Though they didn't live together, Oscar and Alene Johnson, then twenty-three, began to go together in 1959. She became his wife in everything but name and Hill had never been with another woman since.

It is doubtful that Hill had been at the Spring Manor Bar—his next job after the Howard Bar closed—on the day of his death as the presentment said. He and Mrs. Johnson had been together all day. They had visited her mother in the Scudder projects on Broome Street—a few blocks down the avenue from the bar—after which they had returned to Belmont Avenue.

" 'If I was you I wouldn't go,' I told him when he left for work that day," Mrs. Johnson said. "He said, 'The baby got to have milk.' Oscar had joined the union and they were going to have a meeting. He said that if he showed up at the bar he'd be paid. Oscar said if the baby didn't have milk, pretty soon there wouldn't be any food either. He hated to miss a day's work. He kissed me and he said, 'I'll be back, I hope, I hope.' He always used to say that because you could never tell when the bar might be stuck up. 'I'll call you,' that was the last thing he said."

Hill, a tall dark-skinned man who suffered from asthma, spent his last minutes walking up Belmont Avenue.

The quiet, good-natured Hill crossed Avon Avenue where Leroy Boyd would be shot six hours later and where, a block up Avon, Billy Furr would be shotgunned that next afternoon with Joey Bass catching some of the slugs. On down Belmont, Hill crossed 17th Avenue where it had all begun two days before at the Fourth Precinct. He was then in the shadow of the Hayes projects where Mrs. Spellman would be shot to death in her home that next afternoon. Next Hill passed the W. Kinney intersection where the archaic, deserted Krueger Brewery stood like a haunted castle with rock holes punched through its windows. From there it was just two more blocks to the intersection where Cornelius Murray would be shot in a matter of minutes and where the retarded boy, James Sanders, had been shotgunned at four o'clock that same morning.

A short time later Hill was on Springfield Avenue down the hill where police were firing on the Scudder projects. The last person to see him was John Rutledge, twenty-nine, who knew him from his days at the Howard Bar.

"He was a bit in front of me, walking up the hill," Rutledge recalled. "I don't know why he was down there but he was walking up towards the Spring Manor Bar where he worked. I was whistling to make him hear me. There was a boy and girl walking towards me between us. Then I called to him, 'Hey, Oscar!' but he didn't hear me.

"Up at the corner on Belmont there was a police car parked and two policemen standing by it," Rutledge continued. "Oscar kept walking towards the police car. Just then another police car came out of Beacon Street to my right and turned up the avenue. Just as the car got to where Oscar was walking, I heard a shot. Oscar turned towards the car and went down on the sidewalk. When I seen him go down, that's when I took off. I knew the police shot him and I thought they were gonna shoot me too. They shot at me, yeah, I was running. The bullets hit in the street. I ran across the avenue into the street where the police car had just come out of and ran over to South Orange Avenue. When I got there I went back down the hill to High Street and then I walked home. I saw Mrs. Johnson after that but I didn't want to be the one to tell her that the police shot Oscar."

Hill got to his feet after being shot and staggered down the avenue, finally sitting down in the broken-out front of a clothing store. "We were walking up Springfield Avenue when we found him lying in the window," Harry Kearny, former Newark policeman, said. "It looked like he had been sitting there and just fell over into the window. We went into the store through the door and pulled him inside the window. After we sat him up in a chair inside and he had no pulse we thought he was dead.

State troopers said they would take care of the report and send an ambulance. I guess they never made out any report but I'm almost positive that an ambulance did come."

Hill's death remained an unfathomable mystery. Homicide investigators were unable to come up with the location at which he was shot, even though an unidentified photograph of his body lying in the store window was circulated coast-to-coast in the July 28 issue of *Life* magazine. Ironically and sadly, Hill, one of the most peaceful of men, was photographed in death under circumstances that made him appear to be a looter.

Hill lay unidentified in the city morgue for a week, but there couldn't have been any confusion over his identity or address as was reported. At City Hospital in a yellow envelope marked "Oscar C. Hill D.O.A." was his black leather wallet stuffed with names, addresses, and even directions to where Mrs. Curry lived.

"Oscar was supposed to call me at six o'clock," Mrs. Johnson said. "If he said he was gonna call me at six, he always called. I knew something was wrong when he didn't. When he didn't come home either I went and called all the hospitals and jails, even the jail at Caldwell and Rahway Prison. He wasn't at any of them. After everything I called his daughter and she said he may have been out with some fellas. 'No,' I said, 'that's not like Oscar.' I found out he had been killed the next Friday, a week later. 'Oh, God, no,' I said. By that time I knew I was pregnant again. Oscar never knew.

"I never did see him again, I couldn't see him at the morgue because the body had been out so long," Mrs. Johnson went on. "I guess it was all for the best because I was pregnant. I went to one funeral when I was pregnant, my sister-in-law's funeral, and the baby came out retarded. But I cried when they told me I couldn't see him. They sent Oscar back to North Carolina. After he was gone I just couldn't stay on Belmont Avenue no more, I'd be thinking about him a lot. We had a back door and he would always go out the back door to go to work. I'll never forget that day he went out and didn't come back. I used to sit looking at the door. The junkies steal and beat people over the head, why couldn't they kill them? He was such a good man."

Mrs. Johnson moved to Fairmount Avenue not long after and, a year after Hill's death, the baby he never knew he had made was three months old. The family was living on Hill's $238 monthly social security check and, because he was a Navy veteran, a $78 Veterans Administration check. Metropolitan Life Insurance Company said they would pay double indemnity on Hill's death to Mrs. Hill, his legal wife, only if they were certain he hadn't been involved in anything unlawful when he was shot. They paid it.

Cornelius Murray was killed by a bullet which passed through his left chest[4] and was not recovered. He was shot while standing with a group of men in front of a tavern on the west side of Jones Street a short distance from Springfield Avenue. Witnesses stated that they observed what appeared to be two Newark policemen firing at them from a window on the second floor of a vacant building on the northeast corner of Springfield Avenue and Jones Street and also from the rooftop of an adjacent building. When the firing started, the group fled but Murray was hit. Shortly after the shooting, a Newark police car responded to the area to assist State Police officers who were pinned down by snipers on Springfield Avenue near Jones Street. The Newark police explained to Murray's companions that they could not take Murray to the hospital but would call for an ambulance; whereupon the civilians themselves drove Murray to the hospital. The police searched the building on the corner of Springfield Avenue and Jones Street and the adjacent buildings, including the rooftops, but found no one nor any spent shells or cartridges. Apparently, this shooting occurred within about fifteen minutes of the shooting of Detective Toto a few blocks away.

Due to insufficient evidence of any criminal misconduct to any identifiable person, the jury found no cause for indictment.

"The last time I saw him was about ten-thirty in the morning," Mrs. Geneva Murray remembered. "He said he was going over to his mother's grocery store to see if it was all right. They called me from the hospital that afternoon and told me my husband had been shot and I should come over there as soon as possible. I ran downstairs into the street screaming.

"A man stopped his car and told me to get in and he'd take me to the hospital. When we pulled up a policeman on the side of the car put a gun in the man's face and told him, 'Get the hell out of here!' The man explained how my husband had been shot and they called me to come but the cop said, 'Get the hell out of here or you'll get shot.' He drove me back home and I called the hospital. They asked me why I hadn't come. Then they told me my husband had been shot in the foot but they couldn't give me any information. They said the hospital was under martial law.

"I was crying going out of my mind not knowing and I called again and again but they always told me the same thing. Finally, I found out on the third day. A woman told me, 'Mrs. Murray, I feel so sorry for you. I could get fired for telling you this but your husband was dead three days ago.' "

Geneva Murray identified her twenty-nine-year-old husband, Cornelius Murray, Jr., in City Hospital's morgue. When Murray left home he had $126 in his wallet, a diamond ring and a Bulova watch. The only item re-

---

[4] Murray's autopsy report stated he had been hit in the left chest, the bullet emerging from his back. Those who had been with him at the scene emphatically stated Murray had been hit in the back.

turned to his widow was a wallet with thirty-one cents in it. She later found out that news of her husband's death had been released to the newspapers before she had made that last phone call. The corpse was taken to Whigham's Funeral Home on High Street, which handled seven of the black homicide victims, and was buried in Heavenly Rest Memorial Park, Linden, near Newark. His grave site is number twenty-eight, row B, where he wasn't long settled before two detectives from the prosecutor's office visited his twenty-eight-year-old widow.

"They asked me who had killed my husband," Mrs. Murray said. "I told them the Newark police killed him. 'How do you know that?' one of them shouted at me. The taller one was doing all the talking and the other one was quiet. He treated me like *I had killed* my husband. After a while I just asked them to leave. 'You know, we can make you talk,' the tall one said. The other one didn't say anything, he just looked innocent."

Immediately after Toto was hit in front of the projects three men were murdered by the Newark police in cold blood. The jury thought Council was first, Murray second and Hill last. However, it appears that Hill was the first to die. Gunfire directed at him and at John Rutledge was reported as sniper fire. It is also possible that the two policemen standing by their car as Hill approached may well have had something to do with Murray's death shortly after. Because of the difference in radio frequency there is little doubt that Council, the third to die, was shot by Newark police—not troopers. Newark police were first to hear of Toto's shooting and reacted accordingly. Ten to twelve Newark police officers were involved in these shootings of innocent men, either as participants or witnesses. For obvious reasons, *none of them* testified before the grand jury or identified themselves.

The Myth Lives On

Newark Fire Captain Michael Moran was killed by a bullet which entered his left side. Police testimony indicated that the bullet was an armor-piercing cartridge of a common variety that can be readily purchased as can the rifle from which it could be fired. The bullet apparently ricocheted before striking Captain Moran and the identity of the person who fired it is unknown. A witness testified that Moran had responded to an alarm at the above location which had apparently been set off by a bullet which had pierced the sprinkler system in the building. A possible source of this bullet was an automobile that had been driven up Central Avenue immediately preceding the alarm. There were reports of firing from that vehicle at the firehouse on Central Avenue. Captain Moran and his companions were shot at as they attempted to gain access to the building through a second-floor window.

Due to insufficient evidence of any criminal misconduct on the part of any identifiable individual, the jury found no cause for indictment.

Continuing the machine-gun sniper fiction was of paramount importance to the post-riot city in general and the Newark police in particular. To admit that Moran hadn't been killed by a sniper was to lend credence to reports of wild shooting by police and guardsmen in the Hughes Report, which had to be discredited. This could account for the grand jury's misleading treatment of the shooting and the injustice—by insinuation—to Howard Edwards, who was never asked to appear at the probe. The myth of Howard Edwards lived on, more than seven months after he had been cleared.

Slaughter

James Rutledge was fatally shot by police officers while burglarizing the package store annex of a tavern at Custer Avenue and Bergen Street. The county medical examiner testified that the autopsy report showed evidence of four, possibly five separate shotgun wounds in the back and six bullet wounds in the back of the head, any of which could have been fatal. He further testified that, based on the condition of the body tissues, all of these shots had been fired within seconds of one another, almost simultaneously.

Shortly after 5:00 P.M., a car containing four Newark police officers closely followed by several cars of State Police had arrived at the tavern in response to a radio alarm advising of breaking and entering and possible larceny at the location. They found the tavern closed and completely boarded up except for a window on the Custer Avenue side, where the boards had been partially removed. Inside this window, stacks of beer were observed. Two Newark police officers entered the tavern through this window and began to search the premises; they were followed shortly by two State Police officers. All testified that the interior of the tavern and adjoining liquor store was very dark and the visibility correspondingly poor. Their testimony as to what then occurred inside the tavern is conflicting, vague and in many respects contradictory. The consensus of their testimony, substantiated by physical evidence at the scene, indicates that the fatal shooting of Rutledge occurred in the liquor store annex of the tavern and that the victim at the time was behind a counter located along the wall of the store next to the tavern and near the entrance to the tavern. The Newark police, after a search of the tavern, entered the adjoining liquor store with the State Police close behind. As they moved towards the center of the store, which was in extreme but not total darkness, they suddenly observed a man rise from behind the counter, holding a knife in a raised position; the police opened fire simultaneously. The testimony of most witnesses, including officers stationed outside the tavern, agreed that the shots were fired in rapid succession, although a few witnesses reported a pause between the first shots and the final shot or shots.

The testimony of a ballistics expert indicated that at least two revolvers and one or more shotguns had been fired, but none of the spent bullets or slugs could be traced to any particular gun although tests were conducted. Testimony of police radio personnel placed the elapsed time between the first alarm as to "looting" at the tavern and the final report of the shooting of the suspect at only seven minutes.

The jury also heard testimony to the effect that three juveniles, who had accompanied Rutledge to the tavern, were later apprehended in the back room of the tavern some distance from the package store. These juveniles had previously made statements to the effect that they were eyewitnesses to the shooting of Rutledge but they repudiated these statements before the grand jury.

The jury finds that, although some of the testimony was conflicting as to the actual chain of events inside the tavern after the arrival of the police officers, certain facts are supported by the preponderance of evidence heard:

1. A breaking and entering had been committed at the scene of the tavern.

2. Intent to commit larceny was clearly evident from the cases of beer stacked inside the opened window.

3. A knife was recovered near the victim.

After considering all of the facts, the jury found that the police officers were justified in their use of firearms, although too many shots were fired from too many guns. This manifest error in judgment on the part of the police the jury attributes to the conditions within the darkened tavern and liquor store where the officers confronted the suspect. The jury further found no evidence of malice, criminal intent or wanton use of unreasonable force. In the absence of such criminal misconduct, the jury found no cause for indictment.

It has come to the jury's attention that many erroneous and deliberately false accounts of this incident have been published and transmitted to various government agencies and to the public, in the form of leaflets, news accounts and a book entitled *Rebellion in Newark*. Moreover, the jury found that a distorted photo of the victim depicting a complete mutilation of the body, not resulting from the shooting, was distributed in Newark with the inflammatory leaflets attached. The jury finds this act to be despicable and flagrantly irresponsible and designed to inflame unnecessarily an already troubled community. The jury is concerned and believes that adequate steps should be taken by responsible persons in the various agencies such as Newark Legal Services Project and the American Civil Liberties Union to assure themselves that irresponsible and unauthorized persons should not and will not have access to documents and physical evidence, including photographs, which are the work products of said agencies.

For the jury to attempt to justify police conduct in Rutledge's death insults intelligence. We were told the liquor store was *"very dark"* and *"the visibility correspondingly poor"*—yet it was not so dark that six .38 slugs couldn't be placed in back of Rutledge's skull, remarkable marksmanship under the circumstances.

The jury doesn't explain why it failed to probe more deeply into the reasons why four law-enforcement officers gave sworn testimony that was *"conflicting, vague and in many respects contradictory."* It appears to exhibit a permissive attitude toward perjury. The shots—all seventeen of them—were fired *"within seconds of one another, almost simultaneously,"* we are told. This is irrelevant because it would take but a few seconds for police to perform sadistic acts on Rutledge's body. Some witnesses outside indeed reported *"a pause between the first and last shot or shots."* One of the civilian witnesses was Yolanda Spruell. "There was a lot of shots, a pause, and then a lot more shots," she told me. "I was standing on Bergen Street across the street from the bar. I told that to the grand jury."

"The testimony of a ballistics expert indicated that at least two revolvers and one or more shotguns had been fired," the presentment stated. Unless one can believe that Rutledge stood long enough for one officer to empty five shotgun shells in his back, it must naturally be assumed that two shotguns were used. Instead of quoting the obvious conclusions of a ballistics expert that two revolvers had been used, it would have been more helpful for the jury to explain why *both weapons* had to be *emptied,* all twelve .38 caliber slugs hitting Rutledge.

"But none of the spent bullets or slugs could be traced to any particular gun although tests were conducted," we were told. The FBI spent weeks inside Jo Rae's and should certainly have come up with every bullet fired. What happened to them? The police reported receiving only five—short by seven. Contrary to what the jury insinuated in its evasive phrasing, only two of the five slugs had insufficient characteristics for identification. The other three were easily identifiable, having a rifling of five lands, five grooves, right twist. The presentment stated—again misleadingly—that tests were conducted. On what guns were they conducted? Only two revolvers out of a total of four had been fired but these *couldn't be found,* according to the grand jury. This time the FBI found the bullets but the police had unfortunately misplaced the guns that had fired them. Such carelessness, however, apparently failed to concern the grand jury.

Its lack of interest in such matters contrasts forcefully with its barely controlled rage about the use made of photographs of Rutledge's corpse which the jury called *"despicable and flagrantly irresponsible."* That would be a valid attack only if those who made the leaflets understood the process of embalming. Most of those involved didn't know. The issue was a skinny kid who had forty-two holes in him. Now just what is a body supposed to look like after being shot "thirty-nine" times? Danny Dawson, the photographer, testified to the jury of his intentions.

"By the time I got to the funeral home Perry had already started on the embalming," Dawson said. "According to state law they can only keep a corpse so long before working on it. The grand jury was a joke. Zazzali would get people in there and try to intimidate them. I'd answer his questions, then he'd ask the same one again later. I was getting hot. Pretty soon I had to explain what an autopsy was all about and how Perry did it. They tried to make it look like I was paid to take pictures of a mutilated body. It just happened that way. The thing is, you couldn't see the bullet holes with my photos. The body would have looked worse if it hadn't been opened for embalming. As long as they're giving out the news releases, they can play the game."

The grand jury summed up its case not for the public but for the Essex County prosecutor's office. They pointed out the charges of breaking and entering and intent to commit larceny. One more ingredient was needed to justify a fusillade of lead: *"A knife was recovered near the victim,"* the last insult. Rutledge not only had held or thrown the knife but, after being shot seventeen times, had time to wipe his fingerprints off it.

Missing Witnesses, Missing Bullets

In summarizing the circumstances surrounding each of the twenty-two homicide victims, the grand jury found that eight of them (Bell, Sanders, Taliaferro, Mercier, Furr, Hawk, Rutledge, and Gilmer) had either been participating in looting and burglary or were suspected of such crimes and were shot while fleeing. To include Bell was an outrageous disregard of fact. Evidence that Hawk had in any way been connected with a burglary was extremely shaky, as is the jury's portrayal of him attacking at least four shotgun-armed police with a pipe or cable or whatever it was they claimed he had.

Evidence against Taliaferro is also lacking. The jury may get the benefit of the doubt—but not to the extent that Taliaferro can be considered as having been armed. The list stands corrected at six.

Of these six, only Gilmer could be described as "dangerous." Even the police admit that the others were not. It is highly probable that Gilmer—who "pulled out" the mysterious knife after having "hidden" a gun—no more had a knife than did Rutledge or Taliaferro have a gun. He was shot from a moving police car and without any attempt at capture, an important point in state law.

Neither had there been an attempt at capture for any of the others, except for Sanders. There the record is clear: grown men were unable to apprehend a sixteen-year-old retarded boy. So he was shotgunned from a range close enough that seven of nine slugs found their mark.

"Nine deaths [Mrs. Abraham, Martin, Harrison, Council, Murray, Mrs. Spellman, Mrs. Gainer, Mrs. Brown, and Pugh] resulted from gunfire by persons unknown upon individuals in or near their homes or who were innocent bystanders," the jury concluded. Adding the equally innocent Bell, Hill, and Eddie Moss to this list brings the total to twelve. This admission of the jury speaks for itself.

Two other deaths—Leroy Boyd and Moss—were listed as accidental. This may be true for Boyd—a case that will be taken up separately in Chapter 22—but how can direct National Guard fire upon an automobile in which the boy is riding result in an accidental death? The jury could find no category for Hill, and the remaining two, Toto and Moran, were listed as probable victims of sniper fire.

In eleven cases (Mrs. Abraham, Bell, Harrison, Martin, Council, Murray, Hill, Mrs. Spellman, Mrs. Gainer, Mrs. Brown, and Pugh) the killers could not be identified. It is highly questionable whether any effort was made to learn their identities. At least twenty-five law-enforcement officers involved either as triggermen or eyewitnesses—and excluding those shooting at the homes of the three women—refused to make themselves known, thus giving silent testimony to their guilt. This telling fact is completely omitted from the presentment.

Another aspect of the investigation is even more disquieting. Police said they recovered a .38 caliber bullet from Council's skull but that it was too badly distorted for any identification. They said the same about the bullets that killed Hill and Mrs. Abraham. In the Rutledge slaughter only five of twelve bullets could be found and *none of them* could be linked to a weapon, despite identification markings on three bullets and only four revolvers to test. In Martin's case they didn't even admit receiving the bullet or running a ballistics test. It is highly probable that State Police were responsible for Martin's death, just as they were guilty of the wounding of Jimmy Sneed and Karl Green. Those bullets, incidentally, also disappeared.

Authorities acknowledged that nine of the dead victims could not have been charged with any criminal behavior. By coincidence, those nine were among the eleven deaths from "undetermined sources" listed in the special police report of October 24. Police had "misplaced" bullets and had difficulty coming up with reliable ballistic information. The Newark Police Department has never admitted responsibility for the killings of Mrs. Abraham, Council, Hill, Bell, or Murray, and no physical evidence linking police to these deaths is on the public record. Yet the grand jury failed to find this string of "mistakes" worthy of even a slap on the wrist in its presentment.

More alarming than the predictable police errors was the FBI's willingness to become party to it. Awareness that police would be suspected of putting forth something less than their best effort led to FBI duplication of the ballistics tests—at least according to an announcement of intention. No report on these FBI tests has ever been issued.

Not only did the grand jury fail to indict any law-enforcement personnel for their crimes in Newark, but it attacked the integrity of the Legal Services Project, one of the few organizations worthy of praise. The presentment charged that the agency failed to cooperate with the prosecutor's office, furnished material to Hayden and other writers, and had been responsible for the Rutledge photograph and leaflets. The prosecutor's office had suckered the grand jury into using the project as a convenient scapegoat. Their ten paragraphs of critical comment against the project were answered by thirty-nine blistering pages, largely written by Oliver Lofton, which left the jurors looking rather foolish and, in addition, left little doubt who had coached them.

Local PBA president Giuliano, who would run with Tony Imperiale for councilman-at-large in the November, 1968 election, naturally praised the grand jury's work. The Committee of Concern and even the New Jersey Bar Association, however, severely criticized the presentment. "I don't know why the bar head criticized the jury summoned by law," John Page, the grand jury's foreman, replied, "unless he is critical of the whole legal system. We felt that people had confidence in an agency like a jury. We had no ax to grind, only to see that the truth came out and justice was done."

Page, in his naivete, had unknowingly hit the nail on the head. The bar association was not attacking the legal system but rather the grand jury's application of that legal system. As their foreman stated, the jury had been summoned by law; but their presentment ignores evidence and finally made a mockery of the law.

And, for an ironic twist, the law was even used to impede further investigation into the riot's homicides. All of the cases were officially termed "open" and therefore access to most records, including grand jury testimony, is denied.

Only When No Other Means Were Available

Taking up the issue of police use of firearms in *Davis v. Hellwig,* a 1956 case, the Supreme Court of New Jersey ruled:

> A police officer is not even justified in shooting at every escaping criminal to prevent escape. At the common law it was only when the escaping criminal had committed a common law felony and there was no other way of taking him that the peace officer was justified in shooting at him to prevent his escape. This rule obtains in our state. The law does not countenance the act of a police officer in shooting a fleeing offender charged merely with a misdemeanor, breach of the peace or violation of the Disorderly Persons Act,

and the peace officer who shoots such a fleeing offender subjects himself to civil liability to the offender and to criminal prosecution as well. . . . In the Holloway case it was held that the police officer's mistaken belief that the escapee was a felon was no defense. The law values human life too highly to allow an officer to proceed to the extremity of shooting an escaping offender who in fact has committed only a misdemeanor or lesser offense, even though he cannot be taken otherwise.

According to Spina's testimony before the Hughes Commission, regulations regarding use of firearms for the Newark police remained unchanged during the riot. Deputy Chief Redden repeated the same orders over the police radio after 8:00 P.M. Thursday, before any homicides had been committed. In addition to allowing the use of firearms to protect the lives of police officers and others and to prevent commission of a felony, their use would be permitted to apprehend a fleeing criminal who had committed a high misdemeanor—including atrocious assault and battery, assault with intent to kill, burglary, robbery, grand larceny, and breaking and entering with intent to steal—but *only* when no other means of apprehension were available.

Orders under which State Police supposedly operated were more stringent: "to fire if fired upon."

The only specific instructions give to National Guardsmen were to "control the fire" and not to fire at all unless commanded to do so by a senior officer of the guard.

Each of the three law-enforcement agencies ignored its orders. They executed petty thieves. They slaughtered women and children. They murdered innocent men. The jury's presentment amounted to a rubber stamp of approval for murder and manslaughter.

The Essex County prosecutor's office—true author of the presentment on the riot's homicides—had one remaining responsibility. "When the Essex County prosecutor has completed his presentation to the grand jury relating to the deaths that resulted from the Newark disorders," the Hughes Report clearly stated, "a detailed report should be made by him setting forth the results of his investigation in each case where no indictments have been returned."

When Lordi succeeded Brendan Byrne in January, he inherited the duty to fulfill the commission's stern suggestion. Lordi never bothered to turn in any report—a decision that spoke louder than any lies his office could have fabricated.

19

BURIAL OF A RIOT

We Then Proceeded to Investigate Some of the Homicides

"After the riots this past summer, we began an investigation of the various deaths that occurred," Zazzali testified. "Because of the chaos in Newark in many cases we didn't even know where the person had been shot. . . . In a case where a police officer apprehended or attempted to apprehend or caught a burglar . . . if there was a shooting, the police officer made a report. As distinguished from those cases where some people were killed in their homes or a person was killed in a crowd of people outside of, let's say, a project. In some cases the people were brought to the hospitals by friends and there was no record in the hospital as to who brought them in or where they could be found. This caused some difficulty, of course, by way of investigation. . . . Additionally, the police had a difficult time talking to or trying to locate witnesses to some of the shootings."

Thus began a final eulogy for the Newark riot's victims by Andrew Zazzali, the assistant prosecutor responsible for submitting the homicides to the special grand jury. He spoke before the U.S. Senate Permanent Subcommittee on Investigations in Washington, D.C. The Newark riot—and its victims—was finally being laid to rest ten months after its eruption with the pomp befitting a funeral before such an august body. It was interred beside the graves of its brothers—Watts and Detroit—during a detailed four-day ceremony at the end of May. City officials and other pallbearers traveled to Washington with lengthy laments to be entered into the Senate's eternal record. They also brought with them the same old lies to ease the casket into its grave.

"What you are saying is that with all the firing going on, it would not be possible to identify who fired what?" asked Senator Henry M. Jackson.

"In nine cases, yes," Zazzali responded. "These were cases where we know there was sniper fire and return fire by police and/or guardsmen.

"We then proceeded to investigate some of the homicides," Zazzali continued. "Their job was somewhat further complicated because of the various accounts of the shootings that had been published in newspapers, and a book entitled *Rebellion in Newark*. . . . In most instances, the book was erroneous as far as the accounts of the deaths were concerned."

Zazzali also testified to Hayden's lack of enthusiasm for appearing before the grand jury and helping with its investigation into the killings. "At no time did anyone come to the prosecutor's office or the Newark homicide squad and volunteer information on any death," Zazzali said in his prepared statement to the subcommittee. "In all cases, bullets removed from victims were forwarded to a ballistics laboratory. Police officers who fired their weapons were required to deliver these weapons to the homicide squad for transmittal to and examination by the ballistics laboratory."

An illusion of sweating endeavor by the prosecutor's office had been projected by Zazzali, a performance which must have hypnotized his listeners. And Hayden, according to Zazzali, had not only written a mass of inaccuracy and distortion, but had thumbed his nose at the prosecutor's own truthful investigation.

The facts tell a different story.

A first description of the riot's homicides had been published on July 24, 1967 by the *Washington Post*. The newspaper had sent a four-man team to Newark—Leroy Aarons, Hollie West, Ronald Smothers, and William Curry—because, as one reporter put it, it was thought that the Newark press would be less than accurate with its coverage. In all but four cases the work of the *Post* reporters was *virtually the same* as that produced in Zazzali's presentment:

—In the Rutledge case the reporter relied on false statements of the three teenagers who said they had witnessed the shooting.

—In the Taliaferro case erroneous information was taken from a supposed witness who said that a state trooper had shot Taliaferro and then had "finished him off" with another shot.

—There was no mention of Hawk charging at police before he was shotgunned.

—Boyd, according to the *Post*, was shot by a civilian rather than accidentally by police.

A second account of the homicides came out in September, two months after the riot, in *Rebellion in Newark*. In the book Hayden repeated an accurate account of Furr's shooting as published July 28 in *Life* and dealt in detail with Rutledge, reprinting an affidavit of one of the youths that—given the condition of the corpse—seemed believable. Hayden also covered the deaths of Toto and Moran with a hypothesis of the shootings as taken from news accounts and dealt briefly—and accurately—

with the deaths of Mrs. Spellman, Mrs. Brown, Eddie Moss, and Bell. Then, as Zazzali testified, the book listed capsule versions of all the black homicides, virtually *duplicating* the work of the *Post* reporters, including inaccurate versions of the Rutledge and Taliaferro shootings and the disputed versions of the deaths of Hawk and Boyd.

The third and official account of the homicides was released in April of 1968 with the grand jury's presentment. With the exception of Rutledge, Taliaferro, Hawk, and Boyd, its versions—despite a difference in language—were largely *the same* as those previously published both in the *Washington Post* and Hayden's book.

Thus, parts of Zazzali's testimony are distorted and directly contradicted by official documents and witnesses.

First, the prosecutor's office did not show much concern with the riot deaths until a national audience had been exposed by Hayden's book to *previously published* newspaper information.

Second, entreaties for Hayden's help smacked of harassment. Hayden, for example, was asked for the names of the *Post* reporters when he finally did appear before the grand jury. Instead of grilling the subpoenaed Hayden, the prosecutor's office could have bought the July 24th edition which had the reporters' names on the front page.

Third, the prosecutor's investigation appeared more anxious to discredit Hayden's book than to supplement it.

Fourth, Zazzali cited only the four cases in Hayden's book that differed from the versions of his own grand jury, yet he stated that "in most instances the book was erroneous."

Fifth, Zazzali had referred to the nine homicides that were listed in the grand jury's presentment as attributable to "unidentified sources"—Martin, Harrison, Council, Murray, Mrs. Abraham, the three women shot in their homes, and the Pugh boy. In his own presentment, which had been submitted to the subcommittee but had apparently *not even been read* by them, there was not one word of snipers involved in the deaths of Mrs. Abraham, Council, or Pugh. Supposed sniper activity mentioned in the shooting of Martin, Murray, Harrison, and the three women was completely incidental to their deaths. And, also according to the descriptions in his own presentment, Bell, Council, and Murray had been ruthlessly killed by Newark police officers who then refused to identify themselves.

Sixth, white law enforcement officers had been responsible for twenty-one homicides (possibly twenty-two, including Moran) and if Zazzali lacked either information or witnesses it was only because the Newark police, state troopers, and National Guardsmen *refused to identify themselves* and their superior officers had refused to investigate. Why would people from the black community expose themselves to intimidation when police officers who had done the shooting refused to step forward? Even at that, directly contradicting Zazzali's statement, some did approach the prosecutor's office. Was Zazzali's memory so bad he had forgotten the visit of Hank Franzoni with Virgil and Bussy Harrison on the morning of January 22, a meeting concurrent with the death of Homer Mosely? And Franzoni said that witnesses to the death of Isaac Harrison—which he submitted to Zazzali—were never called before the grand jury.

Equally suspicious was any ballistic examination carried out by the Newark Police Department, a group which fired its bullets as carelessly as it traced them.

What could be said for a grand jury investigation of homicides that had gone on for six months and yet could not even identify a dead man—Oscar Hill—whose photograph had been published in a nationally circulated magazine?

As Zazzali wasn't about to volunteer such pertinent information, neither was he inspired by questions from his audience. No less than twelve questions were asked on the photograph taken of Rutledge's corpse, but not a single one on what had killed the youth in the first place. Eight questions were asked on the Legal Services Project and the ACLU which, Zazzali related, had thrown additional roadblocks before his investigation. Fifteen were asked on Hayden and his book, and fifteen others on miscellaneous matters. The subcommittee asked a total of *four questions* of Zazzali about twenty-one black people who had been shot to death during a military occupation. Two of the questions coming near the conclusion of his testimony demonstrated the knowledge they had accumulated:

> JACKSON: What has happened on the other cases? How many people were killed, was it twenty-eight?
>
> ZAZZALI: No, sir, there were twenty-three.
>
> JACKSON: Have there been any indictments in these deaths?

Were There Any Snipers You Were Able to Locate?

The theory of organized snipers, dusted off for another prospective buyer, was brought to Washington by its chief salesman, Colonel Kelly of the State Police. It was left to the colonel to deliver the single most asinine utterance of the entire ceremony: "Fire Captain Michael Moran and Detective Frederick Toto were killed by gunfire. The number of other deaths caused by the fire of rioters is not yet known and may never be fully determined."

Kelly's ignorance was based either on incompetence, stupidity, or another attempt to mislead the subcommittee. His staunch advocacy of the sniper theory may have been founded in his realization that men under his command had slaughtered three women in their homes.

Who were these snipers, anyway? With so many of them, how could they all have escaped? The question occurred to Senator Carl T. Curtis:

> CURTIS: Were there any snipers that you were able to locate?
>
> MALAFRONTE: We have a conviction of a man who fired at a car and killed a woman across the street.

It was Eyvind Chandler's turn again, a man who for ten months had been burdened with the image of Newark's sniper. Unfortunately, he was the only available specimen.

You Don't Know What Disposition He Has Made of It?

The funeral would not have been complete without a psalm or two from Captain Kinney on the great conspiracy theory. His performance, which would be his last, had even been lengthened for the occasion. Included among Kinney's list of conspirators now were Donald Tucker, an organizer for UCC's Area Board Five, Alvin Oliver, a coordinator at UCC, Harry Wheeler, the school teacher who had participated in the Parker-Callaghan dispute, and even Assemblyman George Richardson, a professional politician.

Alas, even Kinney's imagination could not save his performance:

> SENATOR HENRY M. JACKSON (from Washington): As I gather from your testimony, these individuals you have covered in your report were involved in a lot of activities prior to the events of July 13–18, and they have continued to be involved in various activities. But I am not able to get my hands on anything here that indicates that there is a conspiracy in a legal sense that leads to this series of riots and damage. Do you agree?
>
> KINNEY: I agree in part, Senator.
>
> JACKSON: You don't know of any meeting prior to July 13 which would indicate that they were laying the ground work to start trouble there? We have had testimony that conspiracy takes two or more people, generally speaking, and that there has to be an overt act that is connected with the planned arrangement. That is basically what, among other things, you have to prove. As you know, conspiracy is one of the hardest crimes to prove.
>
> KINNEY: I am well aware of that, sir. . . . [In another response] Sir, if I had sufficient evidence to make arrests, I would have made arrests for conspiracy. I do not have sufficient evidence to make an arrest. I do feel that if the evidence that I do have is presented to a county or federal

grand jury, with all the facilities that they have, that I have brought forth the fact these people I have mentioned have conspired.

JACKSON: Then in your judgment, is there evidence available that would warrant calling of a grand jury in Newark or in the county?

KINNEY: I believe my report would be evidence enough to call for a grand jury hearing.

JACKSON: How long has this report been out?

KINNEY: I submitted it last month, about three weeks ago.

JACKSON: Has it been turned over to the district attorney?

KINNEY: No, sir, it is turned over to my superior, Director Spina of the Newark Police Department.

JACKSON: And you don't know what disposition he has made of it?

KINNEY: I do not.

Captain Kinney was just being modest. Other reports have it that his conspiracy theory was eventually transported to Spina's back yard where it fertilized the police director's lawn.

Outraged to learn that Kinney included his name in the list of conspirators, Harry Wheeler sent a telegram to the subcommittee—as did the equally angry George Richardson—and then went to Washington, arriving just as the last shovels of earth were being dropped on the coffin. Wheeler, an uninvited mourner, had to pay his own travel expenses but the thrill of speaking into a microphone had often lifted Harry over far greater obstacles. The schoolteacher arrived late but well prepared, delivering an apt inscription for the Newark riot's gravestone:

Senator [Jackson], first and foremost, I submit that if there has been a conspiracy to produce human upheaval in the past or the present, then those responsible, in my judgment, would include Detective Captain Charles Kinney and his superior, the police director of Newark, Dominick A. Spina.

PART V

The Grass
Won't Grow Again

20

THE CHICKENS COME HOME

I Have Turned the Resignation Down

The word was spread by Sunni Muslims along the ghetto's streets high on the hill several nights before the official news broke. It was ironic that Kamiel Wadud and his followers in red tarbooshes knew long before assistant prosecutors and detectives working out of Joe Lordi's office, some of whom had contributed to the effort to indict Police Director Dominick Spina. Since May of 1968, the special grand jury called to investigate Newark's corruption had been accumulating its information, and on July 25—just after the first anniversary of the riot—it indicted Spina on four counts of nonfeasance in office. It was a bold, startling move that left no doubt that Lordi meant business.

John Redden had also proved he meant business the year before when he said he'd testify before a grand jury. The stand-up Irishman's testimony was instrumental in Spina's indictment.

Spina had learned of his indictment about the same time as Wadud and had prepared accordingly. In the early morning hours a shotgun blast shattered what had thus far been a calm summer, ripping a gaping hole through his living-room window on Highland Avenue. It narrowly missed the police director's head, Spina reported, as he was putting a leash on Nero, his faithful German shepherd.

"Stooping over to put the leash on the dog for a walk saved my life," he said. Spina described how he ran into the hallway after the blast, pulled his gun and charged outside—just in time to see a 1964 black Cadillac with two Negro occupants roar off into the night.

Faithful old Nero! Valiant and courageous Spina!! Together they had survived the only attempted assassination in history with the gunman using number nine birdshot. Newspaper headlines brought Spina the sympathy of dog lovers. Not even the ASPCA came to the police director's aid two days later when even larger headlines announced: SPINA INDICTED ON GAMBLING.

Spina did win support from weekly newspaper publishers Frank Orechio and Ace Alagna. Editorials soothed the Italian community by calling for a legislative probe—not of the police but of the *prosecutor's office*. White support spread and bumper stickers backing Spina blossomed like April tulips all over the city.

Specifically, the police director was accused of having permitted gambling in the city since July 22, 1964. Following the grand jury action, Spina promptly delivered himself to Mayor Addonizio's office where he conspicuously offered his resignation. "I have turned the resignation down," announced Mayor Addonizio, never one to cast the first stone. The mayor promptly issued a four-page statement in defense of the twenty-eight-year department career of his police director. Addonizio also called current gambling laws hypocritical. Who should know better than Hughie?

Walter D. Van Riper, former state attorney general and former superior court judge, took on the task of defending Spina. Dominick issued a flattering three-page statement of self-vindication.

The police director's trial carried over into November with the prosecutor's office carrying out some embarrassing gambling raids while it was in progress. Despite an all-out effort, it was difficult to link Spina directly with laxity in gambling enforcement or the major decline in gambling arrests. Prosecutor's office detectives testified that they had picked up "pass cards" used by certain gamblers to identify their men to police. The symbol of clasped hands on the green cards was identical with the emblem of the Dominick A. Spina Civic Association. After 1963 the club's name had been changed to the Essex County Civic Association, but the members remained the same, including some twenty-five Newark police officers allied to Spina. Superior Court Judge Samuel A. Larner barred admission of the cards as evidence, however, cutting off the prosecution's only direct link between the gamblers and Spina.

The judge directed a verdict of acquittal after the prosecution case had been presented and the jury went home without exercising its judgment. "I just wish they could have gotten him on the witness stand," Redden told me. "The guy's got an ego as big as a house." Spina declared himself vindicated and reaffirmed his faith "in the American system of justice."

I Hope the People Have Faith in Me

Where Addonizio was sitting was none too cool either. With one hand Hughie staunchly defended Spina and with the other he girded his own loins. Newark's mayor, who had already appeared before the grand jury corruption probe in July, was subpoenaed for more testimony. Also called were Dominick Micelli, the assistant business administrator who was identified in FBI tapes as Addonizio's "bag man," and Norman Schiff, former corporation counsel who had found it prudent to resign in April when Lordi first ordered investigation into Newark's municipal affairs. Another official under particular scrutiny was Anthony La Morte, former public works director and at that time executive director of the Municipal Utilities Authority—both jobs attributable to the influence of Mafia kingpin Tony Boy Boiardo.

Ordered to appear with income tax returns, bank books, checks, and checking account records, Addonizio vehemently refused, taking the position that he was a victim of unreasonable search and invasion of privacy under the Fourth Amendment. Addonizio also complained he was being forced to give testimony against himself contrary to the Fifth Amendment. Michael Riccardelli, assistant prosecutor in charge of the grand jury probe, was granted a court order to seize Addonizio's records, but the decision was appealed. LeRoi Jones, an interested observer of law and order, held onto his dream of black Newark as desperately as Hughie clutched his bank books.

The corruption jury's first presentment, released on January 9, 1969, finally struck to the heart of the issue. Earlier presentments had merely called for changes in the police department. This one forcefully advised Spina's removal as director. Once again the jury's decision was leaked in advance, giving Spina time for more theatrics. Two days before its release he announced creation of another gambling squad to be headed by Deputy Chief O'Neill. It made little difference. Mayor Addonizio—who was away on another vacation in Puerto Rico—could no more fire his partner in corruption than he could fire himself.

By this time the jury had been given access to some of Hughie's financial records but he was still withholding others. The state supreme court, upholding his claim, cleared the air:

> The mayor sufficiently stated his belief that the subpoenaed records *would tend to incriminate him with respect to some crime constituting corruption in public office.*[1] It is evident that Addonizio is himself the target of the grand jury's investigation, for it is inconceivable that the records of Addonizio could reveal criminality upon the part of others without also implicating him. When a witness is thus the target of the grand jury's inquiry no more need appear to support his Fifth Amendment claim.

But Addonizio was far from out of the woods. He met Tony Boy Boiardo while vacationing at San Juan's Americana Hotel and, to the

---

[1] Author's italics.

engrossing interest of watching federal authorities, the pair chatted chum-
mily about business conditions while basking in the poolside sun. Meanwhile, even as the grand jury was calling for Spina's removal and Hughie
was rubbing suntan lotion on his hairy exterior, a Justice Department
"strike force" of outgoing U.S. Attorney General Ramsey Clark slipped
quietly into Newark and, after checking the telephones for Mafia-planted
taps, set up shop behind the steel doors of the Secret Service's former
offices.

In late May of 1969, the grand jury again called Addonizio, this time to
answer specific questions about a $14,000 loan from Constrad, Inc., an
Oldwick engineering firm which had done $500,000 in work for the city.
Addonizio was also asked who had paid for renovations on his New
Shrewsbury summer home, a modest $59,000 shanty sitting on ten acres.
The San Juan sun had apparently baked Hughie's brain, causing him
to forget everything but his name and the Fifth, Sixth, and Fourteenth
Amendments.

Then began a three-day marathon as poor Hughie danced around the
Essex County Courthouse, refusing to reply to questions behind closed
doors in one courtroom and being warned in open court he would be
slapped with contempt if he didn't. The tune was becoming monotonous.

Leaving this to simmer for a time, the corruption probe then took up a
$1.7-million federally sponsored New Careers Program which the U.S.
Department of Labor ordered disbanded because all that it was doing
was enhancing several old careers—chiefly those of Addonizio, Spina,
and Councilman Calvin West.

A program intended to help train ghetto people in public service careers
was being used instead as a tool to build political strength through patronage. Sixty to eighty unauthorized positions had been created and filled
by 125 persons who had received a total of $350,000. After five months
in office the program director was unable to explain what his duties were
and knew nothing beyond opening the office in the morning and closing
it at night. Ex-convicts and ghetto youths, instead of experiencing rehabilitation through job training, were being paid to sit listlessly in
storefronts. The grand jury was unable even to find a reliable list of
personnel.

The project director reported that he would no sooner have twenty
vacant positions but that West would swamp him with twenty-five referrals.
Then he would find that twenty to thirty others had been added to the
payroll without his knowledge. At one point, he said, Spina summoned
him to demand that twenty new jobs be created for storefront operations
to be utilized in the police department's community relations program.
The director testified that he had cited a lack of funds and refused. He
was then ordered to Addonizio's office and commanded to place the

group on the payroll. Though it violated terms of the program's contract, he did it.

"The abuses which served to defeat the purpose of a New Careers program," the grand jury said in a presentment, "were the direct result of the political interference of the mayor of the city and certain city officials, particularly Councilman West."

"If acting to keep the city cool is political," commented Don Malafronte, "then I guess we're guilty."

A good guess by the mayor's right-hand man.

Also appearing before the corruption jury during this period was the dapper Paul Rigo, president of Constrad and a partner in Capen-Rigo Associates, an Oldwick consulting firm which had done all the water engineering work for Newark since 1965. These two firms alone had taken more than $2.5 million from the city's Public Works Department and Water Authority for various studies. Being scrutinized at the same time were Valentine Electric and its ace salesman, fifty-three-year-old Tony Boy Boiardo, and other construction outfits from Newark and Mafia-infested Long Branch on the Jersey shore. The main spotlight fell on a stylish, fifty-year-old gentleman of immaculate dress who smoked cigarettes in a holder, drove a Cadillac Eldorado, relaxed on a fifty-foot yacht, and commuted to his eleven-acre estate in exclusive northern Hunterdon County in a jet-powered helicopter.

For Paul Rigo, all this good fortune had descended rather suddenly. In 1963 he had been employed as an engineer's helper with the state. His taste for luxury was excessive for his $9,000 salary. After establishing business ties with Newark, however, Rigo's income quickly caught up.

Though a gourmet, Rigo kept himself trim by juggling money and running back and forth between city officials and Boiardo, to whom he paid large sums to establish and keep an active "relationship" with the city. After paying out more than a quarter of a million dollars to Boiardo, Addonizio, eight members of the City Council, and other officials, however, Rigo became disheartened at the speed with which the money was going out and the delay with which it was coming in. First he made a desperate but unsuccessful attempt to collect some of the $2 million the city owed him for past services. Next he bombarded the city with bills, including such items as salaries for his helicopter pilot and yacht captain. As a last resort, Rigo had the nerve to *sue the city* for $1.9 million—and caught the attention of the corruption grand jury.

Shortly before he was called to testify, Rigo found a note of advice from the Mafia on the seat of his car: "This could have been a bomb. Keep your mouth shut." The advice seemed sound. According to Rigo, he subsequently lied before the grand jury. Then Internal Revenue Service agents began to put the screws to him. "I was in a three-way squeeze—

Boiardo's people, the Essex grand jury, and now the federal people were in the act," Rigo explained. "I was beginning to become desperate. I didn't know who to go to." In November Rigo fled to Acapulco and contacted Justice Department officials in Washington. The next month he told all. With this inside information, Newark's citadel of corruption began to crumble from within.

"I just hope the people of Newark have faith in me," sighed Addonizio sometime between courtroom visits. "I have nothing to say now, but I might have after the investigation is over."

I Am Tired of Innuendo, Whisperings, and Rumor

In early December of 1969—after almost a year of undercover work in the city—the federal strike force was ready to move. The force surfaced under the able guidance of the new U.S. attorney, Frederick B. Lacey. For openers, Newark's entire City Council, other city officials, and Boiardo were subpoenaed to appear before a special federal grand jury while Rigo was in Washington undergoing intensive grilling. Conferences took place between Lacey and the prosecutor's office, which later turned over 5,000 pages of testimony and thousands of documents for federal scrutiny.

Lacey and his men, after plowing through documents, transcripts and contracts, learned that construction costs in Newark, for some reason, ran 20 percent higher than anywhere else in the nation. One water main contract in the city, for example, was awarded to a low bidder for $2.4 million but ended up costing more than $3 million through a series of change orders that eliminated those items on which the company had bid low, taking a loss, and multiplied the items on which the company had quoted high bids in the specifications. LeFera Contracting Company, for another example, had done some work for the city that appeared to require investigation. The company, whose principal had contributed $5,000 to Addonizio's election in 1962, also listed Tony Boy Boiardo as a "trustee." Tony Boy's father, eighty-year-old Ruggiero "The Boot" Boiardo, who—according to FBI tapes—occasionally cremated bodies in an incinerator on his Livingston estate, was listed as a "night watchman."

One Friday, a federal agent visited the company to indicate that its books would be subjected to audit. By Monday the books had disappeared in a burglary that lowered the elder Boiardo's rating as a watchman. Following an investigation, the Newark police termed the incident "suspicious."

By this point three federal grand juries were sitting. The first was investigating Internal Revenue Service employees who had been helping mobsters defraud the government with false tax returns. The second, exclusively focused on the organized gambling network of Essex and Union counties, soon indicted fifty-four men—including two who carried credentials identifying them as special *deputy sheriffs* in Essex County.

The third, dealing with Newark's municipal government, ran into another obstacle when Addonizio refused to testify, among other things, as to whether he was the mayor of Newark. Under the circumstances, he said, the answer would tend to incriminate him. Under the Faulkner Act, some Newark residents thereupon claimed, Addonizio could be removed from office for refusing to answer questions relating to his job before a grand jury. Lame-duck Attorney General Sills was asked to bar the mayor from City Hall, but instead of salvaging a remnant of respect, Sills muttered an excuse and left office as ingloriously as he had served in it.

Philip Gordon, Newark's corporation counsel and first to be called in the probe, quickly admitted having accepted extortion money. Addonizio then announced that Gordon had shared a $4,000 kickback with another official (later identified as Municipal Judge Anthony Giuliano, a cousin of the ex-PBA president and a brother of the superior court judge).

"Ah, ha," said Hughie. "At last we have gotten to the bottom of all this investigating." Addonizio also revealed that his administration had been looking into the very same thing.

"What the hell did he [Gordon] say that for?" said Giuliano.

Soon thereafter Addonizio's desperate bluff was called. On December 17, 1969—Black Wednesday—a federal grand jury indicted Hughie with three of his council stooges, Turner, West, and Frank Addonizio, a distant cousin; a former councilman, Lee Bernstein, who had been kicked out of the South Ward the previous June after a successful recall election; another former councilman, Callaghan, once almost appointed Board of Education secretary; Schiff, the former corporation counsel, and his successor Gordon, an ex-councilman; Judge Anthony Giuliano, another ex-councilman; La Morte, the Municipal Utilities Authority director; Benjamin Krusch, public works director; Mario Gallo, a contractor whose three businesses were hyper-active in the county; and Tony Boy Boiardo himself, with two of his Valentine Electric employees. (Joseph Melillo, the North Ward councilman, and Ferdinand Biunno, Newark's business administrator, were not named in the indictments but, according to later sworn testimony by Rigo, each had also received extortion money. Ralph Villani, the only councilman who hadn't been implicated, was recovering from a stroke at the time his colleagues were cutting the pie.)

All fifteen were charged with violation of the Hobbs Act, one count of conspiracy to commit extortion, and sixty-five counts of actual extortion. From September of 1965 to February of 1969, the indictment stated, they had milked $253,000 from Paul Rigo and Constrad. In addition, eleven of them were also charged with filing false income tax returns. Potential sentences were enough to put Hughie and company away for over a thousand years. "I am tired of innuendo, tired of whisperings, and tired of rumor," Addonizio had said in 1968 when the Hughes Report published the first official inkling of corruption in city hall. "I want facts. I want names. I want places. If there are corrupt men in government, let's find them, those who do the corrupting."

Creating a carnival atmosphere, the mass media once again descended on Newark, uncoiling cables with a joyous dedication. Naturally, Addonizio and his City Hall gang proclaimed their innocence, as did all the other defendants at their arraignment. Only one of the city officials had the decency to resign, Philip Gordon. And for the rest—incredibly enough—it was business as usual, except for Judge Giuliano, whose body the New Jersey Supreme Court removed from the bench. Giuliano joined Chief Magistrate Del Mauro in early judicial retirement. Del Mauro, as disdainful of state Supreme Court dictates as he had been of cab driver John Smith, had been pocketing marriage fees. When his disregard of the high court's ruling against the practice came to light—thanks to the reportage of the Newark *News*—he was invited to Trenton to explain himself. He was also invited to appear before the federal grand jury where he exhibited his grasp of the Fifth Amendment. Del Mauro then resigned, as he put it, for reasons of health. The state Supreme Court put it another way and said that he was suspended as a judge. In January of 1971 the court also suspended Del Mauro from practicing law for one year.

Addonizio and company would have faced the prospect of dangling from City Hall's roof by their toes in other municipalities—which fate they richly deserved—but not in Newark. As a matter of fact, a majority of Newark's "nigger ministers," who could usually be found hanging onto Addonizio's pants pockets, reminded their flocks that Hughie was innocent until proven otherwise and in a straw poll voted overwhelmingly *to return the mayor to office* should he run again. Even a draft Addonizio movement was set in motion to show what support he would have running for a third term. That movement was slowed by the release of more FBI transcripts of bugged Mafia activity—an eight-volume, 1,200-page production recorded between 1961 and 1965 in "The Barn," the Mafia clubhouse of Ray De-Carlo in Mountainside.

As with the DeCavalcante tapes, their predecessors, the transcripts disclosed a staggering depiction of Mafia influence from the governor on down. The mayor and Spina were both frequently mentioned by the mob with great familiarity. Another identified figure was Dominick Capello, Kelly's predecessor as superintendent of the State Police, who had protected the Mafia for two years before retiring. Kelly, then his understudy, emerged personally untainted except for his compromising silence about corruption among the state troopers.

Though Addonizio and the police director had strongly denied such affiliations with the release of the DeCavalcante tapes six months before, this time they decided to forgo the ritual and keep their mouths shut.

The Day That Bum Turned Us Out

Since Spina's acquittal, business as usual also prevailed among Newark police.

When Thomas Pecora, boss of Teamster Local 97 and a reputed Mafia lieutenant, left for a west coast vacation he naturally took along a Newark detective as bodyguard.

In August of 1969 Deputy Chief Anthony Barres, who had moved out of the city two years before, was named to the vacant position of police chief. Many wondered how Barres had bested Deputy Chief Redden, who normally received the highest scores in civil service exams. Insiders believed the test results had been fixed. Redden, for one, was positive of it.

Members of Deputy Chief O'Neill's gambling squad, as might be guessed from the wording of the grand jury's indictment, were taking payoffs. The federal strike force was watching that situation as well. A captain and a lieutenant in the O'Neill squad were seen talking to Harry Serio, notorious Newark underworld figure, in the Office Lounge on the night that Serio instructed a city fireman to follow two IRS agents who had the place under scrutiny. Serio was proprietor of the lounge, a gambling hangout, in which Spina's sister-in-law reportedly had an interest and in which a relative of Police Captain Rocco Ferrante was also involved. Spina's wife was also called in to testify before the federal panel.

Lacey had created resentment and fear in the underworld. Anonymous letters made threats against the U.S. attorney and his family. His mother's home was burglarized. A telephone call to one of his assistants threatened that one of Lacey's young sons would be beaten. Then a top Mafia leader approached Lacey in a Newark restaurant to warn him that certain elements—with which the mobster was not associated—were threatening his son with bodily harm.

The next step was the suggestion that Lacey, too, might be part of the *communist conspiracy* to undermine public confidence in the police. Lacey charged that Essex County Sheriff Ralph D'Ambola—mentioned more than once in the DeCarlo tapes as a go-between for Mafia contributions to politicians—had paid $100 for 2,500 copies of hate literature of this nature and aided in its distribution. Representative John Rarick, an ultra-rightist Louisiana Democrat, then called Lacey *unfit* for the post of U.S. attorney because of his role in releasing FBI tapes and because Lacey's son is a member of Progressive Labor, a Maoist organization. Rarick, either a super-patriot, a fool, or a dupe of the Mafia, came to New Jersey to speak at the annual dinner of the Americans of Italian Descent, at which printed leaflets were distributed claiming that "the Mafia is a myth."

Further investigation of the police department was delayed while the U.S. attorney's office turned its efforts to preparing for a June 2 trial date for the thirteen remaining defendants. Judge Giuliano was already dead after suffering a heart attack at home. Mario Gallo took part in a secret four-hour meeting with Lacey, during which he agreed to seek immunity and become a prosecution witness with Rigo. After the meeting he was accompanied to his station wagon and departed for his Short Hills home alone. Two hours later, at 12:40 A.M., his auto slammed into a bridge abutment on a rainswept highway in West Orange. There were no witnesses to Gallo's death and an investigation failed to turn up evidence of foul play, at least none that was made public.

Paul Rigo, the key to the government's case, was marked for death and was being kept under close watch in protective custody.

Now virtually banished from active police work after Spina's elimination of his gambling squad, John Redden watched and waited from his shelf in the police planning and research department. The last time I saw him, I asked if he remembered the date when Spina had been appointed police director. Redden's eyes met mine and then drifted somewhere high over my right shoulder. Then his gaze dropped to the carpet in front of him. "The only day I remember is the day that bum turned us out," the big Irishman said.

21

LAW AND ORDER

I'm Gonna Blow Your Brains Out

While the summer of 1968 was tedious for Spina and Addonizio, LeRoi Jones was also having some uncomfortable moments due to the zealous law-enforcement of Officer Frank Hunt, who seemed to be making the playwright his personal business. The Newark policeman routinely patrolled Sterling Street in front of The Spirit House, sometimes referring to the neighborhood children as "black bastards" and "little niggers." His greetings to Jones were even more unpleasant.

"I'm gonna take you out before this is over," he yelled to Jones on one occasion and, "I got your picture, I use it for target practice," and "I'm gonna blow your brains out," on others.

Hunt harassed occupants of the house and visitors, entering and leaving. He asked for auto registrations, measured inches from the curb to parked cars to determine if he could issue parking tickets, and ripped posters off the building. One of his favorite tactics was to shine a light on The Spirit House in the early morning, bang on the front door and shout, "Hey, who owns that car down there in front of the house?"

He made a nuisance of himself not only to LeRoi Jones but also to his boss, Dominick Spina. Jones doesn't drive and Walter "Sunny" Kontz, twenty-eight, chauffered the poet's Volkswagen camper, thus coming under Hunt's unremitting surveillance. Hunt stopped the bus at least a dozen times without uncovering any criminal activity. On the night of July 30, in front of The Spirit House, Hunt's doggedness was rewarded with a bit of timely luck: Kontz's driving license had expired at midnight. At 12:30 A.M. Hunt arrested him for driving without a valid license. Jones quickly phoned Kamiel Wadud, and the Muslim leader called Spina at 1:30 A.M. Spina called command post headquarters to order a confidant, Captain Leonard Paradiso, to the First Precinct to insure that nothing happened to Kontz. Jones's driver left jail on a fifty-dollar bond and Hunt soon left the area of The Spirit House.

In the Kind of Game I'm In

Tony Imperiale, a councilman-at-large candidate in the November election, was having a quiet summer—which to him was an unwelcome development. The vigilante's campaign was only stirring when black militants were making headlines, and at the moment Tony had nothing to talk about. This predicament was remedied at 1:00 A.M. on July 25 when three bombs exploded in front of his karate school headquarters on North 7th Street, shattering windows and disrupting what had been—except for the birdshot attempt on Spina's life—a tranquil summer. Two of the bombs went off harmlessly in sidewalk drain pipes and the third—equally harmlessly— under a parked station wagon. Once again the television cameras zeroed in.

"Maybe I should be scared by this but I'm not," Imperiale announced, blaming the bombing on "black militants." "I'm only concerned for my family. I have three of my men guarding them right now. You know, it's funny. They label our organization racist and vigilantes but we've never done anything like this. I'm still looking for someone—the governor or the mayor or someone—to make a statement that this is outrageous."

The next day enough news value remained for the cameras to focus on Imperiale as he turned in his nominating petitions. "I'll never sit on the front porch again unless I know Tony's here," sighed a neighbor.

Yet another "attack" on Imperiale two weeks before the election was even more astounding, raising election activity in the white communities to a fever pitch. As Tony—the only witness—described the incident, "two Negro men" fired a shotgun at him from a passing auto as he walked in front of his Summer Avenue home. The beefy vigilante seems a target almost impossible to miss at such short range and yet—as Imperiale vividly described it—he instinctively dropped to the sidewalk as pellets struck everything in the area except him.

"In the kind of game I'm in anyone could have wanted to do it," said Tony in a rare moment of insight.

Four days after his latest theatrical success, Imperiale was guest of honor at a political banquet. Also, Tony announced that he had cut off his "hot line" telephone connection with LeRoi Jones—which had been set up to control the situation after just such an inflammatory incident.

In a third incident, two black youths carrying a can of gasoline were passing by Imperiale's front steps on the way to their stalled auto when one of them alluded insultingly to the vigilante's relations with his mother. Imperiale—peeved at being called a "motherfucker"—managed to overtake one of the kids in a short foot race. He was charged with assaulting a skinny boy of sixteen years. Imperiale countercharged the boy with threatening to burn down his house.

Nigger, Don't You Know the Mafia Runs This Town

Back on Springfield Avenue, LeRoi Jones was having further problems with Officer Hunt. A chance meeting with the policeman—who was carrying a shotgun at the time—inside a bank led to some bright dialogue.

"Imperiale is gonna clean you people up," Hunt, one of the vigilante's more ardent fans, told Jones.

A one-sided battle of wits ended with Jones remarking, "Without that shotgun you'd be a punk." Becoming emotional, Hunt arrested the hapless Jones, charging him with using profanity and resisting arrest. Back at the First Precinct—captained by Charles Zizza, who had been moved from the racist and graft-infested Fourth Precinct to make way for Williams—the police rummaged around to see what else they could charge Jones with and finally came up with eleven ancient traffic tickets made out to a Leroy Jones. He was also charged with "receiving stolen goods"—the two revolvers he had already been convicted of possessing eleven months before.

The playwright's dashike hung over the courtroom pew and he yawned and fingered his beard as the trial began before Judge Del Mauro. Watching in a rear pew was Imperiale. "Since I'm running for councilman-at-large I would like to learn due process of law," Imperiale said. "LeRoi is a controversial figure like myself and I'm interested in seeing how a controversial figure is handled in court." Tony meant what he said. A few days later Imperiale again appeared in the court in response to the assault charge against him and Del Mauro angrily chastized him for being late. This charge, however, and Tony's countercharge were later dropped by mutual consent. Jones had no such luck. The mildewed traffic tickets and the stolen property charges were dismissed, but law and order prevailed as Del Mauro found him guilty of both of Officer Hunt's charges. Jones was fined $100 and sentenced to sixty days in jail. He appealed this conviction, too.

While Irvin Booker argued and won a new trial on Jones's bank arrest before the county court, the playwright's riot conviction appeal finally came due and Jersey City Attorney Raymond A. Brown challenged it in Trenton before the Appellate Division of the superior court. The state's second highest court ruled that Judge Kapp had indeed prejudiced the jury a year before. "We think that here the dry record shows that the [jury] charge went unfairly beyond mere comment on the evidence," the court declared. "The import of the charge was not only that the judge believed the testimony given by the police, but that he thought the jury should do likewise." The entire case, said the court, hinged on the issue of credibility, whether to believe police testimony that the revolvers had been found during a proper search of Jones's camper bus or whether to believe Jones, Wynn, and McCray had been beaten and the guns used as a cover.

Also thrown out were the two counts of contempt which came at the trial's conclusion, the court ruling that Kapp had failed to give Jones a hearing before finding him guilty.

For LeRoi Jones it was now the second time around. Had five Newark police officers lied on the witness stand during the riot trial? Did the police beat the three defendants? Had Jones uttered "shit" and termed his trial "a kangaroo court"? Did Jones call Officer Hunt "a punk"? Essex County's complacent taxpayers were about to spend thousands of dollars to find out.

On January 15, at the conclusion of a six-day trial without a jury, Superior Court Judge Charles S. Barrett cleared Jones of the charges of loud and offensive language and resisting arrest—much to the consternation of Officer Hunt and the embarrassment of Judge Del Mauro. "I think it was a good decision, a just decision," Jones, beginning to communicate more, told newspaper reporters. "I certainly agree with it and I'm happy about it."

LeRoi was arrested again on March 17 and charged with possession of stolen goods.

A repairman had found a duplicating machine stolen a year before in the basement of The Spirit House and reported it. Whether Jones knew anything about the machine only he knows, but he never got a chance to say. Dismissing the charge after a preliminary hearing, Municipal Court Judge Walls ruled that though the machine was doubtlessly stolen, it had not been established that it was actually in Jones's possession or even if he knew anything about the theft. Tony Imperiale called without success upon Governor Hughes to "review and investigate" an "astounding and shocking dismissal of charges."

Next on the legal agenda was the contempt of court matter with Assistant Prosecutor Zazzali and Judge Kapp among the parade of witnesses before Superior Court Judge Leon S. Milmed. They came to testify as to their knowledge of the word "shit." Had Jones said it or hadn't he? For five days they argued about it and, at the conclusion of the nonsense, Judge Milmed ruled it *didn't make any difference* because the word alone was not grounds for contempt of court. The same was true of the phrase "kangaroo court." The Appellate Division had in effect agreed with Jones's description when it overturned his riot conviction.

This time it was Judge Kapp's turn to be embarrassed as Judge Milmed found Jones innocent on one count of contempt of court and fined him $200 for attempting to leave the courtroom on the other count.

During a morning recess well into the retrial of Jones's riot conviction— a unique case in the annals of Essex County—Detective Andrew McCormick, one of the five policemen involved in the riot arrest of Jones, stood nervously in the courtroom corridor. Perspiration had soaked through his shirt into his suit jacket, leaving large damp blotches underneath both arms.

"McCormick was on the stand all morning," Irv Booker told me. "The master was really working on him."

"How's he doing?"

"Look at McCormick's suit," Booker replied.

"He's sweating pretty hard."

"God damn right," Booker responded.

The master was Ray Brown, a fifty-four-year-old Fordham Law School graduate who was regarded as one of the best lawyers in the East, if not the nation. He had been vice chairman of the Hughes Commission and one of the men responsible for the report's thoroughness. He was good enough to defend the Mafia, as Brown himself put it, "from the best of them to the worst." Brown blended deep knowledge of the law and hard work with a courtroom technique that combined drive, sincerity, and amiability. The work at hand was a matter of making police officers lie on the witness stand, "building little pyramids and hoping the jury remembers them," as Brown put it. LeRoi Jones, the perpetual loser, had gotten himself a winner.

The energetic Irv Booker represented Barry Wynn and the quiet-man-nered John Love represented Charles McCray. Somewhere between them in temperament was Brown, who called himself a black man though his skin was pale. The trio, all black men, represented a complete range of hues as well as personality.

For four weeks the defense persevered, selecting jurors as if their victory depended on it—as it did. Just as doggedly, Zazzali, the thirty-seven-year-old assistant prosecutor, challenged each black person as he was called, *eliminating twenty-six* out of thirty. The testimony took only three weeks. It was the same ghetto street corner and the same Volkswagen camper, but a whole new ball game. Judge Antell ruled as often for the prosecution as for the defense, but even Brown later expressed agreement with the rulings. With an impartial judge and a brilliant attorney the story unfolded just as it had eighteen months before in a Morristown courtroom, but this time the jurors were able to see quite clearly what had happened.

A message over the police radio said that men in "a blue panel truck" *had fired* at police on Springfield Avenue. A half an hour later, near 1:30 A.M., Jones's green camper was halted at the corner of South Orange Avenue and South 7th Street. Brown contended that the five police officers had recognized the playwright and did what came naturally. It is more likely that the police didn't recognize Jones but were aware only of the alien clothing the three men were wearing—their dashikes—and then did what came naturally. Jones, McCray, and Wynn were pulled from the camper and beaten senseless. McCray's right arm was held out by two officers while another rapped it with a nightstick to the refrain of, "Nigger, don't you know the Mafia runs this town?"

The arm was fractured and McCray was also cut on the head. At City Hospital, police even refused to allow their prisoner's arm to be X-rayed. Jones, whose head was being stitched, complained to an Episcopal priest in the emergency room that the police wouldn't allow him to make a telephone call. The priest asked the police about Jones's request. "What about this phony fuckin' priest?" one obese officer asked his colleagues. Meanwhile—as had occurred in the Black Muslim raid—police ripped the interior of the camper to pieces and strewed its contents on the pavement.

The three prisoners were charged with possession of two .32 caliber pearl-handled revolvers which, they testified, they had never seen. Police testified that one gun had dropped from Jones's dashike and the other was found on a shelf under the dashboard. A police ballistics expert testified that neither of the guns *had ever been fired,* a most pertinent point. Ray Brown asked the jurors to believe that the three men had been beaten and had no guns. Zazzali wanted the jurors to believe not only that the defendants had the guns, but also that they had *never been beaten.* Again, it was a case of the prosecution wanting everything. The jury considered the medical testimony and gave the prosecution nothing, taking all of eighty minutes to reject Zazzali's case.

This time Judge Kapp was something more than embarrassed. According to prosecutor's office personnel, his feeling toward Jones was so intense he ordered transcripts of Judge Antell's charge to the jury and pondered over it. Kapp had good reason to reflect. The two unfired revolvers had indeed been in Jones's possession and it was only Kapp's prejudicial charge to the jury that had saved the playwright from prison.

I Will Fight White Radicals as Well as Black Radicals

In October, George C. Wallace paid Newark a visit with a smiling Imperiale in tow, his sound trucks setting law and order to music. The downtown rally in Military Park came off without incident but a confrontation that few saw went unreported. Standing on the sidelines was James Treadwell, a brewery foreman who remembered Imperiale as just another driver in his crew sometime before the vigilante's sudden rise to fame. When leaving the rally, Imperiale caught sight of the stocky black man and approached him with a grin.

"You know I'm no racist, Jim," he called out.

"What are you doing?" Treadwell shouted back. "You got no business down at City Hall shooting off your mouth. You're nothing but a punk!"

The moment of truth was over in twenty seconds. Imperiale patted Treadwell on the shoulder as detectives and three uniformed policemen broke up the crowd which formed quickly around the pair. Through the throng could be seen Imperiale's grinning face and the broad, shaking shoulders of Treadwell, who continued to shout, "You're nothing but a punk!" Imperiale's grin faded to an embarrassed smile as he and his followers marched off.

Imperiale and Giuliano, the PBA president, swept to victory in the November 1968 election over black candidates supported by the United Brothers party of LeRoi Jones. The victors had run on a law-and-order platform. A jubilant Imperiale offered a suitable victory statement: *"We're going to support the police, right or wrong!"*

After the euphoric victory, however, interest in Imperiale waned. At one monthly North Ward meeting during the winter only thirty-five members showed up. "This is one of the worst showings we've had," their leader angrily announced. "Our checking account is down to a dollar thirty-five." To heighten enthusiasm, Imperiale proposed a "battle-line" turnout against school decentralization, adding that Governor Hughes was a "chicken-livered skunk." Some of his audience had more direct action in mind.

"Why can't we kill a thousand niggers?" shouted a middle-aged man with a red face, corduroy jacket, and baggy purple trousers with yellow stripes. "And about fourteen thousand Puerto Ricans?"

"The other way around!" another voice cried out.

"I wish I had all the answers to what the gentleman is saying," Imperiale replied. "I don't like to generalize and condemn all Negroes." Having dampened their merriment during the group therapy portion of the program, Imperiale diverted them with other activities. "Effective tonight we are doubling our patrols," he promised. "Besides, we are increasing our rod and gun clubs. We are going to start practice shooting once a week." Tony needed new issues, and subsequently devised a few.

On January 13, 1969, five months before FBI release of the DeCavalcante tapes, Imperiale announced a new finding: "Anyone who thinks that there is a Mafia in this country or a Cosa Nostra is either a fool or blind."

A few months later, with the same candor, he announced that he would seek a federal grand jury investigation of some municipal and county courts. Some of his people would sit in courtrooms, he warned, to check judges out. A full-scale investigation, he said, would include testimony from members of the Newark police—experts in the field of strange courtroom procedures—whose morale had been bruised because of "yellow-livered judges." Nothing more was ever heard of his monumental purge.

The vigilante and his friend, Officer Henry Martinez, then struck up a business partnership to buy a tavern in nearby Harrison, using their wives' names. "I realize that I am a controversial figure but I hope that Harrison will do what's right by me," Imperiale said as the town council considered his liquor license application.

On May 6, when his application was denied, Tony was less restrained. "I never thought decent people would be subjected to the actions of *quislings* such as in Harrison," Imperiale shouted. "I will fight white radicals as well as black radicals. I think this is a racist action. They are only refusing me because I am Anthony Imperiale. I am Italian and Hank Martinez is Spanish and they are discriminating against us because of it. *Harrison stinks*."

Racing about answering police calls, Newark's new councilman had almost fulfilled his dream of being a law officer and even considered himself a chief of sorts. On the night of June 6, after racing to the scene of a call, he became involved in a heated street argument with Emmett Lewis, a forty-seven-year-old funeral director. The episode ended with Imperiale charging Lewis with threatening his life and inciting to riot and the undertaker charging Tony with assault and threatening his life. The matter also was later dropped by mutual consent. According to numerous witnesses, Newark's councilman and champion of law and order had stood on a corner during the argument screaming, "You fat motherfucker!"

"I remember the first time I saw him," Lewis told me. "Myself and two others were eating in a Blue Diamond restaurant in the North Ward when these three men came in. One of them was Imperiale and he was carrying a shotgun. The other two each had a pistol. At first, you know, I thought they must be the police or something. 'I'm gonna get me two niggers tonight,' Imperiale said. That's the first time I ever saw him and I never forgot it."

In March of 1969, J. Robert Jones, Grand Dragon of the North Carolina KKK, began a one-year prison sentence at Danbury State Prison, Connecticut, for contempt of Congress. "I plan to be a good prisoner," Jones told aides before leaving, "but I mean to tell the warden that there's just two things I've never put up with. That's a pervert and a nigger. And in that order."

Danbury has its share of both but only the latter gave the Klan leader any trouble. It appeared, in fact, that Jones might leave the prison in a hearse. With this in mind, Pete Young, a writer, asked the formidable Muslim Kamiel Wadud to go to Danbury to speak with black prisoners. Injury to Jones, it was understood, would mean death to defenseless blacks in North Carolina, but the Klan leader's safe return would bring KKK influence to bear in releasing several black prisoners in the South. Wadud arranged for protection for Jones. One bodyguard was Bob Young, a black professional light heavyweight boxer in the early 1960's who became Jones's roommate. Bob Jones was finding himself in peculiar company—and glad to have it.

Imperiale was not unknown to the Klansman. Talking to Wadud in the federal prison, the Klan leader asked: "How's Imperiale doing?"

On the fifth day of LeRoi Jones's riot trial, Imperiale showed up at the courtroom with five of his cohorts. "You know," he told "Sonny" Kontz, "Roi and I have had our differences but I think they're trying to give him the shaft in this gun thing."

To congratulate himself for his election victory, Imperiale bought a new Cadillac and a new toupee, both specially equipped. The toupee came with a thatch of hair that fell over his forehead, highlighting a face which had grown plumper. The Cadillac was equipped with a siren, red flashing light, booby traps, and two radios—one for receiving police calls that sent Imperiale racing about Newark like a madman, the other for two-way communication with his North Ward headquarters. A karate school no longer, the emporium of grunt and groan had given way to Imperiale's own little city hall.

Imperiale's new Cadillac was also equipped with twenty-two-year-old Ralph Esposito, the councilman's $6,300-per-year combination chauffeur, pencil sharpener, and heavy. Ralph, the envy of his set, sat alongside his leader in the front seat chewing on a wad of gum and adding a distinct fragrance to the interior. Ralph's sideburns stopped short of his armpits, complementing a perfumed coiffure fluffing down the nape of his neck. His navy blue overcoat was worn over a double-breasted chartreuse suit, with lime shirt and tie.

"What the hell," said Tony of his equipment, "I gotta ride in style."

Good dining had added thirty pounds of blubber to his five-foot-seven frame, rounding him out to 260 pounds.

While good fortune had done wonders for Imperiale, hard luck and eventual success through perseverance had begun to transform Jones. The playwright, who had always claimed the police were liars, had proven his case the hard way. The pure of heart might say that justice had triumphed, but if it hadn't been for Kapp's tirade and Ray Brown's craftsmanship, Jones would have been behind bars. The playwright would have gone to prison for merely having firearms in his possession, while Imperiale bragged with impunity that his group had actually fired weapons during the riot. In truth, a crime had been committed, but the culprits wore police uniforms and were beyond punishment. The experience, as Brown remarked, had its effect on Jones. The playwright wasn't about to start embracing Caucasians or writing poems dedicated to the Essex County court system, but he was now more willing to communicate.

After being released from jail following the riot arrest, Jones and city engineer Ken Gibson had met and talked earnestly about black politics in the city. If LeRoi Jones had anything to say about it, a routine police beating would have as its result the election of Newark's first black mayor.

22

DEATH FOR LEROY BOYD, JUSTICE FOR ALFRED SWIFT

The Only Way I Could Wipe It Was with My Knees

Leroy Boyd was fatally shot in the left side of his back. The autopsy revealed a large irregular lead fragment in the abdomen. Newark police officers testified that they had apprehended six people, one of whom was Boyd, while burglarizing a pharmacy on Belmont Avenue. The suspects, including Boyd, had been lined up against a building when a spectator began to taunt and curse the police officers. At first they ignored him and another spectator pulled him back into the crowd. Other police officers then arrived to assist in the arrest at which time a Newark patrolman was attacked by the abusive spectator. During the struggle, the patrolman's shotgun was accidentally discharged, wounding another patrolman in the arm and fatally wounding Boyd.

Due to insufficient evidence of any criminal misconduct, the jury found no cause for indictment.

Harry Kearny, the thirty-year-old policeman who was attacked, and Shelly Gooden, the twenty-nine-year-old black officer hit when Kearny's shotgun accidentally went off, had arrived at Belmont Drugs in the same radio car. Kearny has since quit the department and Gooden's arm has been saved but will require intensive medical care before he'll be able to use it again. The "abusive spectator" in the homicide presentment was Alfred Swift, a six-foot-three, 196-pound house painter with a police record that included a burglary conviction in Chicago and an armed robbery conviction in Indianapolis. Swift served eight months for burglary and then eight years for the robbery. He had come to Newark in 1947 after serving three years in the Air Force.

Police holding back the crowd of onlookers said they first noticed Swift when he came out of a tenement a few doors down the block, where he had been visiting friends after work. Swift was next seen sitting on the hood of his truck, parked a short distance from the corner, and was again shouting at the police.

"He finally got off the truck and I don't know why but he came at me,"

Kearny related. "There were at least twelve policemen there and I don't know why he picked me out unless it was because I didn't say anything to him. Finally I told him to step back and when he didn't I took a step towards him and tried to hit him with the shotgun to push him back. He grabbed the shotgun and we struggled and it went off. I didn't know right away who was hit because I was struggling for a minute or a minute and a half. Then a couple of other cops came over to help and began rapping him over the head with their sticks. He didn't want to go down but finally he did and we got him into a police car and out of there."

Police accounted for Swift's strange behavior—shouting and then attacking them—by saying he appeared to be intoxicated. Swift's explanation is more plausible. "I was visiting friends for less than an hour," he said. "We were drinking but I wasn't drunk. My truck was parked in front. A truck full of guardsmen pulled up and they lined up in the middle of the street. All I wanted was to move my truck and go home. I asked them a couple of times if I could move my truck. The last time I asked, Kearny told me, *'You have to ask that guy over there,'* just like that. When I raised up my hand to shout to the officer in charge, one of the cops hit me from behind with a blackjack. When I went down another cop hit me with the butt of his shotgun on my forehead."

Swift's explanation—and the scar on his forehead from the blow—are even more believable when considering the tense atmosphere and police "crowd control" tactics. Doubtlessly, Swift was obnoxious and the police felt he had to be contained before he could excite the throng of spectators. And, according to standard procedure, once Swift had been struck it was mandatory that the prisoner be charged with assault to justify the police action. The circumstances of Swift's arrest are identical with the circumstances of Roy Bell's on North 14th Street.

After his arrest Swift was handcuffed and thrown onto the floor of a police car which transported him downtown to headquarters. There, according to the police, he turned into the proverbial wild man. Police said the handcuffs were removed from the prisoner and he broke up the place trying to escape. Swift said he was still handcuffed and was shoved under a desk. Passing police punched him, Swift said, whereupon he became enraged and attempted to fight back. In this case, the police version is an out-and-out lie. When the handcuffs were finally removed from Swift's badly swollen wrists, it was with a hacksaw. Scars on Swift's wrists left from the handcuffs substantiate his account. And the prisoner's version is further substantiated by his bloody work overalls: "My hands were handcuffed behind my back and the blood was coming down my face. The only way I could wipe it lying under the table was with my knees."

Bail was originally set at $50,000 but eventually dropped to $5,000. The longer Swift remained behind bars, the angrier he became about everything, including his court-appointed attorney, Donald Weitzman of Morristown. In February of 1968, after seven months in jail without having been convicted of anything, the forty-five-year-old prisoner was finally released on $200 cash bail. Swift, angry and determined, was set on suing the Newark Police Department. Weitzman, mild-mannered and capable, was worried about just keeping his client out of jail.

The Bullet Hit My Father Instead

However conflicting were the accounts of Swift's behavior, the contradictions were mild when considering the mystery surrounding Boyd's death itself. A *Washington Post* account, which had appeared immediately following the riot, was irreconcilable with the grand jury's report:

> Leroy Boyd was born 37 years ago in Charlotte Court House, Va., but had lived in Newark for the last decade. He had divorced his wife, who is living in Richmond, Va., with their two boys, Richard, 13, and Roy, 11. Richard was visiting his father when the riots began. He recalled that at 6:00 P.M. on Friday, July 14, his father's girl friend (and Richard's godmother), Gladys Baker, asked for a pack of cigarettes. The three of them went to the corner of Belmont and Avon Avenues, searching for an open store. They passed a drug store that was being looted and paused to watch. State troopers and Newark police came upon the scene and called to the looters to come out of the store. An officer told Boyd and Miss Baker to stand against the wall of the building. He held the others, but let them go. Richard joined them as Boyd began to chat with a Negro policeman. Richard said he heard a Negro in the crowd shout, "Hey, you, wait a minute!" and fire a shot, aiming at the Negro officer. Boyd was hit and taken to City Hospital, where he died later that night. Police grabbed the gunman and, witnesses said, started to beat him. Richard recalled that the gunman told the Negro officer that he was his intended victim. An employee at the Irby Funeral Home, where Boyd's body was taken, said he had six .38 caliber bullet holes in him.

During his ten years in black Newark, Leroy Boyd had lived with three different women. The thirty-seven-year-old man, his son, and the Baker woman, the last of the three, stayed together in a second-floor apartment of one of the run-down tenements on Belmont Avenue, just south of Avon Avenue. He and his younger brother, thirty-three-year-old Emmett Boyd, worked together at a paper company in nearby Elizabeth, where Emmett still works.

On the fatal day, Leroy Boyd returned from work after 5:00 P.M. as the city entered its third night of disruption. Boyd and his son, thirteen-year-old Richard, walked to the corner for some cigarettes and found Gladys Baker inside Belmont Drugs looting with four men. Newark police arrived soon after and lined everyone except the boy up against the front of the building. Boyd began shouting that he hadn't been looting and begged the police to release both him and Gladys Baker. After a black police officer spoke for him, Boyd and the woman were released. They stood in front of the drug store talking to the black officer while police waited for a paddy wagon to take the other prisoners to jail. Every minute they waited the crowd at the intersection became larger and more belligerent.

"I was standing on Belmont and I could see everything because the police had everybody pushed back," Boyd's son recounted, substantiating his version of the shooting given to the *Post* reporter. "Just then a thin, bearded man in a blue uniform appeared out of the crowd and fired a gun at the colored policeman standing near my father. The bullet hit my father instead. *'You should be on our side and not their's—I meant to shoot you,'* he yelled at the policeman after he fired. The man was about ten yards away when he fired. Then the police jumped on him and began beating him in the head. They beat him and threw him into the green truck. He was bleeding pretty bad. My father was laying on the sidewalk holding his left side and Gladys was beside him holding onto his arm. 'Leroy, stop playing,' she said. I heard my father say, 'I'm not playing.' He took his hand away and the blood flowed out. They took him to the hospital. On Sunday two days later we read in the newspaper that my daddy was dead. Gladys put me on a bus that same day and sent me home to my mother."

You Could See That Leroy Had Been Shot Six Times

Emmett Boyd had seen his brother for the last time that Friday afternoon around noon at the job before leaving on a week's vacation to Wylliesburg, Virginia, where his sister lived. His brother died at 10:30 P.M. Friday, but Emmett Boyd left Newark on Sunday morning without knowing. That afternoon, before putting Richard on the bus, Gladys Baker made four long-distance telephone calls within one hour from Newark to the home of Boyd's sister, where Emmett had just arrived. She was afraid to talk to the brother and each of her calls was stranger than the one before.

"First she told my sister to tell me that Leroy had been killed," Emmett Boyd recalled. "On the second call she said that Leroy had gone to the store to get cigarettes and had been shot. On the third call she said Leroy had been shot when he got out of the car near the corner. On the fourth call a few minutes later she talked to Richard. She told him that she wouldn't talk to me because she was afraid I'd blame Leroy's death on her."

These telephone calls confused Emmett Boyd, a situation which was later compounded by the Essex County prosecutor's office rather than alleviated. The younger brother headed back to Newark that Tuesday night with undertaker Percy Irby. They arrived about 7:00 A.M. Wednesday and claimed the corpse an hour later at the Beckett Funeral Home on West Market Street. After loading Leroy Boyd's body, they returned to the Irby Funeral Home in Chase City, Virginia, arriving near 9:00 P.M.

" 'Come on, let's go over the body and see how many times he was shot,' Irby said when we got the body inside," Boyd related. "We did, and you could see that Leroy had been shot six times. When I got back to Newark, I went to the prosecutor's office and told them. They said he was shot only once. They wouldn't listen to anything I said. They didn't want to listen."

A month after the riot, a detective was sent to Virginia to talk with Boyd's son. The boy's story remained unchanged. The detective even showed Richard Boyd his gun, asking what kind of weapon the bearded man had fired. The boy replied that it had been a revolver just like the detective's. Richard demurred when shown a photograph of his father's corpse which showed a wound on the left side of the lower back. He contended that his father had been facing the bearded man and was hit in the front on the left side.

Gladys Baker also became part of the investigation. It turned out that she had been charged with murder in 1962 in the death of another man she had been living with, but there had been no evidence and she was released. "Gladys said she had stabbed the man she was living with and she said she would kill my father, too," Richard said. "Once she cut him in the neck with a butcher knife and he had to go to the hospital for stitches. She told me she'd get me if I told the police on her. Daddy said he didn't want to do anything about it."

On at least six occasions a representative of the prosecutor's office visited Emmett Boyd's apartment while he was at work or talked to him over the phone regarding the investigation into his brother's death. The last contact was in December of 1967, five months after the riot. "A detective told me over the phone that Gladys was gone to Jersey City," Boyd said. "He told me that she was going to be arrested for having my brother killed."

Essex County prosecutor Joe Lordi said that every effort was made to find the "bearded man" but he had disappeared, as had the Baker woman. The police did not introduce evidence before the grand jury about the mysterious man. Richard Boyd claimed that this man had not only killed his father, but had done so in an unsuccessful attempt to shoot a policeman. The boy also said that the man had been apprehended and beaten at the scene. Yet, the jury never heard this version of Leroy Boyd's death. Instead, the jurors heard only a version furnished solely by police officers which was so at variance with Richard Boyd's account of his father's shooting that it appeared another homicide altogether.

How Could I Look Like That If Nobody Hit Me?

The man who—according to the prosecutor's office—*had caused* Boyd's death was having problems of his own.

There were three indictments against Swift: one for having caused the wounding of Gooden, listed as an assault on the policeman; another for attempted escape at police headquarters; and a third for an assault on Officer Kearny, not at the scene of the shooting but at police headquarters. This last indictment had been added later by the prosecutor's office and the escape charge was incorporated into it, to be tried at the same time. Because it was believed to be the strongest case, the prosecutor's office decided to try Swift first for the assault at police headquarters.

Swift's first trial was held in April before Judge Sugrue and to have called his chances slim would have been an understatement. As the supposed assault and escape attempt had taken place *inside* a police station, the court had nothing to rely upon but police testimony. The defendant, however, did have several things going for him: an honest detective who testified that Swift *may have been* handcuffed at headquarters, the prisoner's bloody overalls, and a routine mug photo showing his badly beaten condition—and police testimony that *no one* had struck Swift. As was the case at the trial of LeRoi Jones, the prosecution wanted everything.

Swift himself accurately summed up the situation: "In the arrest picture my head was a foot wide and both my eyes were swollen almost shut. I was unrecognizable. They testified nobody even touched me. How could I look like that if nobody hit me?"

After testimony in the three-day trial had been completed, the defendant was further aided by a charge to the jury by Judge Sugrue that explained the validity of self-defense. To everyone's surprise—even to Weitzman, Swift's attorney—the trial ended with a hung jury.

The prosecutor's office then offered to alter the charge to a disorderly person violation in exchange for a guilty plea—a beneficial move for Swift since he had already served more than enough time to cover the likely sentence. But Swift, still set on *suing the police department* for his beating, refused the offering. He later changed his mind after Weitzman's urging but the prosecutor's office, tired of playing cat and mouse, had withdrawn its offer.

Undaunted, the prosecutor's office tried Swift again in November of 1968 on the same charge that had resulted in the hung jury. There were the same police witnesses and the same testimony, but this time Judge Sugrue took no chances on a hung jury. Though the circumstances were identical with the first trial, the judge omitted self-defense in his charge to the jury. Weitzman's objection and Judge Sugrue's rejection of it were exchanged over Swift's blood-stained overalls, lying in a twisted heap on a table before the bench.

"I told Al the best I could get for him was a hung jury again," Weitzman said as the jurors filed out. "It didn't go as well as last time. You heard, we didn't get a self-defense charge to the jury. That's the best we can hope for, a hung jury. I just can't get twelve white people to say the cops are a bunch of out-and-out liars. My feeling is we're home free if we can get another hung jury. Two trials would be enough. I don't think they would want to try Swift again on this charge. And if they couldn't get a conviction on this one, they'd probably drop the other assault charge."

At 4:30 P.M., after being out four and a half hours, the jury filed in to announce that they had found Mr. Swift not guilty. During his long stay in jail, Swift had tried to get rid of Weitzman for another attorney. Now he shook the lawyer's hand and said, "Thank you." For Swift, who kept his thoughts to himself, it was a lot to say.

Swift, however, was not out of the woods yet. Another indictment remained against him, the wounding of Officer Gooden at the scene of Leroy Boyd's shooting—but bringing the matter to trial might prove awkward. For one thing, the prosecutor's office hadn't bothered to find any civilian witnesses to testify on Boyd's death before the homicide grand jury and it would have been difficult for them to find any at this late date. And Swift did have witnesses who would testify to his innocence.

More important, it would be difficult to talk about the wounding of Officer Gooden without including Leroy Boyd, who was supposed to have been mortally wounded by the *same shotgun* blast. For the second time in post-riot Newark—if the prosecution chose to proceed—a riot homicide would be aired in a public trial. Further, for the first time, an entry in the grand jury's presentment would be challenged in a court of law, as Weitzman fully intended to do. The next move was up to the prosecutor's office and would take some time in coming.

I Thought It Was a Bullet

Two years after Leroy Boyd was shot at the corner of Avon and Belmont, Harry Kearny, who became a truck driver after leaving the police department, recalled the scene. "When we got there another officer had already lined the looting suspects up against the outside wall," Kearny said. "The last time I saw Boyd he was up against the wall with the others. He was shouting he hadn't done anything. My job was to keep the crowd back so I faced out towards the street and I never saw Boyd again until the shotgun went off. Then he was laying on the sidewalk holding his left side. By that time the ambulance had already taken Gooden to the hospital. I went up to Boyd and asked him how he felt, like anyone would do. I don't remember what he said but he was talking and didn't appear to be hurt that seriously. I called the hospital that night and the best I could get was he was in serious condition or he was critical, I don't remember which. It wasn't until I testified before the grand jury that I found out he had died."

"Kearny had the shotgun and that's all I know about it," Gooden, his heavily bandaged arm in a sling, said. "Did you ever get hit with a shotgun? Listen, I don't know who or what the shit got hit besides me, that's all!"

An ambulance had taken the wounded police officer but had left a seriously wounded man lying untreated on the sidewalk. In other respects, Kearny's account seems to agree with Richard Boyd's in that his father was not standing against the wall when shot and had been hit from the front. Leroy Boyd's autopsy report only added to the confusion, however, this time over whether he was shot by a revolver or a shotgun. The "large, irregular lead fragment" taken from Boyd's body was turned over to the police but inside the file of the deceased in the medical examiner's office is a receipt for a "bullet" with "apparently buckshot" written in parentheses. The ballistic report listed the fragment as Double O shotgun ammunition. "I thought it was a bullet," said Dr. Edwin Albano, New Jersey medical examiner.

Two years later, the shooting remained vivid in the mind of Boyd's son. Richard, by then fifteen and still living with his mother in Virginia, distinctly remembered the bearded man in a blue uniform who resembled neither Kearny, Gooden, nor Alfred Swift. The boy said in fact that he had even seen the mysterious man around his apartment building before the shooting. "Once I saw him in the alley sticking a needle in his arm from a purple bottle," Richard Boyd said.

Also unchanged was the opinion of the funeral director, Percy Irby.

"He was hit more than one time," he said at his Chase City funeral home.

"Where?" Irby was asked.

"Back, side and the chest that I can remember," the fifty-three-year-old mortician replied.

"Any shotgun wounds?"

"Wasn't no shotgun. They were bullet holes, about a .38."

"How many holes, how many times was Boyd hit?"

"I remember distinctly six times," Irby said.

"Are you certain there weren't any shotgun wounds?"

"I've been looking at shotgun wounds all my life," Irby responded. "It wasn't no shotgun. They were pistol wounds."

A man from the prosecutor's office had also visited the Beckett Funeral Home where Boyd's corpse had been taken from City Hospital. "I can tell you the same thing I told him," mortician James Cofer said. "That I don't remember. I will say this, that I remember there were more bullet holes than just one."

A Clear-Cut Case of Manslaughter

When the prosecutor's office continued to delay action on the indictment charging Swift with assault on Officer Gooden, Weitzman moved for dismissal on November 14, 1969, before Superior Court Judge Giuliano. December 1 was set as a deadline for the prosecutor either to set a trial date or drop the indictment. The prosecutor's office said it would be ready to proceed with the case on December 15, but the matter was again delayed after they discovered they were preparing a case against Swift on the charge he had already been acquitted of more than a year before. After the prosecutor's office straightened itself out, Weitzman was notified a week before the trial date that the remaining charge against Swift was scheduled for dismissal. On December 23 it was finally and officially dismissed.

Weitzman dropped by the courthouse shortly after to pick up Swift's $200 bail, only to find that the escape indictment that had been dismissed and incorporated into the Kearny assault had instead been misfired and was still officially pending. Swift would have to wait for his bail money while the red tape was unraveled, which again raised his ire. And Swift had other cause to be angry. Weitzman explained to his client that the statute of limitations had run out—perhaps what the prosecutor's office had been waiting for before dropping the last indictment—and he could no longer sue the police for his beating and time spent behind bars.

Despite the legal dilemma experienced by Swift and the conflicting grand jury and newspaper reports on Boyd's shooting, the most interesting facet of the homicide results from something the prosecutor's office *didn't* do. Clearly, there should have been a fourth indictment returned against Swift: manslaughter. The grand jury's presentment outlines a *clear-cut case of manslaughter* against Swift since, according to the presentment, he was directly responsible for Boyd's death. It is difficult to understand why the prosecutor's office would move for an indictment against Swift for causing the wounding of one man—Gooden—while ignoring their own official work that blamed a man's death on the same illegal action.

Why wasn't Alfred Swift charged for the death of Leroy Boyd?

Was the bearded man a figment of Richard Boyd's imagination or had the police made him "disappear"?

Of the two accounts of Boyd's death, the prosecutor's office had completely discarded one and it evidently didn't believe its own.

23

A LAST TOUCH OF JUSTICE

From "Friendly" to "Marvelous"

It had taken the judicial system a few years to get around to prosecuting the errant members of the Newark Police Department's auto squad. The five convicted detectives were finally sentenced by Superior Court Judge Conklin in early January of 1969—four years after their extortion activities had begun. It was with remorse and candor that Judge Conklin announced to the courtroom spectators, most of them relatives of the now contrite detectives, that he had considered giving them suspended sentences instead of the ten years behind bars for which they had worked so hard.

The judge did suspend the sentences for the crimes of misconduct in office, neglect of duty and—there is no way to blot it from the record—the act of extortion itself. But for the less devious matter of conspiracy, Judge Conklin apparently had no patience. He dampened the spirits of the gathering by sentencing all five detectives to one year in the Essex County Penitentiary at Caldwell.

The riot's black culprits found the going a bit rougher.

LeRoi Jones, a man who writes nasty poetry, had committed the crime of riding on Newark's streets during the riot while in possession of two revolvers. His punishment, a thorough beating and a sentence of two and a half to three years in prison, was appropriate. Charles McCray and Barry Wynn had no flair for the pen but they were admittedly with Jones and so richly deserved their punishments of one year and nine months respectively.

The less said about Eyvind Chandler, the better. Instead of drawing only an eight-to-ten-year sentence for accidentally shooting Mrs. Jones, he might well have gotten life. Chandler's fate was decided on November 6, 1969, when the Appellate Division of Superior Court rejected the appeal on the severity of his sentence. His attorney, John Francis, appealed further to the Supreme Court of New Jersey. The court refused to hear the case, cutting off the convicted man's last hope.

Poochie Hatcher and Brian Gary, two of the juveniles who had been inside Jo Rae's Music Room at the time of Jimmy Rutledge's killing, appeared in youth court on July 8, 1968, as justice was finally meted out a year after the incident. The boys were charged with breaking and entry and, unofficially, telling lies on how Rutledge had been slaughtered.

Both boys had good reports from their probation officer. And the FBI agents investigating the case had, after the youths had cooperated with them, promised to appear in their behalf. Also, the bar's owner, Joe Campisi, had responded to efforts to have him press charges in his own sincere way. "They're full of shit," he said. "The kids didn't take anything from the bar and the one was killed like that. . . . I told the authorities I didn't want to press charges and I didn't." The probation reports were ignored and the FBI agents never bothered showing up. They sent a letter instead, and it, too, was ignored. That Campisi refused to press charges was also ignored. Sentencing the boys was Juvenile Court Judge Neil Duffy, a former Essex County sheriff and, until his ties with Mafia racketeers were uncovered, a candidate for a federal judgeship. Hatcher was sentenced to the Essex County Youth House for ten days and Gary was sent to Highfields Reformatory for an indeterminate term.

The four police officers who had put forty-two holes in Jimmy Rutledge had been spared any embarrassment that would come from publication of their names.

John Smith had been rude and disrespectful to bona fide police officers. A bleeding head, a broken rib, and a good, old-fashioned rap or two in the groin with a sentence of two to three years would doubtlessly start Smith on his way to rehabilitation.

Smith's unusual appeal on the conviction was argued before the Supreme Court of New Jersey in January of 1970. A month and a half of silence followed while the court considered the matter further. Then, on March 17, the Newark *Evening News* observed St. Patrick's Day by devoting forty-eight square inches of its front page—as a tribute to the Irish—to a string of 348 descriptive adjectives beginning with "friendly" and ending with "marvelous." Buried on page thirty was a short news story with a Trenton dateline, CABBIE'S APPEAL DENIED BY COURT.

Smith's case was appealed further to the U.S. Supreme Court but, in early December of 1970, the court refused to consider it.

Denied Due Process

North 14th Street's Black Muslims had been equally irreverent and those obnoxious individuals were fortunate in getting off with a head busting and a mere eighteen months in jail. Four of the convicted men awaited results of their appeal behind bars: Roy Bell at Caldwell, Dennis Sims at Bordentown, William Jasper at Trenton State Prison, and William Turner, who had been released on bail from Caldwell but ended up in a federal prison camp.

Two years before the North 14th Street affair, Turner had been convicted of draft evasion when Local Draft Board 19 in Newark had shown something less than enthusiasm in classifying the Muslim as a conscientious objector. Despite his appearance in county court and his month stay at Caldwell, the federal marshals had yet to catch up with him on the federal conviction. The twenty-two-year-old Turner returned to his home across the street from 91 North 14th Street after being released from the penitentiary but five months later his luck ran out. He was arrested and sent to Lewisburg Federal Penitentiary for five years because of his religious beliefs. Laurence Orloff, his able public defender attorney, appealed the conviction but it wasn't until February 15, 1970, that the U.S. Third District Circuit Court of Appeals rendered its decision:

> [Turner] . . . was denied due process by the [draft] board's failure to afford him the means to present adequately his claim for reclassification as a conscientious objector. . . . Instead of reaching out to be helpful to him, the board warily maintained its guard against him and declined to give him any assistance, even though he did not know enough to ask for it in the requisite form. It is clear that the clerk would volunteer no information to him and would give him only what he specifically requested.

The freed man returned to Newark in March of 1970. Unfortunately, he had already served fifteen months at Lewisburg's prison camp before the reversal and, in addition, the memory of his beating on North 14th Street was still vivid.

Don't You Guys Know When to Stop?

Of the other Black Muslims, it was easy to feel sympathy for Bell, a soft-hearted slob who had gone for a walk to a neighborhood bar on a summer night and ended up in jail for eleven months. He was a model prisoner at Caldwell, his first experience behind bars. But Bell lost a lot of weight, was suffering headaches after his beating, and evidently missed his wife and children. Between working and writing poetry, he wrote his attorney a letter from cell U-11:

> Dear Mr. Kelly,
> The money for the bail will be ready Saturday. Jessie [Mrs. Bell] is supposed to call you Wednesday to get things lined up so I will be able to leave by Monday. I hope the gentleman that is supposed to sign the bail will not disappoint me. Believe me, he has no worries because I have been in here

almost eleven months and if I ran I would have everything to lose and nothing to gain. I am begging you to do all you can. I want to go home to my
family, I want my freedom. Just to be free for a little while is not too much
to ask. If I have to come back I will and do the rest of my time. I know you
told me not to get my hopes up too high but I am only human. You gave me
hope. Since the day you left all I can dream of is going home to my family.
Please help me for I will always be in your debt.

"I was standing there and I saw the guy laying in the street with his hands
handcuffed behind him," Bell slowly recalled after his release. "There was
blood coming out of his head and I wanted to help. All I can remember is
stepping into the street and Sergeant Fehn pushing me. Then they all
started hitting me on the head. *'Don't you guys know when to stop?'* I
yelled at them. *'Can't you see I'm bleeding to death?'* After that I don't remember anything except my head hurting. At the hospital they stitched it
and they took X-rays after I passed out. I didn't think I was even going to
jail, I thought they'd just sew me up and let me go home. I didn't even
know what I was in jail for. Fehn came up to me at police headquarters and
he told me, *'I'm going to personally see that you get seven years.'* I think
the whole thing was, looking back at it, the Newark cops just wanted to
show off for the East Orange cops."

An Honest Mistake

At the time I had talked to Captain Fausto about the North 14th Street
affair, he told me he wouldn't do anything to alter his defective testimony
about Sims or Jasper. Therefore, I informed Tom Kelly of Fausto's statements regarding false identifications during the Muslims' first trial. I also
informed Kelly of Assistant Prosecutor Riccardelli's statement to me that
Fausto had admitted he couldn't identify anyone, excepting Roy Bell, and
that he wanted the matter dropped. With this new information, Kelly applied for a new trial for Sims to the appellate division based on my affidavit,
this in addition to his initial appeal on behalf of all the convicted Muslims.
In reply, the court directed Riccardelli to submit an affidavit in reply to my
allegation and he honestly did so. His sworn statement agreed with my
own that Fausto indeed had told him he was *unable to make any identifications.*

After these developments it would seem that Fausto was caught in the
middle, but when the hearing for a new trial was held on May 13, he was
taken off the hook in the only way possible—with Riccardelli repudiating his
affidavit. It seemed, the assistant prosecutor testified, that he had somehow
confused Sergeant Fehn with Captain Fausto and it was the sergeant who
had sat in his office stating that he was unable to make any identifications.

This was a surprise coming from an individual as trained and experienced as Riccardelli, Fausto having been the commanding officer at the North 14th Street scene and bearing no resemblance to Fehn whatsoever. Riccardelli now testified that he "couldn't recall" whether Fausto said he was unable to make any identifications. Actually, neither Fehn nor Fausto had been able to make any identifications but only the former declined to do so during the trial.

Fausto was thus saved by a convenient lapse of memory, but it was now up to Riccardelli to explain his affidavit. Judge Lyons, however, was unconcerned about such a trivial matter and quickly dismissed Riccardelli's reversal as "an honest mistake."

A few months later Sims's bail was signed for and on May 16—after ten months in custody—he was released, pending a Superior Court decision on Kelly's original appeal.

We Were Upstairs Hiding

The final mystery of the North 14th Street affair—why William Jasper had been identified and convicted of assaulting Fausto and Officer Tretola —finally unraveled a month and a half after the hearing for Sims. On July 3, the Essex County grand jury indicted four more Black Muslims as having been among the six robbers who had held up the Robert Treat Savings and Loan Association back in 1965, wounded Sergeant Maver, and fired at Mayor Addonizio as he chased after them. The case had been broken when the two men already incarcerated for their part in the holdup—Albert Dickens and James Washington—decided to turn state's evidence after more than three years behind bars and named their accomplices—including William Jasper. Officer Martinez subsequently admitted he had known at the time of the North 14th Street affair that Jasper was suspected of having taken part in a robbery during which the Newark sergeant had been shot. It was now obvious why Martinez had been listed in Detective Scott's report as the only one out of at least thirty policemen who said he could identify Jasper when the Muslim had been hiding inside the house.

William Turner substantiated that Jasper had been upstairs at the time of the attack. "We were upstairs hiding in the front room," he said. "The police broke down the door. I was underneath the door and tried to sneak out with the door on my back. They were beating Jasper and I sort of got their attention. Then they left him and started beating me."

Still behind bars as a result of questionable testimony, Jasper was refused communication with me at Trenton State Prison. It was explained that there was a rule against news media people being allowed to visit inmates.

Eventually Jasper was brought from Trenton to Judge Lyons' courtroom

once again. There he and two others—Robert West, thirty-four, and James
Faulkner, twenty-seven, the gunman who had shot Maver—were convicted
in a trial that closed out the 1965 holdup except for one more suspect
who was already in prison on another charge. Jasper and the two others
were given identical thirty-to-thirty-nine-year sentences for their morning's
work, which had included shooting at Mayor Addonizio. At this point in
Newark's corrupt history—with Addonizio under federal indictment and
using up more of the taxpayer's money—perhaps their greatest disservice to
the city was their bad aim.

It Certainly Took Them a Long Time

The story of North 14th Street developed further on July 10 when the
Appellate Division overturned the conviction of the four Black Muslims
found guilty in the second trial, and it was Judge Lyons' turn for embarrassment. New Jersey's second highest court ruled that Lyons had erred
in not giving the defendants benefit of a self-defense charge to the jury.
Washington, Cogman, Williams, and Turner were granted a new trial. The
prosecutor's office appealed the conviction reversal to the New Jersey
Supreme Court but to no avail. Its decision, coming after Judge Lyons had
retired, further tainted his record:

> At the outset of the jury trial, when defendants indicated an intention to
> rely in part upon self-defense, the judge made plain his view that such a
> defense was not applicable. Moreover, after all of the evidence had been
> presented, he refused to submit the issue of self-defense to the jury for con-
> sideration as a possible basis for acquittal.

The convictions of the four Muslims in the first trial—Bell, Chisone,
Sims, and Jasper—were allowed to stand. Judges Harold Kolorsky, Sidney
Goldman, and Lawrence A. Carton, Jr., Appellate Division judges hearing
the appeal, had received detailed information on all irregularities pertinent
to the case but did nothing to correct the travesties. With little hope of
success, Kelly also appealed to the state's Supreme Court on behalf of the
four men.

The amiable Edward Chisone, a victim of police action that had left his
home in shambles, seemed to accept the court's decision with his usual good
nature.

"It certainly took them a long time," he told me at his home. "I was
thinking they were leaving me alone all this time because I was going to
stick somebody up or something so they could *really* get me and put me in
jail for twenty-five years. If you can't fight what's happening to you, you've
got to just accept it. I had a year of college and the food there was very

bad. As a matter of fact, when I was up in the jail at Caldwell the food was very good. That was the first time I was ever in jail and it's not as bad as they say. The warden walks by and if you say hello to him, he'll say hello to you. He's not an animal, he's a human being just like you are. If you treat him all right, he'll treat you all right. I'll do the eighteen months all right with no trouble at all. If you go to college for four years, that's thirty-two months, right? Well, all I have is eighteen months and the food is much better."

It Was Really Funny Running into Him Like That

The only Black Muslim still unaccounted for two years after the North 14th Street affair was the elusive Mr. Walker. He had matched his own common sense against the procedures of the judicial system and, thus far, had played to a standoff. If Walker had stood trial with the others, he would have been convicted along with his four companions whose convictions had now been reversed. Walker had saved a lot of unnecessary paper work and expense for the county's taxpayers. Even after his narrow escape from the sheriff's deputies, the fugitive continued to drift through Newark's ghetto.

"I saw Walker at a restaurant at Spruce and High Streets eating a bean pie," Chisone related, laughing. "It was really funny running into him like that. *'Strange seeing you in this neck of the woods,'* he said and we both started laughing. He told me after the sheriff's deputies just missed catching him on Wallace Street, he waited until they were gone and then he went back to eat his breakfast."

Everyone But the Police

On December 17, 1969, the state Supreme Court refused to consider the appeal of the four convicted Black Muslims in the first trial. Bell, Chisone, and Sims were directed to join William Jasper behind bars with—if one hadn't signed for their bail—some humorous results: none of them showed up. They joined the errant Mr. Walker as fugitives from justice. Two days later a bench warrant was issued for Mr. Bell, whose soul-searching letter had put some good-natured soul on the hook for $1,000. And on December 23 other warrants were issued for Sims and Chisone, who evidently had decided that Caldwell Penitentiary's food wasn't that good after all. Those who had signed for their bails were also left holding the bag.

Everyone paid for the incident on North 14th Street, from prisoners who had sustained a brutal beating and the well-meaning but naive people who signed for their bails, to the complacent taxpayers who paid for the trials —everyone except the police officers who had precipitated the disgraceful affair.

The four Black Muslims who had been granted a retrial waited while Joe Lordi, Essex County prosecutor, decided their fate. Eventually the indictments were *quietly dismissed*.

Do You Think I Can Sue Somebody?

Howard Edwards' car had been shot full of holes and reduced to junk. He had undergone a beating and the harassment befitting a supposed culprit who had something to do with shooting down an unarmed fireman. He had also remained behind bars for seventeen days without having been convicted of anything. "Do you think I can sue somebody over what they did to me?" he asked, back home in Staten Island.

Edwards was fortunate to be still breathing.

Alfred Swift, the last of the riot's black culprits, came out better than most. As the wild man who had personally wrecked a portion of Newark police headquarters, he had doubtlessly earned his cracked skull and bloody trousers. That he had remained in jail for seven months and was eventually found innocent was regrettable.

I Don't Think It's the PBA's Function

The five convicted auto squad detectives, who had been sequestered on N. tier at Caldwell Penitentiary, had no appreciation of their new residence. The Caldwell facility was used only for short-term prisoners and no trouble was anticipated because of the new residents. Warden John Rush, an able and fair administrator even according to his prisoners, reported that the only threat to the former policemen's safety came on their first day. Black prisoners welcomed the new inmates with catcalls and harassment while they were eating. One of the former detectives went to work in the mason shop, two in the sign shop and the remaining two, appropriately enough, in the auto body shop. Several of the new prisoners had trouble sleeping behind bars. One developed "a stomach disorder." And, to put it in the simplest terms, none of them *liked being in jail*. Something would have to be done.

After but thirty-nine days of confinement, a hearing for reduction of sentence was held in Judge Conklin's courtroom. If the former detectives had been contrite at their sentencing, they now were close to tears. There issued a stream of sad tidings, complaints, soul-searching remorse—everything but an admission of guilt—from the mouths of their attorneys that would have melted the coldest heart.

"This man has been in prison for *two months,*" lamented one lawyer, exaggerating his client's suffering by twenty-one days, "and these two months are like *ten years or twenty years.* By putting him in jail you have given him a taste—and for lack of a better description—of *hell.*"

"I accept the facts as existed and it's a living, twenty-four-hour-a-day *living hell* there in that prison through no fault of Warden Rush or any of his subordinates," announced another of the lawyers.

A full performance followed, including stomach disorders, the use of sleeping pills, inability to eat properly, the deterioration of their families, and the overall "dreadful hardship."

"The sentence that was given to him," Judge Conklin replied to the first lawyer, "was a deterrent—not to him, he will never be back in the police department—but as a public notice that anyone in public office who is corrupt and who has been found so by our jury would have to sustain the punishment that the law imposes. I could have sent him to state prison. They could have gone away for ten years or more. I made it one year and it was a deterrent. I didn't want the Newark police walking around and a fellow going a straight line and saying, 'He's excused, found guilty of it and the guy got away with it,' and 'Look, Judge Conklin put him out in the street.' "

To this staunch position the white-haired judge candidly added:

"There have been attempted contacts by some persons in high places to use pressure upon this judge knowing full well that the matter is coming up for reconsideration. I know counsel knows their judge and I might be a brother rat to somebody but at least I am a straight rat as I try to be and then when I get this letter from the head of the PBA—I thought this was in extremely poor taste for the PBA. I don't think it's the PBA's function."

All was not lost, however, as the hearing concluded with Judge Conklin taking the matter under further study and private meditation. The five tormented former detectives were returned to Caldwell, but they needn't have worried with law and order advocates like the PBA going to bat for them. Here the issues were clear cut.

The Newark riot's black culprits had been guilty of disrespect toward police officers and uncivilized conduct. On the other hand, though the convicted auto squad detectives had extorted at least $9,000 and their crimes were premeditated and arrogant, they had conducted themselves in a *gentlemanly fashion.* Judge Conklin also had to take into consideration that these particular thieves were not only remorseful—because their attorneys said they were remorseful—but at heart basically good men who had been tempted from the straight and narrow. Judges could never guess what thoughts were in the minds of those blank-faced darkies as they were herded before the bench, but the high priests of the court knew that, down where it counted, policemen had to be good-natured men who had come from a long line of good-natured kin.

Blacks like Turner and Swift, though later found innocent, could use their respective fifteen- and seven-month visits behind bars as a civilizing influence. Most blacks had a poor home life anyway. Besides, the convicted men in this instance were *officers of the law*. A week later, while the black criminals brooded over their scars and served their time, Judge Conklin returned the former detectives to the arms of loved ones after they had served a total of *forty-six days* in confinement.

24

THE KILLING OF DEXTER JOHNSON

Tell Your Boy to Put His Gun Away

"My mother told me that Dexter was looking for me," related seventeen-year-old Raymond Boone. "He was planning on buying a car but the fella said he didn't want to sell it. He said that Dexter could go for a ride, though. He knew Dexter, you know, and he gave him the registration and Dexter and I left from the front of my house."

Boone and his good friend, seventeen-year-old Dexter Johnson, a thin, sensitive boy, pulled away up Hunterdon Street on a May afternoon in 1969. They turned left at West Bigelow Street, passed the Fifth Precinct and then proceeded down the sloping hill. "Then the car started to stall and I told Dexter the best thing to do was get back on Hunterdon," Boone went on. "So he made a U-turn and headed back the same way we had come."

At the Hunterdon intersection, a car was parked at the right curb and the Johnson boy, an inexperienced driver, made too wide a turn, hitting the rear bumper of a police car heading in the direction that the boys had come from minutes before. "He didn't hit it too hard, just enough to knock the bumper off," Boone continued. "But Dexter got nervous and when he stopped the car back in front of my house, he got out and ran up the driveway into my back yard."

The two black officers in the car that had been struck believed that the two kids had stolen a car and were on a joy ride, a frequent occurrence in black Newark. The police car made a U-turn and raced after them about 160 yards down Hunterdon, pulling up behind the boys' car in front of Boone's house.

"By the time I got out of the car they were already there," Boone continued. "I was standing on the sidewalk in front of my house and Dexter was gone up the driveway. I wasn't nervous at all but Dexter was the nervous type. I knew we had the registration and everything. I said it loud enough for the cops to hear, I said, 'I live right here in the house, the car's not stolen.' By that time the one cop already had his gun out. 'Tell your boy to put his gun away and I'll catch him for you,' I yelled to the other cop."

A small crowd of young people formed quickly after the police car arrived and they watched as one policeman grabbed Boone and pushed him into the patrol car. The other officer ran up the wide driveway some thirty yards in pursuit of the Johnson boy who, having climbed a three-foot fence, was now in the back yard of an old man named Ellis Williams, who lived next door to Raymond Boone. The frightened boy then went some six yards farther to the rear of the yard where he climbed a six-foot fence and jumped down into the back yard of 203 Peshine Avenue, the next block over. By this time the pursuing policeman had reached the first fence with his revolver drawn. He shouted something and a second later—with two fences between himself and the fleeing boy—aimed and fired. The officer then was seen running to the right in front of the string of garages, looking for an easier way to get into the back yard where Dexter Johnson had disappeared from sight.

The rapidly growing crowd couldn't see what had happened behind the house but they had heard the gunshot and soon learned that the Johnson boy had been hit. What followed was Newark's second eruption since 1967. Explaining it all was a May 20, 1969 story in the Newark *Evening News,* another example of journalism from police reports. This one case adequately reflects why black people have little respect for either profession and why whites, who read once again of a ruthless punk and a valiant police officer, remain so uninformed:

> The killing of a 17-year-old boy by a Newark policeman touched off violence last night in the business area of Clinton Avenue and Bergen Street.
> More than 1,000 persons in the predominantly Negro section were involved. The dead boy was Dexter Johnson of 133 Schuyler Ave. The policeman who shot him was Patrolman Charles Knox. Johnson was a Negro. Knox also is a Negro.
> The shooting followed an accident at Hunterdon and W. Bigelow Streets involving a police car, in which Knox and Patrolman William Burgess were riding, and a car occupied by Johnson and another youth. The youths fled and were pursued by the policeman. Police said Knox *shot Johnson after the youth attacked him with a broken bottle.*
> Crowds began to form after the shooting last night and in a matter of minutes windows were smashed and roaming gangs of youths were looting stores along a three-block area. Police moved in with a show of force carrying shotguns. They began to disperse the crowds.
> Sporadic looting broke out along Springfield Avenue and at Avon Avenue and Bergen Street. The other incidents of looting were isolated and quickly controlled by police. Spina ordered tear gas fired into the damaged stores to prevent looters from entering.
> The igniting incident occurred, police said, when a car carrying Johnson

and Raymond Boone, 17, of 662 Hunterdon Street, collided with a patrol car next to the Fifth Precinct headquarters at W. Bigelow and Hunterdon Streets.

Patrolmen Knox and Burgess chased the youths one block to Hunterdon and Clinton, where the youths jumped from the car and *ran in different directions.* Knox chased the Johnson youth into an alley between 660 and 662 Hunterdon St.

Police said Johnson jumped one fence with Knox behind him. At the second fence Knox ordered Johnson to halt. *Police said that Johnson picked up a bottle and struck Knox twice whereupon Knox pulled his service revolver and shot him.* Knox suffered a cut hand.

Knox called an ambulance but Johnson was declared dead on arrival at Martland Hospital. According to Dr. Rosario Tamburri, assistant medical examiner, the bullet entered the right side of Johnson's chest and traveled through the lung and heart and exited through the left side of the chest. Knox was suspended immediately by Spina.

The *second youth was arrested and charged with juvenile delinquency.*[2]

Other newspaper stories added embellishments to the original incident: the 145-pound Johnson knocking the policeman down twice and kicking him, shouting, "I'm going to kill you, you Uncle Tom," and the officer firing only in self-defense as the boy swung a third time.

"My mother was angry at the newspaper stories," Boone said. "She called one newspaper, you know, and she told them step by step what was wrong. Like, number one, I wasn't ever charged with juvenile delinquency; number two, the car wasn't stolen; number three, I didn't run from the police. Like that, step by step. They told my mother they went by what the police reports said."

"I hope that the community will trust us, that we will do the best and fairest we can under the circumstances," Acting Police Chief Barres—Spina's choice for the job—announced to the black community.

Just Tell It Like It Is

At ten o'clock the next morning, detectives from the prosecutor's office were investigating the scene of the shooting. From witnesses in front of the house such as Raymond Boone, who had noted the police officer's movements on the near side of the first fence immediately after the gunshot, the brief time element involved, the physical measurements of the scene itself and the spot at which the boy's body was found—lacking any powder burns —in the backyard of 203 Peshine Avenue, a clear picture emerged on the basis of circumstantial evidence alone—one far removed from that painted by both Newark newspapers. Still no one came forward who had actually seen the shooting.

[2] All of the italics above are the author's.

Then, looking up from the back yard, the detectives saw an old man looking out of his second-floor window, just as he had been doing the previous afternoon. They talked to Ellis Williams and took the fifty-seven-year-old man downtown where he made a signed statement. That same day, exactly twenty-four hours after the death of Dexter Johnson, I made my own visit to the shooting scene and, standing in the back yard of 660 Hunterdon where the boy had run, I saw the same thing the detectives had seen that morning: An old man looking from his kitchen window.

"I heard all the noise and I was at the window, just like this where I always sit, you see, and I looked down and I saw the policeman come by the end of the garage there and I saw the boy on the other side of the big fence," Williams related. "He looked like he was starting to climb back to the near side and I heard the policeman call to him. I didn't see no bottle and I didn't see anybody attacking the policeman. The boy looked like he was fixin' to come over the fence toward the policeman when the policeman said, 'Halt, motherfucker, you climb that fence and I'll blow your damn brains out.' The boy started to go on the other side of the garage there and the policeman shot him. He fell behind the garage and I couldn't see him anymore. Then the policeman ran along the garages to the right.

"I haven't nothing to say but if you ask me, I'll tell it the way it is," the old man continued. "I'll tell the truth. This morning there were three or four fellas in the back yard and they seen me here looking out of my window. I figure they wanted to know how it happened, I was the only person who saw it."

Ellis Williams, the only person known by police[3] to have witnessed the killing of Dexter Johnson, had come from Columbus, South Carolina, three years before with his wife of some thirty years, Katie. The couple lived with their two sons and six grandsons in the second-floor apartment and, though the old man had a heart condition, he always seemed cheerful.

"Just tell it like it is, so much trouble in this land," he told me on the first of several trips to his home. "No sense making the truth crooked. The point is the boy is dead, he's gone on and I have to go on to meet my Maker and I want somebody to say, 'Well done,' for my children. I went downtown, I told them just as plain as I could what I saw, no hearsay."

There were two more trips for Ellis Williams. The first took him downtown again to repeat his statement before the grand jury as the death of another black boy in Newark was routinely shuffled through what had become an inevitable process. The determining factor of any judgment of the shooting, the most open-and-shut case since the Mathis killing four

---

[3] There was another eyewitness to the shooting whose version duplicated that of Ellis Williams. He, too, had been close enough to hear the policeman's warning to the boy before shooting. But, unlike the old man, he had refused to come forward.

years before, would be the location of the dead boy's body. If the shooting had occurred as the police said, the body would have been found in the rear of 660 Hunterdon. Witnesses on the next block say the body was removed from the rear yard of 203 Peshine Avenue, as police photographs further document. Now, either Dexter Johnson was shot where his body was found or he jumped over the fence after he was dead.

The Newark *News* story, written by Edward Higgins, was taken from initial police reports and clearly depicted the supposed struggle as taking place in the backyard of 660 Hunterdon, a setting at odds with the physical facts of the case. Higgins, as a matter of fact, never knew that the boy's body had been found on the *other side* of the fence, and when told more than a year later, he expressed surprise.

Despite the evidence and testimony nothing more was heard of the killing until April 10, 1970, a year later, when Dexter Johnson's mother filed a suit charging the city of Newark with negligence in the death of her son. The city had been negligent, the suit asserted, in hiring Charles Knox even though he had "inadequate mental, moral and emotional qualifications" to serve on the police force.

Instead of a knife, this time it was a bottle. Again there had been a chase and an attacked police officer and a languid press willing to report whatever it was told. The suspension of Officer Knox was as untrue as had been the case with Henry Martinez. And then the last phase, the grand jury shrugging off a human being's death as nothing. From Lester Long to the Mathis boy and the slaughter of the riot and now Dexter Johnson, the Newark police and the Essex County grand jury system seemed to institutionalize manslaughter and murder.

The ghost of Lester Long was running on.

With only one known eyewitness, the civil suit on behalf of Dexter Johnson ran into trouble. Ellis Williams' second trip was home to South Carolina in a coffin less than a month after testifying before the grand jury. The old gentleman died quietly at home of a heart attack on a Sunday night.

"I reckon it must have been his time," his wife said.

25

A LONG WAY FROM PALM BEACH

Newark's Two Worlds

Two distinct worlds exist within Newark. One of them is rented to the city's poor, a sprawling mass of slums and high-rise prisons. Their disease, perversion, and crime reach to the very doorstep of white Newark—bright, modernistic office buildings downtown, filled by employees who quickly retreat from the city at 5:00 P.M. By nightfall, black Newark is a world of almost primitive behavior, the impoverished living and dying alongside a deserted world of filing cabinets, water coolers, and burglar alarms.

Black Newark has 40,000 units of substandard housing and white Newark has twenty new office buildings which have been constructed in recent years. The blacks have abysmal medical care and archaic, crumbling schools with new medical facilities for them only inching forward and new school facilities not even contemplated. Businessmen downtown, on the other hand, could look forward to five more steel and glass skyscrapers under construction. The poor of black Newark live with the highest proportional rates of infant and maternal mortality, venereal disease, and tuberculosis in the nation. At the same time, white Newark houses two million square feet of office space and the wealth of the country's second largest insurance company complex.

This dichotomy had failed to attract the attention of the mass media prior to the 1967 explosion but, after it was too late, its coverage was plentiful. These efforts were little appreciated by the Greater Newark Chamber of Commerce, the public relations representative of the city's downtown world. The reportage punched to the gut—and Newark's businessmen felt the vibrations in their money pockets.

A good example was a *New York Times* story datelined March 17, 1969:

> NEWARK—A nightmare that haunts many urban dwellers across the country appears today to be turning into a reality in this city of 402,000 people. It is the nightmare of a city finally succumbing to America's catalogue of urban ills, abandoned by its white and Negro middle class and left

to decay and die. What is happening to Newark—the flight of its middle class, its rising crime rate, its racial tensions and its fiscal desperation—is happening to one degree or another in many cities in the United States. Only it is happening to Newark faster.

In the 1930's, when Newark's population peaked at 500,000, nine percent of the city's inhabitants were Negroes. By 1950, with the influx of poor Negro migrants from the South, that proportion had risen to 17 percent and in 1960 to 34 percent. Today, as the middle class exodus continues, the city's population is 52 percent Negro, making it the nation's second major city to have a Negro majority, the first city being Washington.

At least partly responsible for the flight of the middle class has been what is described as a "staggering" and "disastrous" tax rate.

Like many other cities, Newark is unable to find the needed money to begin to cure its ailments. State officials concede that the money is essential, but legislators, many of them representing rural or suburban constituencies, refuse to appropriate. As a consequence, the rate of reported serious crime has risen 26.6 percent in the last year—and shows no sign of abating.

Air pollution stings the eyes of Newark residents and the waters of the Passaic River are gravely polluted. Schools are in trouble, the city's library and museum are threatened with closing and sections of the city remain boarded-up and abandoned reminders of the racial violence that swept Newark in July 1967, exacting a toll of 26 lives and $10 million in property damage.

The evidence of change is apparent everywhere in the city. Weequahic, made famous by the fiction of Philip Roth, once was a predominantly Jewish neighborhood of substantial houses and tree-lined streets. Now it is heavily Negro. Temple B'Nai Beshurun, founded in Newark in 1848 and the oldest and largest reform congregation in New Jersey, built a synagogue in the 1920's at High Street and Waverly Avenue. By the late 1950's, the Jewish population of the area had begun to vanish. Last year, the congregation built an elegant new temple in Short Hills. A similar pattern was followed by the Conservative Temple Oheb Shalom, founded in Newark in 1860. In 1959, it moved to South Orange. And Temple B'Nai Abraham, one of the most prestigious of the Conservative congregations, is now in the process of re-establishing itself in Livingston.

Of the 15 or so Orthodox temples that once served Newark's Jewish community, only two or three remain.

However, the picture is not without some hope. There is some new construction in the downtown business district. Last week, the city announced that a $20 million high-rise office building would be erected as part of Newark's Gateway urban renewal project, and other office buildings are planned for the downtown area.

Gustav Heningburg, the Negro director of the Greater Newark Urban Coalition, agreed that "a sound middle class is necessary in any city" but he said that creating a stable Negro middle class posed problems. "They are trying to get out of Newark just as fast as the white middle class," said Mr. Heningburg. . . . Mr. Heningburg is also skeptical of the motives of his white neighbors in offering to "turn the city over to the Negro." What such a move does, he said, is to put the responsibility for saving Newark "on the backs of the black people."

It's the "In" Thing to Knock Newark

City officials and businessmen complained to the *Times* about the story and the newspaper's Newark reporter, Walter Waggoner, subsequently wrote another piece more pleasing to their tastes. Newark's business community, however, found it difficult to keep up with the barrage of bad publicity that followed. Their city received critical comment not only in other newspapers but also in a nationally circulated news magazine and in a New York television series. Then, when even the *Women's Wear Daily* ran an uncomplimentary story on Newark, the city's big businessmen thought it time to strike back. They unholstered their checkbooks.

In April of 1969 the First National Bank of New Jersey—largest commercial bank in the state—launched an expensive advertising campaign based on the notion that if Newark couldn't get a good press any other way, they'd buy it. IT'S THE 'IN' THING TO KNOCK NEWARK, BUT IT'S THE WRONG THING, announced full-page newspaper advertisements. Every ten days the ads ran in major daily newspapers in the New York–Trenton area. They listed the city's achievements in constructing private and public housing, erecting commercial office buildings, serving as a transportation hub, and becoming what was billed as one of the nation's educational, cultural, and medical centers.

"It [Newark] is one of the oldest of the 'old' cities and one of the newest of the 'new,' one ad claimed. "Its strategic location and the fact that it is the financial capital of New Jersey are assurance that the future will bring continued progress."

The campaign began smoothly enough, but in May its message of progress was contradicted by one of the realities of ghetto life: the police killing of an innocent, seventeen-year-old boy.

Mayor Addonizio, however, described the advertising campaign as a success and, as if to prove it, bestowed a certificate proclaiming "meritorious service on behalf of a new and expanded Newark" upon the man who had headed the drive, First National's chairman, W. Paul Stillman. The bank had spent $50,000 on a campaign to improve Newark's image and not one penny of it went to alleviate the ills which had brought on the muckraking in the first place. The bank chairman, it so happened, had been electrified by the idea while flying back to suburbia from his winter home in Palm Beach.

By September, Newark's status had plummeted so low that it was fair game for even New York City politicians, men with little to brag about. Advertising people working on Mayor John Lindsay's campaign for re-election came up with some television ads depicting Newark as an enlarged garbage dump. A film clip guided the viewer out of the Holland Tunnel and off the New Jersey Turnpike and into Newark via Raymond Boule-vard, arriving at the site of the proposed medical school before demolition in the area was completed. A voice implied that the demolished buildings and barren areas were the result—rather than a cause—of the riot and noted that Mayor Lindsay's efforts had prevented such devastation in New York.

Mayor Addonizio termed the film clip "unconscionable" and shot off a telegram: "I am saddened, John, for you should have discovered by now that there is no gain to be made in public life by sacrificing the dignity and decency of others."

The mayor's sentiments were understated as far as the Chamber of Com-merce was concerned. Undaunted by this newest slap at their billfolds, the city's big business interests followed Hughie's lead.

By the end of the year, the Chamber of Commerce launched a "Program of Work" designed to meet the city's complex problems. The program, details of which were released by chamber officials at a December 16 press conference, was designed mainly as a publicity gimmick. Unfortunately, the publicity gained was once again the victim of circumstance. The day following the press conference, chamber officials opened their newspapers to read that virtually the entire Newark city administration had been in-dicted.

Once the city had been revealed as a haven for corruption and organized crime, Newark became fair game even for television personalities.

"Have you heard? The city of Newark is under arrest!" Johnny Carson announced on his NBC network show. "What a great group we've got tonight! We had a spotlight on the audience and a guy from Newark jumped up and yelled, 'I surrender!!'"

Former *Herald Tribune* columnist Jimmy Breslin, visiting Newark to plug his novel about the Mafia, was contacted by a Chamber of Commerce vice president who had known the writer when they both worked on the *Tribune.* "He asked me if I knew Carson," Breslin jested on a visit to the NBC show. "Whenever anybody asks me if I know anybody, I say no." Breslin continued: "They should just hang a banner right across the street: WELCOME MAFIA!"

The New York *Post* joined the game in February with a story by Perry Young:

Walking down Newark's empty streets any night now, you wonder why a place with all the outlines of a bustling city is open only eight hours a day.

Every day at 5:00 P.M., the people withdraw to the suburbs or into the decaying neighborhoods that have become armed camps of blacks and whites equally afraid to go out after dark.

A police siren echoes out of some side street like an oldtime train whistle in a lonesome mountain valley. You hail the only taxi in sight and stand there while the driver slows down, examines you, and finally stops to ask where you're going. Then, and only then, does he reach behind the bulletproof shield and unlock the door for you.

"Ah, this place is no good no more," he says. Why? "The coloreds are taking over. Me and my wife moved to Irvington and they followed us out there. Used to be a friendly place. Lots of people out then and I could work nights. All you hear now is hate."

An armed guard admits you to the modern high-rise apartment building directly across Newark's main street from City Hall and police headquarters. A hip and happy young white couple in a comfortable apartment on the fourth floor tries to tell you how it is to live as a virtual prisoner in the city at night. In any other city, in any other state, their place would be a lively center of activity. They've marched in all the peace and civil rights marches. But, those days are gone in Newark and they don't even know any of the young black couples in the building.

"Look out there," the wife gestures towards Broad St. "Main Street, Newark. Not a policeman in sight. No taxis. Nobody window shopping. I get home from work in New York before dark and we never go out. Even if we wanted to risk it, there's absolutely nothing to do here after dark."

A recent incident in the couple's lives illustrates the way people live in Newark. The husband had cut a deep gash in his hand and arm in a kitchen accident. Three, four, five calls to the police emergency number brought no response from across the street. The wife, hailing the only taxi in sight, had to plead with the driver to take her husband to the hospital which, like most of the city, is in an area cabbies consider unsafe.

"You're lucky you're white," the surgeon told him. "Otherwise, they would have slapped this together and ruined your hand for life."

After the bloody riots of 1967, most people felt that Newark's mood would change, and hopefully for the better. However, Newark now seems a most dramatic example of the "two societies, one black, one white, separate but unequal," which were foreseen in 1968 in the report of the President's Commission on Civil Disorders [the Kerner Report]. Ask someone about the investigation in Newark and he'll shrug it off. The whites feel the blacks are Newark's No. 1 problem. Since the riots, no civil or social organizations hold meetings after dark in Newark. Even groups like the Red Cross and the Mental Health Association have moved to the suburbs.

Among blacks and whites, the fears of night-time Newark are real enough. And an overpowering *malaise,* tied in with the city's corruption, leaves Newark painfully lacking in spirit.

"I call them Pontius Pilates," says Dean C. Willard Heckel of the Rutgers Law School. "You can see it on their faces every day at five o'clock at the train station: *'I'm through with this city for another day.'*"

No other city in the country has such a heavy percentage of its work force living outside its taxable limits, Heckel says. The city's population is 405,220 and an additional 500,000 come in to work in the city every day.

For the 300th anniversary of the city in 1966, Rutgers vice president Malcolm Talbott wrote that Newark would "come alive" in the next decade. "Nowhere is it *dead* after 5:00 P.M. Newark—1976 is a city that sings." Walking down Newark's deserted streets on a night in 1970, you listen, but nobody is singing. A lone taxi speeds past you and a police siren wails into the emptiness.

Again the business community complained that its city had been maligned. The *Post* story, businessmen felt, had omitted mention of such examples of progress as the Gateway office building-hotel complex and the private construction of 1,400 medium-income apartments.

These omissions could be charged to the *Post* story, but equally omitted was a further unpleasantry. Newark's downtown stores were still thronged, but the old clientele had been replaced by juveniles and adults who stole whatever they wanted. Shoplifting loss by stores like Bamberger's was already alarming and continuing to climb. And though black police and school teachers could be depended upon to maintain the status quo, such was not the case for non-white clerks who understood what was happening and looked the other way.

Business interests had been responsible for the creation of structures that enhanced the city's skyline and kept capital flowing through Newark. The new office buildings also offered hoodlums a better caliber of clientele to mug.

As a last straw, NBC-TV's Huntley-Brinkley Report put together a final blow that made Newark's businessmen moan in anticipation. The film clip described itself as a "death notice" and began with commentator John Chancellor standing in a Newark cemetery with an appropriate message: "Here lie the men who built Newark, resting now in the only good neighborhood in town. This is where you find the upper middle class in Newark today: *in the graveyard.*"

The network issued advance transcripts of the program to newspapers in the metropolitan area and Tom Mackin, the excellent entertainment writer of the Newark *News,* devoted a full column to what he called a program "unprecedented in its unrelieved cruelty" which held "the defenseless city up to national scorn and contempt."

Mackin then listed the $300-million Newark Airport–Port Newark projects under construction, the $50-million Gateway complex, the $150-million medical school and the $60-million development of Rutgers' downtown campus, none of which had been mentioned in the four-minute segment as signs of vitality visible to the naked eye. "Having come to find a corpse, NBC's arrogant embalmers chose to overlook these signs of life," Mackin wrote. "A TV producer looking for a bit of sensationalism can send his cameraman into any metropolis in the nation and find, as Chancellor says of Newark, 'parts of the city seem to have been abandoned by human beings and left to the cats and the rats and the roaches.' "

Mackin's viewpoint was influenced by his residence in Short Hills, as was the case with so many of Newark's businessmen who came into the city to collect paychecks. The columnist's retort, which mirrored the feelings of Newark's outraged business community, was based on the notion of "progress" formulated by that elite group: the needs of human beings trapped and exploited in ghettos were unimportant when compared with office structures and other examples of capitalistic enterprise.

Some portions of the NBC film were right on the mark:

> Newark is about at the top of the list of American cities with its crime rate, and its disease rate, with the number of people living in public housing. It is near the top of the list in the number of people living on welfare. It is almost unbelievable, but one out of every three homes in Newark can be described as substandard—which usually means unlivable. Eight out of every ten houses is over fifty years old.

The advance transcripts which had been sent out and an ill-advised week's delay in broadcast gave ample time for the outraged and the self-righteous to mobilize. A North Ward citizens club sent angry letters to the Federal Communications Commission and the president of NBC. It also announced it would seek an injunction to make the postponement permanent. The group's chairman then went to Washington to enlist the aid of New Jersey congressmen in keeping such a disastrous view of Newark from nation-wide viewing. Councilman Imperiale's first reaction was to threaten NBC with a few busloads of demonstrators who would camp on the network's New York doorstep.

Also complaining, loudly, were the Chamber of Commerce and, of course, poor Hughie, who said the film was politically motivated and nothing more than "character assassination."

NBC, beginning to feel the heat of a growing controversy, announced that it was canceling the segment. The following day, an editorial in the Newark *Evening News* crowed: "Good night, David; good night, Chet." Thereupon, the network, apparently feeling that it was being mocked for its capitulation, announced that the film segment would be adapted to run at some future time. It never did, however.

A final twist was added to the NBC controversy when the Frontiers Club of Newark looked around for someone on whom to bestow its 1970 Distinguished Service Award. The competition was somewhat sparse but there, standing in the forefront with Addonizio's "certificate of merit" which had been given in honor of his $50,000 jingle, was Stillman, First National's chairman. The wealthy gentleman, who also happened to be chairman of the board of the Mutual Benefit Life Insurance Co., received this latest tribute on the day after NBC re-announced its intention to broadcast the Newark segment. Though not on hand himself, another of the bank's executives read his prepared statement at the Military Park Hotel to an enthused audience: "Something like this should cause us to renew our determination that those who would knock Newark simply do not know what they are talking about."

The Whorehouse's Blushing Virgins

While Newark's business leaders looked with distaste on such journalistic efforts, they could have nothing but praise for the *Evening News* and the *Star-Ledger,* the city's two daily newspapers. Their appreciation, however, was not shared by the U.S. attorney's office. "I, for one, found it difficult to understand how blatant, arrogant corruption can exist as long as it did in Newark without devastating exposures by the press," Lacey stated during a speaking engagement.

Thus did the two local newspapers assume their rightful positions alongside Newark's businessmen as the whorehouse's blushing counterfeit virgins. The city's press and its businessmen pretended innocence of the corruption and were oblivious to non-whites who lived under conditions of subtle genocide. At day's end, editors and reporters joined the businessmen in their haste to flee Newark. The relationship of the business community and the newspapers was underscored in the Chamber of Commerce's perfumed periodical, *Newark!* Even as Lacey was delivering his remarks, an issue featured lengthy interviews with the editorial hierarchy of both newspapers. The article left little doubt that they were as far removed as ever from the realities of black Newark:

> What they [the two newspapers] hold in common, and what remains unchanged, is a philosophy geared to impartial and objective news coverage. Between them, they cover every event of any significance for Newark or the area.

Governing coverage of all types of stories in the *Star-Ledger* was the belief that events must be "approached with an objective mind, with the idea of presenting whatever happens as it really is," said the *Ledger*'s managing editor, Henry Stasiuk. "We believe in 100 percent objectivity," the *Evening News*'s executive editor George Kentera said. "We don't believe that reporters should be advocates, but that they should gather as much pertinent information as possible, evaluate it and put it together in as complete a way as possible."

There was another reason, however, for both newspapers' staunch reliance on the doctrine of "objectivity."

If it seems ironic that angry whites like Imperiale and ghetto residents led by LeRoi Jones both charged the local press with failing to meaningfully communicate their respective positions, it is only testimony to both papers' spineless editorial policy. News which might be inadequately and inaccurately reported in the *Evening News,* would be completely ignored by the *Ledger,* a sad product of the Newhouse chain which had the reputation of being little more than "the administration rag." Both newspapers seemingly hoped Newark's corruption and callous disregard for human rights would *disappear* if ignored long enough.

Why had the newspapers in Newark stood idly by during years of corruption?

Why had they failed to take a strong editorial stand as the bungling city administration drove the city toward a riot?

Why had the Newark press failed so miserably during the riot itself and why did it allow the lies to stand despite the reportage of the *Washington Post* and the Hughes Report?

Would the lies of the Dexter Johnson killing have evolved if the press had done its job after the shootings of Lester Long and Walter Mathis?

Would there be any changes in the future?

Yes, indeed.

The latest innovation at the *Star-Ledger,* the article continued, was the elimination of reporters to specific police beats. "We find crime stories getting repetitious," the *Ledger*'s editor Mort Pye explained. "A reporter on the beat, just to justify his own existence, picks up third-rate kinds of things and the paper starts to look like a police blotter. Of course, we cover any major stories that develop."

The *Evening News,* on the other hand, reported that it didn't consider crime news as news unless it was "tied in with sociology."

Both philosophies could be reduced to practical translations. White people living throughout the state would be spared the usual run-of-the-mill stories as Newark's blacks robbed, raped, shot, and knifed one another.

"As long as people have young dogs, there'll always be a newspaper," one *Evening News* executive asserted during the interview.

26

LIKE A BITTERSWEET REFRAIN

A New Quality of Life

With the riots in Newark, Detroit, and other cities in 1967, the country experienced its fourth consecutive summer of serious racial unrest. White suburbanites, long oblivious to the ghettos and to the evils they contained, feared the worst and bought guns. From coast to coast, the nation was angry, anxious, afraid—and pessimistic. It wasn't until the night of July 27, 1967—two years after the Watts explosion—that President Lyndon Johnson, speaking while Newark and Detroit were still smoking, addressed himself to the problem. It was time, he said, for a commission to study the situation. Johnson then announced the formation of the Kerner Commission, a group of distinguished individuals which was not only to study the causes of racial unrest but to suggest comprehensive programs designed to deal with it. One of many interested listeners was Senator Robert Kennedy, who heard Johnson's address with friends in his Washington office.

"It's over," Kennedy said. "He's not going to do anything."

"What would you do if you were president?" the senator from New York was asked.

Kennedy thought for a moment and then began:

If I were president, I'd take advantage of the power of the office. I'd call the heads of the three television networks and ask them to be here tomorrow morning. I'd tell them it's their duty to their country to produce a two-hour documentary to be run as soon as possible—in prime time—which would show what it's like to live in a ghetto. Let them show the sound, the feel, the hopelessness and what it's like to think you'll never get out. Show a black teenager told by some radio jingle to stay in school looking at his older brother—who stayed in school—and who's out of a job. Show the Mafia pushing narcotics. Put a candid camera team in a ghetto school and watch what a rotten system of education it really is. Film a mother staying up all night to keep the rats from her baby.

The president is the only man who could get them to produce that show.

Then I'd ask people to watch it—and experience what it means to live in the most affluent society in history without hope. Government can't cure all the problems, but the president isn't a prisoner of events—he can act. Then I'd collect data on what this means in every major city. In New York, ghetto children lose between ten and twenty points on their IQs between the fourth and eighth grades—those statistics should be available for every city. Then I'd call meetings—one a day, if necessary—of people from every major city. Maybe there are fifty such cities—maybe more. I'd find out who has the real power and I'd ask them to the White House. The mayors, ministers, bankers, real estate men, contractors, union officials—everybody who really has power in a city—not just elected politicians. I'd talk to these groups; I'd show them the facts—in their city. And I'd say, "Gentlemen, this is your problem and only you can solve it, your city will fall apart in a few years and it will be your fault—and I'll say it was your fault."

They would figure out their own solution. If the problem was schools, let them raise the money for schools, or modernize, or bus the kids, or change the zones. I wouldn't care—just do it. If it was unemployment, make new jobs. They could do it by cutting profits, or by tax incentives, or by using government programs. But I'd make it clear that this can only be solved in the community—and that they had no time to spare.

As it developed, Kennedy was far from alone in his conviction that the time for drastic reform was long overdue. The Kerner Commission's finding —that America represented two distinct societies, one white and the other black, separate and unequal, that were drifting further and further apart— was too forthright for President Johnson's political tastes. The Kerner Report was supplemented by other governmental and private reports which seemed to be warning the country that virtual civil war was imminent.

Whatever other rationalizations existed for not facing the problems, politicians could no longer claim ignorance as a defense. Johnson's "Great Society" rhetoric hadn't been realized. His successor, Richard Nixon, retreated to a policy of "benign neglect." While tossing off a promise of "a new quality of life," Nixon's priorities were not what Kennedy and the Kerner Commission—or any others with humanitarian ideals—had in mind.

Examples of "benign neglect" were plentiful. The president vetoed a health, education, and anti-poverty appropriation and opposed hospital construction because he regarded them as inflationary. At the same time, Nixon was willing to spend $53 to support the education of each American child and $20,000 to kill each Viet Cong. He remained fascinated with IBM missiles, supersonic transport planes, and future rock gardens on Venus and Mars. Closer to home, Nixon was determined that if the Confederacy and its racism were to endure, it would do so under the Nixon-Agnew banner rather than that of Wallace in the 1972 presidential election.

The crisis was at its worst in Newark, a city still faced with severe hous-

LIKE A BITTERSWEET REFRAIN

ing problems, miserable schools, pathetic medical facilities, and corrupt courts and police. The problems of New Jersey's largest city had been detailed by the state's own commission study, the Hughes Report. Outlined were steps which should be taken to begin the long cure. Federal and state "doctors," however, had other ideas.

In 1968 the city received $47 million from the federal Department of Housing and Urban Development to acquire and clear land for various urban renewal projects. The following year the city required another $48 million to develop 220 of the wasting acres, but President Nixon and the new Republican administration felt otherwise. In December of 1969, after a seven-month freeze on federal funds, Newark officials learned that they would receive but a pittance of those desperately needed funds. Seventeen of the city's urban renewal projects were slowed or halted completely. The same fate befell badly needed Office of Economic Opportunity programs. Newark's Model Cities program, the usual grab bag of goodies for rising "Negro executives" sponsored by the federal government to keep the natives quiet, was more fortunate. Federal backing came through in January of 1970—just as the project was ready to close its doors. Two months after the reprieve, its director resigned. "The city administration's notorious reputation for corruption repeatedly short-changed the city on federal and state funds," he contended.

In May of 1970 the federal government announced it would come through with $52 million for the city's urban renewal projects. By this time hundreds of vacant buildings and more than 200 acres of deserted land had turned portions of Newark into a virtual ghost town.

Construction of low-income housing in the post-riot city was non-existent. Nevertheless, acquisition of property continued for the proposed Interstate Route 78 and the Route 75 Midtown Connector. It was intended that this $70-million, two-and-a-half-mile, six-lane expressway would rip through the heart of Newark's Central Ward—eliminating $13 million in tax ratables, two public schools, and the homes of 9,000 to 15,000 people. Plans for the connector went back ten years and specific blueprints had been laid out in 1965 at a cost of more than $1 million by Mayor Addonizio and city officials. The Newark Housing Authority and the New Jersey Transportation Department were responsible for relocating those families displaced by the proposed roadways. Thus far, 1,200 families had been moved out of their homes by Route 78. Four hundred of them were relocated by the local agency. Unfortunately, no one knew *what had happened* to the other 800 families.

The black community's anger made the new roadway the most serious public issue since the medical school fiasco. The Emergency Committee to Stop Route 75 demanded that all property acquisition cease until low-income housing could be built to accommodate those forced out of their homes. With the riot a vivid memory, this time the city agreed.

I Have Them Read Comic Strips

The Hughes Report had stated that the shortcomings of the ghetto school system were a cause of unrest and recommended a state take-over. This suggestion was rejected. Since 80 percent of the 80,000 school population was non-white—72 percent black and 8 percent Puerto Rican—few outside of Newark cared if *anything* was ever done. The Hughes Commission had found the city's schools in an advanced state of decay and by 1970 the only change was an additional two years of deterioration. The waste was apparent in ways other than physical: as many as *90 percent* of the grammar school children were now below the national reading norm. Newark was primed with social dynamite—functional illiterates—who were unemployable.

"I teach English literature but I realized from the very beginning I had to throw out Shakespeare," a Weequahic High School teacher said. "I tried getting the kids to read newspapers. Too difficult for them. Finally I was able to have them read the comic strips. Will they graduate? Of course they will. There's no room for them to stay here."

"A child was brought into my office with a rat bite she received while eating in the cafeteria," a school nurse reported. "I called the board offices and someone there said something would be done about it but nothing ever happened."

In May of 1969, a Philadelphia non-profit research outfit released results of a $72,000 study financed by the Office of Economic Opportunity. Their report charged the school administration with rushing headlong into programs without adequate planning. It also accused the state and federal government of contributing to "the financial rape of Newark," criticized the local press for its coverage of education problems, and recommended that the Board of Education share power with the community.

Efforts to improve the educational system, however, only seemed to underscore the system's ineptitude.

The Board of Education invested $38,000 in a program structured to improve reading skills of pupils in twenty-seven schools. Not only did the project fail to make any improvements, but the reading level attained was actually *surpassed* by students not using the program. The board then invested another $33,000 for a second trial.

Another experiment brought thirty-eight elementary pupils from hard-core poverty areas in Newark to the well-to-do borough of Verona. Its purpose was to provide an environment that might correct some of the serious educational deficiencies of the children. In May of 1969 a Verona citizens' group succeeded in having the plan canceled.

Two teachers' strikes in the 1965–66 school year had failed to settle anything and only prepared the way for more serious difficulty. On one side, angry voices from the powerless community demanded control. On the other, the teachers—70 percent white and fearful of losing tenure status and promotions—resisted. The Board of Education, an unimpressive group with the exception of some non-white members like Harold Ashby, was caught in the middle. Confrontations among the teachers, community, and school board became common. Lack of adequate books and supplies, double shifts, and overcrowding produced disagreements aimed at unpopular teachers and administrators. As these confrontations continued, the fears of white teachers increased.

The fighting at Vailsburg High School in May of 1968 and the three-day black student boycott were followed by increased community pressure for more black representation in school administration. A badly split school board subsequently voted to break its contract with the Newark teachers and elevated eleven black teachers to supervisory jobs in violation of prescribed promotional procedure. White teachers, many of them hacks with seniority and a great majority of them suburbanites, were shocked. When their contract expired in February of 1970, the teachers walked out. Their strike was a carefully executed walk-out planned by professional organizers of the American Federation of Teachers who couldn't have cared less about what impact their action would have on the community. The school strike, longest and most bitter in New Jersey's history, lasted four weeks. It was marked by the arrests of 200 teachers picketing in violation of a permanent court injunction won by the Board of Education, and the exchange of threats during negotiations by union representatives and school officials. At its climax, Mayor Addonizio pressured the Board of Education into a "sell-out" contract which the black community could not possibly live with. The contract, considered by the federation to be one of the strongest—if not *the* strongest—it had ever obtained throughout the country, brought generous pay raises to the teachers—which the parents didn't feel they deserved and the city was unable to pay—and additional formulas on grievances and teacher assignments that thwarted community control of the schools.

One of the contract's clauses called for binding arbitration, and the Board of Education, amateurs in dealing with polished trade union negotiators, lost one arbitration case after another, including one on nonprofessional chores. As a result, the Newark teachers were home free with what was probably the most sweeping nonprofessional chores clause of any school district in the entire country:

The board and the union agree that professional employees shall be released from assignments involving nonprofessional duties so that they may devote the time within their work days to rendering professional service to their schools and students. In order to effectuate such relief the board agrees to employ an additional 252 three-hour aides in the elementary schools to perform duties in conformity with their job description.

Teachers who were willing to supervise children in playgrounds and cafeterias were ordered not to by their union. Parents who were worried about their children running free out of the classroom were frustrated. White suburbanite teachers, whose home towns didn't grant such contract terms, were content. The black community was angry. In effect, the teachers' strike perpetuated the irrelevance of the school system for the city's black children. Once again the children had lost. Apparently unconcerned, many of them celebrated by staying out of school yet another day.

Newark's future generation was going to bed hungry and waking up cold. They were being abandoned at City Hospital and being stuffed into the Essex County Youth House until it was ready to explode. They were eating paint from the walls of their slum apartments and suffering lead poisoning. They were smoking marijuana and shooting heroin like there would be no tomorrow. They were learning about sex in the dark stairwells of housing projects, inside abandoned cars, and in rubble-strewn backyards. They were being burned in fires; they were crippling themselves falling from the roofs of abandoned buildings; and with few play areas they were running in the streets and being hit by cars. One four-year-old boy was found hanging by the neck in an abandoned building off Bergen Street, a death sentence carried out prematurely.

The inevitable harvest was reaped. In March of 1970 a prominent Mountainside resident drove into the jungle in early evening to collect rents at his fourteen-family apartment building. Police found him an hour later slumped on the front seat of his car with a bullet in his head. Two nights later, a fire set by two teenagers in a slum tenement a few blocks away took three lives, two of them eleven-year-old children. A month later, two youths rode around the city robbing and terrorizing black pedestrians in a bizarre crime spree that left several victims with bullet wounds and one dead. Two other black teenagers enjoyed a sunny Saturday afternoon less than two weeks later by slaughtering a harmless, white taxi driver in the Weequahic section.

Assault Upon the Dignity of Man

Despite a reported $50 million being spent in proposed construction for new facilities at five of its hospitals, Newark still had the highest sickness, accident, and death rates in the state. "Health and medical services rendered to residents of Newark are in general disgraceful and result in residents of New Jersey's largest city having a death rate almost one-third higher than the state average," stated the New Jersey Health Planning Council.

For the fourth year in a row, Newark led the state in cases of gonorrhea even though, the state health commissioner said, City Hospital was not even reporting its gonorrhea cases. Newark ranked *seventh* in reported cases in a national survey of 159 localities. The situation was reported to be "a venereal disease epidemic" by the health commissioner.

On February 11, 1968, the board of trustees of the New Jersey College of Medicine and Dentistry at Jersey City announced it was giving up previous demands for 150 acres of Newark's ghetto. Now, after a riot, it would settle for only fifty-eight acres.

An agreement made early that year stated that the medical college would assume control of City Hospital, spend $2.5 million for its renovation, and open 2,600 jobs to the black community. The agreement also provided that at least a third of the journeyman workers and half the apprentices on the construction site of the new college would be non-white. In addition, sixty-three acres of the now unwanted land would be turned over to a community group, the newly formed Newark Community Housing Council, to develop as it saw fit.

The medical school took control of City Hospital in July of 1968, an institution then described by the New Jersey Division on Civil Rights as "merely an extension of the ghetto condition, grossly substandard, dehumanizing and a stoic assault upon the dignity of man."

Difficulties at the hospital continued.

A training coordinator was fired because, he charged, he had attempted to set up training procedures to enable the poor to become employees at the hospital. An employee grievance committee later reported that they were forced to share toilet facilities with hepatitis and tuberculosis patients; medical examinations were being made in full view in wards; some patients were naked because of a clothing shortage; and junkies were bringing heroin into the hospital to drug ward patients, who walked out of the hospital to get their own fixes when their visitors didn't show up.

One illustration of the Civil Rights Division's comments was the case of Sidney Jackson, who came to City Hospital at 9:30 P.M. on a Saturday night after falling from his third floor porch. The badly injured man sat in the emergency room until 5:30 A.M. and was finally sent home without treatment. Jackson died the next day. Another cause for alarm was a fourteen-year-old South 10th Street girl who took an emergency ride to City Hospital and became the victim of a white ambulance driver's attempted rape. Despite numerous previous similar incidents, he had been allowed to remain at his job.

Construction on the new medical school, meanwhile, was proceeding anything but smoothly. The first labor agreement permitted work to begin on interim buildings but this harmony was short-lived. In June of 1969, community leaders said that minority employment quotas were not being met and demanded that federal funds be cut off. Community leaders wanted non-whites to receive on-the-job training and the labor unions wanted instead to train apprentices in vocational schools. The building contractors, caught in the middle between state hiring specifications and provisions of their own written agreements with unions, just wanted to hide. Two months of negotiations proved fruitless. When the talks broke down, the medical school site was like much of the rest of black Newark: a wasteland.

The taking of construction bids was postponed to give building contractors time to test in court a law requiring minority group workers to be employed on the job.

Another front was opened in January 1970, when the Newark Black and Puerto Rican Construction Coalition asked the U.S. Department of Labor to undertake a full-scale investigation into discrimination in the hiring of minority group laborers on publicly financed projects. "Promises were made that the building trades would provide many job opportunities for minority groups," Gus Heningburg, chairman of the group, said. "To this date, it has not proven true. A continuing source of frustration and hostility in a city which is in the throes of crisis at all levels still exists."

The hearings were held in March and, after two days, the federal panel retired to evaluate the testimony. Their report, released three months later, said that non-whites are "seriously under-utilized" in union and non-union jobs in the Newark area. It also said that minorities are acutely under-represented particularly in skilled and semi-skilled construction trades. This unstartling revelation had been pointed out by the pickets at Barringer High School *seven years* before.

As had countless groups before them, the federal panel advised state labor leaders to formulate a "strong plan" to remedy the situation. No such plans were formulated—strong, diluted, or otherwise.

The stalemate continued as Governor William T. Cahill inherited the medical school problem in 1970.

"Today I saw the contrasts in Essex County," Cahill had said as a candidate following a walking tour of the Central Ward—a favorite pastime of politicians looking for press coverage. "I walked the streets of the Central Ward. While critics may say I did it for publicity, that is not true. I saw the scars on the buildings. I saw the scars on the human beings. I saw what can happen to a great city."

Cahill may have seen but it didn't take him long to forget. In his first press conference, the new Republican governor announced that there would have to be "modifications" of the medical school plans. He explained to reporters it was a time of "tight fiscal conditions" and "fiscal realism." In late April, the Newark press reported that the medical school complex would *never be built* as originally planned. Cahill hastened to deny such reports. Not many in Newark believed him. Months passed and nothing was done. For Newark's poor blacks it was just like old times, like a bittersweet refrain. After years of tension, of haggling over the proposed medical facility while people died for lack of adequate care, after a riot and its legalized murders, the medical school site was a deserted ruin. Even the sixty-three acres given to the black community for its own development lay wasting years later.

Gus Heningburg charged that Governor Cahill and other state officials had made "a political decision" not to force the building trades to take in black workers. Heningburg, an articulate man, also charged that political pressure prevented the New Jersey Division of Civil Rights from taking court action against contractors and unions for their discrimination. "The Civil Rights Division takes on issues which the governor tells them they can take on," he stated. "The Civil Rights Division has investigated discrimination charges in the building trades in New Jersey for years and they have reached a point where the minority guys who have been fighting this problem won't even talk to them anymore because they know full well they've got enough information to go to court and they haven't done it."

The lily white unions and lack of action spoke even louder than Heningburg.

A Prologue to Tragedy

Though Newark's City Council did not have the power to act on any of the Hughes Commission's far-reaching proposals, it did show that its heart was in the right place. The post-riot councilmen came up with the idea of making black juveniles carry identification cards—as they would in South Africa or any other occupied territory. Another idea was the canine corps. When these ideas were abandoned, the council voted to protect white residents with $309,958 worth of social rehabilitation tools: thirty-nine pieces of military equipment, including jeeps, vans, and armored vehicles; tear gas grenades, riot shields, 280 bulletproof vests, armored suits, forty large caliber rifles and—of absolute necessity—fifty rolls of barbed wire.

Another Hughes Report recommendation, that the state also take over Newark's municipal courts, was also ignored. Assembly-line justice rolled along downtown, though there were refinements. The spectacle of prisoners marching into the courtroom in chain gangs had been eliminated through construction of an exit from the cell block. Now the prisoners bided their time while herded together in wire cells outside of public view. Another change was the absence of the errant chief magistrate, Del Mauro, who had retreated to the sanctuary of the Housing Authority. He was replaced by Harry Hazelwood, Jr., who, despite his tenure with the establishment, could be described as an able black man.

In other ways, however, it was business as usual:

"You can always tell when the fix is in," one attorney explained. "That's when the judge yells and screams but does nothing to the defendant."

"What do these councilmen know about who is qualified to be a judge?" asked a former magistrate. "One [Turner] was a copy boy on a newspaper when he was elected. Another [Imperiale] runs a karate school."

"Keep your mouth shut," one magistrate shouted at a lawyer typifying the court's protocol. "You're better off not wasting time."

"You've made so much money you can afford to be fined," said another magistrate. "Does it pay to talk so much to save fifteen dollars?"

Two more magistrates were subsequently investigated for pocketing illegal fees and found it to their advantage to resign. The vacancies caused further disorder and backlog of cases in the municipal courts.

Another recommendation of the Hughes Report, that a civilian review board be established to protect ghetto residents against transgressions of the Newark Police Department, was *never even considered*. In all, the Hughes commissioners had submitted a list of nearly a hundred recommendations for action by the city and state government which would relieve the chaotic conditions in Newark. The Hughes Report, ironically entitled "Report For Action," became a study in non-action. Predicting its own reception, the report added a warning:

> The mood in our cities clearly indicates that commissions like ours will have outlived their usefulness unless action is forthcoming from their recommendations. Our disadvantaged communities must see far more tangible evidence of a commitment to change than has emerged so far, or the summer of 1967 is likely to become a prologue to tragedy, and the time for study and planning will have run out.

Just as the rest of the Hughes Report, this warning, too, was ignored.

Like Old Times

In February of 1969, the Newark press again announced that Arnold Hess would retire as secretary to the Board of Education and that the able black man Wilbur Parker would replace him. "I haven't reapplied for the job, but I guess my application is still in," the gentlemanly Parker responded. "I don't know of anyone else interested in the job."

Thereupon, Mr. Hess apparently changed his mind again and decided to remain at his job.

At the same time, a frayed old photograph of a gray-haired man in a black beret haunted the squad room bulletin board at the fifth precinct. "This is a picture of Colonel Hassan," the typed caption read. "It is believed that he is now residing in the Fifth Precinct area. If he is observed, attempt to locate his address or the address of any place he is frequenting."

So it was like old times. Valentine Electric was awarded yet another Newark Housing Authority Contract and the Mafia-connected company also had its share of the Gateway project downtown. Ironically, Valentine had even landed contracts for all electrical work on the $18-million new county jail and courthouse.

Examples of the arrogance which had been shown by the Newark Police Department's auto squad were also abundant in the post-riot city.

The Fifth Precinct's twelve-man vice squad accounted for a large number of arrests following its organization in November of 1967. Some of its members, however, were equally adept at disposing profitably of the confiscated heroin. In May the squad's leader was arrested for giving away a few decks of the narcotic to the wife of a pusher. Despite witnesses who gave statements to the prosecutor's office, other squad members who were selling much larger quantities of the narcotic were never touched. In addition, no member of the defunct squad *was prosecuted* and they remained police officers in good standing.

Members of a First Precinct burglary ring involving at least fifteen policemen, including a superior officer, also were keeping themselves busy stealing. In October of 1970, after years of operation, the group finally came under investigation. The involved police patrolled the downtown area and worked with employees of a burglar alarm service. Policemen first set off the burglar alarm at a desired location and waited for the company representative to arrive. Then, while he waited to reset the alarm, the police looted the store.

It was doubtful if any of the policemen would ever be punished for their crimes but for ghetto residents Newark-style law and order continued unabated.

More then a score of blacks were sent to their graves, a good share of them by trigger-happy black police officers. They were shot when they ran. They were shot when they didn't run. And they were shot in confrontations and brawls which were dubiously reported in the local press. In one incident, a tipsy off-duty black cop shot and killed an innocent bystander during a tavern disturbance. Newspaper accounts painted the police officer as a battered hero. Another off-duty black cop, this one thoroughly drunk, shot and killed a drunk who had talked with the officer's girl friend at the Howard Bar on the strip in August of 1969. The policeman's brother, an employee at the bar, was holding the drunk from behind at the time. The death bullet passed through the drunk's body and also wounded the brother. The Newark *Evening News* reported this homicide as a battle between a courageous police officer and a maniac who had attacked him first with a barstool and then with a knife. The headline read: ASSAULTS COP, IS SHOT DEAD.

Newark's two most notorious policemen—Gasparinetti and Martinez—also continued in their accustomed style.

Gasparinetti, the motorcycle officer, was involved in several boorish affairs at tumultuous City Council meetings and was at his best form in two assault cases. In March of 1968, Gasparinetti assaulted a one-armed Marine wounded in Viet Nam, James May, who was subsequently cleared of loitering and resisting arrest charges in municipal court. The grand jury, however, refused to indict Gasparinetti for assault and he continued on his bullying way. Two months later he was the leader of a tipsy group of off-duty policemen who had been drinking when they attacked three black youths with a baseball bat in Italian land on Bloomfield Avenue. Gasparinetti was listed as defendant in these two civil suits against the Newark Police Department.

Martinez, not as obnoxious an individual as Gasparinetti, just happened to hit someone who was of a mind to do something about it. While frisking a twenty-year-old black youth in August of 1968, the police officer rapped him on the back with his nightstick—an almost routine procedure in black Newark. The youth, who suffered no serious injury, was charged with assaulting Martinez. He was convicted in municipal court before Del Mauro, who was running true to form, and the conviction appeal was handled by none other than Leon Kapp, who also acted predictably. In January of 1969, however, the Appellate Division of Superior Court overturned the conviction. The court's ruling made Del Mauro look like an ass and did nothing to improve Kapp's reputation. Martinez was subsequently named the defendant in a $125,000 civil suit.

Another black policeman held up a dice game in May of 1968 and shot one of its participants. He was arrested immediately, and indicted for extortion, robbery, and atrocious assault and battery a year later. In May of 1969 the officer pleaded not guilty to all charges. Nothing more was heard of the matter, nor is there likely to be. The policeman, who owns a bar illegally and subsequently was also indicted because of a liquor license application, was merely shifted from the fourth precinct to work in the cell block at headquarters. He remained on the city payroll.

Armed robbers and hoodlums killed one black policeman, wounded four other officers, and slaughtered nearly a score of white store owners and cab drivers. As a natural consequence, two innocent blacks—one of them a skinny, seventeen-year-old kid—were shot by jumpy store owners afraid for their lives. The grand jury, perpetuating its philosophy of white domination, failed to indict the whites involved.

The situation in post-riot Newark was typified in two unrelated incidents on the night of February 6, 1970: junkies beat a seventy-four-year-old landlord to death and police executed an unarmed, sixteen-year-old burglary suspect.

White Society Condones It

Conditions in Newark had changed much in the three years following the riot. The housing shortage was worse and buildings termed as substandard could be described as rotten. Miserable schools were more miserable. Pathetic medical facilities were more pathetic. And Newark's court system and its police were conducting business as usual.

"Why can't history's most affluent, technologically advanced society act to make the black man a full participant in American life?" *Newsweek*'s special report had asked in 1967. "The answer is a meld of ignorance and indifference, bigotry and callousness, escapism and sincere confession. But the inescapable truth is that so far America hasn't wanted to."

The Kerner Report had its own reply to the question a year later:

> What white Americans have never fully understood—but what the Negro can never forget—is that white society is deeply implicated in the ghetto. White institutions created it, white institutions maintain it and white society condones it.

After two more years, the rear end of the Nixon-Agnew elephant duet premiered the new song: *"If you've seen one slum, you've seen them all."*

27

ON SECOND THOUGHT

While Newark's business community was unconcerned about blacks who had been shot to death and maimed during the riot, it was very interested in property loss. Owners of stores that had been destroyed or looted during the eruption had to be compensated. More than 3,000 plaintiffs were merged into 450 individual damage suits against the city. In April of 1969, the matter was brought before Superior Court Judge Larner in a single case which would test Newark's liability for the damaged and looted stores.

There were two potential cases for liability:

1. City officials had been negligent for failing to take adequate precautions before the eruption and, once it began, they had also been negligent in failing to call sooner for the aid of the State Police and National Guard.

2. There was liability for damages under an 1864 Civil War state statute if the plaintiffs could establish that a "riot" as defined by the statute had occurred.

Riding on the trial's outcome was the possible loss of $7 million which would plunge the city deeper into fiscal chaos.

In his first ruling, Judge Larner stated that Newark *could not* be sued for its lack of preparation and foolhardy handling of the riot. The plaintiffs had not established, said the judge, "a *prima facie* case of negligence." In the second ruling, however, Judge Larner stated that the city *was liable* under an archaic statute intended for use in the post-Civil War period.

The plaintiffs would have to wait for a year or two, however, while the city appealed Larner's ruling to the Supreme Court of New Jersey.

Judge Larner's decision, a clear example of the oft-revealed gap between reality and courtroom logic, saved Mayor Addonizio and his city administration from being held responsible for the riot. In November of 1968, Judge Larner had also saved Spina the embarrassment of presenting a defense during the police director's malfeasance trial.

At the same time, official Newark's view of the riot had shifted somewhat. The year before, Captain Kinney had testified before HUAC and the Senate subcommittee that the eruption was largely the result of a gigantic conspiracy and now the city's office of the corporation counsel, represented by former counsel Norman Schiff, took quite a different tack. The eruption in Newark hadn't been a riot at all, but rather a "rebellion" or "insurrection," resulting from social ills, said Schiff. What actually took place, Schiff continued, were "spontaneous outbreaks of hostility not directed against any particular objective."

At long last, the truth was now a matter of record: the city of Newark agreed that the riot had been exactly what Tom Hayden had said it was two years before.

The Harvest

PART VI

The Harvest

28

A NEW MAYOR FOR NEWARK

You Can Fight City Hall

"I have promised to work toward that great day in 1970 when we shall elect a talented, progressive, and imaginative black mayor who will be able to give Newark an honest, moral, and people-oriented government," said Reverend Horace Sharper. "The election proved that you can fight City Hall and if your cause is just, you can beat the hell out of City Hall. . . . Today we took the first step toward a new Newark."

With these triumphal words, a black politician proclaimed the arrival of a new mood in Newark.

The fifty-four-year-old Sharper, winner of a dramatic South Ward recall election in June of 1969 that ousted Addonizio cohort Lee Bernstein, declared war on City Hall. Sharper was hardly in his seat before he began to condemn city officials for meddling in the federal New Careers Program and called for the *resignation* of Mayor Addonizio and his spokesman Don Malafronte. His fellow councilmen, long used to a live-and-let-live philosophy and to scratching one another's backs, sensed Sharper's victory as an omen of things to come. Ahead was the 1970 election with real alternatives possible, not only for the mayor's office but for all nine council seats.

Black Newark's new mood gained momentum in November with a black and Puerto Rican convention which excluded white delegates. The three-day gathering was originated by LeRoi Jones and designed to nominate non-white candidates who would represent their communities instead of themselves in the coming election. The convention—which separated "blacks" from "Negroes"—yielded a group of candidates whose community concern would demand fundamental change.

More than 300 delegates chose a council ticket that included activists Earl Harris, Sharpe James, Reverend Dennis Westbrooks, Al Oliver, Ramon Aneses, Donald Tucker, and C. Theodore Pinckney, the last two the United Brothers candidates defeated in the at-large election of the previous year. Kenneth A. Gibson, thirty-eight-year-old engineer, won undisputed backing for the mayor's job.

The unlikely mayoral candidate was a stocky, mild-mannered man who grew up in the city and earned his engineering degree over a ten-year stretch in night school. After working as a civil engineer for the New Jersey Highway Department and then for the Housing Authority, Gibson received a Greater Newark Chamber of Commerce Young Citizen Award in 1964 and joined with business leaders to form a Business and Industrial Coordinating Council. In 1966, to the surprise of many, he made a belated bid for mayor. Insiders believed that Leo Carlin, the ex-mayor attempting a comeback, had paid for the Gibson campaign to draw black support from Addonizio into a run-off election with Carlin. Nevertheless, Carlin was subsequently defeated. This time, however, there would be no last-minute quality to Gibson's campaign. He had been quietly preparing since his 1966 defeat, and the riot had accelerated his efforts.

Though both Addonizio and Imperiale naturally attacked the convention as a *racist gathering,* other attacks by non-whites may have been more damaging, particularly those of two other mayoral aspirants, Harry Wheeler and George Richardson.

In 1962 Wheeler had been nicknamed "The Milkman" because of his questionable handling of schoolchildren's milk and cafeteria funds. The Board of Education belatedly discovered that Wheeler, a teacher at the school as well as the man responsible for cafeteria receipts, had a three-year shortage of $631.58. Wheeler said it was all a mistake. The board said it just wanted the money. Harry made good on the deficit but was subsequently relieved of his bookkeeping chore.

Richardson's position as mayoral candidate, on the other hand, was legitimate. He and Gibson had helped form the Business Coordinating Council. He was a founder of the United Community Corporation and of the Greater Newark Urban Coalition, a group predominantly composed of white politicians and business leaders that was formed in the post-riot period. Continuously involved in community affairs, he was more personable than Gibson and had more political know-how. Yet, like the house Negroes before him, Richardson had offered himself for sale. He had looked the other way for slumlords. He had traded his State Assembly vote to the corrupt Kenny machine of Jersey City. He had deserted the people he lived among for white bourgeois success. And he had also crossed the color line in bed, further offending the black nationalists.

At Newark's time of crisis, a man with the intelligence, ability, and temperament to lead a black revolution had become its enemy. Richardson remained officially out of the race but was busy planning a "spontaneous draft movement" for himself meant to split the black vote. Richardson represented no change in the usual brand of Newark's politics—he was just a darker shade of it.

As the divisions among non-whites grew sharper, Al Black, former chairman of the Human Rights Commission, allied with Richardson. "We are here to tell all our black and white brothers and sisters throughout the nation," Black said in mid-April at the Overseas Press Club in New York, "that Newark's Black and Puerto Rican Convention was not only racist, and therefore immoral, but it was also a hoax that tried to hoodwink the black people of Newark and the nation into supporting a predetermined choice."

Black's statement was a reply to a group of national figures—including Representative Shirley Chisholm, Herman Badillo, Ossie Davis, and Gary Mayor Richard Hatcher—who had called on Richardson to *drop out* of the race, a sign of the national attention that Newark was getting.

Some other calls for unity were less polite. Willie Wright, who had dropped a similar plan for selecting a black mayoral candidate earlier for lack of support, charged that the convention had been rigged and declared that he was running for a council seat without the group's support. His office was smeared with red paint and the windows broken. Some Wheeler associates, meeting in his Hansbury Avenue home, left to find their car tires slashed. Richardson's luncheon talk before Newark businessmen was heckled and a meeting of his draft movement ended in the stench of smoke bombs. Meanwhile, Jones's followers were breaking windows, ripping down signs and defacing political posters with zest. Both Wheeler and Richardson were also smeared in anonymous leaflets that had the malicious honesty of Jones.

These incidents raised further doubt about the so-called assassination attempts on the lives of Spina and Imperiale. The dangerous black militants, the supposed would-be killers, were acting much like mischievous juveniles with their paint and smokebombs—and blacks reserve their more ruthless tactics for their own people.

It Is Not My Nature to Quit

Anthony Imperiale had announced his candidacy a full year before the election. Characteristically, it came during a public berating of Mayor Addonizio inside an Italian restaurant in the North Ward. His campaign bounced between a legitimate attack on the city administration and pointless rhetoric, as when he called Jones a "loudmouth pipsqueak" after the playwright had the audacity to question his Marine discharge. Imperiale opened his downtown campaign headquarters in a flourish of noise and banners, including one in Turkish that said, according to Imperiale, "Truth, Honor and Courage for Mayor." The accurate translation was

"Vote for Mayor," but none of Imperiale's followers understood the Turkish language. As a matter of fact, few of them seemed to understand correct English.

Mayor Addonizio's federal indictment failed to deter his intention to run for a third term. On January 29, with city employees propped around his office in a well-planned demonstration of support, he declared his candidacy. "I am running because it is not my nature to quit when the going gets difficult," Addonizio said. "I have acted at all times with a sense of respect and honor for the trust my fellow citizens placed in me and I swear to each of you today that I have never committed a single act in public life to betray that trust. I would not—and I could not—offer myself for re-election and I would not—and could not—face my children if I had."

The burlesque ended with several women employees breaking ranks to hug and kiss Hughie, after which he quickly exited through a side door, refusing to submit to press questioning.

Addonizio then resigned from the Newark Urban Coalition on the pretext that its executive, Gus Heningburg, had participated in the "racist" Black and Puerto Rican Convention. Addonizio worked at creating the image of a moderate candidate between the "white racist" Imperiale and the "extremist" Gibson, who was being labeled as a tool of LeRoi Jones.

"I will be very interested in hearing what his platform will be," said Imperiale in one of his more cogent attacks on the mayor. "What will he tell the people about the fact that three-quarters of the land in Newark became vacant and untaxable during his administration? What will he tell the people when they ask him why the Board of Education under his administration is the worst in the history of Newark? What will he tell the people when they ask about the crime rate in Newark that is out of proportion? What about the fact that Newark has the highest infant mortality rate in the country? What about the civil disorders? The community is corrupt. Organized crime has the run of the city and the narcotics problem is unbelievable."

In addition to an "Italian backlash"—a determination of Italians to vindicate themselves by winning the election for Addonizio or another Italian candidate—the other major political result of the federal indictments was the emergence of more white candidates. These enhanced the chances of a black candidate to make the June run-off election if no candidate received the necessary majority on May 12. Addonizio helped add to the field of candidates when he angrily summoned Fire Director Caufield, a rumored mayoral aspirant, to his office.

"I told Addonizio I hadn't decided if I was going to run or not," the fifty-one-year-old fire director said. "I also told him I could not and would not under any circumstances support him for mayor. I told the mayor he had lost confidence and faith of most of the people." Caufield, administrator of one of the few effective agencies in Newark, was then fired. The unemployed Caufield announced his candidacy shortly afterward. "This city doesn't need an Italian mayor, a Negro mayor or an Irish mayor," he said. "It needs a mayor for all the people."

Believing, as did Addonizio, that stepping down was a virtual confession, the other indicted councilmen joined their mayor in the charade of another campaign. RE-ELECT WEST: HE STOOD THE TEST, posters inexplicably proclaimed. "The sixties represented the smoke screen for a political assassination of our government, but we together will not let them wipe us away as we move into the seventies," West said at his opening campaign dinner. "This is our only insurance."

"I sincerely hope I will have the privilege of running once again with him," Addonizio, an honored guest, said of his accomplice, "and I hope that Councilman West and Mayor Addonizio will again walk the streets of Newark."

If the U.S. Attorney's office had anything to say about it, Addonizio and West would be walking together into the federal pen at Danbury.

With three of its members under federal indictment, Newark's ruling body began the do-or-die business of buying votes. With the trial ready to commence, victory in the election for Addonizio and company was more important than ever. Even a sequestered jury would eventually learn of the results and be psychologically swayed by a political defeat. Though the city was on the verge of financial collapse, the City Council voted pay raises for sixteen Finance Department employees, including one of Addonizio's main female supporters. Early in April, a month before the election, Addonizio and his cronies announced that 3,600 city employees would receive a $1,000 raise, spread over two years, the first $600 to come a month after the mayoralty run-off in June.

Only Imperiale and Sharper opposed it.

Mayor Addonizio, now an embarassment to the city's big business interests, was becoming desperate for campaign funds. City employees were being invited to demonstrate their enthusiasm by buying three-dollar tickets to a May cocktail party. Whenever someone refused to pay, the solicitor listed his name in a deliberate attempt at intimidation. His opponents charged that Addonizio was even using federal funds and personnel from Model Cities and rat programs for his campaign. Having bought or pressured city office employees, Addonizio and company then turned to the police and fire departments. By mid-April they approved an expansion in both groups that would result in thirty-six promotions and thirty additional firemen, a package expected to cost the city $400,000.

Again, only Imperiale and Sharper refused to go along.

Newark's insurance and big business complex, which had put nearly

$1 billion into downtown office construction and were anxious to protect their investment, faced the election with apprehension. Their money and backing might swing a city election—but whom to support? They looked at Addonizio and frowned. They took a glance at what Imperiale was likely to produce as mayor and cringed. They looked at Gibson and saw visions of black bogeymen stampeding down Broad Street with spears. Caufield was a good man, but the wrong nationality. The business community wanted an honest local Italian for 1970 and a scrubbed, docile, sell-out Negro for 1974 when the city would be overwhelmingly black.

They were at an impasse when, presto—out of the spaghetti fields stepped one Alexander Matturri who, though a state senator living in the North Ward, had been virtually unheard from through the city's torments. Matturri was better known in Italy than in Newark. He had once been knighted by the Vatican to the Order of the Holy Sepulchre, was a former chairman of Boystown of Italy, and had been appointed by President Eisenhower as U.S. conciliator in post-war Italy. He was doubtlessly honest, which for an Italian politician living in the gambling-ridden North Ward was a rare virtue, indeed. Here was the man to restore confidence to the business leaders and respectability to the Italian community.

Matturri stepped into the most hard-fought election in the city's history with $15,000 from Newark's moneyed Italians bulging from one pocket, proof of knighthood in the other, and purity in his knapsack. His motto was equally impressive: "You're in the grip of Crime, Taxes, Corruption . . . but Matturri can free you. NEWARK NEEDS MATTURRI FOR MAYOR." According to some reports, Republican contributors from Newark's largest insurance companies had not only financed Matturri's bloodless redemption but had pressured the new Republican governor, Cahill, to push the knighted Italian into the race with the promise of an eventual judgeship should his bid to redeem Newark be unsuccessful. According to more reliable reports, Matturri was the sole choice of Newark's wealthy Italian hierarchy and business interests, who were told by their state Republican leaders that aid was coming only if their local people could get Imperiale *out* of the election, which they failed to do.

Results of a poll sponsored by business leaders in late February—before Matturri had begun hard campaigning—caused concern in City Hall. The poll of 1,500 city residents in all five wards found Gibson leading with 34 percent and Imperiale trailing with 24 percent. Addonizio was third with 16, Caufield next with 14, and Richardson fifth with 10 percent. Matturri was credited with 2 percent and Wheeler wasn't mentioned. Although the pollsters. Oliver Quayle and Company, had come within two percentage points of calling the 1966 election for Addonizio, a spokesman for the mayor called the figures merely an attempt to "discredit" him.

With the power and machinery of his office, and a surge of Mafia money behind him, however, the Addonizio campaign soon began to pick up momentum under the banner of PEACE AND PROGRESS, two commodities indeed scarce in Newark.

Addonizio had the advantage that many voters, including some blacks, didn't know what to expect with Imperiale or Gibson, but had been given patronage during Addonizio's eight years. He also had what LeRoi Jones called his "house niggers," such as Reverend Levin West, now UCC president following the death of the beloved Tim Still, who succumbed of a heart attack on the first anniversary of the riot. "There is a national conspiracy against the Italian people," West proclaimed alongside his mayor in the North Ward, "and if you don't get yourselves together in this election, you'll never be together." Another "house nigger," Deputy Mayor Lewis Perkins, appeared in the Central Ward on his mayor's leash to warn that "blood will run in the streets if this man isn't reelected."

A funny thing happened to Tony Imperiale on his way to the election. He dropped his gun in the second-floor hallway of City Hall—directly in front of the mayor's office he hoped to occupy. The gun went off. The slug ricocheted off an elevator door. A councilman's wife fainted. Someone shouted to startled onlookers, "Tony dropped a gun." And Imperiale just stood there ashen faced. The gun had dropped from beneath his coat when he embraced Mrs. Calvin West, proclaiming himself "your friendly militant."

When investigation began, however, the gun was long gone. Mrs. West, who had reported seeing a gun on the floor when first questioned, now denied it and said *the noise* had caused her to faint. However, a dent in the elevator door and a spent bullet, found lying some twenty feet from where Imperiale had squeezed Mrs. West, were in evidence. "I don't carry a gun," said Tony. Two full days later he and his lawyer and campaign manager, Sam Raffaelo, went to police headquarters for questioning. Finally, one week after the incident, the mayoralty candidate made a public statement.

"What happened was that I went to say hello to Mrs. West and I hugged her and suddenly there was a loud noise," Tony explained. "I was pale and I was really scared and hardly anything ever scares me . . . I was so scared I became pale . . . I got sick . . . I thought somebody had taken a shot at me."

About four months before, Imperiale explained, a fortune teller from Italy had predicted that he would suffer "a rough campaign" and that he would be the target of a bullet if he continued his pursuit of the mayoralty. "I wonder," Tony mused out loud, "could the City Hall gun incident really have been a realization of what that twenty-four-year-old fortune teller told me?" Apparently, others were wondering too.

The second Quayle poll—this one paid for by the mayor—was taken in mid-April. Since January, Gibson had lost two points, but remained a strong front runner with 32 percent. Addonizio had picked up nine points and moved into second with 25 percent. Imperiale, dropping seven points after his little accident, had fallen into a tie with Caufield at 17 percent each. Matturri, with 5 percent, had passed Richardson who had lost seven points and had but 3 percent. Wheeler was last with 1 percent.

Addonizio was rooting for Gibson. Though most likely to come out on top on May 12, the engineer would lack a majority and, since he could be branded an extremist, Gibson was the least likely of the three black candidates to beat the incumbent mayor in a run-off.

Addonizio prudently ducked out of joint appearances with other candidates, screwing up many intended programs. And a twenty-five-dollar-per-plate Chamber of Commerce breakfast on April 29 reflected the insipidity of Newark's businessmen. In the only appearance of all seven candidates together to submit to questioning, nobody could think of a worthwhile question.

Spina, a politically powerful man, waited until the last days of April before appearing with Addonizio at a rally. Perhaps the move came because of Imperiale's announcement of the previous day that he would name a replacement for Spina, or possibly Spina's boss told him that he had been silent long enough. Or perhaps it was because of the Quayle poll that Spina felt it time to make a move. Whatever the reason and however late the hour, Spina lent his immense dignity to an absurd speech. The police director of the city of Newark stated that his own previous indictment, the federal indictments of Addonizio and his councilmen, and the fervent activity of the federal strike force were all the work of a vast "political conspiracy" seeking to *discredit* Addonizio. Speaking inside a Park Avenue tavern to 250 persons, Spina said the conspiracy began in 1966 when it became clear that Addonizio's gubernatorial ambitions had to be squelched.

"What the hell did corruption have to do with a riot in this city?" the police director asked.

The Hughes Commission had answered Dominick's question three years before, but evidently the police director didn't get the message.

Imperturbable and subdued, Gibson carried on a low-key campaign with a quiet persistence that won many admirers, both black and white. The most exciting incident of his initial campaign came when his car, a 1964 Chevrolet with 67,000 miles on it, broke down in the middle of Broad Street. Gibson accepted this mishap as he would most others—with a shrug. His methodical manner and quiet confidence contradicted the extremist image the Addonizio and Imperiale camps were trying to hang on him. Actually, such attacks brought sympathy from moderate whites who worked in New York and ordinarily took little interest in local elections. Gibson's white support—to Imperiale's surprise—was spreading.

Harry Wheeler's change of heart and Richardson's floundering helped Gibson and black solidarity.

Wheeler dropped out of the race two days before the election and began campaigning for Gibson, a City Hall job both deserved and assured should Newark elect its first black mayor. George Richardson, on the other hand, was second only to Gibson in campaign spending but had run one of the most listless, rag-tag campaigns imaginable. This added to the suspicion that Richardson was not his own master. As the situation grew hopeless and he still refused to bow out, there could be little doubt of it.

Al Black returned to the fold of black unity with a 3:00 A.M. telephone call urging his candidate to withdraw on the night of Wheeler's turnabout —but to no avail. Richardson had dug himself a hole and refused to climb out. His best hope now was that his vote total would be so small that it wouldn't make the difference in Gibson's lack of a majority. His future in Newark depended on whether the new breed of blacks had short memories.

It's Us Against Them

Richardson netted but 2,000 votes in the May 12 election, finishing last. Matturri finished ahead of him with 5,000. Caufield, with 12,000 votes, was not far behind Imperiale who received 14,000 in a third-place finish. Addonizio, his extortion-income tax evasion trial hovering above him, compiled 18,000 votes—only 20 percent of the electorate but good enough for second place and a spot in the June run-off. Quayle's poll had been rather accurate, except for a major underestimation of the Gibson vote and his white support. He received 38,000 votes, a strong 43 percent of the ballots cast. Gibson won by landslides in the black Central and South Wards, came in first in the predominantly white West and East Wards and even finished a respectable third in the Italian stronghold of the North Ward, where Imperiale ran first. Tony, finishing a long campaign in the same comic style in which he had declared his candidacy a year before, refused to concede defeat and asked for a recount.

Three out of four councilmen-at-large candidates nominated by the Black and Puerto Rican Convention—running bracketed together as the "Community Choice" slate—topped a record field of twenty-nine candidates. The able Earl Harris led the field, followed by Tucker and Pinckney. Ramon Aneses finished fifth, still in the running.

In the Central Ward election, Reverend Westbrooks outdrew the walking catatonic, Irvine Turner, by more than two to one, even with six other candidates running. And in the South Ward, Sharpe James, another black convention candidate, finished on top. Reverend Sharper ran third and was out of the run-off.

LeRoi Jones and other convention organizers and participants, such as Curvin and Heningburg and attorney Ray Brown, could look upon their work with pride. Six of their seven nominated candidates were still in contention. No candidate in the May 12 election received the required majority, however, and the run-off was set for June 16.

The electorate now had to choose between an honest man who happened to be black in a city more than 65 percent non-white, and an incumbent who had virtually enveloped Newark in graft, corruption, and their by-products.

A second city-wide choice would be between four energetic and enterprising black convention councilmen-at-large candidates—Harris, Tucker, Pinckney, Aneses—and four men bracketed together under Addonizio's "Peace and Progress" slogan: Ralph Villani, now seventy years old and ailing after a stroke; Michael Bontempo, also seventy, who had been bought by the Mafia in the 1962 election and who actually lived on the Jersey shore, and like Villani was an Italian establishment dotard who hadn't even bothered to campaign; Anthony Giuliano, fifty-two, former career detective with the Newark police who brought into the election a renowned Italian family name and an intellect that couldn't crack an egg; and Calvin West, the mayor's favorite Negro.

"We have given them something new," said Jones, now known among his followers by his Islamic name, Imamu Amiri Baraka. "We ran collectively. Now we got *them* running collectively. Have you seen their new posters with the colors and all the pictures the same size, just like ours? That is an example of how rock-'n'-roll was born."

Unfortunately for Addonizio, his trial was scheduled to begin in Trenton on June 2, two weeks prior to the election. It began as scheduled, despite repeated pleas for a change of venue to Newark and a postponement until after the election, the latter motion going all the way to the U.S. Supreme Court where it was unanimously rejected. Addonizio was forced to stand trial in Trenton during the day and return to Newark for early evening and night campaigning. The new tack of his campaign was to run against LeRoi Jones. Its tone was that Gibson as mayor would mean Jones as police director with Newark's schools and streets taken over by black savages who would rape women and children. Such warnings, adroitly using some of Jones's own poems, were mailed and distributed to white residents living in the North, West, and East Wards.

"It's us against them," Spina echoed, "black versus white . . . a matter of survival."

These were the tactics to which Hughie and Dominick had descended.
Gibson won endorsement from New York gubernatorial candidate Howard Samuels, Representative Shirley Chisholm, Adam Clayton Powell, Coretta King, Reverend Ralph Abernathy, Dick Gregory, Reverend Jesse Jackson, and Senators Clifford Case and George McGovern.

Addonizio had the endorsement of his fellow defendants, his wife, God, and . . . Anthony Imperiale.

Imperiale, who may also have received a divine summons—or a job offer from a more worldly source—forgot the issues he had so often spoken of, such as poor schools, crime, and corruption. He reduced his message to the issue that had spawned him, the only force he really stood for: white racism. With a choice between Addonizio, whom he knew to be a thief, and Gibson, an honest black man, Imperiale revealed himself. At a press conference Imperiale described himself as "a man of destiny" and supported the man he had called corrupt. His constituents, who joyously applauded his action, revealed just as tellingly what they stood for.

As for Matturri, the less said the better. The man who had valiantly charged forth to battle corruption and redeem Newark, wouldn't endorse either candidate. If saving Newark required supporting a black man, it was too much trouble. Alexander would sulk in his tent.

But John Caufield, despite lavish offers from Addonizio, not only endorsed but campaigned for Gibson. When hired goons cursed and spat at Gibson and Caufield in an effort to provoke a major incident, Gibson's blacks held back from retaliation and Addonizio's hopes for racial trouble came to nothing.

One violent incident did occur, however. Its details may appear familiar. A mysterious shotgun blast was fired into a building, this time through the living-room window of Reverend West, Addonizio's second-favorite Negro. The pellets—which again were birdshot—were poorly aimed and embedded themselves in the ceiling. As it turned out, West had been in the basement at the time of the shooting tending to his barking dog. Spina, the "victim" of an identical attack two years before, was, appropriately enough, one of the first to reach the scene. No one knew more about dogs and birdshot than Spina.

Don't Let This Happen Again

As the run-off election drew near the single most vital issue of the campaign—the control of the Newark Police Department—was drawing into sharp definition. It had first emerged in a campaign poster, a photograph from the July 28, 1967 riot issue of *Life* magazine, showing Joey Bass, Jr., the boy who had been shot when police killed the fleeing Billy

Furr. The boy lay in a pool of blood as a pot-bellied white police officer walked past with a shotgun in his hand and a cigar in his mouth. The message read: "Don't Let This Happen Again. Register—Vote." Once again, LeRoi Jones had shaped the words that the Negro politicians—excepting Gibson—were afraid to speak.

The PBA called the posters, now hanging all over the ghetto, "hate literature." The laughable Human Rights Commission thought they were "not calculated to appeal to a voter's better instincts." As for Gibson, the determined candidate reached not only to the gut of the campaign, but into the heart of black Newark: *"If I'm elected and I ever find evidence of any indication of that kind of thing by a policeman, I'll have him brought up on charges of murder."*

They Need Have No Fear

For LeRoi Jones, who had been there for the entire ride, it was now the end of an era and the beginning of a new Newark. After the polls had closed and as the first votes were being counted downtown, one hundred black youths crowded into the playwright's headquarters on Springfield Avenue and High Street to await the results. They had worked hard together through the long and often hectic months. Now they sweated together in silence inside the cramped storefront as their leader prepared to speak to them.

Three years before, Jones had been beaten bloody by Spina's police and laughed at by the police director himself. Now a black man was being elected mayor of Jones's city largely through the playwright's efforts, and Gibson had publicly stated his first act as mayor would be to have Spina "clean out his locker." For Jones it had been a transition from frustrated rage to significant participation.

"I have been a lot of places in my time and done a lot of things," Jones had written five years before. "And there is a sense of the Prodigal about my life that begs to be resolved."

Now, in 1970 post-riot Newark, the Prodigal had come home. And as the diminutive man stood there in front of Newark's new restless blood, it seemed as if his gentleness had also emerged during what must have been a moment of great personal fulfillment. "It looks good," he said quietly. "Some of the brothers here will talk to you while we wait."

With Jones on the small stage in the rear of the building were other national figures, including Floyd McKissick and Chicago's dynamic Reverend Jesse Jackson, who interjected a few moments of silent meditation into his eloquent talk.

"We will win," Jackson, a large, powerfully built man, told the black youths. "And they need have no fear. We will never treat them as they have treated us. The real test is just beginning because now we must walk with dignity and prove ourselves."

The night before on a New York television news show, Tony Imperiale predicted there would be trouble in Newark whether Addonizio or Gibson won the election and that black "goon squads" had been imported from the South for the occasion. Instead, there was only the commanding figure of Jackson telling Newark's inheritors they had to walk with a new dignity and pride, while at Addonizio's headquarters in the North Ward there were cries of "Hughie's beating the nigger." First returns had put Addonizio ahead. Not long after, however, the joy of his supporters was replaced by mounting anger as they watched blackboard totals that showed Gibson closing the gap and their time of power slipping away. When it was clear that a black man would be the next mayor of Newark, they took out their frustrations on newspaper reporters and television cameramen, beating several of them, throwing glasses and breaking cameras. Also, in the finest Italian tradition, they wrecked part of the restaurant. If the goon squads were from the South, it was southern Italy.

Downtown, near City Hall, police closed off blocks of Broad Street to accommodate thousands of jubilant blacks and the whites who joined them in wild celebration.

"You're here because you have no choice," Reverend Jackson told the black youths back on High Street. Then, looking at Jones, he said, "The thing that's great about Baraka is he *chose* to be here."

Gibson's win was decisive, topping Addonizio by 12,000 votes, and it was white support that had made it possible. Caufield's integrity was the major factor in the election. A black man was elected mayor of Newark by some 10 percent of the white voters who were fed up with corruption. The Italians did everything they could to prevent it. Almost every registered voter's name was used. With forged signatures former North Ward residents were back again voting. Other residents showed up at the polls only to be told they had already cast ballots. Some voted twice. People who had died five months before also cast ballots. There were at least 4,000 questionable ballots for the "Peace and Progress" slate in the North Ward alone, not enough to keep Gibson out but enough to elect Bontempo and re-elect Giuliano and Villani, diluting the full flavor of the black revolution.

Had the election been formally protested, there would have had to be a costly process involving handwriting experts, briefs and court costs, and eventually another election with the plaintiffs bearing the tremendous expense. After two elections, Tucker, and Pinckney and Aneses, the councilmen-at-large candidates, were out of funds and they accepted the loss. Only Gibon's fourth-at-large candidate, Earl Harris, was voted into office.

Two other black convention candidates, Sharpe James and Reverend Westbrooks, also triumphed in their respective wards.

Because White People Don't Want to Be There

Louis Turco, who had been re-elected in the East Ward, was subsequently voted president by his fellow councilmen instead of Giuliano. As far as Sharpe James and Earl Harris were concerned, Turco was the lesser of two evils. At least Turco was a young man with some intelligence, though viewed by many as a vain opportunist who was grooming himself for state politics.

Instead of voting for qualified, dedicated black and white candidates, it was shameful that Newark's citizenry settled for such as these. Villani shouted incoherently at council meetings and at times didn't seem to know where he was. Turco wrote a letter to Governor Cahill pleading municipal poverty and at the same time put in an order for a 1971 Buick limousine with eighteen extras—including a stereo tape player—which would cost tax payers $6,000. Bontempo, whose civic virtue had changed little since the 1962 election, also made known his interest in Newark. "I want a raise of ten thousand dollars and I want it now," he said. "I want it all on the table and none under the table."

Caufield was subsequently returned to the fire director's office by the new mayor. Aneses was appointed a deputy mayor. Tucker, the most hard working and community conscious of all the candidates, was named a program director in Model Cities. Wheeler was rewarded for his astuteness with a one-hundred-dollar-a-day job as a manpower consultant with the Community Development Administration. Al Oliver was named executive director of UCC.[1] Judge Walls was appointed the new corporation counsel and Irvin Booker, Jones's attorney at his first trial, replaced Walls on the bench. And Junius Williams, another community activist who had been mentioned in Captain Kinney's list of so-called subversives, was named to replace Malafronte as the director of Model Cities.

There was no "housecleaning" in Newark following the election, however, far from it. Making these relatively few appointments took Gibson three months. The new mayor was as prudent in victory as he had been sedate during the campaign, and the slowness with which he made appointments angered many followers. Gibson was not only lacking in vengeance, but he was generous as well. Harold Hodes, the executive director

---

[1] Oliver proceeded to arrange contracts and set up programs without consulting Jones's people—or the board of trustees for that matter—and he was subsequently fired.

of the Human Rights Commission who tagged along after Addonizio on the campaign route like a pet, was allowed to remain at his post for five months. Of more interest, Don Malafronte was allowed to hang around for months after the election, a decision which caused further consternation among Gibson's people, particularly Bob Curvin, because Malafronte had written Addonizio's more slimy speeches. Even after his services were terminated on August 14, Malafronte insisted on coming into the Model Cities office drawing vacation pay.

"He's just a guy who likes to be in on things and I don't know what we can do about him, unless Junius [Williams] calls a cop and has him put out of the office," said Gibson.

Reverend West was soon voted off UCC's board of trustees and out of its presidency as supporters of LeRoi Jones and his Committee for a Unified Newark at last wrested control of the anti-poverty agency. David Barrett, a strong Jones supporter and community activist, was voted president in his place. Jones's followers quickly began a purge of all non-supporters with even Jesse Allen, the former associate of Tom Hayden, losing his job.

The appointment of a business manager was of major importance in restructuring the collapsing city, and Gibson left no stone unturned to find a man who would be dedicated to the task. Finally, after a nation-wide search, the new mayor named fifty-four-year-old Cornelius Bodine, Jr., as his choice for the job. Bodine was the former business manager of Sioux City, Iowa, and had eighteen years' working experience. He was also an innovative, aggressive, and honest man who had special interest in urban renewal. Nevertheless, many had hoped that Wilbur Parker would get the job and some, more concerned with black identity than practicality, became disillusioned.

Parker was eventually named to fill a post created specifically for him, deputy secretary to the Board of Education. He would be, ironically enough, Arnold Hess's assistant and would accede to the secretary's job when Hess finally did decide to retire.

Naturally, Spina was removed as police director and assumed his former job as deputy chief—after having said before the election that white policemen would rather quit than work for a black mayor. The ex-police director, upon stepping down, said he was thinking about writing a book. In his version of what had happened to Newark, Spina would probably play an Italian Peter Pan and the evil Captain Hook would be portrayed by Lacey.

In future years, ghetto children throughout the country would be taught in their civics classes that Gibson's victory was an ultimate triumph of the democratic process, an additional proof that the system works. Jones had evaluated the situation long before more accurately:

One city will fall to black people peacefully, one will fall by force of arms. Newark will fall because white people don't want to be there any more, and they will voluntarily want to leave. I mean, things come together, they break up, they come together on a higher level, they break up. Things are young and strong, they struggle, they achieve some kind of solidarity—they get comfortable, they get lazy, they die.

29

THE POST-RIOT CITY FLOWERS

Lock Them Up If You Have To

During the hectic campaign, Gibson had described organized crime in Newark as being in a business relationship with the city. Addonizio's administration had been selling licenses to operate, he said. Gibson further explained that mobster activity, particularly narcotics, would be curtailed if such licenses were *revoked* and the Mafia was told its services were no longer wanted. This evaluation was oversimplified. No one explained what would happen when the Mafia refused to accept cancellation of its contracts.

Some of those associated with Gibson weren't about to cast the first stone.

One of the phalanx of off-duty black police officers who accompanied Gibson as bodyguards during the campaign was the cop who had killed the drunk at the Howard Bar. Two key members of the old United Brothers still politically active in the city were heroin pushers. There was even some pressure from many in the black community, including LeRoi Jones, for Gibson to appoint a black police director. Such a move would have, in a short period of time, increased graft and brutality by the black police who would have felt they could get away with just about anything. If there was one group who had less respect than white police for the black people in Newark, it was the black cops. And the thought of a black police director keeping white segments of the department in check is humorous.

The Mafia, however, had its own ideas about who should be the new police director.

Gibson hadn't been inaugurated yet when he was given the word that the police director's job was worth $15,000 to the Mafia. He was also notified that it would be the usual 10 percent for the new mayor on city contracts. Gibson publicly rejected both offers. The mob's choice for police director was the same man Spina had preferred as police chief,

Anthony Barres. Gibson ill-advisedly sought out a black police director instead and fate was kind to Newark when he was unable to find one. He offered the job to three experienced black men in various parts of the country and all three, realizing the cooperation they were likely to receive within the Newark Police Department, refused.

Gibson then nominated Deputy Chief Redden for police director and the nomination was passed on to the new City Council for approval. Bontempo made it no secret that Spina had called him several times, once at 1 A.M., to make sure he voted against Redden's appointment. Spina also made similar calls to other white councilmen and, in a private caucus vote, the Redden nomination was rejected seven to two with even the black Central Ward councilman, Reverend Westbrooks, going along with the majority. Only Earl Harris and Sharpe James, who would prove themselves the most proficient men on the council by their future actions, voted approval of the honest Irishman. Appointment of Redden was a must if Newark was to be cleaned up, and it was a troubled Ken Gibson who spoke earnestly with the council members before his inauguration ceremony. Harris then reintroduced the nomination and, on their first public vote, Redden was approved by a seven-to-two vote with unenlightened Westbrooks and, naturally, Anthony Giuliano, still voting no. The haggle to get Redden appointed caused Gibson to be half an hour late for his inauguration.

Spina's fears about Redden were well founded.

Before the police director's office had even been repainted, Redden had revamped the entire department. It was a strategic move that included job changes for twenty-five top officers and more than 170 transfers within the department, at least temporarily disrupting the flow of graft money. Redden also authorized all his appointed division commanders to make personnel changes within their commands without consulting him, and some veteran detectives found themselves in uniform back inside a patrol car. Thus did Spina's system of political patronage come to a halt. The confrontation was not viewed by supporters of Hughie and Tony as being between integrity and corruption, however, but rather as a power struggle between the Irish and Italians.

Police officers who had made graft a way of life, paying off new cars and even buying homes in the suburbs, besieged Councilmen Giuliano and Bontempo, both former career policemen, with complaints. The raging Bontempo was named chairman of a committee which was to investigate the transfers. At a private meeting in Redden's office the police director laid it on the line:

"That third precinct is the hell-hole of the world. Mob people walk in and out of there like they own the place. They even use the police telephones. The place stinks from top to bottom."

Giuliano and Bontempo had nothing to say when Redden was through.

Attempted retaliation took the form of another appeal to public gullibility, as was the case with the "assassination" attempts on Spina and Imperiale. This time hate mail was used. Italian police officers subsequently received anonymous hate letters at their home addresses. Naturally, blacks were blamed for the despicable deed. If only a few had been mailed out, this conclusion might have been plausible. Reportedly, hundreds of policemen received the letters, however, and because home addresses of policemen are classified information, it was likely that police leaders themselves were behind the bid for sympathy.

Redden issued one order to his new commanders: "Clean them up. Lock them up if you have to."

The police director sought a new image for the department and himself initiated the investigation of the First Precinct burglary ring, turning over all information to the prosecutor's office. Free-wheeling graft and corruption which had been allowed to flourish during Spina's reign were being threatened. Spina had also refused to discipline officers who were harsh with minority groups, despite specific pleas from the black community. Redden handled the problem differently. For one, Gasparinetti's ass was removed from his motorcycle, forthwith. Reverend West, the police department chaplain, was severed from his last tie with the new administration when Redden fired him.

Redden also ordered all cigarette machines removed from the precinct houses, a vending service which had been rendered by Mafia chieftain Jerry Catena's tobacco company. "The department was not receiving a large enough commission," Redden explained.

Not stopping with his own investigation, Redden called on the federal strike force headquartered in Newark for help. While effective internal investigation of his department was at best difficult, federal agents could act autonomously. Two veteran policemen with more than forty years service between them, one white, the other black, were subsequently caught red-handed with shakedown money extorted from narcotics pushers and arrested. It was thought that the two uniformed officers wouldn't believe they were being approached by federal agents and Redden personally joined in the arrest to prevent a gunfight. "They were in a state of shock," Redden commented.

A few days later, a thirty-four-year-old black policeman was indicted for attempting to shake down another narcotics pusher for $1,000. The prosecutor's office, remembering the officer as one who had escaped unscathed from the Fifth Precinct's corrupt vice squad the year before, had evidently decided to draw the line. In early April, three more white policemen—two of them lieutenants—were also indicted by the county grand jury on charges of attempted extortion and atrocious assault and battery.

The three officers had tried to get money from three narcotic pushers and had beaten one of them.

Redden's efforts at "cleaning house" within the department alarmed many high-ranking police officials in Newark and gave all members of the department cause for reflection. It got to the point where some police officers were turning down graft.

How Arrogant the Conspirators Had Become

Addonizio's new pastures, meanwhile, were far from green. The Newark extortion trial moved into July with Lacey using Paul Rigo's testimony to give the ex-mayor and other defendants a slow roasting. Ex-councilmen West, Turner, Bernstein, and Frank Addonizio, all of whom had been defeated in the election, were granted postponements. They couldn't, however, have looked forward to their day in court what with the evidence that was being piled up against poor Hughie.

Of the others indicted on Black Wednesday, Schiff was granted a postponement due to a heart ailment. Tony Boy Boiardo suffered an apparent heart attack during the latter stages of the trial and his case was severed from the trial. Evidence against Callaghan, who had confessed before the grand jury, was so strong he pleaded guilty to income tax evasion and also dropped out. Charges against Ben Krusch were dismissed for lack of evidence after the prosecution had presented its case.

Of the fifteen men originally indicted, two had died—Gallo and Giuliano—seven had been granted postponements, charges against one were to be dropped, and only ex-Mayor Addonizio, LaMorte, Gordon, and Boiardo's two men, Anthony Biancone and Ralph Vicaro, went through the entire eight-week trial.

"How callous, how brazen, indeed how arrogant the conspirators had become. . . . The way they were going, the obstacles they had overcome, the success they had had, the fruits they had gathered made them arrogant and indifferent to the public attitude," Lacey summed up for the jury after flawless prosecution by himself and his chief assistant, Herbert Stern. "I recall the pious words of Mayor Addonizio that he decided to give Newark the benefit of his years in Congress. What a way to arrest the decline of a city. What a way to act the role of a savior."

Addonizio also heard himself described as "a man of easy conscience and flabby pride" before the jury went into deliberation. Only five hours later the jurors returned to the Trenton courtroom to announce that the defendants were guilty on all sixty-four charges.[2]

[2] Two counts of the 65-count extortion indictment were dropped by the prosecution during the trial.

"I testified on the stand and I told my story," said Hughie with emotion. "The jury evidently didn't believe me. I can only say I'm terribly disappointed. I will appeal."

I Refuse to Be a Party to Colossal Deception

And as Newark's first black mayor took office in the near bankrupt, racially tense city, Tony Imperiale was there to lend what assistance he could. Speaking before his North Ward group and the United League of Italian Americans, another group which experienced his leadership, Imperiale declared "war" against the press and the insurance companies which had, in his view, made Gibson's election possible. Imperiale also began a movement to do away with the mayor's office. Instead of a mayor and city council, Imperiale now wanted to return Newark to the five-man commission form of government the city had discarded sixteen years before and had again vetoed in 1960 when the alternative had been on the ballot. Tony was still marching backward.

"This is not directed at Gibson," he explained.

Shortly afterward, Imperiale announced he was forming a coalition of conservative groups to fight his declared war on the Gibson administration. He said he planned to invite all right-wing groups to join him— including the John Birch Society and supporters of George Wallace.

"If racism means to be against communists, to be against those who advocate anarchy, then I'm proud to say I'm the head of a racist organization," Tony declared.

Imperiale also announced he would ask Newark's six white councilmen to meet with his group. If any of them accepted his invitation, it was not for public knowledge. A week after declaring war on the new administration, a new announcement from Imperiale reported he had met with Gibson in "an attempt to open the channels of communication." Now Imperiale was saying he only wanted "the same things for Newark as Ken Gibson wants." He added that he was "tired" of the tension that existed in the city. Who was the real Imperiale? Perhaps not even Tony knew. The spotlight which had followed him for three years was swinging away, and Tony was chasing it.

In the ensuing months, Imperiale's name dropped completely from the news and an event of considerable drama was needed to restore it. Accordingly, in the early morning hours of December 12, an Army demolition team from Fort Monmouth was called into Newark to handle a third "attempt" on the former councilman's life and limb. This one, even more suspicious than the others, bordered on the asinine. The culprits had somehow circumnavigated the booby traps on Imperiale's car and placed two sticks of dynamite under the hood. Had the dynamite exploded, police said, the car would have left the ground. Imperiale's orbit of Newark had been prevented, however, because his cunning foes had neglected to hook the dynamite to the ignition wires, a necessary prerequisite for blast-off.

Imperiale blamed the "radical element" for this latest assassination attempt and said that he would confer with Police Director Redden and Essex County Prosecutor Lordi. He also said he would seek an investigation by the FBI. Imperiale did everything but supply a clue as to the identity of the culprits or even volunteer a possible motive.

A review of this latest Imperiale show in the *Evening News* was not good:

> The "apparent bombing attempt" was further confused by the fact that Imperiale said the Newark Police Department received anonymous calls warning that the dynamite had been placed in the vehicle.

Tony's latest performance—like the dynamite—didn't go off.

Unemployed, Imperiale reopened his karate school, ran a North Ward volunteer ambulance service, and founded his own firm, Imperiale Public Relations of America, Inc. The letters which had been written to Italian police officers and Redden's transfers gave Tony his first clients. In *Attack!*, a right-wing newsletter, he threw down the gauntlet once again:

> I ask my readers to forgive my diversion from the article I originally had intended to write. However, a dastardly act is being committed against our police officers of Italian-American heritage here in Newark. An abusive and indecent letter addressed to them has been circulated in the city of Newark. The letter is too filthy and vulgar to publish, but it is available upon written request. Recently Italian-American police officers have been the target of unwarranted criticism and harassment in the city of Newark. I charge these unprovoked and irresponsible acts of vilification to the mayor and councilmen of Newark. It appears that once again and more firmly entrenched, the wicked and evil minds of radical and communist-oriented groups are spewing their poison letters.

Imperiale concluded his column:

> So I say to my fellow patriotic Americans, do not despair, rather let us stand side by side. I implore each and every reader of this Newsletter to join hands with us in our fight for survival in a nation that radical and left-wing elements attempt to divide. We shall overcome and defeat the madness and sickness that pervades in the minds of the conspirators that are intent on destroying our communities and our nation.

Imperiale was again heard from early in 1971 when he resigned from the Model Cities Neighborhood Council, a position he had held since his election to the fifty-two-member board in 1968. The council's chairman was not unhappy, particularly since the group hadn't seen much of Imperiale for two years.

"I could give the usual accepted and trite reason but that is not my style," Imperiale wrote in his letter of resignation. "My honest reasons are two-fold. I refuse to be party to colossal deception and to be associated with the many personalities on this board whom I deem beneath my concepts of ethics and integrity."

Always leave them laughing, Tony.

You'll Be Able to See Signs of It Shortly

LeRoi Jones, meanwhile, in a September interview, was enjoying his own style of fantasy:

> Remember the themes of grass roots songs not too long ago. . . . "I 'aint got no money, I 'aint got no future, I 'aint no good." Remember how during the same period our so-called intellectual turned his back to his people and transformed himself by taking over the habits and ideas of the alien culture—he became white. He tripped out. [Frantz] Fanon tells us that it is political power that allows culture to flower. When this happens you can sing root songs about a great many other things than, "I 'aint got nothing." When you are expanding culturally you can sing about positive things, sing about building and creating, and sing about a bright future. . . . The creation of a sympathetic environment, which exists in Newark, will help the intellectual to deal with his traditional culture. He will begin to pursue new directions that will hook up to his African culture, which is expanding in a very positive way. We now know that it is possible for the concept of Afro-American culture to flower. You'll be able to see signs of it shortly.

In Newark, Gibson's election sparked the rallying cry, "It's nation building time." Political control, though far from complete at this stage, was the starting point for a "cultural flowering" that would result, Jones hoped, in fulfillment of a black identity and control of all municipal institutions by the communities they serviced. The drab Spirit House was redecorated with bright coats of black and green for the occasion, while the playwright moved out of the hardcore ghetto to a large house on South 10th Street and assumed the unofficial title of director of culture. The conductor of the New Jersey Symphony, a black man, was subsequently chided by Jones and urged to vibrate with fewer European tunes and more African music. The blackest exhibits at the Newark Public Library, the playwright pointed out, were the people who mopped the floors. Likewise, the John Smith-Pocahontas exhibits at the Newark Museum were as trite as they were irrelevant. "White colonial art," commented LeRoi. "Take a look out your window at what's going on and get with it." And Jones said that if Newark's Essex County Jail was stuffed with a steady flow of black prisoners, why shouldn't it also have a black warden and a Muslim chaplain? The playwright's main concern, however, was with an educational system that was turning out functional illiterates, and it was here that his contribution was most meaningful.

The African Free School, which Jones had established and guided as a community service at the Spirit House for three years, had at last received recognition. The playwright's program was federally funded and given a one-year trial period for thirty children at the Robert Treat Elementary School. The Board of Education's assent to the program distressed both white and black conservatives. While Jones had formulated a curriculum to develop black identity, together with academic and emotional achievement by youngsters from blighted areas, critics recalled some of LeRoi's more distressing anti-white poetry and dreaded the result.

A black cultural flowering in Newark would take many years, but the city's culture of poverty was reaping yet another harvest.

During Gibson's first day in office, a thirty-one-year-old woman was stabbed by an angry lover after he kicked in her apartment door in the early morning hours on Bergen Street. Her nine-year-old son watched. The woman, a hardcore junkie, subsequently refused to identify her attacker for police. At the same time, another woman was shot by a man who demanded to enter her apartment. Police arrested a thirty-six-year-old Belmont Avenue man the next day for the killing. He had a record of more than twenty arrests, including aggravated assaults and another murder.

In the weeks that followed, another black man was stabbed to death on Bergen Street by four teenagers. Two more were shot at the intersection of 11th Avenue and South 8th Street. Police, who found a baseball bat at the scene along with the two bodies, believed that the shootings were the result of a difference of opinion. During the same night, a fifty-one-year-old man attempted to break up another argument between a black man and woman in front of his home. He received a knife in the stomach for his efforts and was D.O.A. at City Hospital.

Blacks, in addition to slaughtering each other, also continued with their own periodic executions of whites after Gibson's election.

A fifty-three-year-old retired New York City policeman and his son-in-law, a detective on the same force, went to a party in Irvington. The older man left alone and was eventually found lying in the Central Ward with fifteen stab wounds. It took several days to identify the corpse because the wallet had been cut from his trouser pocket. A week later, a twenty-year-old college student was shot by one of four black juveniles on a downtown campus. He, too, was D.O.A. at City Hospital. Newark officials and the Chamber of Commerce prided themselves on downtown college construction while the students lived in fear once the sun went down.

For LeRoi Jones, Newark was to be the Mecca of a nationwide black cultural renaissance. Afro hair styles and African clothing were everywhere. The sound of Swahili became more frequent. The throb of drums reverberated into the early morning darkness. Jones undertook the monumental task of re-educating black people in their heritage. A new hymn to black beauty was being sung in Newark, but its singers were far too few. After the curtain came down, heroin, poverty, and crime continued their oppression. Jones and his followers were in a world all their own while the overwhelming majority of Newark's black residents were too busy living even to begin to understand what the playwright was talking about. It seemed to many that Jones had reverted from his meaningful role of political innovator. For Jones, however, blacks living a slow death first had to achieve a cultural identity.

As far as Imperiale was concerned, the niggers were still taking over Newark.

Now it could be argued that Jones and Imperiale had something in common after all: an ability to lose themselves in their own illusions.

The Butcher Shop of Newark

City Hospital, meanwhile, was also undergoing a dramatic transformation. Previously described as an "assault upon the dignity of man," the facility was now being called the "butcher shop" of Newark by no less than twenty-four community groups. The groups demanded a conference with Governor Cahill and, after an unfruitful meeting with one of the governor's aides, threatened to *take over* the hospital.

Their complaints included "great rigidity and frustration" in grievance procedures for employees, hostile attitude of supervisors, "exploitation and intimidation" of workers, and overall racist behavior. The hospital was charged with having leaky, unsafe pipes, unsanitary toilets, and rodents and vermin. Its elevators carried cadavers, dogs, infested linen, and food along with infectious patients and visitors.

The groups demanded dismissal of the hospital's new boss, the president of the New Jersey College of Medicine and Dentistry, the hospital's administrator, and the director of personnel. They also called for a federal investigation and withholding of federal funds until the probe was completed. Ironically, a deadline of Christmas Eve was set for state and federal action. Had He a choice between City Hospital and a stable's manger, Christ would have fared better in the latter.

It Is Now a Question of Desperation

While Redden had an impossible job on his hands, Gibson and his new business administrator, Bodine, were faced with their own "flowering."

Addonizio and company's parting gifts to Newark came to light during Gibson's first month in office. In their efforts to remain in power, the old city regime had dumped the problem of finding $17 million for 1971's school budget in Gibson's lap. Then there was the $4.3 million for teachers' salary hikes which had been generously passed by the City Council. On top of these headaches, Gibson was also confronted with a state urban-aid cut of $900,000 because of Addonizio's manipulations with the tax rate in the attempt to get himself re-elected. Under Trenton's formula, the city would be penalized because Addonizio's tax rate had been deceitfully raised by only a few points. This pay-later philosophy worsened his black successor's plight. Newark was also to receive a cut in state money because Spina had come up with figures that showed the city's crime rate as *decreasing*. This was a development that occurred, coincidentally, only when Addonizio was running for mayor.

Thus, while Gibson was struggling to raise Newark from the quicksand, his feet were sinking.

Newark faced a staggering 1971 budget deficit of $42 to $63 million. The city's agencies, such as they were, would continue to operate until the final crisis but the schools might not be open even that long. By mid-November, Gibson announced that the Board of Education would run out of money by the end of the next month and, unless drastic action was taken, Newark's entire school system would be forced to *close down*. On the same day, the press in Trenton reported that Gibson's effort to raise funds with a new tax package was receiving an expected chilly reception from the state legislature.

Gibson's proposed tax package included a state take-over of City Hospital, a tax on fuel at Newark Airport—and either a 2 percent income tax for those who lived and worked in Newark or a 2 percent business-paid payroll tax.

Of the two taxes, the income tax was more equitable. It would be based on earnings—if there were no earnings, there would be no tax. The payroll tax, on the other hand, would be applied to every business regardless of whether its earnings were large or small, or even if the business was operating at a loss. Thus, a 2 percent payroll tax could represent as much as 100 percent of the earnings.

"It's very difficult to operate a city with a $60-million deficit," Gibson observed. "It's now a question of desperation. We must have money. The legislature must be convinced that the problems of Newark are the problems of the state."

Among the legislators Gibson was talking about were those who had derided the Hughes Report. Some were the representatives of those who drew paychecks in Newark and then quickly disappeared to suburbia. With some exceptions, the legislature was comprised of insensitive, narrow-minded politicians who looked upon Newark as an economic enterprise surrounded by a crumbling zoo. A report during the mayoral campaign from the Race Relations Information Center at Nashville, Tennessee, had aptly speculated that the election of a black mayor would be the equivalent of turning a dead body over to a black undertaker.

The leader of Essex County's Assembly delegation was candid in announcing his feelings on Gibson's chances of success: "If the city of Newark is bent on a Kamikaze mission, I don't feel any responsibility to provide the airplane."

So much for the support of the county's politicians.

What backing did Gibson have in Newark itself for such taxes? Would the city's business interests agree or volunteer corporate taxes to save the city? Would the big business complex rise to the occasion at long last to make up for generations of greedy selfishness and neglect?

Donald MacNaughton, the chief executive of the Prudential Insurance Company and the Chamber of Commerce's new chairman, announced that he "hadn't decided yet" whether or not he supported Gibson's plea for an income tax. Despite this clumsy sidestepping, Newark's blushing counterfeit virgins continued to play their role. Business and professional leaders were *near unanimous* in their opposition to any income tax. After all, the business community had graciously volunteered to increase the salary of Bodine, the new business administrator, by $10,000 over a four-year period. As far as a payroll tax was concerned, however, the Chamber of Commerce's position was very precise. Its members screamed like stuck pigs.

Governor Cahill also manifested his sincerity. At first he promised Gibson that he would support any "responsible" tax package to save Newark. On second thought, however, the governor was more prudent. No sooner was the first promise out of Cahill's mouth when he qualified it by saying he would recommend any proposal which was "politically feasible." The translation of this trite phrase was that the legislators lacked the moral courage to face their state's urban problems.

At the height of the crisis, the Newark *Evening News* and the *Star-Ledger* entered the fray wrapped in cloaks of self-righteousness.

A *Star-Ledger* editorial chastized the legislature for its "shocking indifference" and offered the astounding revelation that Newark's problems weren't going "to disappear by some miraculous stroke." But did the newspaper back the income or payroll taxes? This was one "miraculous stroke" the *Star-Ledger* wouldn't touch with a telephone pole. The *Evening News*'s editorial at least approached the issue:

> This [income] tax for the first time would have compelled the hundreds of thousands of non-Newarkers who earn their living in the city to help support the many services of the city they enjoy during their working hours. Along with Newark residents, they have been demanding more and better services—but paying for them, it develops, is another matter.

The *Evening News* also outdid the *Star-Ledger* by calling some of the county legislators "cowards"—harsh language for the newspaper—and by questioning Governor Cahill's sincerity during the crisis. There was no doubt that the editorial's conclusion also had the bite of truth:

> The proposal for a business payroll tax is only the newest in a long sequence of attempts to evade responsibility. Its application may gain a little time before the ultimate disaster and thus votes for some cowardly legislators. But in the end the disaster will be of larger proportion and thus all the harder to cure—if a cure is possible at all.

Both newspapers agreed that the state's legislators were either cowards or irresponsible. Critical comment on those closer to home, however, was unsurprisingly absent. Newark's press, for one reason or another, didn't have *one word* to say about the Chamber of Commerce whose members filled its pages with advertisements day after day.

Eventually, the state legislature authorized Newark's City Council to impose a slew of new taxes which were expected to bring in $45 million. Governor Cahill, upon signing the tax package, let his feelings get the better of his sense of political practicality. He let Nixon know what he thought of the President's philosophy. "I suggest once again that the time has come for the President of the United States to redirect the priorities of this country," Cahill said. "Housing, health, education and the myriad problems of urban America cannot wait much longer."

Included in the tax package were an occupancy tax for businesses which rented office space in Newark, and a 1 percent payroll tax for corporations. Almost every major business in the city was aghast at the prospect. The new taxes, however, not only fell $20 million short of bridging the budget deficit, but they might drive out established businesses and frighten away new ones. Far from a life-saving device, the tax package was expected by many to seal the lid on the city's financial coffin. Rather than acting responsibly by initiating an income tax or state-wide corporate tax to save Newark, the state government had handed the city a shovel with which to dig its grave.

Paul Stillman, the financial potentate who had been awarded Addonizio's good citizenship wreath, was the spokesman for the embittered businessmen. "This levy [the occupancy tax] would be devastating and potentially ruinous to the high hopes for our city's future," he moaned in a telegram to Mayor Gibson. "Newark is breaking faith with businesses that have chosen to remain in Newark."

In January, an independent accounting firm hired by Mayor Gibson released its efficiency report on City Hall. It said that Newark's municipal government was all screwed up. Also in January, the U.S. Department of Housing and Urban Development issued a report on the Newark Housing Authority. This report said that the housing authority was screwed up. It strongly recommended that the housing authority straighten itself out if it expected to get any more money from the federal government. Investigation by another federal grand jury was imminent. A few hours after HUD's report was released, a State Health Department doctor said that the public health inspection system in Newark was also screwed up. As a matter of fact, the doctor said the city's system, or lack of it, was worthy of "criminal action." The month was complete when Mayor Gibson, frustrated on City Council inaction on the tax package, appeared on a New York television show and announced what being mayor of Newark was like.

"I think the majority of the City Council would like to do business as usual, as it had done in Newark for many, many years," he stated. "It has to be corrupt. Business as usual in Newark in previous years was corrupt. So the question is whether or not I get *any* judges unless I appoint their friends to judgeships or whether or not I make their friends detectives."

Would Gibson receive approval of his proposed tax package if he did accede to certain requests?

"Yes," the mayor of Newark replied, "but then I'd be subject to jail like the previous administration."

The councilmen, already angry at Gibson because they weren't getting any patronage jobs to hand out to their constituents, became more angry. Blacks up on the hill were angry at Gibson because his white police director was shutting down all after-hour gambling and drinking clubs. Newark had gone from a totally corrupt administration to an honest one and many people of Newark were unhappy at the change.

The Welfare of the Animals

On February 2, Superior Court Judge Samuel Allcorn, Jr., awarded the city $37,500 in damages from the Associated Humane Societies of New Jersey because of a "corrupt understanding" between the society and former South Ward councilman Lee Bernstein. Addonizio's cohort had seen the handwriting on the wall in his forthcoming recall election against Horace Sharper and had taken out a bit of "insurance" for himself. "The court is satisfied that the contract of March 25, 1969, had its genesis in a corrupt understanding by which Mr. Bernstein would receive employment and be supplied with a regular source of income in the event his political tenure (and income) were terminated by the recall election of June, 1969," Judge Allcorn said. Bernstein had landed a $15,000-a-year job as the Humane Society's executive director in exchange for "help" in negotiating a deal that brought the society a five-year, $95,000 contract.

Judge Allcorn stated that this was a "corrupt understanding that undoubtedly was conceived in the mind of Mr. Bernstein but to which other members of the Board of Trustees of the defendant Humane Societies nevertheless gave their prior approval and assent."

The judge also had a few kind words for Bernstein's fellow councilmen:

"The evidence also points strongly to the conclusion that those members of the City Council of Newark, who were present at and participated in the executive session of the conference of March 18, 1969, were privy to (if not also party to) this corrupt understanding between Mr. Bernstein and the Humane Societies."

Included along with Bernstein were two members who were still seated on the City Council, Louis Turco and the still lovable Ralph Villani, and the others who were subsequently turned out of office, Anthony Giuliano, Joseph Melillo, Irvine Turner, Calvin West, Frank Addonizio—and even that self-proclaimed protector of the people, Tony Imperiale. Judge Allcorn noted that Turco and Frank Addonizio had not only participated in the corrupt contract as councilmen but had served on the board of the Humane Society as well.

"My main concern is the welfare of the animals," Bernstein responded.

Justice, however, continued to be as slow-moving and lenient with Newark's white transgressors as it was harsh and unbending with the blacks. The aforementioned politicians suffered only the possible embarrassment which came from the court record. After his political defeat, Bernstein lost his job at the Newark Housing Authority due to a civil service job reclassification but Frank Addonizio had better luck. The former councilman, who had yet to answer for 65 charges of extortion, as well as charges of conspiracy to commit extortion and income tax evasion, refused to allow this latest "impropriety" to deter his remarkable career. Frank took a civil service test, finished last in a group of 13 applicants, and was awarded a job with the Essex County Welfare Board a month after Judge Allcorn's decision. His new position? Frank became a fraud investigator.

Let the Son-of-a-Bitch Walk

What help could Mayor Gibson expect from his City Council in the effort to sustain Newark?

The new mayor had brought to Newark the expertise of Cornelius Bodine to revamp the antiquated city government. Originally, the council had agreed to the proposed reorganization after wringing from Gibson a pledge not to go ahead with the economy dismissals of 490 city employees. On second thought, the council viewed the efforts of Bodine and Gibson as an attempt to "circumvent the powers of City Council" and repeatedly rejected them. Gibson had proposed seven new taxes and the council cut the package to three. The council then created a disastrous bureaucratic logjam by refusing to authorize creation of a Division of Special Taxes, which was to process the funds, because the new office was a part of the mayor's governmental reorganization. While the council members preened their feathers, Newark's finance director viewed with dismay the growing mountain of unopened mail containing tax returns. The council, more interested in its own selfish motives than guiding Newark from its ills, was in itself antiquated. Rather than guiding the city, the City Council was proving itself a threat to Newark's survival.

What did Newark police think of their new black mayor?

On Christmas Eve, Gibson planned a tour of the city's hospitals to cheer up the bedridden. Unfortunately, his car broke down and he used the police radio for an assistance call. A reply was not long in coming: "Let the son-of-a-bitch walk."

Mayor Gibson had success in at least one endeavor. A concentrated seventeen-week cleanup drive resulted in removal of 2,700 truckloads of debris from streets, lots, and alleys and a trophy in the national cleanup contest. It seemed, shortly, that the old garbage had been removed only to make room for the new garbage.

While Newark was falling apart, the United States government was sponsoring an invasion of Laos and an Apollo 14 astronaut was playing golf on the surface of the moon. Earlier, on the cratered streets of Newark, Mayor Gibson officiated at the ribbon-cutting ceremony at the opening of the heralded $5-million Gateway Hotel—the Chamber of Commerce's pride which had been constructed by lily-white labor unions. The façade of the structure, fittingly enough, suggested a medieval castle. Missing were the battlements, moat, and drawbridge which would protect its wary inhabitants from the restless natives.

30

THE KILLING OF RICHARD OWENS
AND A PROMISE

Richard Was Really Something

The Newark *Star-Ledger* was the first to announce the passing of Richard Owens:

Two Newark patrolmen shot and killed a 35-year-old man last night after the man allegedly resisted arrest.

The dead man was identified as Richard J. Owens Jr. of 62 Cyprus St., Newark.

Patrolman Lancelot Owens (no relation) and Alfred Harris said they shot the man when he leaped from his auto and ignored their orders to put up his hands. They said Owens had gone into his glove compartment moments before and emerged from the auto with his hand held behind his back, as though concealing a weapon.

Police gave this account of the incident:

Margaret Winn, 29, of 290 Schley Street, reportedly was beaten unconscious by Owens in her apartment. When she came to, she rushed to a nearby phone booth without shoes or coat, and telephoned police.

Patrolmen Owens and Harris met her at the phone booth. As the three approached her address in the patrol car, Miss Winn identified Owens, in his car, as the man who had beaten her.

Owens attempted to drive off but was blocked by the radio car. As the patrolmen approached his car, intending to arrest him for atrocious assault and battery, Owens rolled up the window. One of the patrolmen kicked in the window and ordered him to get out. Owens jumped to the passenger side of the seat and reached into his glove compartment. He leaped out of the car with one hand held behind him.

The patrolmen ordered him to stop and put his hands up. When he kept coming, Patrolman Owens opened fire. When that failed to stop him, Harris fired. Then a second shot from Owens brought him down.

Owens was pronounced dead at the scene with a wound in the chest and one in the lower abdomen.

Miss Winn was treated for multiple contusions and a head injury and was admitted to Martland Hospital for X-rays and observation.

The man who had been involved in the near fatal fight with two white policemen in 1967 (Chapter 5) had survived only to be killed by two black officers of the law three years later under remarkably similar circumstances.

Richard Owens had come to Newark about six years before from Fort Deposit, Maryland. He soon met Mrs. Margaret Winn. The twenty-three-year-old woman had three children and was separated from her husband. She and Owens became lovers. For Owens, a handsome, sometimes charming man who also had an explosive temper, it was not a novel experience. Richard stood six feet, three inches, weighed 240 pounds, and loved women and eating, in that order.

After meeting Margaret Winn, the affairs of Richard Owens are a puzzle that defies assemblage, but the key piece, Mrs. Winn, was always on hand. She was the first and last woman in his life. In between Owens' frequent visits to the Winn apartment on Schley Street, he managed to marry twice, once illegally, and to stay with each woman only a matter of weeks. He had reunited with Miss Getter, the woman who had almost caused his death in 1967. She returned with him to Newark from North Carolina where she had gone with their young son and they again lived together in an apartment on 18th Avenue. For Owens, a hard-working man who always had a job, money was never a problem. This relationship, however, didn't last long either, and soon Owens was back with Margaret Winn. Eventually she bore him a son.

"He married two women and he never really left me," she recalled. "Richard was really something. He was a big-hearted person and women were always chasing after him. I think he was lonely most of the time. He just couldn't say no. Richard never could get himself together. I kept on waiting but he never could."

For five years, Owens either lived with Margaret Winn or came and went as he pleased. Only once did he lose his key to the apartment.

"It happened a few months before he died," she said. "When I found out that Richard had gotten married, I knew we didn't have any future together. I told Richard he couldn't come anymore and he had to give me the key. He said I couldn't order him out of the apartment and I called the police just to show him. When the police came, Richard made a phone call to his lawyer, Solondz, and Solondz told him he had to leave the apartment. If the police didn't let him make the call there would have been trouble. Richard was like that. When he knew he was wrong and you treated him right, he cooperated. There was no argument with the police that time. He gave me the key and he left quietly. A while later, I gave it back to him."

Months later Mrs. Winn received official notice from a Newark lawyer naming her "the other woman" in a divorce action brought by Owens' second wife. They had married in June of 1970 at Sumter, South Carolina, where he wasn't known, and had returned to Newark. For Margaret Winn, it was the last straw. She told Owens they were through. Ironically, Mrs. Winn couldn't, in this instance, be legitimately named in a divorce action because Owens was not legally married to the woman in question. He had never even told Margaret Winn of his first marriage.

At approximately seven o'clock on the night of November 23, Richard Owens appeared at the apartment to find company sitting in the living room, another man whom Mrs. Winn had just started seeing. She had never gone this far before. For Owens it was an emotional crisis.

"Richard didn't become angry at first," Margaret Winn remembered. "He asked my friend to leave as nice as could be and he left. Then he grabbed me by the neck and choked me. I fainted. When I came to he hit me but Richard couldn't help himself. Then he pulled me outside to his car. I think he was going to crash it into a tree and kill both of us. He said something like he didn't want to go on. I broke away and ran to the liquor store around the corner. The man inside the store phoned the police for me. They didn't come and he phoned again. All I wanted was to go to the hospital. I knew what had happened to Richard before and the last thing I wanted was something like that to happen again. I never wanted them to arrest Richard. When the police car came I asked them to stop by the apartment to make sure my kids were all right. Richard had waited for me to come back and was just getting into his car to leave."

Ordinarily, the follow-up newspaper story on such an incident would be more accurate and have additional information. During the lapse of time before Newark's afternoon paper went to press, reporters should have checked the story independent of police sources. The Newark *Evening News* version of Richard Owens' death was, nevertheless, not only inept but irrational:

A man reportedly sought in connection with an assault and battery charge was shot to death last night when he attempted to flee from two Newark patrolmen in the Weequahic section.

Richard J. Owens, 35, of 62 Cyprus Street, was pronounced dead at the scene after being shot in the chest and abdomen.

Detectives Charles Harris and Alton Smith said the incident occurred when Owens leaped from his auto and attempted to run from Patrolmen Lancelot Owens and Alfred Harris in front of 286 Schley Street.

The patrolmen approached Owens after Margaret Winn, 29, of 290 Schley Street, identified him as the man who moments before had beaten her unconscious in her apartment. The detectives said Owens reached into the glove compartment of his car and then jumped from the vehicle holding one hand behind his back as if he were carrying a weapon.

The patrolmen said they ordered Owens to stop and, when he ignored them, fired three times.

How, a reader might ask, was Owens hit in the chest and abdomen while running away?

They Were Angry at Richard

Actually, Owens was shot in the right thigh and in the chest. The first bullet passed through and the second wound proved fatal. The wounded man was handcuffed and lay on the cold cement for about twenty-five minutes before an ambulance came. Instead of being brought to nearby Beth Israel Medical Center, Owens was transported to City Hospital. He died there of "massive hemorrhage" at 9:00 P.M., approximately an hour and forty minutes after the shooting. Medical personnel had worked to save his life for fifty-five minutes. Their efforts would have commenced sooner except for a police regulation which forbade carrying wounded civilians in patrol cars.

According to the first newspaper story, Owens was advancing and in the second version he was running away. The location of the body, lying alongside the brick wall at 286 Schley Street, proved both accounts false. It was Owens who had been retreating, his back facing the wall. Mrs. Winn, sitting in the rear of the police car some 25 feet away, had watched the drama unfold:

"They told Richard to come out of the car but he rolled up the windows and locked the doors. He wouldn't come out. If they had let him alone and talked to him, he would have come out but not when they did him like that. I think if the younger cop hadn't kicked in the window the tall one, Harris, would have shot right through the glass. Richard jumped into the back seat like he was afraid they were going to shoot into the car. He finally got out of the car on the curb side. He never went to the glove compartment like the police said and he didn't have anything in his hands. He was moving his arms back and forth to stop them from putting the handcuffs on. Richard was near the wall there and Harris just got angry and shot him. I saw Richard grab his chest first and Harris shot him again when he was going down, like bang, bang, bang, real fast. It was an emotional thing. They were angry at Richard like men get angry because he wouldn't do what they were telling him. They didn't have to shoot him. They were just angry and they forgot they were policemen."

Fired from the Same Weapon

Officer Harris, forty-three, a thirteen-year veteran of the department, was described by fellow officers as being a friendly man. Like Richard Owens, he stands over six feet tall and has a strong build. Also like Owens, Harris has a temper. He declined to comment on the shooting. Lancelot Owens, his twenty-five-year-old partner who had been on the force a year and a half, is of medium build and height. In comparison to Harris, he projects a happy-go-lucky attitude that was far from altered by the shooting. Owens was amiable and talked freely.

The younger policeman said that both he and Harris had immediately opened fire when Owens had "leaped" at them from the car. They fired, Officer Owens related, because they believed their stubborn suspect had "something" in his hand. Officer Owens said there had been no struggle outside of the car. The first shot, according to the policeman, was fired by him and missed. The second shot came from Harris who was standing near the front of the deceased's car and hit Owens in the thigh. A third shot, hitting Owens in the chest, came a split-second later and also was fired by the younger policeman. Officer Owens insisted that he had fired the fatal bullet and not Harris. According to Margaret Winn, the only witness who would come forward, Officer Owens had been holding the handcuffs and was standing to the right of Harris. Mrs. Winn couldn't say if the younger policeman had even drawn his revolver, but she was certain that Harris fired at least twice.

A critical aspect of the episode—like the killing of Dexter Johnson—was the location of the body. If Owens had been shot near the wall where his body certainly fell, it was implausible that he had done anything other than resist passively, as Margaret Winn described. Neither policemen claimed Owens had struck them at any time. The official police version was that Owens had been coming forward when shot. How did the police explain the discrepancy between where they said Owens had been shot and where the body was picked up for the trip to City Hospital? Officer Owens vividly described how the deceased had staggered from ten to fifteen feet before falling.

Officer Harris may or may not have fired the fatal shot but Mrs. Winn's account of the shooting was otherwise verified by an independent pathologist, Dr. David Spain of New York City. Dr. Spain performed a post-autopsy on the corpse. According to his report, the two bullets that struck Richard Owens had the same trajectory and were fired as if from the same weapon. Further, the flight of the projectiles was approximated by Dr. Spain as being from four to five feet.

He Didn't Have Anything in His Hands

Homicide detectives visited Mrs. Winn at City Hospital and followed the usual tactics connected with police shootings. "They wanted me to say that the other cop did the shooting and not Harris but I know it was Harris. They kept on asking me, 'How could you be sure it was Harris?' They also wanted me to say that there was something in Richard's hands. He didn't have anything in his hands."

Mrs. Winn also related that one of the police who had arrived after the shooting walked through her apartment and disappeared into the kitchen. He remained there a few seconds and then left the apartment without a word of explanation. Some time after, Mrs. Winn missed a bread knife and still has been unable to find it. She may never see that particular policeman again but, in the event of a civil trial on the Owens shooting, she might see the knife again.

Other police at the Fifth Precinct told Owens' sister that he had been shot when he came at the two officers with a screwdriver.

Treatment of the dead man's property was also routine. Owens had about $170 in his pocket when shot. Police verified that the fatally wounded man had "a bundle of bills." By the time Owens' corpse left City Hospital his money had been returned to the family, a total of ninety-two cents.

The Ghost of Lester Long

Mayor Gibson could not prevent Newark's blacks from maiming and killing one another in their frustration. Neither could he save them from miserable suffering and death at City Hospital. But blacks had habitually been the victims of wanton shooting at the hands of the Newark Police Department and callous injustice in the courts and about these the new mayor *was expected* to do something. When asked during the campaign if he would establish a civilian review board if elected, Gibson declared, "I will be my own review board." The black mayor had also promised to charge with murder any police officer who killed illegally.

Gibson and Police Director Redden naturally took note of Richard Owens' death in the newspapers. Attorney Morton Stavis, who had been retained by one of Owens' sisters to look into the shooting, sent them a reminder:

> The enclosed is a copy of a press report from yesterday's Newark *News* which tells of the shooting to death of Mr. Richard Owens by two Newark patrolmen.

A very preliminary investigation of the facts of the current situation indicates grave doubt as to the occurrence of the story as told by the police, and regardless of their story, there is most serious question as to whether any reasonable exercise of police practices required that Mr. Owens be killed.

I submit that the only way to deal with a matter of this sort in which a citizen of Newark is killed or seriously injured by a police officer is to have an automatic investigation, independent of the police department, and, especially where there is a killing, the officers should be suspended at least from duties in relationship to the public pending such investigation.

I am not suggesting that the police officers be pre-judged, but I do believe that the approach that I have proposed is appropriate in the interests of community confidence in the police force.

As it turned out, Stavis seemed to be the only individual in Newark who was concerned about Owens' death and what it meant to the city's non-whites.

At the time of the shooting, Mayor Gibson was involved in a struggle with the state legislature for funds to bail the city out of its hole. He was doubtlessly aware that adverse publicity from another shooting death would not do the city any good. Gibson did nothing about the killing.

For Police Director Redden, it would have been a matter of disciplining black officers while his predecessors had failed to take action against white police who had been involved in questionable homicides. Redden, despite his integrity and the concern he had shown over the needless homicides during the riot, was silent. His staunch adherence to rules and regulations would, in this instance, be put aside. After past occurrences—such as the shootings of Lester Long and Dexter Johnson—it had at least been announced to the press that the police involved had been suspended. This was a tactic whose sole purpose was to appease the black community. Actually, the officers were merely given desk jobs and taken off the street. In this latest shooting, however, Officers Owens and Harris were not only not suspended but continued with their normal patrol duties.

Newark's three black councilmen, Gibson's running mates on the "Community Choice" ticket, may or may not have forgotten that community but they certainly forgot Richard Owens. Indeed, all three men were totally uninterested and only vaguely aware that there had even been another shooting.

LeRoi Jones, the man who should instantly have recognized that Richard Owens' death represented a crisis for the new Newark, was busy dabbling in the world of black nationalism. At the time of Owens' death, Jones was organizing a black boycott of products imported from Portugal in retaliation for the attack of Portuguese mercenaries on Guinea. Newark might disintegrate in crime and perversion, but its black residents would make LeRoi happier by using fewer Portuguese olives. Jones didn't approach Gibson and demand that the black mayor make good on his campaign promises of protection for non-whites. He did, however, manage to get one of Gibson's aides to appear at the press conference called to announce the playwright's boycott—a position Gibson quickly retreated from when angry members of the Portuguese community showed up at City Hall.

The city's two newspapers, once past their erroneous reporting of the Owens shooting, never mentioned it again. And, what would seem to be surprising, no one did anything to remind them. Bob Curvin, one of the most conscientious community leaders in the city, was working for a Ph.D. degree at Princeton University and had left Newark. Others had faded into the background, perhaps under the mistaken assumption that with a black mayor they were no longer needed.

While the Owens shooting quietly passed into history, Mayor Gibson named Irv Solondz—the attorney previously involved with Richard Owens and with the deaths of Lester Long and Bernard Rich—to fill one of the vacant magistrate's benches in municipal court. This choice demonstrated Gibson's intention to see justice done for black Newark. Solondz was not only on the local board of trustees of the ACLU, but he was a virtual affiliate of Morton Stavis—the nemesis of the Newark Police Department. And if this wasn't enough to recommend the thirty-five-year-old white attorney, his nomination was denounced by the Newark lodge of the Fraternal Order of Police. With Solondz joining Gibson's other appointee, Booker, the municipal courts atmosphere would have changed from "law and order" to "law and justice."

Such councilmen as Bontempo, Giuliano, and Turco could, naturally, be expected to vote against Solondz's appointment. Gibson's appointee was not only initially rejected by these politicians, however, but by *every* member of the City Council—including the three black men elected on Gibson's ticket.

It was reported in the press that the councilmen were irritated because they read of Gibson's selection, rather than having been personally notified by the mayor beforehand. It was also reported that Solondz's liberal leaning had much to do with his rejection. The situation, however, was not as simple as this. Behind the scene, Gibson's right-hand man on the council, Earl Harris, took credit for getting the votes to block Solondz. His reason for thwarting Gibson was that Solondz had refused to donate campaign funds to the councilman before the election. Self-interest had already replaced altruism as the motivation for one of the leaders of the black revolution.

Gibson realized Solondz's potential impact on the court and stubbornly resubmitted the nomination. The council just as stubbornly again rejected

Solondz, this time the vote splitting six to three along a more predictable line—color. The three blacks on the council eventually backed Gibson, as they should have in the first place, but the six white men would have none of it. Instead of a judicious man such as Solondz, the council eventually approved the nomination of Harry Del Plato for the municipal court bench. Del Plato lived in Bloomfield. He also was a nephew of Ralph Villani.

The rhetoric of LeRoi Jones and others on black unity and the "new awareness" had faded into something quite old as the blacks proved to be as politically conscious as their forerunners. The joy of Gibson's election had dissipated into lethargic indifference while racism was still a factor on the council. Through the maze of lies and misery, the ghost of Lester Long still ran. There was a new day in Newark, one more ghost, and another broken promise.

31

LET IT BE

Jesse Jacob and Carole Graves

Shooting victims of the police were not the only ghosts in Newark as Hugh J. Addonizio continued to haunt the ill-fated city. The former mayor's sellout contract in the 1970 teachers' strike had been signed at the expense of the Newark Board of Education and the non-white communities. The contract, which was to expire in February of 1971, set the stage for a massive confrontation. A new cast of characters joined Newark's unfolding drama.

First, there was Jesse Jacob, a forty-four-year-old housing manager with the Newark Housing Authority. Jacob, a former director of Newark's parent-teacher association, was a staunch advocate of community control. Black and muscular, he was often boorish and arrogant but could be gentle and patient. A hero to the black community, to many whites Jacob was a black devil in collusion with LeRoi Jones to steal the minds of innocent children. He had testified in the contempt of court hearings against the teachers in the 1970 strike and had served copies of the court's permanent antistrike injunction won by the Board of Education. Mayor Gibson, who owed his election to the black community, Jones, and John Caufield, did what they all wanted by appointing Jacob to the Board of Education.

After taking office, Gibson appointed two other blacks to the board, Charles Bell and Mrs. Helen Fullilove, and a Puerto Rican, Fernando Zambrana. Already seated was another black woman, Mrs. Gladys Churchman, and with a five to four non-white majority the Board of Education at long last was representative of Newark's altered population balance. The board itself took this phenomenon a step further when it elected the aggressive Jacob president, a move that disturbed the Newark Teachers Union and its thirty-two-year-old president, Mrs. Carole Graves.

Mrs. Graves, who was born and raised in Newark, was an attractive, level-headed, long-suffering, seemingly imperturbable woman with a pleasant manner and voice. She was also black and was thus the perfect union representative for such a situation. All of this could be seen quite readily on television, which media she used to advantage. To many blacks, however, Mrs. Graves was only a "show window Negress." It was because of her that the union could refute the claim that the strike amounted to a racial confrontation. Throughout the school controversy Mrs. Graves and Jesse Jacob could not help but emerge through the mass media as the protagonists—the sweet, gentle Negro fighting courageously for her union and the rabble-rousing, bullying nigger catering to the dangerous black militants.

Negotiation Strategy

From the beginning there was no doubt that Jacob and the Board of Education felt that the teachers would not strike, and with good reason. First, the funds of the Newark Teachers Union had been depleted after paying $44,000 in fines for the last strike. Second and more important, the board was armed with the permanent injunction against another teacher walkout. It was thought that those leading youth to knowledge would not openly flout the law. Jacob viewed the situation as one in which the black community could wipe out the previous contract with its binding arbitration and non-professional-chores clauses. He moved along those lines. Negotiations on a new contract which were to start in October never got under way until the end of December. This was felt to be "negotiation strategy." Even then, Donald Saunders, the board's chief negotiator, might as well have been speaking Swahili. As far as the union was concerned, that's exactly what he seemed to be speaking. The inconsequential banter that took the place of honest negotiation was viewed by the board as further "strategy." It was obvious that the Board of Education had committed itself to break the Newark Teachers Union's hold on the education system and, with a little luck, break the union itself. As far as the black community was concerned, no group deserved it more.

On the other hand, the union and its leader, Mrs. Graves, did not want a strike, particularly an illegal one against the non-white communities. Their 1970 walkout had been carefully planned but such was not the case this time. The union leadership put off a strike vote until a few hours before the old contract expired. They met with Mayor Gibson through the last night and all believed an agreement had been reached to extend the old contract temporarily. Jesse Jacob felt otherwise. He said the contract would be extended only over his dead body. Numerous anonymous phone calls promised such a development. The threats had no validity and, when the old contract ran out, the teachers had no contract.

Newark's teachers, who had to bear their share of responsibility for one of the worst educational systems in the country, were faced with a choice: fulfill the first requirement of their vocation by continuing to teach or go out on an illegal strike against backward schoolchildren who desperately needed them. Roughly half of 4,300 teachers chose to be criminals. This new message of law and order could not have been lost on all the city's non-white children, even if relatively few of them could read.

Superficial and Banal

On the day the teachers' strike commenced, the *Star-Ledger*'s "Reporter at Large" columnist went to Trenton and wrote a charming story on women's liberation. The *Evening News* daily columnist stayed home and wrote a column on Groundhog Day. It consisted solely of Woody the Groundhog's letter to the newspaper. Both Newark newspapers covered the strike tactfully and rationally. The reportage was accurate and, as always, superficial. The city's press covered the crisis as if it were taking place in a distant, alien country, which was no surprise considering that the majority of editors and reporters were also suburbanites who had much in common with the teachers. Editorials in both newspapers were banal. Reporters from New York were plentiful and equally superficial.

Network television crews from the big city also descended on Newark once again. They found the black community angry and surly. Striking teachers were pleasant and cooperative. The blacks were ignorant people who didn't give a damn about the newspapers or any of the other media that had stood by while their people had been slaughtered.

Labor Against Management

The bitterness of the strike was set shortly after its beginning when a group of teachers were badly beaten as they left the union headquarters. Non-striking teachers in white schools were not allowed to enter and these buildings were virtually closed down. Teachers who refused to strike were threatened and some were attacked. Mrs. Graves was repeatedly threatened and her car was burned. The majority of black teachers, near 40 percent of the union membership, refused to strike. Black schools in the Central and South Wards remained open, partially staffed by black teachers who had been run out of the white schools. The children, however, were not necessarily being educated. Many high school students signed in during the morning and then played basketball. Others went downtown to shoplift. Striking teachers picketing the black schools were called names and returned their share of slurs. Some of them were pushed around and harassed. They were fortunate not to be killed. If looks could kill, they would have been.

Throughout the strike more than 50 percent of the system's 80,000 children had no formal education. Police reported that incidents of juvenile delinquency had risen by 15 percent. Instances of adult delinquency were far greater.

Tony Imperiale, a champion of law and order, again showed up on the illegal side. In black Newark he was given credit for single-handedly closing down the First Avenue School in the North Ward. Actually, the school's parent-teacher group was not ashamed to take credit for that deed and also for barring non-striking teachers. Nevertheless, when it came to Imperiale and the illegal actions of the ward's white residents, the police seemed to be looking the other way. Imperiale also appeared at rallies for the teachers and unlimbered his tonsils with usual gusto. The strike according to Imperiale: Gibson had sold out the white people in Newark; LeRoi Jones was an idiot; the Board of Education was comprised of idiots; and Mayor Gibson was also an idiot. Unprepared for the sudden call to duty, Tony developed a hoarse throat.

A supporting cast of hundreds was unveiled through the mass media, the community versus the teachers. Led by such outlandish rallying cries as, "The union wants to commit the worst crimes ever perpetrated against the children of Newark," "Don't let them murder our children," and "The teachers are barbaric," the mothers acted as if they believed what they were saying. They were angry, crude, uproarious, and often obscene. They were also justified.

There were dedicated teachers both white and black who would never strike; other blacks who were afraid to strike; and a majority of whites who didn't give a damn about their vocation or Newark's children. It was the latter who refused to enter the schools. They were largely milky-white suburbanites who were driven by reports that if Jesse Jacob had his way they would be transferred or even forced out of the school system. Their fears were correct. Jacob wanted to get rid of every teacher in the system —black or white—who didn't care first about the children.

The depth of the confrontation far exceeded the tissue-thin coverage of the media. The blacks wanted to control their own schools and the teachers who taught in them. For them it was a chance to fight back against the agony and frustration of the many Lester Longs, inhuman living conditions, a rotten police force, a history of corrupt government, Parker–Callaghan, the medical school, and the bitterness remaining from the riot. If they couldn't win any other way, if they couldn't control any other facet of their ghetto lives, the blacks would at least control their children's education.

The Newark Teachers Union, on the other hand, wanted more power over the education system, more money, and a welfare fund. Here was a union leadership which equated teachers instructing children with assembly-line workers in a factory. Mrs. Graves herself accurately summed up her position: "People usually have an image of me as a little old lady in tennis shoes. What I really am is a labor organizer. All I'm trying to do is represent labor against management."

The Newark Teachers Union, Local 481 of the American Federation of Teachers, wanted to impose a traditional trade union contract on a demoralized, deteriorating educational system. While their counterparts in affluent communities such as Short Hills, Scotch Plains, and Maplewood were involved in all aspects of their teaching duties and responsibilities, the teachers in Newark found it demeaning to supervise children in playgrounds and lunchrooms. That the children were black and the city bankrupt revealed the union's calculation. Newark was thoroughly polarized once again and the tense, emotional climate was similar to that of the June mayoralty election.

Gus Heningburg, who had the interests of the children at heart, volunteered his services as a mediator. He soon ascertained—correctly—that neither side cared about the immediate needs of the children and he bowed out. Jacob saw to it that Mrs. Graves and two other male union leaders were sent to jail with six-month contempt-of-court sentences. Mrs. Graves, canonized on the spot, became a chocolate Joan of Arc from that moment on. White parents would have called Jacob even more vile names but they had exhausted their vocabularies. The black community was further delighted when the board suspended 347 teachers for walking on picket lines. Negotiations, if they could be dignified with such a description, dragged on as new characters were pushed to center stage, Dr. E. Wyman Garrett and John Cervase.

Garrett and Cervase

Dr. Garrett was a ruggedly handsome, thirty-seven-year-old obstetrician and a former member of the Board of Education who remained active in school affairs. His three-year term on the board had expired and such was the doctor's attitude toward the Newark Teachers Union that Jesse Jacob could be viewed as an adequate replacement. Color Garrett black. The most colorful character in the strike, Garrett stood near six feet tall, was built like a football player, and had a nose resembling a professional fighter's. His educational qualifications belied his conduct and demeanor, to put it mildly. The doctor was angry, threatening, and an articulate, uproariously humorous speaker. As a former board member, Garrett knew where the bodies were buried, and he sometimes made life miserable for John Cervase, a sixty-year-old man who was undergoing his fifth year on the board with nervous, twitching hands.

Cervase, a slightly built man with pale, watery eyes, was looked upon as an arch conservative who seemed to oppose Jesse Jacob on every issue. This in itself was enough to incur the wrath of the black community, but Cervase had a knack of delivering public utterances that drove blacks to frenzy: "Teachers are shortsighted and dissipate their energies squabbling among themselves when faced with a handful of hostile extremists who would take over the school system and revolutionize it. You should be more concerned with combating LeRoi Jones and his crowd, who are trying to grab control of the school system for their nefarious ends and indoctrinate the children against the American system and its institutions which guarantee freedom to all."

Cervase, who had no accurate knowledge of precisely what type of freedom the impoverished in Newark were actually experiencing, was oblivious to self-determination and the struggle going on in his city. Nor could Cervase understand why non-white children living in conditions of genocide *should* be told that the "American system and its institutions" were directly responsible.

The school board member was particularly critical of LeRoi Jones's African Free School and believed it to be a damaging experience to "innocent children." His consistent complaint—and warning—was that Jones represented little more than himself as far as Newark's blacks were concerned. There was some truth to this charge, but what Cervase and many others failed to realize was the strength of two truths. First, Jones's small group was the most influential faction in black Newark. Second, his influence had derived from his having moved into the vacuum of ghetto powerlessness and lack of inspired leadership.

Sitting in his beautiful home on one of the city's last white strongholds, the Forest Hills section of the North Ward, Cervase viewed blacks as a numerical quantity that was fast turning the once beautiful Weequahic section in the South Ward into a garbage-strewn mess. Viewing community spokesmen such as Jones and Garrett and others who spoke up as "black militants" and self-proclaimed leaders who were far from the solution, Cervase made himself part of the problem. Blacks called him a bigoted racist. Actually, Cervase was a liberal-minded man who for many years had acted diligently without pay on the board of directors of the Essex County Urban League. At the Board of Education meetings Cervase was publicly mocked, hissed, insulted, and laughed at by blacks. Then, speaking at a rally for the teachers, such was his unimposing style Cervase was also booed by the whites. He was just another of the well-intentioned hopelessly lost in the dynamics of change.

By this time, even Ken Gibson was beginning to wonder if he knew where he was.

Bell, Don't Sell Us Out

Mayor Gibson was caught in the middle from the outset. On one side were the pre-election propaganda flyers charging that if elected he would turn Newark's education system over to LeRoi Jones. On the other side were the entreaties of spokesmen for the black community to be given control over the schools. Gibson's initial decision was to leave the matter in the hands of the Board.

Cervase was subsequently honored with the Essex County Civic Association's annual humanitarian award for his "outstanding performance during the 1971 school crisis." At a Board of Education meeting, Cervase's meaningful participation was also recognized by the black community. He was awarded a pair of "black militant finder" binoculars to aid him in his efforts to make Newark safe for civilization.

After failing in his attempt to ward off the impending strike, Gibson bowed out. The mayor wasn't personally involved in negotiations again until March 19 when he, union and board representatives, and a state-appointed mediator were sequestered on the tenth floor of the Downtowner Motor Inn in the new Gateway complex. Frustrated, the state mediator packed his bags and left the talks on March 25. Gibson then appointed a three-member mediation panel with equally dubious results. Finally, on April 1, after private conferences in his office, the mayor got his board members to agree to watered-down versions of the binding arbitration and non-professional-chores clauses. The vote was five to four, with Jacob, Mrs. Churchman, Mrs. Fullilove, and Zambrana voting no. Bell, the only other non-white on the board, voted with the majority at the informal meeting—and soon found himself in the spotlight.

Charles Bell was a docile, mellow, slightly paunchy black man whose vote was the pivotal one in the controversy. Such were his gentlemanly nature and deportment that even angry whites found it difficult to vilify him. Although only twenty-eight years old, Bell's beard, posture, and mannerisms reminded one of a middle-aged college professor. He was, appropriately, the assistant director of education for District Council 37 of the State, County and Municipal Employees Union, AFL-CIO, in New York City, which union position naturally brought him under great pressure during the strike. Would Bell stand up for the black community where he lived? Or would he protect himself by siding with those who gave him his paycheck, as had so many "house niggers" before him?

All that was needed now to end the teachers' strike was the Board of

Education's formal ratification of the proposed contract and, if one believed the Newark newspapers, the ten-week strike appeared to be over. White residents, who had pushed out non-striking teachers while shutting down their own schools and who could have opened them any time they pleased, screamed, ironically, for the strike to end. Blacks who had previously begged not to be sold out now demanded that their Board of Education represent them. The Newark Teachers Union, being fined at a rate of $7,500 per day, waited impatiently for their own ratification meeting which was to follow directly that of the board. The 1971 teachers' strike had reached its climax. What followed was the most tumultuous public hearing in Newark's history, outdoing even those during the Parker–Callaghan and medical school confrontations.

A thousand spectators, more than half of them black, stuffed themselves into the City Council chambers for the public hearing. A large number of the whites were teachers who stood in the rear. Blacks chanted "Cervase must go," and the teachers responded with, "Jacob must go." Dr. Garrett, the first speaker, who took forty minutes to complete a ten-minute statement with the loud interruptions of the crowd, set a harmonious tone for the oratory: "You honkeys run your schools the way you want to on your side of town and we'll run our schools on our side of town."

Garrett was followed by other black speakers who addressed themselves to Charles Bell, repeating another message from the black onlookers, "Bell, don't sell us out." There were a few whites who braved the trip up to the microphone but they were hooted and shouted down. After a few hours of this brotherly love, brawls between teachers and blacks broke out in the chamber. Blacks were carried bodily out of the room by a phalanx of police. Guilty whites were pointed out by shouting spectators and they, too, were dragged out. It was democracy in action. Whites screamed insults at blacks and the blacks responded in kind. The nine members of the board tactfully evacuated their chairs and they were quickly replaced by spectators who stood on top of the elevated benches to watch the mayhem.

At the height of the disorder, Dr. Garrett demanded to see the notes of a *New York Times* reporter and was refused. Several black men then grabbed the reporter around the throat, punched him in the stomach, and took both his notes and a wallet containing $40. At least two of the culprits were Board of Education security officers who were there to insure order. After their unique peace-keeping effort, the public hearing was adjourned until the next night at the larger Symphony Hall, where the acoustics were better.

When the ratification vote was finally taken, Bell replied to the impassioned pleas of the blacks with quiet dignity: "There is no such thing as victory for either party. You are damned if you do and you are damned if you don't. But the point is that you had better make a damned decision. There comes a time when we do not totally personally agree but my vote must reflect the people I represent. Tonight is such a position. There comes a time in life when one must not do what is best but what is necessary. I must vote for the survival of a city and therefore I vote no."

Bell's vote was followed by no votes from Zambrana, Mrs. Churchman, and Mrs. Fullilove. Jacob eloquently supplied the fifth and decisive no vote: "If this be the year of attrition, *let it be*. In the oft-used words of the Negro spiritual . . . free at last, free at last, great God Almighty, free at last. I vote *no!!*"

The almost totally black audience erupted in unrestrained joy. Jacob adjourned the meeting and then, weeping, embraced Bell.

It was Dr. Garrett who again supplied an anticlimax, though this time his role was involuntary. The doctor and one of the men who had robbed the *Times* reporter were arrested together shortly after the hearing's jubilant conclusion. Garrett was charged with interfering with a news reporter in violation of a state statute. A few minutes before, Councilman Westbrooks had also been arrested when he hadn't responded quickly enough to a police order to clear an aisle. Neither man was harmed by the police. The two arrests, nevertheless, prompted a news conference the next day as LeRoi Jones finally stepped from behind the curtain to center stage.

LeRoi and the Zombies

LeRoi Jones may have changed his name to Imamu Baraka but he was still LeRoi: "Redden must be fired. The majority of the community is fed up with this racist turkey. Last night his goonish savages arrested black councilman Dennis Westbrooks allegedly for blocking an aisle at Symphony Hall during the voting on the teachers union contract. . . . Redden cannot control the zombies Spina trained to eat black flesh."

Jones, adhering to his own timetable for black Newark, again called for a black police director and more black police who would be "sympathetic to the community." He couldn't have forgotten that many black police were thieves and punks who equated manhood with carrying a gun. He couldn't have overlooked the fact that a significant number of non-white police victims were being killed by black officers. But Jones seemed to be saying that even bad black cops were better than bad white cops. And white police would scoff at a black director just as they scoffed at a black mayor and would feel free to victimize blacks, as LeRoi well knew. Newark needed a black police director like it needed another Addonizio; the city needed more of what blacks called "nigger cops" like it needed a plague. Jones once again had ignored reality for the sake of his own illusions. By participating in such theatrics, Jones, Westbrooks, and Garrett hurt their own credibility and inadvertently gave credence to the shouts of such as Imperiale that "police brutality" was a myth. This was, however, the least of the harm accomplished by the inappropriate news conference.

As foolish and ill-conceived as the arrest of Westbrooks had been, Jones had made a blunder of his own by pressuring Mayor Gibson to remove Redden, by most standards a superior police director and, perhaps, the one man who could have immediately answered the demands of non-whites for a more honest police force. While the playwright had remained tactfully on the sidelines during Gibson's mayoralty campaign, his timing on this occasion was wretched. The rejection of the teacher contract was anything but the stepping-stone to a blacker Newark that Jones evidently believed it to be. Jones scared the hell out of the business community, which was now led to believe that "Jones's crowd" wanted to take over the police department as well as the school system. The pre-election white scare-propaganda seemed to be coming true. Further, the playwright virtually joined forces with the Newark Teachers Union itself in undermining Gibson as the union distributed vicious pamphlets predicting another riot and calling for Gibson's recall.

Not the Proper Thing to Do

"As mayor, I now appeal to all the citizens of our community to help me resolve this dispute," the mayor announced in a New York television address. "Only the moral pressure and action of the people can create an atmosphere which will lead both sides to a fair and just settlement." Gibson put his reputation on the line as he launched a drive to generate public support for a compromise agreement and called on residents to put pressure on the Board of Education and the union to end the strike. Thousands of leaflets from the mayor's office added to the pressure.

Gibson's compromise agreement was virtually the same as had been discussed at the beginning of the strike and it was bad enough for the union immediately to deem it, "eminently fair, reasonable, and just." Mrs. Graves was released from jail for further negotiations. The Newark Teachers Union, sensing victory and above pressure, or, for that matter, conscience, announced it was prepared to continue the strike and further picketing. Jesse Jacob found he had a new adversary: "The mayor has attacked the board because now the board has to deal with a television speech rather than the union. It was not the proper thing to do."

All of Gibson's pressure fell, naturally, on Jacob and the four other board members who had rejected the proposed contract. Zambrana, employed by the Greater Newark Urban Coalition, which depended on funds from big business for its existence, changed his vote. Charles Bell also sat down but was still fired from his New York union job. Mrs. Churchman and Mrs.

Fullilove, independent and unreachable, announced with pride that their vote was still no. Jacob, black to the end, also voted no. The vote was now six to three in favor of ratification and the Newark Teachers Union had won.

Mayor Gibson, who had inadvertently gained prestige for ending a crisis, was pathetic in its aftermath. "I want to say to you, Carole, and to you, Jesse, that we have a long way to go."

"We've come through it with our heads held high," said the computerized Mrs. Graves.

"The children just got kicked in the teeth," said Jacob.

We Don't Want Criminals

Out on the ghetto's streets the messages were more realistic. Teachers came back to school flashing smiles and victory signals for the television cameras. "Nigger teachers" who had abandoned their people were not embarrassed to join them. Under the agreement, the 347 suspended teachers were allowed to return with the others. Their victory, however, was costly. Striking teachers had lost $3,000 in salary and Superior Court Judge Allcorn ruled that the union owed $255,000 in court fines. The union attorney responded that there was only $75 in the treasury. Judge Allcorn replied that the union should have thought of that before it went on an illegal strike. The teachers' smiles faded altogether when Judge Allcorn further ruled that the fine would be deducted from their salaries and union dues.

Many teachers attempting to return to black schools were barred from entering by irate parents and community groups. "The parents didn't go on strike," said one mother. "It was the teachers who created all the problems. If the proper action had been taken against the teachers, they would have been fired. Now these lawbreakers want to return to the schools but we don't want criminals teaching our children."

Most of these teachers were eventually transferred. Some of those who were allowed to return to their classrooms achieved their end when they prompted children to walk out of the schools with placards reading, "We Want Our Teachers Back." The victims of the longest school strike ever in a major American city laughed and cheered.

Newark had passed through its first crisis since the election of a black mayor. The 1971 teachers' strike was a power struggle pitting the black community and the Newark Board of Education against the Newark Teachers Union for control of the education system. It was a confrontation between the middle class and the poor, the white and the black, those who had the power of organization against those who were just awakening to what power meant.

Fearful whites viewed the strike as an attempt by LeRoi Jones to purge the school system of teachers who wouldn't comply with an "extremist philosophy." For some blacks it was a battle to free their children's minds from white oppression. Such complexities were beyond most black mothers, for whom it was only a time during which their children learned nothing. For LeRoi Jones himself the strike was a necessary step toward a separate black culture. It was "nation-building" time, the start of a long journey to black identity for a black city. If the white teachers were all gone at journey's end and their replacements were inadequate, if the children couldn't count, no less understand geometry, if they could speak Swahili but not English, if they didn't even know enough to stop destroying their schools and neighborhoods with vandalism, disruption, and violence, so be it. The journey had many victims and it would have many more. They would join those who had already been forgotten.

32

HURTIN' ON THE INSIDE

He's Never Been the Same Since

During the hard-fought campaign, LeRoi Jones's group had hung one of its posters showing the wounded Bass boy on the outside of Brown's Floor Waxing Service on Hawthorne Avenue—not knowing that the flesh and blood Joey Bass lived directly across the street. Joey, fifteen years old and only in the eighth grade, saw the color poster and recognized himself as the youngster lying in a pool of blood on Avon Avenue. He didn't understand what it was all about. Neither did his mother and father. The Committee for a Unified Newark had gotten permission from *Life* magazine for use of the photo but no one asked Joey's family how they felt about it.

"He got out of the hospital but he's never been the same since," his mother related. "He don't be sick or nothin' but his leg gives way under him. He fell down comin' home for lunch the other day and messed up his eye. Then he fell going to the store. The left leg just gives way beneath him."

"I didn't know no riot was going on because it wasn't where I was," Joey told me, trying to recall when he had been shot. "How did I get shot?" he absent-mindedly repeated the question. "I don't know. I was walking in the street, that's all I remember."

From the celebrity of *Life* magazine's cover, Joey Bass had returned to a life of anonymity. Somewhere downtown in one of those office buildings, however, there were intentions for his future. The lawyer handling the case of Joey Bass, Jr., versus the city of Newark, an accidental shooting by the Newark police, was in no hurry. After all the boy was a minor and not affected by a statute of limitations. Finally, on April 18, 1969—twenty-one months after the shooting—the suit was filed in Essex County Superior

Court. It had taken so long, the lawyer said, because the "climate" for such a legal action had not been right.

"He can't walk flat anymore," the mother said. "Joey walks on his toes and wears out the front of his shoes. His eye is a little crossed, too. And the fingers on his left hand curl up sometimes, stiff-like. He can't use his left hand too well, not like he should. I took him back to the clinic and they didn't do a damn thing but talk with him, so I didn't take him back no more. He's not hisself. He doesn't move the same, you can tell the way he walks."

Joey Bass had been hit by two Double O shotgun slugs which had missed Billy Furr, one in the left thigh and the other in the neck. The first was still embedded in the boy's leg and the second slug had passed almost completely through his neck and protruded under a small lump of flesh on the right side.

Action on the Bass boy's civil suit was expected in two more years or so.

They'd Say I Sold Him Down the River

The uncomplicated issue during the Bernard Rich civil trial before Superior Court Judge Alan B. Handler was that either four policemen had used excessive force and were negligent or that they hadn't and weren't. The youthful Rich, rather wiry and strong at six feet one and 175 pounds, had been in excellent health when put into his cell but something at the other extreme when removed. The jury, which had five days of testimony to consider the two alternatives, witnessed an outburst from Rich's sister while one of the police was testifying. She stood up and called him a murderer. Naturally the jurors were instructed to disregard the outburst. Evidently, they did.

The police officers said—under oath—that no one had even struck Rich. The jury, which found for the defendants, never had an opportunity to hear another piece of testimony from a disinterested witness. An alcoholic in an adjoining cell remembered that when Rich was being carried from his cell, the police rather carelessly slammed his head into a cement wall. He later signed a statement for the police saying that he hadn't seen anything, perhaps because he was a frequent visitor to police accommodations.

Benjamin Bendit, who replaced Solondz as Mrs. Rich's attorney, was offered a settlement of $5,000 at one point. The widow, acting with dignity, turned it down.

"Bernard's family blamed me for signing the complaint he was arrested on," she said. "If I were to take the money, they'd say I had sold him down the river again for a few dollars."

The Kendrick Arrest

Albert Portee, one of Shirts Kendrick's accomplices who had been arrested at the time of Kendrick's shooting in 1965, remained out on the street after having jumped bail. The narcotics possession charge he was running from was subsequently dismissed. If Portee still believed he was a wanted man, however, he certainly didn't allow it to cramp his style. In February 1969, Portee became involved in an argument with fellow ghetto resident Melvin Akbar Howard on Clinton Avenue. He ended the argument—and Howard—with a shotgun blast. Portee was convicted of manslaughter a year later and was subsequently sentenced to eight to ten years in state prison.

The man who had killed Kendrick, Detective Harold Schwankert, could only nod knowingly and remark, "I knew they were dangerous men." Notoriety from the episode had dissolved, and for Schwankert, a kindly man many in Newark had regard for, it couldn't have been quick enough. Schwankert's health was failing and he walked with two canes due to an arthritic condition in both legs. Early in September of 1970, he visited my home in Newark because he was concerned with what was being written about the Kendrick killing. During my talks with the aging detective, he objected to the phrase "Kendrick shooting." Schwankert said the incident should be referred to as the "Kendrick arrest."

Other than expressing this feeling, the old man declined to comment on any specific aspect of the shooting. Did Schwankert really see a gun inside Kendrick's car before the chase? The answer remains with him. A few weeks after the visit he died of a heart attack.

Balogh Will Get His Some Day

"If Walter had done what they said he done, I wouldn't have done nothing even though they killed him," Mrs. Mathis said, recalling the death of her son five years before. "We're fighting because they were wrong. My people wanted to do something about it to get even. They were mad about how Walter died, but we said we'd fight it with the law."

"I see Balogh riding around on the streets," the father said. "I could walk right by him and I wouldn't do nothing to him. I have nothing to say to him."

"Balogh will get his some day, the Lord will take care of him," the mother added.

John Balogh, one of the detectives demoted in Redden's shake-up of the police department, was back in a patrol car working out of the Second Precinct. His short, stocky physique, craggy face and raspy voice lent themselves to an unfair labeling in the aftermath of the Mathis killing. Balogh had moved onto Morris Avenue in the Central Ward when the neighborhood was all white and he remained there when it was all black. His was the only white family in the vicinity and other policemen at headquarters made fun of him because of it. "I want my kids to grow up knowing how other people live," he once said. Balogh was also one of the first in the department to ride in a patrol car with a black partner. It was ironic and sad that Balogh ended up with the "nigger hater" label.

"If I had looked the other way when I was told about the drunk being mugged, I would have been brought up on charges," he said. "If there's a fuckin' thing in my life, I'm a cop and I don't care what I get involved in, I do the job. I don't think about the shooting anymore at all. If you let that knock you down, you're no good anymore. You don't belong out there on the street. I'm a cop twenty-four hours a day. I'll be there till I die or I'm retired. Or unless somebody shoots me first."

"It's a clear-cut case," said Nathan Kurtz, attorney handling the Mathis suit. "All we have to prove is that Balogh shot the boy in the back. That won't be hard. You've seen the photographs of the body, nobody has talked about them before. I have a few questions I can ask Balogh. I doubt if he'll even testify."

In December of 1970—five years after the killing of the Mathis boy—the damage suit against the Newark Police Department was settled out of court. The price on Walter Mathis' life was fixed at $11,000, the same figure the family had refused a year and a half before. Newark's press compounded the travesty when it failed to report the final word on the killing of Walter Mathis. He would only be remembered by the white public as the boy who had been shot to death by an embattled police officer while resisting arrest.

I'll Be Glad When It's Over

After the U.S. Supreme Court refused to consider John Smith's appeal, he remained home in Salisbury, North Carolina, while attorneys representing him filed a writ of habeas corpus to keep him out of jail. His attorneys, Harris David and Carl Broege, who had written his appeal brief, planned to start all over again in the federal court system, raising the same constitutional issues that the state courts couldn't afford to consider seriously. By this time, however, further legal efforts on the forty-three-year-old man's behalf appeared useless and only postponed the three-to-five-year prison sentence Judge Lyons had imposed two years before.

"I just wish it was finally resolved," Smith said. "It's been a long time.

I'll be glad when it's over and I can pick up the pieces and get something done. It's hard to look back at the riot objectively, my view would be slanted. Law and order? I think it's pretty weird, that's all I can say about it."

Since returning to North Carolina, Smith had worked as a laborer in a cotton mill and as a helper on a beer truck for about seventy dollars per week. He came back to Newark in January of 1970 when he thought his civil suit against the Newark Police Department was ready to proceed. The case was postponed indefinitely, however, and Smith and his twenty-year-old brother started back south in a 1957 Ford. Their trip was delayed when the car blew two tires and punctured the radiator after ramming into a snow-covered dividing island near the entrance to the Pulaski Skyway.

That Was Cold-Blooded What They Did

Of all the Black Muslims from North 14th Street, William Turner's case was unique. Like the others, he had suffered a brutal beating and spent a month at Caldwell Penitentiary. But then Turner had been convicted of draft evasion and sent away again to a federal prison. Both convictions were reversed. Justice had triumphed, but Turner, who had a scarred head and the memory of sixteen months in custody, had little regard for it.

"What could I say when all those police started coming?" he said, standing on his porch across the street from where it had all happened three and a half years before. "Wow, I thought, something is getting ready to happen. I couldn't just walk out because all the police were standing in front. That was cold-blooded what they did, cold-blooded. They wouldn't stop beating us. I forgot how many stitches I took in my head. I hear now they're trying to give police officers more power. I guess they just want to be able to legally kill people they don't like."

Turner looked across the street at 91 North 14th Street. "I think they have enough power right now," he said.

I Knew They'd Never Believe Me

Mrs. Geneva Murray had been one of the lucky next of kin to the riot victims. After her husband, Cornelius, had been murdered by the Newark police on Jones Street in front of the R & R Bar, the twenty-eight-year-old widow was able to collect on his $1,000 insurance policy. On reflection, however, the company refused to honor the double indemnity clause because Murray's death had been "mysterious." There was another $500 policy that Murray's mother had taken on him and she gave these receipts to her daughter-in-law to pay for the funeral. The expenses came to $1,410.10. This left the widow with $89.90, no husband, and three children, sitting in a worn apartment on Wainwright Street.

In addition, two of the kids had been hospitalized. The family was living on Murray's $377 monthly social security check and it was far from enough. It was all on Geneva Murray's shoulders and they were fragile. Her face was pale and drawn and she was troubled with abdominal pains. For a year before her husband's murder, the family had lived in the four-room apartment. Now the landlord said the place had to be redecorated, children weren't allowed anymore, and the family had to get out.

"I went to sleep that second night after Cornelius left not knowing whether he was alive or dead," she recalled. "Then I heard a voice calling me in the dark, 'Geneva . . . Geneva,' and I woke up. It was a woman's voice. The room was crowded with people who stood around the bed, so crowded there wasn't room for anybody to sit down. They were all shapes and sizes and they wore dark clothing. It was dark and I couldn't see any of their faces. They stood there moaning like something terrible had happened and I got scared and pulled the covers up over my head.

"The next morning I felt different," Mrs. Murray continued. "I felt almost relieved, I just knew Cornelius was dead and I didn't have to be worrying about it anymore. Right after that I called the hospital and the girl told me he was dead. I never heard that woman's name who was calling to me in the dark but somehow I knew her name was Hattie Gainer."

Mrs. Murray went to her husband's wake with her mother-in-law and, as she stood over the casket, she became faint. "I had felt strange ever since I heard that voice calling my name," she said. "Then I was sitting there next to the coffin and I said, 'I wanna go in the other room.' My mother-in-law made a motion with her finger around her head like I was crazy but I said, 'Take me in the other room, I gotta go and see something. . . . I want to see the body in the other room.' I knew who the body was, I just knew it was the dead person who had called to me in my bedroom. I stood over the coffin in the other room and I said, 'That's Hattie Gainer.' Then they read somewhere in the room the name, 'Hattie Gainer.' After I went out of that room it was the first time I smiled since Cornelius was killed. I just felt better but I didn't know why. I never told anybody this before because I knew they'd never believe me."

In her hand Mrs. Murray clasped the stub of a pencil and on the bed alongside her were classified ads marked with crude circles. She had been looking for two months for another apartment but she couldn't make it with the three children. Then the landlord raised the rent from eighty to one hundred to make her look harder. The city had no further communication with Geneva Murray after having sent the two prosecutor's detectives to interrogate her. Having killed her husband, it was content to leave her alone.

Go Look for Him

Brian Gary was released from the reformatory after serving six months for having attempted to steal beer during the riot—and for telling lies about the death of his friend Jimmy Rutledge. He returned home to Newark on Christmas Eve with a vivid recollection of shotgun blasts.

"We heard the shots," he told me. "They were saying, 'Die motherfucker, die you black nigger,' and all kinds of nasty names. If they wanted to kill him they should have just shot him without all that bullshit."

Theoretically at least, Rutledge's death was still open for further investigation. It was left to the FBI to lower itself one more notch by showing the interest with which the agency approached the case. Two agents visited the Trenton apartment of Rutledge's mother on a pursuit of law and order. It seemed one James Rutledge, Jr., had failed to show up for draft induction and the FBI wanted the boy's mother to tell them where he was. At first she said that she was shocked. Then she had become angry.

"I told them to go look for him," she related.

I'm Just Lucky I Didn't Get Killed

Alfred Swift was found sitting with a drink in a corner of the Park Cafe, a small, dingy bar off Clinton Avenue where he often came. The bar was four blocks over from Belmont Drugs, where Leroy Boyd had been shot more than three years before.

"It's all stacked against you," the forty-eight-year-old man said. "There are a lot of policemen, white and black, who have a tendency to exempt themselves from the law. Because he's a policeman, he's right regardless of what happens. I haven't got no reprieve from all the whippin' and all the time in jail I was away from my family. I'm just lucky I didn't get killed."

The muscular, six-foot Swift explained that when he had been younger, he was involved in a lot of bar-room brawls and fights. Now, Swift said, he was older and things had changed. "It makes more sense just to walk away," he said.

Dexter Just Got Scared and Ran

Dexter Johnson had lived with his mother, fifteen-year-old brother, six-year-old sister, grandmother, and his step-grandfather, Reverend Albert D. Wright, in an area removed from the hardcore ghetto on Schuyler Street. His death had been carelessly reported but the *Evening News* did justice to his funeral:

> More than 200 persons attended funeral services at the Israel A.M.E. Church yesterday for Dexter Johnson, the 17-year-old boy slain Monday by a Newark policeman following an alleged altercation.
>
> The Rev. Bynum C. Burton, pastor of the church, conducted the nearly hour-long services, assisted by the Rev. Isaac J. Kilby, pastor of the Grace A.M.E. Church of Crosswicks. Mr. Burton referred briefly to the youth's death as "unfortunate" and said that he would "not attempt to go into the details." However, he urged those present to "not get angry."
>
> Both clergymen offered words of consolation to members of the bereaved family as well as offering prayers. Mr. Burton also gave thanks in behalf of the family. He also discussed the "uncertainty of life" as he consoled the family and friends.
>
> Two nurses were in attendance during the services to minister to several persons who became hysterical.
>
> After the services, a 29-car entourage followed the hearse bearing the youth's flower-decked coffin and a car carrying 19 floral wreaths to Glendale Cemetery, Bloomfield.

"Dexter never did do anything bold, he was very mild," Raymond Boone, his friend who had been with him in the borrowed car, recalled. "Really, he was weak minded. You could tell him anything and he'd believe you. He was a beautiful person. You'd do things to him and expect him to get fighting mad, but when you saw him again he had forgot all about it. He was a simple person, that's all. He wasn't doing anything. Dexter just got scared and ran."

The twenty-nine-year-old policeman who had killed the Johnson boy, Charles Knox, had been portrayed by the press as a beset hero who had been forced to do his duty. The prosecutor's office and grand jury had kept this in mind and must have questioned Knox gently. At any rate, the police officer didn't care to test his memory with me as to the details of the shooting. Officer Knox angrily refused any statement whatsoever on the death of Dexter Johnson and ordered me out of his home.

Knox was subsequently promoted to detective and, in December of 1970, announced his candidacy for president of The Bronze Shields, the Newark Police Department's fraternal order of black policemen.

I Never Wanted Them to Hurt Richard

Finding a casket large enough to hold the bulk of Richard Owens' corpse had been a problem and the one the family members knelt beside at Whigham's Funeral Home was too small. The gray, felt gloves on the deceased's huge hands were also too small. Owens' mother and father had come from Maryland for the viewing and three of his brothers and two sisters, only one of whom lived in Newark, were also there. The body would be taken home and the entire family, two more brothers and three sisters, would be at the funeral at Fort Deposit. A guest book at the far end of the carpeted viewing room was filled with the names of friends and well wishers who had met Richard Owens during his five years in Newark.

The dead man's estranged wife, Barbara, sat quietly on a corner sofa in the large room. No one knew where his second, illegal wife was and few if any in the family even knew that Owens had married not once, but twice. Eva Getter, the young woman who had prompted Owens' near fatal fight with the police three years before, had remarried and taken his young son back to North Carolina. It would be some time before she learned of her former lover's death, if she ever did.

Richard Owens' brothers stood uneasily in front of the casket while Margaret Winn, the first and last woman in his life, lay uneasily in a ward bed on the eighth floor at City Hospital. Her eyes were almost swollen shut and her face was puffed.

"I never wanted it to be like this, I never wanted them to hurt Richard," she murmured, starting to cry. "Once the cop kicked in that window, Richard wouldn't listen to anything. If you wanted Richard to do something, you could never do him like that. You couldn't make him do anything when he was mad. I'm not going to the funeral home. . . . I couldn't stand to see him, I just couldn't stand to see him like that."

"My father has a heart condition," a sister said at the funeral home. "He was so excited when he got here he would have killed those police if he had gotten the chance. My brothers were so angry they wanted to do something. Richard should never have been killed. What if one of those cops came here?"

"That would be one of the last things he'd ever do," a brother said angrily, looking over at the handsome, wax-like giant lying in the casket.

"A man getting killed is a serious thing," Officer Harris said, "I can't talk about it. The police department has regulations about that. Let me have your phone number and if I can talk, I'll call you."

"They worked on him quite a bit when we got to the hospital," Officer Owens related inside my car. "They had a hard time finding a vein to pick up his heartbeat. They cut him on the arm and they cut him on the side. I stood there watching. They had to open that cat up, man. They gave him an electric shock that made him jump on the table. Nothing. The cardiograph machine was going on the heartbeat. It got slower and slower. . . . There he goes. . . . That was the ballgame. I was gonna go over to the funeral home. That would have taken balls, man, big balls."

We Have a Different Viewpoint than White People

There was no one to speak for Lester Long, but his ghost was indeed still running. Officer Henry Martinez, an unsuccessful City Council candidate in the May election, appeared with Tony Imperiale at a political rally and vividly described his version of Long's shooting for an enthusiastic audience. Other remembrances—such as photographs of Long's corpse and the puddle of blood on the sidewalk where he had fallen—were meant to speak for him but remain mute inside a folder within the Newark Police Department. It was the Long shooting which had begun an era in June of 1965. Also in the folder are photographs of the corpses that followed him—Kendrick, Mathis, the Sanders boy, Rutledge's perforated remains, and Dexter Johnson.

These police photographs cry out for publication. Had they appeared in these pages, for the first time the brainwashed public would have had the opportunity to view the more grisly aspects of what is commonly termed "law and order." With so many secrets to hide, the Newark police were not about to volunteer the material. On November 19, 1970, I was arrested across the street from police headquarters while attempting to buy the photographs from a police officer. The charge, bribery, will eventually be decided on its merits. My arrest for attempting to make public photographs of victims of the police points an accusing finger.

These photographs, like grand jury transcripts which describe such events, remain filed away as confidential material. The system, thus protected by law, demands that these official records remain secluded from the public.

Little as that public may care about victims such as young Michael Pugh, it cares nothing at all about his forty-five-year-old mother, the last riot homicide relative to be located.

"I'm not really bitter," the quiet, dark-skinned woman said. "I know it was a soldier that shot Michael but it doesn't make any sense being bitter. When they had that investigation downtown, they said they weren't even shooting, that it was snipers. I guess we're just different than white people. Our people get killed and beaten up all the time. We have a dif-

ferent viewpoint than white people. . . . You be hurtin' on the inside
but we can't do nothin' about it. We just have to live with it. Inside you're
just hurtin' but you just got to live with it."

It Is Impossible to Estimate the Impact

On September 22, 1970, Hugh J. Addonizio and his four accomplices
were back in Trenton before Federal Judge George H. Barlow for sentencing.

"These were no ordinary criminal acts," the judge said, looking down at
the convicted men. "These crimes were not the product of a moment of
weakness, nor inspired by the defendants' desperate financial circumstances,
nor the result of some emotional compulsion. The crimes for which Mr.
Addonizio and the other defendants have been convicted represent a pattern
of continuous, highly organized, systematic criminal extortion over a period
of many years, claiming many victims and touching many more lives. Instances of corruption on the part of elected and appointed governmental
officials are certainly not novel to the law, but the corruption disclosed here
is compounded by the frightening alliance of criminal elements and public
officials, and it is this very kind of destructive conspiracy that was conceived, organized and executed by these defendants. The criminal acts of
these defendants were as calculated as they were brazen; as callous and
contemptuous of the law as they were extensive. Nor can these defendants'
criminal conduct be measured in dollars alone. It is impossible to estimate
the impact upon—and the cost of—these criminal acts to the decent citizens of Newark and, indeed, of this state, in terms of their frustration,
despair and disillusionment."

Grouping the conspiracy conviction and sixty-three specific instances of
extortion together because, in Judge Barlow's words, "I regard these acts
as representing a single continuing pattern of criminal activity," the judge
sentenced Addonizio to ten years in prison and a fine of $25,000.

Biancone received an identical sentence. LaMorte was given ten years
and a $10,000 fine and Vicaro was sentenced to twelve years and a fine of
$10,000. Gordon was sentenced to three years in prison. Callaghan, who
had pleaded guilty to income tax evasion when the prosecution produced a
canceled check made out to him, was given a one-year sentence and began
serving the time immediately. Addonizio, Biancone, LaMorte, and Gordon
remained free on $25,000 bail pending an appeal which would guarantee
their freedom for at least *two more years*. Vicaro, described by the prosecution as "the hit man" of Boiardo's group, was denied bail and immediately
taken into custody.

During the trial, Lacey had shown the jurors how Addonizio and Boiardo had stolen at least $1,500,000 with their phony supply company. The prosecution had proved beyond doubt the extortion figure named in the indictment, $253,000. There is no way of knowing what other activities the conspirators were involved in, how much they actually did steal, or even how much Addonizio had stashed away. Outside the courthouse in the bright sunshine, Hughie once again insisted in front of television cameras that he was *innocent*. During the trial, at his almost daily press conferences, such empty assertions were acts of pragmatic desperation. Addonizio had been convicted of stealing from the very citizens his administration had sentenced to a slow death in the prison of Newark's rotting facilities. His protestations of innocence were a pathetic clinging to a now transparent arrogance. Hughie stood revealed as a mealy-mouthed liar.

In late November the Justice Department in Washington bestowed $300 awards on four of Lacey's assistants for their excellent work during the Addonizio investigation and trial. Lacey's right-hand man, Stern, who would succeed his boss when Lacey was "kicked upstairs" to a federal judgeship, was rewarded with a Distinguished Service Award and a check for $500. Although the federal government had shown no undue concern for what Addonizio and company had left behind, getting rid of him and some of Newark's corruption was worth $1,700 in bonuses.

After a Riot

The Clinton Hill neighborhood where Tom Hayden and his NCUP group had hoped to spark a social revolution had changed much in seven years. Buildings that had been corroded with age were now withered and decaying. Many tenements were boarded up ghost houses and, while authorities played at their urban renewal game, restless teen-agers played by their own rules and set fire to them. K's Restaurant, where Hayden and I had met in the winter of 1968, had been smashed in the disturbance following Martin Luther King's murder and had never reopened. Dexter Johnson was shot to death around the corner on Hunterdon a year later. Other stores were wiped out in the eruption that followed, some for the second time since the 1967 riot. Over at Avon and Badger, where Hayden's people had marched for a traffic light and where Billy Furr and Joey Bass had been shotgunned, urban renewal's bulldozers had leveled the entire block. Liquor was still a big seller in the neighborhood. The corner store, Mack liquors, naturally was the last building scheduled to be torn down. There was still no traffic light at the intersection.

A year after Gibson's election and four years after a riot found the city more immersed in a jungle atmosphere than ever before. Heroin was everywhere, destroying young minds and bodies in ever increasing numbers.

Blacks cut, shot, and mugged one another with abandon. Even Mayor Gibson's father became a victim when he was attacked by a gang of hoodlums as he walked near Clinton Avenue. The elder Gibson was badly beaten and ended up at City Hospital. The sixty-year-old man had fought back with a pen knife and two of his attackers joined him there. Hoodlums and junkies also slaughtered more white merchants and black residents. A black policeman was shot to death by his girlfriend and another black officer was shot to death in a bar-room argument. Police Director Redden replied to disgruntled black residents in the South Ward in his own forthright manner: "During the previous administrations, year after year, we all watched as this city tumbled down to the point where it is now. And if you think that I or any member of this administration is going to turn this town right around, you've got another think coming."

Neither was anyone going to disturb the amicable relationship between the Newark Police Department and the Essex County Prosecutor's office. Exposure of the First Precinct's burglary ring led to a few newspaper headlines and little else. Only two of the thieves were indicted and they all remained police officers in good standing. While victims of Newark's riot had little but bitter memories to cling to, the policemen even managed to hang onto most of the goods they had stolen.

As Tony Imperiale had stated on numerous occasions: "There is a dual system—one set of rules for the blacks, another for us."

Imperiale had unknowingly stated the truth but it was Gus Heningburg who knew precisely what he was talking about. "The system is geared to protect the protectors of the system," Heningburg said.

For Imperiale, Easter Sunday knife attacks on white women and children had been replaced by a newer fantasy. What did Imperiale see for the future? Was he expecting another riot? Yes, indeed, but with modifications. This time the riots would be countrywide with blacks moving into the suburbs attacking utilities, water supplies, and covering the highways with sniper fire. Tony even had their route mapped out: "They can't come through the North Ward, of course, so they'll push out through Vailsburg (in the West Ward) and work their way into the Oranges and other suburbs."

The niggers were not only taking over Newark, now they wanted to take over the suburbs, too.

After the killing of Richard Owens, the police evidently decided that Gibson and Redden would be no different from their predecessors and they reassumed their role as executioners. Seven more blacks were shot to death for suspected or petty crimes during Gibson's first year in office, five of them as they ran. One was a sixteen-year-old boy running from a stolen auto. Another was a fifty-two-year-old man who became involved in a bar-room scuffle with an off-duty black detective. He arrived at City Hospital in critical condition with a bullet hole in his back and died shortly afterward.

A third victim was an eighteen-year-old youth suspected of assaulting a black woman with a gun, according to police. "Patrolman Derek Akridge, Martin Goldman, and Lancelot Owens chased him through a vacant lot and then over a fence at 124 Hillside Avenue," the Newark *Evening News* reported. "A patrolman cornered the youth, who pulled a knife and attempted to attack the police officer. The patrolman, and two others who saw the attack, fired their revolvers and the suspect fell." The dead boy, Charles Paul, had no gun. Neither did he attack anyone with a knife. Nor had the police "cornered" him. Eyewitnesses who saw the shooting said that Paul's crime was running. The Essex County Medical Examiner's office seemed to concur. It said that the youth's life ended when a .38 caliber slug entered his brain after piercing the *back* of his skull.

Police said that the Paul killing was but one of six homicides over the February 20 weekend in Newark. It was the only homicide given coverage, such as it was, in the *Evening News*. The newspaper also carried a wire-service story from Philadelphia on the "execution" of two white policemen by blacks. The *Star-Ledger* also carried the Philadelphia story but spared its readers the details of the local bloodletting. The new philosophy of the Newark press produced readers who were as ignorant as ever of life in black Newark.

In May, Steve Negler of the New Jersey ACLU made public a letter to Mayor Gibson charging that police brutality was still very much a part of Newark and was being treated by the police with a "business as usual" attitude since the black mayor's election. Negler's sincerity was evident in that the letter had been sent the month before and its contents were made public only when *ignored* by the mayor's office. "Until now we have maintained a public silence in the face of mounting evidence that police brutality in the city of Newark has in no respect diminished in the past nine months," he wrote.

Police Director Redden could not be reached for comment. Mayor Gibson was vacationing in Puerto Rico. Newark's two newspapers again proved themselves worthy. The *Star-Ledger,* as usual, editorially ignored the ACLU charge. An editorial in the *Evening News* responded that Negler's letter had "the clear markings of an over-reach." A week later, a seventeen-year-old Puerto Rican suspected of stealing a car was shot to death by a Newark police officer. He was a runner. Police said the dead youth had a knife which they had mistaken for a gun in the darkness. The familiar official refrain.

Genocide also continued for Newark's non-white children. One seven-year-old boy was crushed by an elevator in a housing project and critically injured. Two days later, a nine year old plunged to his death down an elevator shaft at another high rise jungle. A thirty-seven-year-old black mother lost one young son at City Hospital in November of 1970. Early in February, she buried her remaining three-year-old son. Cause of death in both instances was lead poisoning from paint eaten from the walls of her apartment. The woman had lost her two children. It naturally followed that she also lost her aid to dependent children allotment. Her home was next. Her black landlord, who happened to be president of the Newark Model Cities Community Council, began eviction proceedings when she was no longer able to pay the rent.

Governor Cahill and Newark's businessmen had also changed little in their outlook on the city's non-white residents. They had more important things to think about than black children sentenced to death or wasted lives. While the bitterness of the school confrontation continued to polarize the city, and the schools themselves creaked with age, the governor—with strong support from Newark's business community—pushed ahead with plans to build a $200-million, gigantic sports complex in the Hackensack Meadows to lure the Yankees and Giants out of New York City. There were, in addition, other signs of progress. Governor Cahill cut the state welfare budget by $15 million and, four years after the riot, the New Jersey College of Medicine and Dentistry finally got around to picking up the deed for the barren Central Ward land where the new medical college was supposed to be constructed. Priorities had been established once again: the well-to-do would be able to eat roast beef while watching professional sports; Newark's children were left to eat paint and watch desperate foot-races between muggers and their prey.

Also, the Justice Department at long last responded to the persistent efforts of Gus Heningburg by filing discrimination suits against white construction outfits working on the Gateway complex. The federal government had finally decided to move after most of the project had been completed and action on the suit was expected in a year or two. Newark's new skyline, whatever it was, would be mired in old mud.

With a black mayor, Newark's agony was complete. Unlike his cunning predecessors, Gibson offered an honest directness and little back-room savvy. Far from a political animal, the new mayor had no sooner been in office when he announced that he would work for his city for four years and then retire from the political scene. No one felt the disillusionment more than Gibson himself as he faced the reality of just how powerless the mayor of a black city could be.

He hoped to improve the disgusting living conditions and the federal government looked toward Mars. He wanted to improve the sad school system and the state government was more interested in a sports stadium. He would at least save children from genocide but all he could do was lament their deaths. He attempted to reorganize the municipal government and his own City Council fought him at every turn. He wanted to impose an income tax for those who made their money in Newark and the big business leeches and petty state legislators wouldn't hear of it. It was Gibson's hope to act in the interests of the people who had elected him and instead he found himself a captive of the business and real-estate interests that controlled Newark.

Gibson had specifically promised to prevent the execution of non-white residents by the police and this was his most total, abysmal failure. With the Italians in power there had been corruption, but voices had been raised against the slaughter of blacks. Civil rights activists had now all but vanished from the scene. Black politicians were as disinterested as their worthless white counterparts. Now there was silence as non-whites continued to be shot down like animals.

Black was beautiful in the small cultural sphere of LeRoi Jones, but Baraka's influence over UCC was turned into a battle over control of the federal green stuff. A coalition of disgruntled blacks—whom Jones called neo-colonialists—formed in an unsuccessful attempt to gain control of the federal antipoverty agency from Jones's supporters. The disgruntled forces, largely composed of former supporters of Addonizio and Richardson, remained on the outside looking enviously in. A year after Gibson's election, there were old players in a new game, as well as new players in the old game. "House niggers" had been replaced by slick Negro entrepreneurs, hustling fast-time Charlies playing the Model Cities game, show-window Negroes and nigger landlords. The enemy now came in all colors for the residents of black Newark.

A Last Trip

From the home of Joey Bass on the 400 block of Hawthorne Avenue, the ghetto street slides down the long hill through the violent world it services. It creeps past a bar where a black policeman attempted to stop a robbery and was shot down and past the scenes of hundreds of shootings and knifings. Further along is the deteriorating building which once was Stash's Restaurant, one of the favorite eating spots in the city, where my father brought me as a sixteen-year-old kid to celebrate winning a Golden Gloves championship in 1955. The Avenue completes its trip to the bottom of the hill, choked with the litter of fast-living, hard-loving, and long-suffering black people. At its foot, they flock into the White Castle, where the family of Eddie Moss had been headed when the youngster was slaughtered. Stash's was now an empty shell, while an eating place with piles of sixteen-cent, greasy hamburgers had enlarged to four times its former size. As the hours dwindled away into the first light of morning the night people of black Newark would come out of their violent world for a brief stop, the smell of cooking hamburgers and onions permeating the stale air.

She stood behind the counter, a brown girl with wide hips and pointed breasts. The white uniform was open at the neck, the girl's nipples pressing against the dress. Her butt was round and firm, moving to the sound of a transistor radio, the driving beat of Aretha Franklin's "Don't Play That Song for Me."

There were four feet between her and the man in the tan raincoat on the other side of the counter and he was whispering to her. Standing there face to face, he was asking for her body as a black man would. She gave him a hard look out of dark eyes but said nothing. The man leaned forward against the counter and continued to talk. Soon the girl began to look amused. Now her hand pushed against her stomach, making the breasts arch forward even more, and then ran across the front of the uniform. "Shit, what you got I can't get somewhere else?" she said. The man, black Newark's perpetual lover, persisted and the girl began to smile. Even though I was standing right next to him, I couldn't make out what the man was saying to that girl but she was smiling more now, to be sure.

Between them was nothing but the smell of cooking onions and the promise of passion on a bed somewhere in the corroding ghetto, of which the brown girl was so important a part. She was black Newark, a night's promise of no tomorrow, perhaps redeemable with yet another black baby for the post-riot city.